ENGLAND IS

The village under snow

ENGLAND IS A VILLAGE

By

C. HENRY WARREN

Illustrated by

DENYS WATKINS PITCHFORD

ASHGROVE, PRESS, BATH

This edition published in Great Britain by
ASHGROVE PRESS LIMITED
26 Gay Street, Bath, Avon BA1 2PD

Originally published in 1940 by
Eyre and Spottiswoode

ISBN 0 906798 34 5

This edition first published 1983

Printed in Great Britain by
Hillman Printers (Frome) Limited

For Heinz

FOREWORD

THIS chronicle of village life was mainly written during the two months of comparative calm which were destined to be the sinister prelude to total war. Moreover, the calm was emphasized, at least in the countryside, by coincidence with one of the bitterest spells of winter weather within living memory.

For a few weeks Larkfield (as I have called the village) experienced something of that self-sufficiency which was the basis of English rural life in the days before Enclosure.

And now, as I write this introductory note, every vestige of that calm has been shattered. Larkfield watches the approach of happenings which have no equal in terror or frightfulness. And meanwhile spring unfolds with a completeness only matched by the completeness of the winter that preceded it: the English countryside puts forth her loveliest and best to front the enemy, like "a kneeling angel holding faith's front line."

Already the Larkfield I have tried to picture in these pages wears the aspect of a dream . . . but it is a dream that must be kept before our waking eyes when the horrors that sought to blind us are past. For it is from the ashes (if such must be) of the Larkfields of England that our phoenix strength shall rise.

England's might is still in her fields and villages, and though the whole weight of mechanized armies rolls over them to crush them, in the end they will triumph.

The best of England is a village.

May 1940 C. H. W.

CONTENTS

Chapter One	*page* 1
Chapter Two	21
Chapter Three	39
Chapter Four	51
Chapter Five	63
Chapter Six	79
Chapter Seven	99
Chapter Eight	117
Chapter Nine	131
Chapter Ten	145
Chapter Eleven	155
Chapter Twelve	173
Chapter Thirteen	191
Chapter Fourteen	209
Chapter Fifteen	225
Chapter Sixteen	237

ILLUSTRATIONS

The village under snow	*frontispiece*
Snowdrifts by the roadside	*page* 13
Telegraph pole	19
Promise of Spring	33
House martin	37
Timber and plaster in Essex	45
Harvest-bottle	49
A corner of an old barn	57
From any English hedgerow	69
Sheaf of oats	87
The end of the day	93
Pigeon-house	97
Children call them the Keys of Heaven	105
The village carpenter's handiwork	127
Essex cart	130
Coming home from the fields	135
Winnowing fan	144
The lane and the barn	149
Mutz	153
Wild Campion	165
Scythe in apple-tree	171
With glove and bill-hook	179
Mare and foal	189
Broken windmill under the stars	201
Corn dolly	208
By the mill-pool	217
Kneading trough	224
A flock of peewits	229
Rookery	235
The setting sun that brings the labourer home	247
Essex thatch	250
Signpost	251

Chapter One

I BEGIN this story of an English village in a wartime January that will be remembered in Larkfield as long as there are any of us alive to remember it and to talk of it. And it will not be of the war we shall speak. Indeed, during these last seven days, the war, for most of us, has been little more than a not very circum-stantial rumour penetrating our homes by radio and (occasionally) by newspaper.

Not that, as a village, we are any more callous or unconcerned than other villages, but that, like most country people, our interest is mainly reserved for the things we understand, the things we know about by direct experience. War, for instance, first came home to us, as something that really had happened, when the telegram arrived announcing the death at sea of Mrs. Chayters' only son. Before the morning was out, everybody in the village knew of that tele-gram; and from that day onwards, U-boats, though none of us had ever seen one, were a dreadful reality—they had killed a man we knew and left a weeping mother in our midst.

But for a week now, war has been pushed into the background again by a much more immediate reality: the drama of its far-away happenings has been dwarfed by a much more actual drama here at home. Hardly an aeroplane has dared our skies for days. Even the soldiers from the neighbouring anti-aircraft camps have some-how been less in evidence. And although our volunteers still keep their punctual shifts at the local observation point, we have been too much engrossed in other things to give them the attention their patient service merits.

For days we have been almost cut off from the outside world—a community of some nine hundred souls huddled together in a white waste of snow. "Snowy Tuesday," some of the old folk say, recalling with peasant exactitude a bitter fall in 1881. Others call it "Black Tuesday." Snowy or black, however, we of a younger generation have hitherto been a little inclined to doubt their tales of outlying farms and cottages that were isolated for a week on end and of snow that drifted so high it was possible to walk over the tops of the hedges. Such things do not happen, here in the kindly south. So we said, and credited their tales to the proneness of old people for exaggerating the happenings of years gone by. Let them boast, it does no harm, anyway!

But now the same thing has happened in our own time. There *are* farms and cottages in the "uplands" (as we say, though nowhere hereabouts is more than three hundred feet above sea-level) that neither the baker nor the grocer nor even the postman can get near; and all around the village there *are* drifts of snow in the sunken lanes so high you can walk over the tops of the hedges. Thus humbled, we shall perhaps listen a little less incredulously in the future to the tales of our elders. And no doubt we, in our turn, shall seem as prone to the exaggerations of old age when we tell of the snows of this white January.

It is one of the merits of village life, as well as one of the penalties, that we are, even in the most propitious days, so closely inter-dependent one on another. And when such inclement weather as this shuts us away from the world, we are even more closely united. If there was kindness among us before, it is more than trebled now. If there was envy, hatred or malice, it seems for the moment to have been forgotten. Perhaps there is an element of fear compelling us to this unstinted kindness, a faint echo in us from the days when, to an extent not even the severest hardships can inspire to-day, men and women were forced to find safety in communal endeavour. Or perhaps it is nothing more than excitement, engendered by a spectacle in which, whether we will or no, we are all compelled to play our part. The same dead sky hangs over us all, day after day. The same snow comes flaking down on the just and the unjust alike. And the same uncanny silence fills us all, even to the most unsusceptible among us, with premonitions of we know not what.

Before the snow came, we used to be wakened in the morning by the sound of men going off to work. Voices below the Causeway told us that Tom Crutchly and Arthur Small were passing one another on their bicycles as they pedalled out of the village in the early dusk. "Nice mornin', Tom!" "Aye, it is that." And then silence again, broken only by the sound of the stream purling by the roadside. But once Tom and Arthur had gone by, punctual as the sun itself, others would soon follow.

It was amusing to lie abed, pleasantly half-awake, picking out the passers-by by the mere weight and rhythm of their tread. Easiest of all to recognize, of course, was Sam Merriman's, the blacksmith. At any time Sam shuffles rather than walks; but when he goes across to his forge, first thing in the morning, his heavy boots are still unlaced and then his usual shuffle would sound even sprightly by comparison. Kettle in hand, he ambles down the road to the forge, to boil some water for the morning cup of tea; and it is with this first unbuttoned appearance of Sam that the day really begins. His loud voice and his louder laughter, as he greets whoever comes along, are the cock-crow announcing the dawn, and any sounds and voices, earlier than his, are mere shy, hesitant bird-calls, timorously awaiting the master-herald of all. Sam has a word for everybody and everybody has a word for Sam; and those he does not meet in the road itself, he calls up to in their bedrooms: nobody is allowed to sleep on once Sam has appeared on the scene.

But now it is all quite different. No Tom or Arthur goes pedalling past, called from bed each morning for a pittance on some far-off farm. And when Sam does appear, the day is already so far advanced that nobody could rely on such a belated cock-crow. In that cold silence when the snow throws its first white light on to the ceiling, it is almost as if the end of the world had happened overnight, and, unaccountably, we were the only souls left alive in a blank and muffled world. At last, however, there are voices—voices unnaturally clear, and as it were suspended, because unaccompanied by the sound of passing feet, in a vacuum. And then, once we are up, we see what all the mystery is about. There is nothing the snow has not clung to and changed past all knowing. Roof and tree, road and garden, all have been fashioned anew in the night by a hand of miraculous cunning and to the whim of a mind that loves not colour.

And down by Mark Thurston's cottage, under the knot of elms we had thought so friendly and so familiar, half a dozen men have suddenly appeared from nowhere with a couple of horses and the village snow-plough. Monkish in their sacks, which they wear over their heads, the two corners tucked one into the other, the men handle the cumbersome implement that has lain on the grass by the roadside all the year, its massive shares decorated with cowslips in spring and hidden under a foam of kexes in summer. While some of them attend to the harnessing of the horses, others stand by, flinging their arms about like flails, in an attempt to stir some sort of warmth in their shivering bodies.

Whereupon, of course, Mark appears at his door, with not even a jacket to shield his seventy-seven years, and, what really is unusual, without his cap. No old farm-hand ever dreams of going about with his head uncovered, any more than he would dream of picking a bunch of wild flowers ("*them* ol' things: now if they was taters, I'd understand"), and so there is always a suggestion of nakedness in the sight of a hatless villager, his pale, unsunned brow contrasting so vividly with the remainder of his ruddy, weathered face. In Mark the oddness is emphasized this morning by the reflection of the snow on his high, shining forehead. With both hands thrust deep in his pockets, he watches the men struggling with their plough.

"Bless us, Bob," he says: "it's a rummy sort of furrer you'll draw this morning. And hadn't you better stick a twig o' something in Gipsy's forelock to keep them ol' flies away?"

But nobody takes any notice. Mark's little jokes are not always as keenly appreciated as he thinks they are; and anyway, the men are too cold this morning to pay attention to him. "Now then, Gipsy! Come up, Dimint!" And the hooded men follow their cumbersome plough up the road, cleaving a wide furrow through the snow that curls over and breaks, like the ploughed stubble in autumn. Mark turns away, shutting his door behind him.

For awhile yet the village maintains its empty silence. Double-thatched now, with straw and snow, the cottage roofs project their picturesque angles against the deadened sky. Over Goose End the ruined windmill flaunts its broken sails, set at Miller's Pride till they fall and ill able to support the weight of snow lodged on their upper edges. Gardens there are none, and every bush is a frozen fountain. Our meagre river, running through the centre of the village, is indistinguishable now from the Green that rims its banks. At other times, it alternates swiftly from a convenient mirror (beloved of photographers) for the reflection of the surrounding cottages to a muddy stench that causes the passers-by to pinch their noses in disgust; but to-day both mirror and stench are sealed in ice.

Buried somewhere beneath its white, unruffled surface are the inviting slides that traverse it from end to end—slides where the children of the village have enjoyed themselves as never since they were born and where even the farm-hands, returning from the fields in the early dusk, could not resist the temptation to drop their bicycles against the bridge and take a flying turn or two before they went home to tea. Later on, no doubt, somebody will brush the snow away, or at least enough of it to uncover the precious slides. But it will be beyond their power to restore the simple sport to the pitch of ecstasy it engendered all last week and the best part of the week before. For then there was a moon. And while the frost dropped silver stars on to the roofs and spun from every branch and twig a hoary lace that only the morning would discover, lads and girls, and children who should long ago have been abed, sped over the glassy river, wings at their heels, and filled the blacked-out village with their laughing voices.

The Green is the hub of the village and much admired by our visitors. Four roads intersect it, pale ribbons that cut the green grass into unacademic triangles; and the meeting-place of these four roads is a narrow brick bridge adequate enough for the trickle of water which, in summer, flows underneath it, but totally inadequate for the amount of traffic which such a convergence of roads must necessarily cause.

However, it is a charming bridge in its simple, unhistoric way, and the number of accidents its inadequacy has so far occasioned is not yet sufficiently impressive to stir our Parish Council to do anything about it. Not that we have ever urged the Council to do anything about it. On the whole, we are a conservative people and (often quite justifiably) suspicious of innovations. Besides, from time immemorial the bridge has been the haunt of such old men as Mark, who, turned out of the pub before their argument has reached a satisfactory conclusion, may surely be allowed to lean somewhere and finish their talk in peace?

But now there is nobody leaning against the bridge. There is nobody anywhere. Then one by one people begin to appear. A door opens, and a woman wrapped up in a shawl tied over her head like a rabbit's ears picks her slow way across the Green; or another door opens, and a man with a broom makes a futile effort to brush back the snow that has heaped over his step, like Canute trying to push back the tide.

The two butchers' shops, apparently, do not deem it necessary to open this morning; and the grocer's shop, whatever activities may be going on inside, presents an obstinately inhospitable front.

Only the post office is open. For Miss Dickson, though nobody would guess it from her jocular manner and her warm-hearted concern for the welfare of all of us, is a Civil Servant, and the Civil Service allows no concessions, or few, to the whims and eccentricities of country behaviour in general. Snow or no snow, business must go on as usual in the post office—or as nearly usual as the circumstances will allow. For even in the post office punctuality has been nullified by this heaping snow. The mail-van has not yet managed to get through to the village, and the postmen, who dare not do the sensible thing and go home for a hot drink and a second breakfast, must make the best they can of an enforced idleness, kicking their heavy heels on the floor and flinging their arms about, till Miss Dickson's imperilled sweet-bottles rattle on the shelves and even she can hold them in good humour no longer.

Nor is it only the postmen who are a little ruffled in temper by this unaccommodating weather. Tradesmen, tired of running their cars up roads that lead nowhere but to a blank wall of snow, are all inclined to be a little brusque these days. And as the first novelty wears off, even the farm-hands, stolid enough as a rule, are getting weary of being sent so far afield, spade in hand, to help the unemployed dig away the drifts.

Only in Goose End is there no appreciable sign of petulence. And the cause of such geniality, of course, is Sam Merriman. For Sam all this is welcome holiday: no horses to shoe, no spare parts to mend, nothing to do but exactly what he chooses to do. And what he chooses to do is as nearly nothing as makes no difference. Late to rise, therefore, at last he comes out into the roadway, shuffling along and kicking up the powdery snow like a ten-year-old. Carrying his broom over his shoulder, he volunteers to sweep anybody's snow away for them; and what his endeavours lack in effectuality, they certainly make up for in jocularity.

"Now then, midear: what can I do for you?" And he begins brandishing his broom about, as if the gestures of a magician were what the heaped-up doorstep needs, and not good hard work.

"Did y'ever see the like? They say it's nigh as high as a haystack over by Gilbert's Rise, and goodness knows when they'll taste baker's bread agen over at Vetches."

Sam continues to pat the snow with his broom, then stops altogether and says:

"Could you keep warm last night, midear? I couldn't, nohows. I said to missus, 'This is a rum 'un, if ever there was one.' It *was* cold. And do you know what she remembered me of? Well, I'll tell you."

It is no kind of weather to stand on the doorstep listening to Sam's tales and so he is invited inside. "Just for a minute, then," he says, and brings his broom in with him. He sits on the chair nearest the door, where he always sits, because he must keep one eye on what is happening out in the roadway. The fact that the door is shut now makes no difference: this is his chair. He hangs his cap over his knee, a childlike smile spreads over his broad features, and his ample body sags at once into complete and solid silence. He says nothing.

And then, being asked what it was Mrs. Merriman had reminded him of in the night, "O aye," he says, "I was forgettin'. Well, it was a terrible cold night, not so many years ago—and I suppose the cold last night must have put mother in mind of it. We 'ad two little ol' pigs that time: proper little dears, they was. And it got so cold I said to the missus afore we went to bed, 'Whatever'll us do with them little pigs out there, mother? We can't leave 'em out there all night.' So I went an' fetched on 'em in, and we wrapped 'em up in flannel, and we took 'em to bed with us. Mother had one along o' she and I had t'other along o' me. When I woke up in the mornin', I couldn't see my little ol' pig nowheres; so I felt down in the bed-clothes, and there he was, dead as a nit! S'pose I must a-laid on 'im in the night. But mother, she'd got her's all right. Now what d'you think of that, eh?"

And as if there is now nothing else to stay for, Sam puts on his cap, takes his broom, and opens the door.

"That sky do look reg'ler full of it," he says. "I reckon us ain't seen the worst yet."

Sam is quite right. By noon the snow is falling again as fast as ever, only this time it is accompanied by a driving, searing north-easterly wind. In fact, to say it "falls" is quite inaccurate: it blows along, horizontal with the ground, so that men walking with their backs to it are completely snow-covered on one side and have hardly a flake to show on the other. Spectacular as the village itself is, the really exciting scenes are in the roads and fields outside. Half a mile away is a world away now, for there are several places where the snow-plough would be useless and where nobody has yet arrived to dig a way through. And even where the spade and shovel have been hard at work, leaving an abrupt wall of snow on either side of the road, this latest gale is closing the drifts over again.

I find myself fascinated (it is the exact word for it) by the mere action of this silent drift-formation. With the small snow blowing over the fields at I know not how many miles an hour, melting in my ears and on my eyebrows, I stand watching the deathly masonry being piled up before me. So many of the narrower roads and lanes about here are slightly sunken between the cornfields and, as I watch, it is easy to see how these fields are being all but denuded of the snow that is blown off them and deposited in the lanes. The high walls, chopped out by the spade, have long ago lost their angularity: a lean lip is being formed on top of them and grows fatter as I watch, till it hangs in an evil pout. Already the shelving snow protrudes a quarter of the way across the top of the tunnel, it grows every minute, and I can see that before evening the whole lane will be blocked up again. And how silently, intently, irrevocably, the building goes on!

The snow blinds me. The wind whines. I had forgotten the war, and even now it is not our war I think of, but the war in Finland, where men freeze to death as they stand, one clutching at the collar of his coat, another trying with one hand to staunch the wound in his stomach; and I almost think, as I watch the remorseless, evil activity of these millions upon millions of infinitesimal flakes, that perhaps I have come just a mite nearer the reality of their suffering.

And yet it is all so incredibly beautiful. English hedgerows, those gestures of largess so frowned upon by the efficient agriculturists of to-day, have never lacked for poets to sing the praises of their tangle of June roses, or their singing birds, or their autumn galaxy of berries; but I wonder to-day why no poet (at least that I know of) has sung the praises of their boughs garlanded with the January snows. Perhaps it is for sheer lack of words. At any rate, roses and birds and berries are child's play, when it comes to putting them down in words, in comparison with these extravagant waves and billows of snow that ride over the hedges just now. Where there were boughs and branches, there are now tethered clouds of snow, fantastic flounces of snow; and underneath, where the rabbit had its hole and must now sit cowering in a warmth that still is not warm enough to satisfy his shrunken body, there are blue-mouthed caverns more mysterious even than those where the sacred river Alph ran "down to a sunless sea."

The cold sings in my head and reluctantly I return to the village. Though the snow is deeper now, and the wind colder, there are more people about. Somebody has brushed away the snow from the slides on the river, and a follow-my-leader trail of children, the girls shrieking and the boys expertly silent, skims from one end to the other. Young blood is easily roused and these heady children are much too absorbed in the new-found pleasures that every day provides now to stop and consider its possible uniqueness in their lives.

Very different is the attitude of some of the bunched-up adults, picking their dangerous way from this shop to that, panic-driven to store up while they may food against even worse days. Food, however, is not half so urgent or difficult a problem for us as water.

It is one of the lesser ironies of progress that, while we have electric light in the village, a radio set in every cottage and 'buses

Snowdrifts by the roadside

four or five times a day to take us the eleven miles between here and the nearest town, we are still dependent upon pump and stream for our water. Most of us, at least for the greater part of the year, prefer it so. We cannot see why on earth we should pay for water, when all we need do is dip a bucketful out of the stream or take a few turns at the pump. It stands to reason, we say, that water which has travelled miles through "the Company's" pipes cannot possibly be as good as water pumped straight out of the clean earth. We count for nothing the handiness of being able to turn on a tap and have your water ready to hand. And why should we, when gathering round the pump, pail in hand, is such a pleasurable occupation and so prodigal of friendly gossip? Summer evenings would not be half so enchanting if we could not saunter down to the pump and fritter away in talk of this and that the last, easy minutes of a heavy day. And I know that, for myself, if I were asked to name one of the most pleasantly characteristic country sounds, I should say the lazy, monotonous squeak of the pump handle in the hot dusk of the summer night.

But just now all the village pumps are frozen—and have been for days. On being informed of our predicament, the Council sent out orders to Mr. Peck to unfreeze the wells. But Mr. Peck was engaged on other jobs and so did nothing about it. Even in the best weather, eleven miles is a fairly safe distance away, and now, with the roads almost impassable, it is perfectly safe: no sanitary officer is likely to come prowling around to-day. So Mr. Peck, who is himself so often at the mercy of those in high places, uses his advantage and obstinately keeps us waiting. Even if he did crack the cement round the wells and apply his blow-lamp, he knows the chances are that the pumps will be frozen again to-morrow: then why not let them wait until to-morrow anyway? So, I suspect, he argues; and every hour we make the slippery journey across to our particular pump in vain.

However, it's an ill wind. . . . And I am glad that the one to benefit this time is Widow Fields. By some miracle of Providence, that would seem after all to have a special care for poor widows, Mrs. Fields' pump has remained unfrozen. Revealing an unexpected commercial acumen, she therefore charges one penny a pailful and prodigally sets a limit to nobody. Mr. Peck's obstinacy is her advantage; and I confess I find it hard to believe her when she cocks a sad eye up at the skies and says, "Well, I *do* think it's about time it stopped freezing now."

In the tap-room of the Wheatsheaf, some half-dozen men, old and young, are savouring their precious midday respite over a mug of beer. Mark is among them and speaks for the older generations: not so much by general consent, maybe, as by force of character. For one thing, words come easily to Mark and so he invariably gets in first. Then there is Luke Negus—a lad more useful with the tractor than the horse, but none the less a genuine countryman for that. He speaks for the younger generation.

Just now Mark and Luke (I know the juxtaposition sounds incredible, but such it is; and anyway, the only apostolic thing about them is their names) are sponsoring a conversation that has somehow evolved itself into a sort of impromptu game.

"And how do you tell a fox's track?" asks Luke, posing a query on behalf of the lads sitting at the same trestle-table with him.

"That's easy," comes Mark's ready response: "a fox has got five pads an' his tracks follow one another in a single line."

Score one for the old men.

And then: "Can you tell where a rat's been in the snow?"

It is the young men's turn to show their detective skill. "It allus drags its tail," says one of Luke's company: "it leaves a line between the footprints."

Score one for the young men.

"What is it, then," asks Mark, "as leaves a lot o' convicts' arrows wherever it goos? And all in a single straight line."

Everybody seems to know this one, probably because there is nobody here who has not gone beating with the Squire's shooting-party at some time or another.

"Pheasant," says one. "Partridge," says another. And the score is equal on both sides.

Thus the game continues: the badger with its four pads in a double line, the stoat with its two-by-two dimples ("ever so pretty it looks, going straight across the snow," says Luke), and so on, until suddenly, unexpectedly, the sport has played itself out, and, before anybody knows how or why, we are all listening to Ben Tetlow's account of how he, and a lot more men, forty-nine years ago, took days digging through the snow-drifts that filled the sunken lane over Gilbert s Rise: "'T weren't no hill at all then," says old Ben, not a little surprised to find himself suddenly the focus of the company, "only one great big ol' lump of snow. We weren't short of wukk that winter, I can tell 'ee. And you may say it's nasty, heavy ol' wukk clearing away the snow; but it's a lot better'n doing a day with the stick-an'-a-half—that's what we used to call the flail," he adds, for the benefit of the ignorant youths of to-day. "I tell you, you don't know what wukk is, not these 'ere days."

"Come on, boys," says Luke, "let's get on with our job. I don't know whether it's what Ben would call wukk, but I reckon it's got to be done. Come on." They file out into the snow, leaving Mark and Ben to enjoy the fruits of victory.

"Just one more drink," says Mark, as the grandfather clock wheezes in the corner, preparatory to striking two: "I *think* there's time."

Ben has much more to say yet; and although the audience for whose special ears it was intended has gone away, he talks on. Mainly he talks to himself now, for neither Mark nor any of his cronies seems to be interested: the merit of the old days and the old ways is to be able to talk about them, not to have to listen to others talking about them. And so Ben's undoubtedly interesting recitative gets lost at last, submerged in a general conversation (which Mark has manœuvred) about the damage the pigeons are doing, this bitter spell, in the gardens.

And yet, as I come away from the Wheatsheaf into the silent, one-toned village, some of Ben's words still remain obstinately in my mind.

"We had to do pretty nigh everything for ourselves, then," he had said. "And for why? Because there weren't nobody to do it for us."

"And if we couldn't have done it for ourselves," he might have added, "we should have gone under." Perhaps that is one of the best things this snowy isolation has done for us: it has put all of us on our mettle—we are learning to do things for ourselves. And those things we cannot do for ourselves, we are learning to do without. In a minute degree, Larkfield recently has been more like a village used to be, I suppose, in the days before it began to ape (not very successfully) the towns. In the days before the windmill was a curiosity. In the days before radio and electric light and tinned food encouraged dependence. Old men such as Mark or Ben remember something of such days. Not much—but at least the sad afterglow of the self-supporting village. But for Luke and his friends, indeed for all of us under fifty, the village as a self-contained unity, baking its own bread from its own wheat, curing its own ailments from herbs gathered in its own hedgerows, is a fact out of history-books. And I cannot help thinking it is something of a pity that it should be so. Our newspapers don't arrive and we are vexed at their non-appearance. Our radio sets give out and we rush to the garage for a new accumulator. And we don't even like walking in the dark streets without a torch to show us the way. Are all these things so considerable an addition to our freedom, I wonder, that we ought not to count as loss the lack of self-reliance we have paid for them?

But for the snow it would be already dark. These are topsy-turvy days anyway, and the sky shines under our feet. And it is apparently a better sky than the one that normally should shine over our heads, for twilight will linger on an hour beyond its time, loath to leave a world so lovely. And so empty. Not a single cart has risked the roads all day. Even the motor-cars have consisted of little more than the milkman and the baker and such as were compelled, by a strange mixture of profit and duty, to go as far afield as they could. Now they too are home.

For once the pedestrian has the village to himself—a pleasure bestowed just when he is most unwilling to avail himself of it. A few cautious stragglers shuffle along the Causeway, and I have to scan their faces (for overcoats have suddenly appeared on bodies that never wore them before) to see who they are. But white masks are all I see; till "Good night to 'ee: good night!" proclaims the persons who wear them.

Chapter Two

BENEATH the snow, that regiments everything into a uniform prettiness, the houses of Larkfield are as various and individual as the men who, down four centuries or more, have built them. They range from half-timbered cottages, neatly capped with straw thatch, to council houses, whose staring brick uniformity is a sorry indictment of this year of grace, nineteen hundred and forty. The former, even where their owners have neglected them, wear their age with dignity; but the latter have been ignominiously pushed out of sight, as if their approvers knew beforehand how rapidly (despite restrictions which, as one tenant put it, "don't even let you go to the privy in peace") they must deteriorate into a slum.

Every local style is represented in the architecture of Larkfield: from the Congregational chapel, with its Dutch façade hinting of the Flemish weavers who came over to enrich East Anglia with their craft, to the church, with its dog-toothed Norman doorway reminding us of those armoured knights who were our last and most considerable conquerors; from the steeply gabled butcher's shop by the Green, whose clustered chimneys crown as fair a piece of Tudor building as any round about, to the scores of four-roomed cottages under whose thatch generations of farm-hands have each night forgotten in sleep the ache and poverty of the day.

Thatch, in fact, is our special pride—though you would see no cause for pride just now, while snow, that other leveller, lays an equal pall on straw and tile alike. And well may thatch be our special pride, for this village lies in one of the richest corn-belts of the country: seen from an aeroplane, or even from the top of the church tower, Larkfield is a picturesque hotch-potch of angular roofs bundled together in a wide expanse of cornfields. Thatch is as apt to us here as limestone tiles to the Cotswolds; and although perhaps it is on the decrease to-day, it is still our most predominant roofing. Wherefore I find it strange that, in an 1848 directory of the locality ("under a lucid arrangement of subjects") the list of Larkfield craftsmen contains no mention of a thatcher. Four blacksmiths, yes, and two wheelwrights; a saddler and seven shoemakers (how the clay tugs a man's boots to pieces!); a cooper, a glazier, and even a "machine-owner"; but no thatcher. To-day there are two thatchers resident in the parish; and the Squire, whose many tenant-farms, I suppose, make him impatient of their well-known procrastination, has imported a third from Bedfordshire.

All craftsmen are notoriously independent: if they are not allowed to do a thing in their own time, they certainly will not do it in anybody else's. Their own satisfaction is the clock they work by; and you may as well try to make your garden plants blossom before they are ready as try to force the pace of a true craftsman.

So it is with thatchers. November gales may blow your roof off, and leave you to sleep beneath the stars; but Thatcher Wright will not come to your aid until he thinks fit to do so.

You walk out to his cottage and attempt to stir his pity with a recital of the plight you are in. "Ah, I dare say," is all he says: "there's everlastin' o' folk been after me these days. Dunno when I *shall* get round to you."

Exasperation dies down, and you even get used to sleeping under the stars. And then, one morning, when you had given up bothering any more, a load of straw arrives from somewhere and is shot down in your garden. It blocks the view, but there is a compensation: your rooms glow with a golden light. Then Wright himself arrives, crippled with the Old Man (as he calls his rheumatism), a bundle of spics and uncut hazels under his arm and a few tools tied on to his bicycle.

From that moment your house is a centre of attraction in the village. Perched on his ladder, with his game leg stuck out over the gables at so precarious an angle that your heart almost misses a beat to see him, he is greeted by everybody who passes; and although he always has something to say in return (usually sardonic), I have never yet seen him pause and turn from his work to see whom he was addressing.

In the days before the towns drained the blood away from the villages (offering errand-boys higher wages than farm-hands could earn) every thatcher had his assistant, whose job it was to draw the straw, cut the spics, load the yealms in the greip, and in fact do anything that might prevent the thatcher from wasting time by going up and down the ladder. Wright, in common with most other thatchers of to-day, has no recognized assistant. But he has three handsome, stalwart daughters. And sometimes, when the Old Man gets too "opstropulous" (as he says) he will bring his favourite daughter along with him: a silent, hefty girl with a head of fly-away hair as golden as new straw in sunlight. Expertly she trims the hazels and combs the straw; and as Wright calls to her from the ridge, where he sits in the sun shearing the scalloped pattern that runs from gable-tip to gable-tip, like a shepherd astride some monstrous golden-fleeced sheep at shearing-time, I think he sometimes wishes she had been born a boy.

It is, I know, a matter of some envy with him that Fremlin, his rival thatcher in the parish, has a son to assist him. True, Albert is more witty (in a bucolic way) than helpful. He spends most of his time, while his father gets on with the job, mimicking the more outstanding of our very mimickable community. Or, if it is not people, then it is birds and animals. Somebody in the village has heard the cuckoo—ten days, as every native knows, before he is due to arrive: it is only Albert. Or somebody's cockerel develops an unusual exuberance and crows throughout the livelong day: it is only Albert.

"A fool of a fellow, if ever there was one," says Wright, in no position to appreciate such homespun talent. All the same, he is probably thinking what a pity his own assistant can't be called Albert.

So the thatch grows. Always providing, of course, a wind does not intervene. No thatcher will work in a wind. Perhaps he has secured all the yealms in place, and nothing remains to do but the finishing-off—the straw to be trimmed round the eaves and over the dormer windows, the withy pattern to be woven along the ridge and gables, and so on; but as long as the wind lasts, the thatch must wait. The straw hangs over the windows, tousled as a beggar-boy's fringe; and every time the door is opened, another handful of straw-ends blows across the room.

But at last the thatch gets finished somehow, and Wright ties his tools on to his bicycle, flings a straight leg over the saddle, and disappears, leaving behind him a litter of hazel-chips and a garden where every plant grows straw.

How dandy the house looks now! Time, and the weather, will draw the gold out of the thatch and mellow it to a basic grey, as various as the light that falls upon it, rose at sunset, pink at dawn, moody as the sun and rain themselves. But just now—there it is: a new toy for all the village to pause and admire: an invitation to every homeless sparrow in the neighbourhood.

Or will it prove to have been an invitation to the martins, instead? For my part, that is what I sincerely hope. Two years, now, the martins have tried their best to bring up a family under the shelter of my eaves, and two years they have been routed. Will they try again?

It is not only that almost every other house in the village has its quota, and more than its quota in some cases, of the "lov'd masonry" of this favourite bird: but that to have martins building under your thatch is to have money coming into your house—and who so unworldly as not to enjoy the prospect of that? What should have given rise to the sentiment that one bird brings good luck and another ill, who knows?

"Have you ever seen a white blackbird?" Jim Adams asked me the other week, pausing, axe in hand, where he was felling an ancient ash. "If ever I see another," he went on, "I shall shoot it."

For all his bushy black brows and his gipsy eyes, Jim is a mild young man at heart, and so I was a little astonished at the amount of ferocity he put into his words.

"Why, Jim?" I asked.

"Because they bring nothing but what's bad," he replied.

From the story that followed, it appeared that a white blackbird had made itself very much at home in the cottage (now pulled down) where Jim lived with his busy young wife and his nigger-haired little girl.

"I suppose our Dot made a fuss of it," said Jim. "It was always in and out of the place. You couldn't keep it away with a broom."

Then Jim's young wife fell ill. The next he heard of the white blackbird was at Mrs. Rugby's. She had to be taken off to hospital. Then it appeared over at Joe Ferring's; and he fell off a load of straw and nearly broke his neck. So the tale went on: wherever the unlucky bird made its home, tragedy invariably accompanied it.

"Yes," said Jim, "if ever I see another I'll shoot it," and he brought his axe clean down upon the wound of the ash-tree, as if in emphasis of his intention.

Poor blackbird! "White as sin (as Andrew Young says) to your black kith and kin"—and to some countrymen as well, to judge by Jim's sad experiences.

But to return to my house martins. It was two years ago last May they made their first attempt to build under my eaves. I had watched other martins in the village, by hundreds, nesting and mating and scurrying round the houses, filling the summer heat with a twittering sound as of far-off water; and—I admit it—I was jealous. Why not *my* eaves? And then one morning there was a whirling and flashing past my window, like blown snow-flakes, and an incessant small bickering. The martins had arrived! I went outside to see. Already the work of building had begun. Close by one of the projecting joists of the roof, on the east side of the house (where certainly the air is not "delicate," as Banquo observed it should be), several dark mud-blots showed where the martins had secured the plinths and main uprights of their nest.

Most of that morning I spent watching the birds at their incredible task. By noon, however, they had little more to show for all their efforts than when I first caught sight of them. I think it is Coward who notes that a certain amount of play and aerial courtship invariably accompanies the initial stages of building: there was certainly much more play than work going on that morning. They would flurry in and out of the eaves, brushing past the wall in narrow arcs, twittering ceaselessly; and then, unexpectedly, one would settle. With her arrowy tail sucked tightly against the plaster, she turned her head this way and that, as she clung there, watching the brief assaults of her lover, and often her body would be so curved that beak and tail-tip made a complete half-moon against the wall. If the male bird managed to keep away long enough at a time, she would make a momentary effort to get a little work done, jabbing the clot of mud with her beak, kneading it in, and busying herself as a good housewife should. But her endeavours never lasted for long. Soon her companion would return, swooping up to her side with little *tchucks* of annoyance, as if he were luring her away. Come, time enough for house-building to-morrow!

That was in early May, when the celandines shone in the ditches and brimstone butterflies drifted like petals from the budding boughs. Once the martins got down to work in earnest, the nest was soon completed—a work to match the Pyramids themselves in cunning and audacity. It was a grand welcome-home, those days, to see, just above my door, a white-throated martin looking down at me with bright, intentful eye. I grew accustomed to the sibilant, soft music of those birds, as they flashed past the window and they gradually became the essential focus of that spring in my garden.

Then June took me away and the house was left empty. And when I returned in July, I knew at once that something was wrong. Martins, by the dozen, flickered over the roof and ransacked the evening sky for food; but they were not my martins; or, at least, they had nothing to do with the nest over my door. At first I thought perhaps the birds had hatched their eggs and the fledglings had already flown; but when I looked at other nests, in near-by eaves, where the martins had been busily building long before mine came on the scene, I was convinced that this could not be so —for there the youngsters were still thrusting their yellow gapes out of the nest-hole, clamorous for food and yet more food.

It was a straw sticking out of my martins' nest that first betrayed the truth. And then a sparrow-face appeared at the opening, chirruped saucily and disappeared inside again.

I know there are people who have a special affection for sparrows: they are so impudently indomitable, thriving where more delicate birds would perish, insouciant, undeniable, the *gamin* of the skies. Well, I give them all that and more; but still I do not like them. And if I did not like them before, how shall I like them now, when they have turned my martins out of house and home? My thatch had been wired to keep them away; but no, that did not defeat them. Those sparrows were determined to be my guests. If they could not get into the thatch, at least they could turn the martins out of their nest and make themselves at home there. Anyway, who *are* these fanciful weaklings that must needs hurry off south directly the cold weather comes? Come along, we'll show them who's master here: the nasty foreigners!

And so—well, the long and the short of it was that that cheeky face peeping out of my martins' nest made me see red. Saint Francis, who loved the house-sparrow equally with the nightingale, forgive me: I took a pole and poked the nest, till it fell in broken shards to the ground. That will teach you, I said; though of course it didn't.

Next morning the impossible seemed to have happened. My

martins were returning! The same swooping up under the eaves, the same soft chuckling as of a hidden burn, the same giddy spiral-flights past my window. Then they would cling against the plaster, probing with their needle-beaks the ruins of their home. The sun shone on the pansy-blue of their backs, and breast and throat gleamed like snow. Their long, tapering wings were crossed above them, like the slim, folded wings of Fra Angelico's angels. And they chattered unceasingly. Out of the blue sky more martins appeared and joined them, pricking the morning with a multitude of small cries, glissading down the air and briefly inspecting the ruins as they passed. It seemed as if my martins had called all their friends and neighbours to come and help them to decide the momentous question whether, even at this late stage, they should build a second house and rear a second family. What finally decided them, I do not know; but after that one morning of frenzied consultation, they never came near the place again.

Next year, the same thing happened. With the celandines came the martins. A few feet away from last year's sad reminder, they built another nest. Again there was the bright eye looking out at me every time I passed. Again I was called away. And again the ragamuffin sparrows turned them out. So now I am wondering will the martins give me a third chance to get rich? Will they try again next spring?

Next spring! But nobody dares to think of next spring and what the war may bring for us with the warmer weather and the lengthening light. Thanks be, then, for the respite of these shivering days that shut away the fear of what may be.

Meanwhile, the martins, whom the spring will bring, whatever else it takes away, are far over the seas, and our native birds must endure the rigours of a record English winter. Fluffed out to twice their size, they look well-fed enough; but in truth their crops are well-nigh empty. On the radio last night a bland announcer's voice might have been heard encouraging us to feed the birds. It was, he said, a form of war-work. If the birds died, the crops would suffer next summer and we should suffer too. How many right things, these topsy-turvy days, are done for wrong reasons! We must feed the birds, not for their sake, but for our own. Well, so long as the birds are fed, that, anyway, is something. And maybe a habit will be started that will not cease: in the end we may feed the birds for their own sakes.

That was the way we thought about another war-measure: the evacuation of children. Like most other villages, Larkfield had its sudden influx of children from the towns. In those warm, end-of-summer days, the village rang with unfamiliar voices. There were difficulties and disappointments. Two worlds suddenly clashed, and the impact, to say the least of it, was uncomfortable. But there was also hope of compensation. How country life would change these pale-faced children! It had taken a war to do it; but at least the heritage would not be wholly evil, if afterwards we could point to a regenerated youth. And as we watched the colour come into those children's cheeks, and saw their limbs grow stronger every day, we began to believe the end of slums was in sight after all.

But alas, things did not turn out like that in the least. As the weather grew worse, and the bombers failed to arrive, the children one by one drifted back to the towns. The villages were themselves again. And so were the slums. It would almost seem that lasting good cannot come accidently: straws, for all the proverbs, will not save drowning men.

And as with the children, so with the birds. Anyway, I know I much prefer Jim Adams's reason for feeding the birds. He does it because he likes to do it. He loves the birds. And so does his wife and his little curly-haired daughter. When spring comes ("the flower that always makes me feel best," says Jim, "is the snowdrop") father and daughter will walk round the hedges in the evening, when work is done, looking for nests. Back home again, Jim will empty some small egg from the peak of his cap, for Dot to add to her growing collection. "We never take more than one," Jim says, sternly; "and then only if we haven't got one like it at home." Well, I dare say the birds would allow him so much at least, if their memories could stretch back as far as this bitter winter and the scraps of food he put out for them in his garden.

Sometimes I have heard Jim spoken of in the village as "soft." There is no very serious criticism implied in the speakers' words, for they know well enough how good a worker Jim is on the land; and one farm-hand is always quick to appreciate in another the deep store of inherited (rather than acquired) knowledge that lies behind all the tasks of good husbandry, ploughing, sowing, stack-making, and so on. No, it is not any inherent inability in him that they deplore, but a tendency to indulge the poetic. Birds'-nesting is all very well for boys and wild-flower gathering for girls, but a married man should have done with such things.

I have noticed it is usually the younger men who imply this lack in Jim. The older men sit back and say nothing—as if they did not altogether agree but were compelled, out of timorousness and their own tendency towards a similar indulgence, to keep quiet.

It is, shall we say, an expression of the spirit of the times. The young countryman of to-day, though he goes to the cinema at most once a week and is still leagues away in thought and feeling from the young mechanic in the cities, has nevertheless become enough affected by the modern attitude to put on at least some of the hard, protective armour with which men and women seek to shield themselves to-day from the pain of too much feeling. The armour fits him ill, as yet; but with combine-harvesters in the field and electrically milked cows in the shed, he is gradually learning to wear it with more ease.

Jim, however, will never learn how to protect himself from his feelings. His vulnerability shines in his black eyes. Yet his critics are wrong to impute this tenderness in him to "softness." Like his own favourite snowdrop, that rears its fragile head through the ice, his strength is in the very nakedness with which he dares to bare himself.

Jim is, in fact, that increasingly rare person, the genuine young

Promise of Spring

countryman. There is a certain loneliness in him, a proud isolation, as a result. He would have been more at home with the farm-hands of fifty and sixty years ago. They would have felt as he feels. But now they are old and outmoded, and Jim must walk a good deal alone.

His sense of this isolation is perhaps revealed in his shyness in first conversations; but once contact has been made, the shyness falls away and you find yourself talking with one whose interest in the land is a living thing, a responsibility even, echoing back to the days when every countryman, however poor, was master of his own few acres, his own few strips. Owning nothing (scarcely a pig in the back garden) the farm-hand of to-day has no sense of responsibility to the land. And where there is no responsibility, there is no intimacy. No wonder Jim walks alone! Such an intimacy with the land is the very breath by which he lives. It explains that tendency to indulge the poetic which his fellows are inclined to deplore, that tenderness which is only another name for his sensibility to the living earth.

"I wouldn't work in a town for anything," I once heard him say. "Whatever you do there hasn't got any *life* in it. Here, everything has got life in it."

Jim is not ashamed of his sensibility to the living earth, any more than his forebears, far back, were ashamed of theirs. Indeed, daily, though perhaps unwittingly, he encourages a like sensibility in his child. To him a dunnock or hedge-sparrow is always a Hedge-Betty, a thrush is a Mavis, and a flower of the lesser bindweed is a Hug-me-Tight; and in speaking their names so natively, he proclaims immediately his kinship with the long-dead men who christened the goldfinch King Harry, the owl Billy Wixey, and the harebell Our Lady's Thimble. Such names are a lot of nonsense to the majority of the modern generation of farm-hands. Standing there in their dungarees, by the side of their tractor, its oil spattered on their faces and its fumes caught in their hair, they would feel awkward to be heard speaking these old poetic metaphors.

How many times, for instance, in the Wheatsheaf, have I heard some old man (Jim's spiritual brother of fifty years ago) speak vivid, homespun words that have merely evoked a giggle from his young listeners.

"If you want to get your rights in this parish," said Mark, the other day, voicing one of his pet criticisms of the way things are to-day: "if you want to get your rights in this parish, you've got to be either crafty, or wicked, or a downright liar—and goo about lookin' like a farden kite with its tail blew off! Don't, nobody'll take a mite of notice of 'ee."

And all the response he got was: "Mark's a proper comic, so he is," the speaker's own language being as devoid of poetry as a marrow of meat.

In the diminished numbers of its genuinely responsible young farm-hands, however, Larkfield is no worse off than any other English village up and down the country. Possibly it is even a good deal better off than many. No railway runs through our village and the nearest town is eleven miles away. We have no cinema and we have no dance-hall. Several of us have never seen the sea, although it is only some twenty miles away. And Jim was not conscious of anything unusual in his confession to me one day that he had never seen a mountain: "I used to think they was like this," he said, moulding an imaginary single peak with his hands, "but I suppose I'm all wrong about that!"

The depth of a man's knowledge is not to be measured by the number of miles he has travelled—as every second tourist to-day bears witness. Travel broadens the mind, we are constantly being told; but there are some things better measured by depth than by breadth. And experience is one of them. Jim has never seen a mountain and old Mrs. Cook has never seen the sea; but the daily lives of both of them are an ample witness of the intensity of experience of which they are capable.

Our isolation, therefore, is not without its advantages. Among the older generation (for whom, still, all that is not Larkfield is foreign) it has preserved a goodly measure of that sense of responsibility to the land which was the very basis of our greatness half a century or so ago; and among the younger generation it has at least kept alive a more hopeful semblance of that responsibility (for all Jim's comparative loneliness to-day) than might otherwise have been the case. Some villages have not even their Jim.

And certainly we are fortunate in the number of old people still living among us, women like Ann Bright who brought up twelve children in a four-roomed cottage on wages that, at their best, never exceeded seventeen shillings, men like Mark Thurston who at seventy-seven are in possession of a vitality and an integrity that colour every word they say, to give an example to such as care to follow it.

Ann stands in her doorway taking the sun and watching the world go by. "Yes, I'm feeling as happy as all the birds!" she says. And she means it too. And, hearing her words, how can one not be glad to be living in Larkfield to-day?

Chapter Three

WHATEVER the villager makes of his church to-day, there it stands, towering over his cottage, as powerful in its masonry, if not in its appeal, as it was hundreds of years ago. He may seldom go inside it, but it is part of his life now, like an apple-tree in his garden that has been there ever since he was a boy. Perhaps he makes no more use of his church than as a clock. What's the time? and he opens his back door, cranes his neck, and reads the hour between his neighbours' thatches. Or he passes it every morning on his way to work, and there it is to greet him again on his return at night. Or he hears its bells blowing across the fields to him as he walks behind the drill.

"The wind's gone round to the west again," he will say, glad of the sound for its welcome news of coming rain.

Such usages may be secular, but may they not somehow serve more than a secular purpose? The mere fact of the church, so persuasively in evidence every day, telling the hour for him and prophesying the weather, perhaps helps to keep alive in him some echo of a faith more alert in earlier times. Willy-nilly, he is a child of the twentieth century, and the twentieth century is a faithless one; yet there is a possibility that faith will not wholly die in it, while church bells chime across the fields to tell the time of day.

In Larkfield to-day, as in most other villages, it is mainly the women who attend the church: they are more traditional than the men, more timorous of breaking with the past. And so it is upon them that the vicar chiefly relies for his meagre congregations and upon them that he spends the greater part of his clerical endeavours. Except maybe for a funeral, whether of a relative or some lifelong friend, the men rarely enter the church at all. They may still touch their caps to the vicar when they pass him in the street, but it is usually in obedience to a respect they learned (or, rather, had thrust upon them) when they were young: the ghost of an old habit instilled in the days when such deferences were compulsory.

"It were forced religion in them days," says Mark: "we *'ad* to goo to church. And if it wasn't parson as compelled us, it was Squire. But we got the better of 'em sometimes, for all that. We used to hang round the church porch a-Sunday mornin', waitin' till Squire drove up in his carriage an' pair. 'Mornin', Thurston,' he'd say: 'mornin', Tetlow,' and time he'd gone inside and was kneeling down in his pew, we'd be on our way home agen, to set the taters, or somethin' like that."

Nowadays, relieved of compulsion, the men no longer even make pretence: they just stay at home altogether. Called upon to defend their attitude, they might very well make use of another of Thurston's remarks: "Religion ain't just goin' to church, now is it? It's how you live—leastways, that's how *I* see it."

Nevertheless, there is one occasion, apart from funerals (which anyway are attended perhaps as much out of deference to the dead as out of respect for the living) when men may be seen, in plenty, walking up the church path at the summons of the bell. "Harvest festival," I remember one non-churchgoing farm-hand saying to me: "harvest festival? That somehow ain't *like* church, not to say church, is it?" And the implication was, I imagine, that with the corn and the flowers all around him, the hearty singing and the rather more informal air of the whole service, he felt at his ease; and ease is a feeling few farm-hands associate with attendance at church.

At harvest festival the fields are brought inside. Everything a man's eye rests upon, then, is familiar. This is the corn he has tended all through the year, from green blades piercing the first fall of snow, to rustling ears swept down by the binder; these are the marrows and flowers and apples from gardens just like his own. No need for his thoughts to get mazed at the prospect of some frightening after-world, while there are these real and very familiar things all around him—Tom Clissold's potatoes, pride of the village allotments, Baker Swift's crisp brown loaves, and those shaggy dahlias, nursed so carefully all through the winter to blossom at last in his own back garden. The very smell of the church at such a time is comforting and friendly, a blend of all the scents that surround him at his work. Yes, it is all actual enough and close to every day. Why, somebody has even brought a dozen sugar-beet, and there they lie in a neat pyramid, chopped and scrubbed, to remind him (as if he would be likely to forget it!) how his fingers have ached with the cold, till he could almost have cried, and each boot has weighed a ton, as he stood out there in the bitter fields cleaning the roots of leaf and mud and pitching them up into the tumbril. "Harvest festival? Well, that somehow ain't *like* church, is it?"

So the majority of the men feel; but with the women it is rather different. The church necessarily occupies a larger place in their lives. Not only because they mainly comprise its congregation, but because, one way and another, it subtly controls several of their most considerable pastime activities. Such activities (like the Women's Institute that has become so firmly established in every village) may advertise themselves as strictly non-sectarian and non-political, but the theory is scarcely maintained in the practice.

It cannot very well be otherwise. The village women, it is decided, need entertaining, need educating, need organizing. Very well, and who else is there to do these things if not the women of the "leisured" classes? In every village there are the equivalent to the Squire's wife, the retired Colonel's wife, the Vicar's wife, the pensioned Anglo-Indian official's wife, and the elderly spinster daughters of some dwindled aristocrat: on these the work of entertaining the village women, educating and organizing them, is bound to fall. They have the time on their hands, they have the money, and quite often they have the genuine aptitude and inclination. But they are, almost without exception and by the very nature of things, Church of England and Conservative; and even with the very best intentions in the world, they cannot help colouring the organizations they control with the hues of the Church and Party they support.

Unfortunately, the Church and Party they support are largely propped up on the idea of class-distinction. However unintentionally, therefore, a suggestion (if no more) of condescension informs the activities of these leisured women on behalf of their presumedly inferior sisters. But their inferior sisters are no longer quite so uncritical of condescension as they used to be. Conservatism dies hard where the people live mainly on and by the land; but even the remotest villages, these days, are slowly shaking themselves free of every vestige of servility. Such condescension implies a denial of the villager's proper pride and he is quicker to defend that pride to-day than he was a quarter of a century or less ago.

"Is Sam at home?" the retired Anglo-Indian official inquires of the blacksmith's wife. "Mr. Merriman is over at the forge, sir," comes the prompt reply, dignified and without emphasis. The quiet rebuke is unmistakable.

On the other hand, Sam himself, the very next day, will lapse into something at least reminiscent of the old servility. The Squire, in one of whose cottages he lives, calls and asks him to give lodging for a few days to a timber-valuer who is coming down to assess some trees on the estate. Sam hates lodgers, because they are a severe restriction on that simple liberty which, at seventy, he has just managed to achieve. Nevertheless, he agrees. Afterwards, of course, he complains. "Then why did you say yes?" he is asked. "Well, I live under 'im, don't I?" he replies: "what else could I do?"

But in any case there is a difference here between Sam's lapse

Timber and plaster in Essex

into near-servility and his wife's quiet insistence on her pride: liberties taken by the Squire and liberties taken by the retired Anglo-Indian official are not at all one and the same thing. Merely by virtue of the long-standing position his family have occupied, the Squire is allowed to encroach at least an inch or so on Sam's liberty without giving undue offence: there is a bond between them, forged through long generations. But the Anglo-Indian official has no such tradition to sanction his assumption of intimacy.

Indeed, the Squire is in quite a privileged position. Perhaps, in this respect, Larkfield is more fortunate than some villages. Our Squire is not only Squire—and local Member of Parliament and Chairman of This and Manager of That—he is also farmer. Four thousand acres is the extent of his estate and it includes most of the major farms in the parish. Some of these farms are rented out, others are worked by foremen who live in a few rooms of the vast, half-timbered farm-houses put at their disposal; but one of them, the Home Farm, is the Squire's special pride—and the pride, also, of the whole parish.

Mention of this farm, and of the good husbandry practised on it, occurs in several old farming books; and Arthur Young himself wrote in praise of the methods employed on it by one of the Squire's ancestors. If you want to see ricks neatly trimmed as they were in the days when the farm-hand's "task" included a hundred and one little jobs neglected to-day for lack of time or inclination or ability, go to the rickyard of the Home Farm and see how the score of ricks there, some round, some oblong, some set on iron staddles, proudly proclaim the joy of a job well done. If you want to see a ploughman draw a straight furrow across half a mile of field, go to the Home Farm fields in autumn when the ploughmen rip open the long stetches in the stubble and leave them wavering across the undulating land like ribbons flicked out in the wind. And if you want to be assured that the "old-fashioned" farmer still exists, loving his land as he loves his wife, go and have a word with Mr. Saling, the Squire's Home Farm foreman. You will probably find him wandering round the fields somewhere, on his way from superintending one job to superintending another, and as you walk by his side you will notice how he continually steps a stride or so out of the way to dig up some dock or thistle (for his walking-stick is also his "spud") that his keen eye has seen while you have been talking.

And all this evidence of careful husbandry—Mr. Saling and his spud, the neatly trimmed ricks, and the straight furrows wasting so little at the headlands—is the Squire's pride, as it was his father's before him and as we all hope (not quite so confidently as we might wish, perhaps, for even the stoutest tradition is apt to snap these days) it will be his son's after him.

No wonder, therefore, if the Squire wins the respect of the village and is allowed a certain amount of licence even with Sam. It is generally claimed that the days of Squiredom are over; and goodness knows there are enough forsaken mansions up and down the country, their dead eyes staring across the ruined park, to give grounds for such a claim. But Arley Hall at least still stands intact among its fertile acres. Its Tudor brick façade, rosy as a peach under the rays of the setting sun, still maintains a gallant defence against the enemy. Progress makes no conquest there. In all its great length and breadth there is no bathroom, and the servants (hard to get and harder to keep) must each evening carry up dozens of oil-lamps from the kitchen.

Such obstinacy in the face of forward-moving time may seem crass or merely apathetic. Arley Hall belongs to the old order and it is just being wilful to pretend it doesn't. Maybe, we say; but we are not quite convinced. We do very well under the Squire and would be sorry to see him depart; and we certainly do not wish to see Arley Hall converted into some screaming girls' school. Squiredom, it seems to us, depends upon the Squire. It can be a good thing and it can be a bad thing. And if it is asking too much of poor human nature to count upon a sufficiency of good Squires to justify such a scheme, then we can only say that in Larkfield, at any rate, we are fortunate. Another Squire might make us think differently; but so long as the present one justifies his place in the grand tradition of his fathers, serving his land and the people who work on it, we are satisfied.

Yes, we do very well under our Squire, thank you; and some of us have seen quite enough of the way things work under the up-to-date, impersonal system that is prophesied for us not to prefer to be left alone. As countrymen and countrywomen we know the value of the personal as compared with the impersonal, and we willingly accept the possibilities of error that such an attitude entails. Our daily contact with growing things has taught us this much. While we may, therefore, let us keep our Squire, because at least he reminds us, in a world of increasing statistics and bureaucracies and government from afar, of a communal life based upon the discipline of personal relationship.

And let us also keep our church. For many of us it may be little more than a timepiece, a weather-glass, an imposing piece of architecture with a chilly and rather musty interior. But there it is —the most powerful reminder in all the village of that slow pyramid of life of which we are the insignificant apex.

The leaning tombstones in the churchyard are a salutary warning, each time we pass by them, of our own relative unimportance: the lowly mosses and the humble lichens are sufficient to blot out our names when we are gone.

Chapter Four

IF the church, then, is there to cater for our spiritual needs, the pub is there to cater for our bodily needs. The one undeniable and yet somehow remote; the other equally undeniable but not at all remote. Church and pub, spirit and body—and it is perhaps not without significance that whereas the one is mainly frequented by women, the other is mainly frequented by men. The village pub, indeed, is the farm-hand's club.

I should, of course, say "pubs," for in Larkfield there are four of them. And they flourish as the green bay-tree. It is true that my directory informs me that, in 1848, there were six pubs in the village; but what is the loss of two pubs in a hundred years?—particularly when it is recalled how large were men's thirsts in those days. A man took his ten-pint harvest-bottle with him into the fields and would have thought himself extraordinarily hard done by if the farmer did not supplement this with liberal supplies from his own farm-house brew.

To have retained four pubs out of six, therefore, is not too bad. And when I say they flourish, I particularly have in mind the Wheatsheaf, over against the village green. Some of us, more unprogressively minded than most, are inclined to think it has perhaps flourished too much of recent years. In the old days there were only two rooms and one of them was obviously not for use. Sometimes a stranger would make a mistake and open the wrong door, but a first glimpse of the sedate plush furniture inside and a first sniff of the uncirculated air were usually enough to make him hastily withdraw.

A pub should be entirely democratic, and nobody could have claimed that the Wheatsheaf was anything else in those days. We all used the same room, shared the same fire, sat on the same worn, shiny forms, and studied (if ever we were so unoccupied or bored as to notice them) the same battle-pictures and sale-bills on the wall. If we were disturbed by the fact that Mark spat liberally (and, it must be said, accurately) into the fire, only just missing our coat-sleeves as he did so, then the remedy was in our own hands—we could at least move out of range. And if Ben Tetlow became more garrulous than usual, or launched again on a yarn we had already heard more times than we could possibly count, well, it was a simple and effective antidote to invite him to a game of dominoes. Ben may not concentrate on many things, but one of them is certainly dominoes.

Now everything is changed. Instead of two rooms there are three; and all of them are for use. Furthermore (and perhaps this is the innovation we jibbed at most) all are labelled: Saloon Bar, Visitors' Room, and Tap Room. "It's as bad as the Army," I heard Mark say, as he stood watching the workmen painting the white lettering on the doors: "officers and their wives, men and their women."

Not that the labels were necessary. I cannot imagine Mark walking by mistake into the saloon bar, with its tile-topped tables and its satin cushions on the chairs. Rose-pink satin cushions are not Mark's idea of pub-comfort, and so he and his cronies sit round the trestle-tables in the tap-room in monkish simplicity, and no doubt in time they will feel just as much at home there as they did in their old den in the days before the renovation. As yet, even in the austere tap-room everything is still a little too new, too clean, too shiny. Mark, for instance, is not quite sure about spitting into the handsome new fireplace; and when, carried away by his own exuberance, he so far forgets himself as to do so, the action is invariably followed by a wrinkle of pained apology on his shiny forehead.

As for the visitors' room, I have no idea who uses this inner sanctum—if anybody does. When the alterations were first completed, Tom Clissold, our proud landlord, showed me over the building—the tap-room, the bar, the saloon, and then, with the air of a magician about to produce out of the hat the most astounding surprise of all, the visitors' room. He opened the door and I peered inside: to have entered would have been more than I dared and clearly more than Tom expected. But the brief view revealed such an assembly of new furniture and brilliant china vases, dyed pampas grass and brass fire-irons as immediately suggested the windows of a furnishing shop in the Tottenham Court Road. And I confess I still find something more than a little incongruous in the thought of that paint-plush room at the core of a Larkfield huddled under the simple stars.

Commercially considered, of course, Tom's improvements were made just in the nick of time. Hardly was the new paint dry on the doors, or the new bottles temptingly displayed above the bar, when war was declared. A couple of anti-aircraft units were dumped down in the neighbourhood and naturally the very first explorations of the soldiers led them straight into the Wheatsheaf. Tom's saloon bar has never been empty since. What was panic and almost pandemonium at first, settled down after a few weeks into a steady and profitable routine.

In fact, prosperity is in the very air at the Wheatsheaf these days, and Tom's smile grows with each succeeding week. Even this unprecedented weather has been to his advantage, for the camps are cold and the duty tedious, and inevitably the soldiers seek what solace they can find in the bottles and barrels of the Wheatsheaf. Some have brought their wives with them and some their friends, and as many of these as Tom's bedrooms will accommodate are now additional aids to his prosperity.

The military influx, moreover, has given Tom an importance over and above his status as landlord of our most considerable pub. Tongues, even soldiers' tongues, are set talking by good drink, and he can hardly help himself if, fulfilling his pleasant and profitable duties, he overhears a thing or two not perhaps meant for civilian ears. He knows; and of course we know that he knows—by mysterious nods and becks and hints he sees to that. But Tom is far too wise a man, and too patriotic an Englishman, to divulge what it is he knows. "A careless word may send thousands to their death": so reads the warning on his walls. Well, he at least will not be guilty of homicide. Maybe whatever he knows amounts to nothing that matters; but by keeping it to himself, at least he adds something to his stature. And remembering that gleaming visitors' room, I think perhaps he needed an additional cubit or two.

Only in the bare-boarded tap-room has the war so far made no appreciable difference. Perhaps it is because, as yet, so little has happened to bring the fact really home to us. Perhaps it is because the *habitués* of the Wheatsheaf do not fundamentally understand why there should be any need for anything to "happen." They understood the last war well enough, or at least they thought they did. Many of them took part in it—including Mark, who disguised his age and joined the Army Veterinary Corps. And if the War Memorial on the green outside the pub (defying history with its plain assertion that the war lasted from 1914 to 1919) no longer rouses any very pronounced feelings in them, at least they thought the struggle it commemorated was inevitable and righteous enough at the time.

It used to seem to me, in those fateful months preceding the actual declaration of war, one of the most hopeful signs of progress that nobody in the Wheatsheaf (or in any other village pub I chanced to walk into) ever showed anything but dislike at the prospect of another war. "If they want me, they'll have to fetch me this time," was the most frequently heard comment. Certain things began to

A corner of an old barn

be recalled: kindnesses met with from the enemy, lies told at home, and a vague conviction that, whatever might be the differences between one nation and another, they certainly did not justify the barbaric slaughter of war.

"I expect if you was to go over there," I remember Tom Clissold saying, who had never been beyond these shores, "you'd find them there Germans pretty much about the same as you an' me. Leastways, they're wonderful fond of their beer, I'm told, an' I reckon that counts for *some*thin', don't it?"

In spite of increasing provocation, goodwill was still the characteristic attitude of the nameless thousands that make up the Larkfields of England. War could not happen again.

But it did. And gradually I noticed a change in the men's attitude. Instead of "If they want me, they'll have to fetch me," now it was, "Well, I suppose I'll have to go." No enthusiasm, no conviction: merely a dull acquiescence in the inevitable.

And in spite of the obvious barbarities of the enemy abroad and the persistent propaganda of the authorities at home, this is still very much the attitude to-day. Not that the men talk a lot about the war. An illustrated daily paper lies on the table, shouting some new sensation from its two-inch headlines; but few bother to pick it up and read it. The voices of the soldiers in the saloon bar drift round the corner; but we cannot see the khaki, and the stray words sound peaceful enough. So our conversation follows the course all country conversation invariably follows: the weather, the crops, the new tenants over at Vetches, and local matters in general. Sometimes a concession is made in favour of matters of more national import, such as the ill-management of "this 'ere rashoning business" or the scarcity of pig- and chicken-food ("They tell us we've all got to keep a pig in the sty," says Luke Negus, "but they don't tell us what we're goin' to feed 'em on"), but even such national matters are only viewed from a purely local viewpoint.

It would be difficult for a stranger to tell, from the average conversation in the tap-room of the Wheatsheaf, that we are at war. These men are incorrigibly peaceful. The land is their whole life; and war, until it enters their very homes, remains essentially a secondary consideration with them.

How different, for instance, is their attitude to the black-out, compared to the attitude of their brothers in the towns. Perhaps Mark Thurston's comment, the other day, sums up as well as any the general reaction of such born-and-bred countrymen.

"I don't like it," he said, "and I shall be wholly glad to see the back of it. When my missus has got into bed, I like to slip back the curtains, so's I can lie and look outside, time I ain't asleep. I like to see the moon through the window, and my ol' tree, and a little owl a-sittin' on it—whoo-ee! whoo-ee! That's being alive, that is; but this 'ere's like being dead. You might just as well be in your coffin."

Smart as the Wheatsheaf is, and admirable its service, there are nevertheless times when my loyalty to Tom wavers and I find myself gravitating towards another pub on the edge of the village. Inevitably a pub takes its colour from those who regularly frequent it. It is their club and owes its character to their many tics and foibles. But sometimes even the tics and foibles of Mark and Ben and the rest are powerless to resist the imposition of an alien character on the Wheatsheaf. Usually this only happens at week-ends and in summer. Then our tidy (but never too tidy) green is all but obliterated with motor-cars and picnic-parties, and the Wheatsheaf is crowded to the doors with young men and women who have come out into the country for the day. The Wheatsheaf's regular customers are silenced before such a happy, voluble crowd. Indeed, they are hardly visible. And at such times it seems only courteous to clear out of the way altogether and leave our guests to the unimpeded enjoyment of their visit. To-morrow we will return and clear up after them; but to-day we will leave them in full possession —in fact, there is no alternative.

On such occasions, therefore, I quit the urbanized atmosphere of the Wheatsheaf and take my drink at the Three Horseshoes.

There will be no crowd there (Harry Clark, the landlord, would not know how to deal with it if there were), and every voice will have a familiar tone about it and every word a native twist.

The Three Horseshoes is less a house than a honeycomb: to draw a plan of its oddly shaped cells and passages, every one on a different level from the other, would be quite beyond my power. One thing these cells and passages have in common, however, and that is a certain severity. There are no rose-satin cushions in the Three Horseshoes; nothing but good, honest wood. And there is nothing progressive about Harry. He is only half, perhaps only a quarter, the landlord of the Three Horseshoes; the rest of him is a blacksmith. And when, in his own good time, he comes to bring you your beer, he brings quite a lot of his forge in with it. The yellow end of a home-made cigarette (constantly being lit and as constantly going out again) hangs from his lower lip; soot colours the rest of his face and his lithe, strong arms; and instead of a barman's apron he wears a bit of old leather, cut to ribbons and seared with fire.

In fact, the landlord of the Three Horseshoes has always been half that and half something else; and one of Harry's predecessors has left behind him a local reputation which, however skilled a craftsman he may be, the very nature of the times will deny to Harry himself. Many a craftsman, dead and buried these fifty years or more, still keeps his memory green in the village by some work of his agile hands—a field-gate here, good for another quarter of a century, a neat piece of house-thatching there, or even a scrolled latch in some out-of-the-way cottage window where mass-production frames have not yet been introduced. And so the memory of Natt Witherby the cooper still lives on, kept green by those oaken harvest-bottles (kegs, as some call them, or costrels) of which he was the master-maker in the locality.

Not that many of Natt's harvest-bottles are still to be seen. Here and there you may find one hanging on a rusty nail in some cottage outhouse, its iron hoops falling away, its paint weathered or gone altogether, and its leather handle and trimly shaped vent-pegs as irretrievably lost as the dark, shining bullock's horn from which its owner drank his beer in the harvest field. But for the most part, Natt's bottles have been broken up and burned, and Natt is remembered less by the sight of them than by the reputation they earned in years gone by.

Harry may have all of Natt's skill in those strong hands of his, but he has to spend it on such severely circumscribed jobs as the mending of stoves and grates, the riveting of cart-wheels, and the patching-up of factory products which the craftsman in him abhors. His fate is the fate of most village blacksmiths to-day, but at least he is more fortunate than most in having his little pub to fall back on. His customers may not be many or very profitable; but they are his friends. All the week they must more or less look after themselves and be content with only an occasional visit from Harry, who stumbles in from the forge for a moment just to see how things are going.

But on Saturday night, washed clean of soot and with a whole cigarette between his lips, he is a host in a hundred. It will be strange if Ned Freeman is not there with his accordion, and many a forgotten country song comes to life over the glasses of beer. And even after closing-time, when his customers should all be gone, Harry sits on in the cloudy tap-room, discussing the mysteries of life with a few chosen cronies.

"No, Jim, you don't want to go home yet awhile. Drat the missus! I should a-thought you had enough of her jaw all the week. Why, I'm only just beginnin' to wake up! Did you see that bit in the paper the other day. . . ."

But Jim resists the lure of the landlord's intriguing conversation and goes home. And Harry is left alone, dreaming while the last embers fade.

Chapter Five

AS I look out on the snow, dinted only with the feet of birds, I think that if there is one person in Larkfield whom it must please, more than another, that person is surely Charlie Beslyn. (Sam I leave out of count. Almost everything pleases Sam, providing he is in the mood.) More than once I have heard Charlie Beslyn complain at the fleeting nature of the English snow, no sooner come than gone again.

"It always used to rile me, when I was a nipper," he said, "because I never could get up in time to see the snow before somebody or something had spoiled it."

To see the snow before the dirt had smutched it, however little, was Charlie's boyish ideal, and somehow he never could manage it. The poet in him, even then, longed for perfection, complete and entire, and it "riled" him that perfection should always remain just beyond his reach.

Well, if unsmutched snow is still his symbol of perfection, he has had plenty of opportunities to see it lately. Charlie lives about half a mile outside the village, and every field he can see from his windows now must be covered from hedge to hedge with pure, driven snow. No need to get up at dawn, lest somebody's nailed boots should spoil it before he can enjoy it: all day, and day after day, it keeps its white perfection. Charlie should be happy now.

I had known him a long time before I learned that he was a

poet. Perhaps I should have guessed. That he was no ordinary farm-labourer was clear enough at the very first glance. Lean-cheeked and unshaven, he looked at me with black eyes of diamond brightness. Those eyes were keen and missed nothing, and their brightness was perhaps less of laughter than of avidity—an avidity to drain the honey out of every moment, every thing. His hair (I have never seen him wear a hat and that alone sets him apart from his fellow-countrymen) was inextricably tangled over a high-domed forehead that later reminded me of another rural poet, though immeasurably his peer—John Clare, "the Peasant Poet of Northamptonshire."

I first got to know Charlie, however, through casual conversation, as a middle-aged countryman who "farmed" his garden, and lived with his sister in a thatched and tiled cottage outside the village. Indeed, our conversation in those days was nearly always confined to the garden; and yet, even then, there were hints in his words, gleams of a muddled mysticism, flashes of original thinking, that set him apart from other men. Even his attitude to his garden was original and quite unlike the strictly utilitarian attitude of most cottagers. Its crowded acre combined beauty and use in a most unusual way. Flowers and vegetables grew together, dahlias bloomed among the cabbages, the foot-long tassels of Love-lies-bleeding trailed over the turnips, roses climbed the apple-trees, and giant sunflowers of incredible diameter peered with phoebus-faces here, there and everywhere.

If there was order in Charlie's garden, and I believe there was, it was an order devised entirely by himself to please his own individual whim. He has an old wireless set and, for all I know, may listen regularly to the comfortable voice of Mr. C. H. Middleton; but if he does, it is certainly with no slavish intention to follow that omniscient gardener's advice. In gardening as in everything else, Charlie obeys his own laws. He will give you, and freely, slips of this and seedlings of that; but if you ask how to treat them, all he will probably say is: "Well, *I* always dibble them in somewhere shady for a start, and dust a pinch of soot round them—but maybe you will find a better way." Experience is the only schoolmaster he trusts; and in the same way as he has learnt everything for himself, so he would like to see other people trusting in nobody but themselves. The result, so far as his own garden is concerned, is admirable. Some would say he has green fingers; but Charlie himself would say it was all a matter of common sense—and faith in his own ability.

I remember a talk I had with him one day in autumn. His cottage lies well back from the road, shut away from passers-by by the whole width of his crowded garden. I heard his ladder rustling among the gay, withered leaves; he was gathering his apples. I opened the rickety gate under the ivy-tod, walked up the cobble path, and made my way round to the side of the cottage where I could just see his weathered face and shining eyes peering at me out of the apple-boughs. We talked for a while of this and that, a conversation as desultory and peaceful as the autumn afternoon itself, while the red and yellow leaves fluttered to the ground and the leviathan sunflowers, with their lesser constellations of buds, put the weakling sun above to shame. Then Charlie clambered out of the apple-tree and, setting his heaped-up basket among the windfalls that were scattered over the dark earth, came over to me in silence.

"Do you read poetry?" he asked. Assured that I did, he then added: "Maybe you write it, too?" And when the proper basis of understanding was thus secured, he put his horny fingers in his waistcoat pocket and produced a folded sheet from a small exercise-book. "Read this," he said, "and tell me what you think of it."

In a bold, straightforward handwriting three verses were written on the grimy sheet. I do not remember their entire contents, but I do remember that the first verse sang of violets ("that's Alice, when she's ten"), the second of daffodils ("that's Alice, when she's fifteen"), and the third of roses ("that's Alice, when she's twenty").

I suppose there are few minor situations more embarrassing to the conscientious than to be given some verses to read and then to be asked, by their author, for a candid criticism. Inferior verses are bound to mean more to the poet who writes them than to the reader who reads them: the former at least knows what fine emotions he intended to convey, and those emotions surround his verses like an aura which only he can wholly divine. Of course, one could behave like the Rev. Twopenny, of Little Casterton, to whom Clare sent his early poems in the hope that this worthy gentleman might help him to get them published. Mr. Twopenny merely sent the poems back again "with a cold note stating that he had no objection to assist in raising the poor man a small subscription, though the poems appeared to him to possess no merit." Clare retaliated later by lampooning the clergyman in some witty couplets that made good use of his unfortunate name; and perhaps Charlie would have revenged himself on me in the same manner, if I had adopted a similarly tactless attitude.

Instead, by as happy a route as I could discover on the spur of the moment, I led the conversation away from the particular to the general, and before either of us really knew what was happening we were engaged upon a discussion concerning the diverse nature of verse and poetry.

It was during this talk that I first discovered how far afield Charlie's interests roamed beyond the confines of his flowery garden. Milton, I happened to say, was an example of the entire poet. "Now there," Charlie replied, "I don't agree. I think *Paradise Lost* is a poor sort of poem: most of it is full of words I can't understand, anyway—and there's no *life* in it."

Somehow this brought up the subject of music. "I dare say you'll think differently," said Charlie, his diamond eyes brightening as his mind grew heated with the ideas that delighted him: "I've my own notions about music. You see those trees over there" (and he pointed towards some yellowing willows slanting over the pond beside his garden), "well, *they*'re music to me. So's somebody leading a good life. Or a child picking flowers in the fields. All that's what I mean by music."

From any English hedgerow

And when the conversation, following its own inconsequent course, came back again to poetry, Charlie said: "My favourite poet is Shakespeare. There aren't many evenings go by but I read something or other out of one of his plays. I wonder if you know this bit?"—and then, not so much to impress me by the intimacy of his acquaintance with the playwright's work as to share with me his obvious delight in it, he quoted, giving each slow word a native accent that Shakespeare would surely have relished, Jaques' speech on the seven ages of man.

I suppose Charlie is somewhere about fifty years old. He has never lived anywhere but in this same cottage, which was his father's and his grandfather's before him. His father was one of the last, hereabouts, of those small cultivators whose doom was sealed with the advent of Enclosure. From him, no doubt, Charlie inherits the iron determination with which he still makes his stand against a world of big-scale farming for profit.

Exactly what he lives on nobody knows, yet he never seems to be in want. Occasionally he may get an order for a score of hurdles from some farmer who happens to be old-fashioned enough to prefer them. He sells a few vegetables and apples to his neighbours; and once or twice during the course of the year he may lend a hand to some smallholder in the district. On the proceeds of all this (and perhaps on such savings as have survived from the days before the last war, when he rented an orchard and kept a fair number of chickens) he and his sister live to-day, maybe meagrely, but certainly happily.

Indeed, Charlie is one of the most truly happy men I know. His life may be circumscribed but it is full. Change and variety from the outside world he never seeks: he does not even bother to go as far away from home as the village. Many a time I have asked him if he would not come along and see my garden—a matter of ten minutes' walk; but he just smiles and says, "I don't know, I never seem to have the time."

Though he is something of a recluse, there is nothing shy or withheld about him, once you get to know him. In conversation he is brisk and vivid, and he is in close touch with every aspect of the immediate life around him. Every dawn sees him out in his garden.

"That's the time I like best," he says; "everything is fresh then, and new. Even the air seems cleaner." (Not that it could ever be called dirty, in so open and uncontaminated a spot.) "I like to go and stand down there by the pond and see the primroses reflected in the water. And there's nobody about anywhere: only me and the birds and the animals."

If Charlie does venture beyond his garden (other than on those rare occasions when he goes away to work), it is usually at night.

"I was up by the cross-roads at Robin's Head at midnight last night," he once said, "and whose voice do you think I heard? Yours!" Now Robin's Head is at least three-quarters of a mile away from my house, as the crow flies; yet when I recollected what I had been doing at midnight, I found he was certainly right. A night of extraordinary starry brilliance had persuaded me out into the garden; and Charlie, with an ear as keen as a Red Indian's, had heard my voice if not my actual words.

Another midnight walk he told me of was to a place locally known as the Churchyard. It is a meeting of four green rides, far out in the middle of the fields, with not even a barn near by, much less a church. The place is legend-haunted. There is a pond, rush-fringed, close by and in summer the air smells sweet of thyme and marjoram.

"They've a saying round here," said Charlie, "that if you go to the Churchyard on midsummer night, and stand by that little pond at midnight, you'll hear bells chiming. The sound is supposed to come from some church bells buried in the water. Old Tom Selby will have it there was once a church there, and others will tell you the same. Some say it's where they buried those who died of the plague, donkey's years ago. But nobody seems to know the rights of it all. Anyway, I thought I might as well go and see if I could hear the bells!"

Charlie's laugh made it clear he had gone less in expectation of hearing any bells chiming in the water than because the lonely, haunted place attracted him as just right for a midnight walk. He would certainly have it all to himself.

Although there is this streak of fancifulness in Charlie's make-up, he nevertheless mostly keeps strictly to facts. Of a bundle of books I once gave him, ranging from anthologies of poetry, through Henry Williamson's *Tarka the Otter*, to Samuel Butler's *Erewhon*, it was the last that most forcibly appealed to him. The poetry books he prized in the main because they provoked his own gentle muse, whilst he relished *Tarka the Otter* for the multitude of its close, natural observations which he could check and query from his own intimate knowledge of nature. But *Erewhon*, I found, was something entirely after his own heart. Butler was a rebel, Butler said audacious things. And Charlie, who, in his own quiet way, is also a rebel, sometimes likes to suppose that he too is saying audacious things.

"I'll tell you what I've been thinking," he said one day. "Most people hold that selfishness is a bad thing, but I don't agree. When you've *earned* a thing by your own work—whether it's a flower in your garden or a thought in your mind—you *ought* to be selfish about it. That's good: what's bad is envy of things belonging to somebody else, things you haven't earned for yourself."

The value of such remarks may not be in their profundity—most of Charlie's sayings are apt to sound platitudinous until you recall the fact that they spring from his own individual thinking. They are original enough to him; and, like his verses, they are perhaps more calculated to thrill the teller than the told. I think Butler pleased Charlie because he was so eminently sane. He took nothing for granted. What tradition and the pundits agreed was final was not final for Butler until it tallied with his own conviction. And I think Charlie saw in himself another Butler, testing everything by his own experience, accepting nothing at second hand. His opinions, if faulty or even trite, are at least his own. It is imperative to bear this in mind when talking with him, and more than once I have had occasion to remember what Edmund Blunden wrote of Clare, "Tact was essential if you would patronize him: you might broaden his opinions, but you dared not assail them."

Modern education will see to it that there are very few Charlie Beslyns in the future. To achieve such contentment, in a world bounded by an acre of clay, will be difficult indeed when every country child has been perfectly moulded into the urban pattern which modern methods of education are designing for him.

Charlie digs in his garden. He pauses a while, and a robin comes and perches on his fork. He looks around him—these are his flowers, his apple-trees, his cottage. Every sound yields up its meaning to him, as he stands there listening in the still, sunny afternoon; and his eye, bright as the robin's, misses nothing of the small, eventful movements that are going on all around him. If, in such a simple scene, he is happy, it is because, by desire and by tradition, he is satisfied to suck the nectar from whatever flowers may come his way. Utterly self-reliant, and disciplined to the fewest possible needs, I think I can honestly say he comes as near as any man I know to the power of seeing "a world in a grain of sand, and a heaven in a wild flower." And for this power he has absolutely nobody but himself to thank—himself, and the enigmatic fate, perhaps, that caused him to be born of simple country stock.

To be country born and bred must count for less and less as the years go by: it counts for less already. Here, in Larkfield, in common with most other villages to-day, as soon as the children are comfortably able to make the journey, they are whisked off by 'bus to the nearest considerable town (in this case eleven miles away) where they attend an up-to-date school complete with every possible amenity that modern educational theories can devise. Since the town is so far away, the 'bus, which must needs make a circuitous journey in order to pick up the children from outlying villages, leaves Larkfield at eight o'clock in the morning. Some of the children have half an hour's walk before that, and another half an hour's walk when the 'bus deposits them on the green at five o'clock in the evening. Thus their homes become little more than dormitories to them and they have less and less opportunity to indulge that busy idling, in lane and meadow and wood, which is the basis of every country child's development, an education such as no school can possibly improve upon and a sure foundation for that after-contentment which makes Charlie Beslyn the happy man he is.

Nor is this the only, or perhaps even the worst, penalty which must be paid by these country children who are the compulsory victims of the increasing trend towards a centralized education. Spending so considerable a proportion of their time in the towns, they must inevitably adopt town habits of thought and feeling. They mix with town children, playing and working with them throughout the day. They are taught by teachers who, whatever the consequent advantages may be, are at least at a disadvantage in their enforced remoteness from those peculiar qualities that characterize the rural mind. And in their free moments they rush into the streets and dawdle about the sixpenny stores and the cinemas, and so forth.

At the moment all this is not so important as it will be presently. The age at which the children are sent away to the town schools is now from ten years to eleven; but presently, as the system gets hold, and easier methods of transport are devised, the central schools will open their maws wider and country schools will become a thing of the past.

And then where shall be found a genuinely country-minded child? Hygiene is no wise substitute, in the long run, for hours spent in the open air, nor lessons in trigonometry and biology a profitable exchange, at such an age, for an education that comes as much from sauntering round the fields with a ploughman father as from the teachers themselves.

Where the children are educated (however inadequately, from the pedantic point of view) in the countryside that is their home, at least some of them may grow up preferring the country to the town, a farm-hand's job to a mechanic's. What is more, it is just in those first fifteen years that they will realize, if ever, the love of the land that is their heritage. A good farm-hand, or even a good farmer, does not acquire his most valuable knowledge of the land in school or college; and he is severely handicapped when his contact with it is cut short in those early, precious years. We complain that men cannot be induced to stay on the land these days, even when they like the work and are so eminently adapted to it. Are they any more likely to prefer it, one wonders, when the whole of their training is framed to thwart their initial advantage and to encourage them away from it?

And so I suppose we must make up our minds to accept a future in which the villagers will all speak the same standardized speech and in which the land is farmed by men trained in town laboratories. Well, I suppose it will be a more efficient world than now—if efficiency is your aim. But for my part, when I talk with Charlie in his garden, among that fruitful and pleasing higgledy-piggledy of flowers and vegetables, I cannot help believing that efficiency is a dead thing in comparison with such purposeful individuality.

Towering over Charlie's cottage is a walnut-tree. It must be over forty years old, because he says he planted it when he was a boy. From an insignificant two-leaved stick to a multitudinously branched tree, bearing all the winds of heaven, he has watched it grow, year in, year out; and if any man can be said to know a tree, that man is Charlie and that tree his walnut-tree.

In spring, on his way across the garden to feed his hens, he will snick off one of the oily leaves and press it against his nostrils: the very breath of the young year is there, in that bruised tender bit of green. And in autumn, when the leaves begin to spin and fall, he will take a long pole and thrash down what nuts he can reach, leaving the rest to fall of their own accord, so that he may shuffle the ruck of dead leaves aside and enjoy a second crop. All seasons and all moods he knows that tree. As he sits by the fire in winter, pencilling some sentiment in homely verse, he hears the wind flailing its bare boughs; and in summer its ample shade is his cool retreat at noon.

I do not wish to give the impression that Charlie is sentimental about his tree: it is perhaps typical that, although it is among the best-loved things in his garden, he keeps his winter-wood stacked untidily against its trunk to drain, and pens his chicken under its shade in summer. But then, there is no sentimentality in Charlie's attitude to anything in nature. There is his walnut-tree, and he accepts it; and use and beauty are inextricably twined in his enjoyment of it. Forty and more years he has known it; and as it broods over his cottage now, sturdy and slow and fruitful, it might well be considered an epitome of his own life, deep-rooted in one place, rich in its strong individuality.

One day, just before this snow first fell, Charlie asked me if I would lend him a history-book. Not, he stressed, one that was little more than a string of dates with their appropriate events, but a detailed history of the reigns of Richard II and those monarchs immediately preceding him.

I was a little surprised at the request. What new adventure of the mind was he embarking on now? Then he explained.

"You see," he said, "I'm thinking of re-writing Shakespeare!"

A twinkle from those black eyes somewhat relieved my momentary embarrassment. All the same, I knew that he was not wholly joking.

"I think Shakespeare got King Richard all wrong," he continued, "and it's up to somebody to put things straight again. The dead can't speak for themselves and so I'll try to speak for them. *Have* you got a history-book like I said?"

And what, I would like to know, is one to do about a man who wants to re-write Shakespeare?—even one of the thirty-seven plays. You may reply that if Charlie, in his youth, had been whisked off by 'bus to the Central School (and thence, maybe, to the High School, and thence, again, to the University) he would have acquired a perspective that would have corrected such errors in taste.

I agree. But a Charlie Beslyn, educated through High School and College might very well have lost, for all his gains, just that one quality which is to-day his abiding solace and makes him the full man he is. Charlie is an example of the natural man, and the natural man will certainly offend the canons of the school-men.

Anyway, nobody will suffer because he is to-day sitting before the fire in his English igloo re-writing *The Tragedy of King Richard the Second*; and he himself may learn quite a lot by doing so.

Chapter Six

WRITING verses is not the only accomplishment of which Charlie Beslyn could boast, if boasting were his pleasure. He also plays the piano. Perhaps that is too positive, too forthright a description of what actually happens when Charlie draws a chair up to his fretwork-panelled piano and picks out his favourite melodies, note by note. His own description is better: "Of course it's only a while-time," he says; "I'm no pianist."

But the merit of Charlie's piano-playing is not in proportion to its dexterity: he plays because he likes the sound of the notes, and because he likes the way they gradually fall into a recognizable sequence under his hesitant touch. And that, I contend, is merit enough. There are more proficient pianists in the village, but I honestly doubt if their enjoyment is keener than Charlie's, as his rough, unagile fingers stumble over the yellowing keys. His enjoyment in his music is the same as his enjoyment in his verses: both may be untutored, and, indeed, rather infantile, but they nevertheless spring from the pure source of all aesthetic pleasure.

I have never yet been able to persuade him to play to me. With diffident pride he will show me his verses, but apparently as yet he has less confidence in his music. All the same, without his knowing it, I have occasionally heard him play. Sometimes, of an evening, as I passed by his cottage, I have heard him trying to marshal the obstinate notes into a melody, and I have stayed a while out in the roadway, listening.

"I heard you playing the piano last night," I will say to him the next morning, when I find him digging in his garden.

"Could you make out what I was playing?" he will ask, smiling rather anxiously, like a child eager for praise which he fears he may not have earned.

"Of course," I answer; "it was 'Drink to me only.'"

"That's right," comes Charlie's happy reply; "so it was." And his simple pleasure is a joy to see.

Yes, Charlie's performances may be meagre enough, judged from an artistic point of view, but they represent something quite unique in the equipment of the average village.

Larkfield, not unnaturally and certainly not unkindly, treats them as rather a joke; but then so many things about Charlie are a joke to the villagers. How should they realize that here is a bud of culture vainly striving to break into flower? Culture is something quite outside the ken of most of them—and I am speaking particularly, of course, of farm-hands and their families. And so they smile at Charlie's efforts at piano-playing, or whistle loudly when they overhear him from the road. They go home and turn on the wireless. There's music for you! Symphony concerts and chamber-music, organ music and opera, anything you want, and all for the turning of a knob. The Wurlitzer throbs in the front room, rattling the china in the cupboard and filling the place with oceans of sound. How shall Charlie's fumbling melodies, one note now and another ten seconds later, compete with such expert performances? And yet I swear they are worth all the radio sets in the village and should be honoured for the heroic fight they put up against the victorious onslaught of Music at Second-hand.

Perhaps Larkfield is more than usually philistine in the matter of music. There are villages in Wales and in the North where it seems to be as natural for the people to sing as it is for them to speak. This certainly cannot be said of us. I have heard it ingeniously suggested that this dour songlessness may have something to do with the clay on which we live—clay that pulls the heart out of a man when he must struggle with it every day of the year. But for myself I doubt whether there is anything worth a second thought in this pretty theory. There was plenty of singing here once upon a time.

"They say times are better now," I remember one old man here saying to me, "with less work and more play. They say we worked so hard and so long that we hadn't any time left to enjoy ourselves. I dunno so much about that. Why, in them days, after ten or twelve hours' scything in the harvest fields, you'd hear men go home at night singing; and it weren't always for the beer inside 'em, either!"

And only yesterday Mrs. Trugget was telling me of the dancing and singing that used to go on over at the Pig and Whistle. "They cut the floors up no end with all their carryings-on," she said. "They used to dance to—

> I'd rather have a guinea than a five-pound note.
> For the guinea would sink and the fiver would float:
> So I'd rather have a guinea than a five-pun' note!

and all sorts of nonsense. And the bricks were all worn thin as paper with the tread of their feet."

Well, you can count yourself lucky, these days, if you hear so much as an accordion in the pubs round about here, and I never yet heard men coming out of the harvest fields singing. Evidently something has taken the song out of the people.

Every now and then, of course, the old vocal conviviality comes alive again. I remember such a resurrection of song some eight or nine weeks after the outbreak of war. We had gone into Castle Oliver in the local 'bus that shakily plies the seven miles between here and that quiet little town on market days and Saturdays. On market days the 'bus is full of farmers and their wives bent on business, but on Saturday it is full of villagers out to enjoy themselves. With money in their pockets, they crowd into the 'bus, spend the afternoon trailing round the streets and listening to the Cockney Jews touting their wares in the Square, and then visit the little local cinema in the evening.

There was a full moon that Saturday night, and Castle Oliver, as we walked through its blacked-out streets on our way to the waiting 'bus, between the gabled and overhanging houses, might have jumped back through the centuries to medieval days. There was none but pedestrians in the streets, shuffling and whispering in the moonlight, and the peaked roofs, clear-cut against the winter sky, reminded us of the drawings by Dürer. Then we all clambered into the 'bus, settled ourselves down, and began the darkened journey home.

No sooner had we got outside the little town, to where the thatched cottages stood in moonlit isolation among the fields, when somebody started to sing; and at once the whole 'busful of happy passengers joined in. With dimmed headlights we crawled through the winding lanes, while the searchlights flowered from their long stalks in the sky around us, and the singing grew to such a volume that it seemed we must be heard miles away.

Only now and then did it cease, when the lights went on and the 'bus stopped to let somebody down. "Good night, John; good night, all!"—and then, with the dousing of the lights again, the singing recommenced. And the songs we sang? Mostly they were the favourites of the minute, tunes popularized by the various radio dance bands in the frantic attempt that was being made just then to discover patriotic marching tunes for the troops. We didn't always get the melodies right and we couldn't always remember the words; but our singing nevertheless served its purpose. Some mood of unusual happiness had communicated itself to us—maybe from the full moonlight outside, or, who knows, from the novelty of a 'bus ride in the early days of the wartime black-out—and we had need to sing. And for once we responded to that need, without let or hindrance, as Mrs. Trugget's dancers did and those harvesters coming home from the fields.

Such vocal conviviality, however, is unusual. It seems we have lost the very desire to sing. And such attempts as have been made, at one time or another, to bring music into Larkfield have rarely met with much success. There was, for example, Mrs. Glow, whose whole life, one might say, was spent in a missionary endeavour to teach us the delights of good music. She played the organ at the church and gave pianoforte lessons to such as could afford her admittedly modest fees. She even composed music and once (at her own cost) achieved the dignity of print. "Ivydene: a Waltz. Composed by Ada Glow, *née* Huggins. Copies to be had of the Author." She kept a tin trunk full of copies of her waltz which she sold, at a handsome discount on the printed price, to her pupils. But they, alas, never amounted to many, with the result that when she died, worn out in an uneven struggle against the forces of darkness, the tin trunk still remained half full of clean, mint copies.

Perhaps the peak of her proselytizing endeavours was reached one day when she was asked to provide some *entr'acte* music for a play that was to be performed in the village. The play was intended (or so the performers themselves had previously advised us) to be hilariously funny; but either the acting was very bad or we were very dense, for laughs that evening were few and far between. Nor did Mrs. Glow help matters much by playing the slow movement from Beethoven's "Sonata Pathétique" between the acts. But, as she afterwards said, "One had to do what one could to raise the tone of the occasion."

That, in fact, was just where Mrs. Glow failed with us. She did not know it, and she certainly would have refused to admit it, if somebody had pointed it out to her, but her failure was largely due to the fact that she was much too intent upon improving us.

She should have taken a leaf out of the book of one of our neighbouring villages. There is still music in Toddington, and plenty of it, too. Captious residents in the place are even heard to declare that there is too much of it, especially on summer evenings, when the vicar conducts his little brass band out on the green. On those practice evenings the village heart-beat quickens, as the well-known tunes surge over the hill. There is no point in talking, then: the only thing to do is to keep quiet, or sing with the band. Down in the valley the men pause in their gardens. "There's Freddie's band at it again," they say, trying to catch the tune as it flows down to them in waves.

"Freddie" is the vicar, and he would be the very last person to object to such familiarity. He organized the village brass band, whose members are drawn solely from the workers—the blacksmith, the shepherd, old Fairy the stockman, and the lads who ride off to the jam factory each day on noisy motor-cycles—for no other reason than because he knows there is nothing so tonic as being able to make a loud noise. When inviting subscriptions from the Hall, of course, he said a band would help to hold the village together; but his honest reason for undertaking the adventure was that he knew it would be a handy means of letting off steam. He is fond of letting off steam himself. It never occurred to Freddie that, for instance, the music might improve the villagers: to act the part of cultural ambassador was never in his mind.

So the band was started and soon became a great success. There was never much finesse about its performances, and neither Freddie nor his bandsmen ever showed much desire to tackle music that wasn't chiefly noticeable for its good, broad tunes: the broader the better. In matters of expression, maybe, it ran to extremes: its "louds" were loud enough to blow the walls out, when it practised in the schoolroom, and its "softs" were a whisper to melt the heart, and the alternations between these two extremes were swift and dramatic.

However, the band achieved its purpose, and achieves it still. Like Charlie Beslyn's piano-playing, it may be no more than a "while-time," with no pretensions to professionalism and no aspirations to culture, but it is something the village does for itself and loves doing. Mrs. Glow would have considered it vulgar; but the point is that, whereas her efforts in Larkfield came to nothing, Freddie's, in Toddington, prosper with each succeeding year.

The trouble is we have no leader, nobody willing to take such matters in hand, no exuberant Freddie to push brass instruments into our hands and to gather us round him on the village green. There are men and women of talent among us, even, so the papers say, of genius: a playwright, an actor, a singer, and so on. But they are not perhaps the right persons to lead us: they are with us (if only for week-ends), but not exactly of us.

And even if they were the right persons, they have no time for us. An actor whose voice is known and admired on both sides of the Atlantic, and a playwright whose plays are certain winners—how may we reasonably expect them to spare their precious minutes for the likes of us? We are one with the trees and fields among which they come, in luxurious motor-cars, each week-end, to relax after the ardours and endurances of a week in town. We see them pass in the street, shining, fleeting presences; but we never think of them as one of ourselves—we wouldn't dare.

And so, for lack of a leader, we go songless, save for such untutored outbursts as in the 'bus that night coming home from Castle Oliver, and bandless, save for the second-hand music doled out to us over the radio; and such actor talent as there may be among us seems doomed to hide its light for ever under a bushel.

Even in the matter of book-reading we are not much better off. If the roofs were lifted from all the houses in the village to-night, at this very minute, I doubt whether half a dozen people would be discovered over a book. Mind you, I would not by any means count this necessarily to our discredit as a community. There are times when I find myself heartily in agreement, for instance, with Jack Deeping's remark to me one day when I talked with him in the rickyard up at Brock's Hole. He was cutting out some hay for fodder. Somehow the talk came round to flax, its culture and its possibilities to-day. Jack paused, his thick knuckles clenched over the handle of the hay-knife.

"I dunno," he said; "some says one thing, and some says another. I was readin' all about it in the *Farmer and Stockbreeder* the other day. But there, you could read a book as big as this here haystack about it and be no wiser—till you'd tried it out for yourself."

All the contempt and suspicion of the farmer and the farm-hand for mere book-learning was in his words. "A book as big as this here haystack!" The countryman's knowledge is gained at first hand and the subtle vagaries of nature have taught him that, until he has tried a thing out for himself and made it part of his own immediate experience, he had better not put much trust in it. No doubt this way may seem to waste a lot of valuable time. No doubt it makes him obstinately conservative. But it also makes him sure. What he knows, he usually knows beyond all contradiction, because he has proved it by his own experience. His own experience, in fact, is the touchstone by which he has learned to judge all things; and books, however wise, however time-saving, are not his experience but somebody else's. Though they be as big as "this here haystack," they count for nothing beside his own direct and personal experience.

There is much to be said for such an attitude and, of course, much to be said against it. At its worst it may make a man ignorant and sottish; but at its best it may make his character sweet and wholesome as an apple. There are old men and women in Larkfield in this year of grace, nineteen hundred and forty, who cannot even write their own names, let alone read what someone else has written; but for sheer beauty of character—sheer soundness of character—I would not know where to look for their equal. Certainly I would not look for it among the so-called wise men of this world. Statesmen are wise, but look where their wisdom has led us! Scholars are wise, but how often they miss the truth!

And that is what I mean when I say I do not altogether count this lack of book-learning to our discredit as a village community. When I talk with some of our number who *do* profess to be book-lovers, I do not feel convinced that they are thereby much superior to those who don't.

Mrs. Crosbie, who lives in one of the larger houses in the parish and occupies at least some of her considerable leisure in organizing the various activities run in connection with the church, receives a library book regularly every week, by post. She may be reckoned as one of our more knowledgeable book-readers. When I last spoke to her, she was busily engaged in getting through *Gone with the Wind*. She evidently found it hard work. "It's such a *very* long book," was the most sensible comment upon it I could evoke from her. On another occasion she declared, with perfect ingenuousness, that it was essential to read such books in order not to feel "out of things" when one was invited to dinner and a game of cards.

Of course it would be foolish to claim that Mrs. Crosbie represented the summit of village pretentions to literary culture. Nevertheless, she is far from being unique.

How much preferable, I cannot help thinking, to be like the majority here, and read no books at all!

Or, better still, to be like old Mrs. Whillum, who lives in a thatched cottage on the outskirts of the village and sits all day sewing under the eye of her sailor husband looking down at her from his black frame on the wall. At least, she used to sit sewing all day; but either her hands got clumsy from the pain of too much rheumatism in her knuckles, or the ladies in the village who used to bring her work have found that they must do without her help until the war is over; for now she has less and less to do, though the Hall still sends her curtains and chair-covers to be mended on occasion and there is usually some cottager who wants a pair of inherited trousers adjusted to his measurements.

But she always used to be so busy that somehow I never even supposed she had time for reading books. All day she sat over her sewing-table, with yards of chintz flowing away from her and swamping the little front room with billows and waves of gay colour. But the other day I found her sitting at the table with a book.

It was *Pilgrim's Progress*.

"Not that I've much need to be reading it again," she said,

"for I almost know it by heart. Now *he* went through something, didn't he?"

I picked up the coverless copy and looked at some of its extremely fanciful illustrations. She had read it she did not know how many times, she said, because she loved it and because there was nothing else to read.

"Mrs. Stowe sent me up some books a while since," she continued; "here they are." And she showed me a collection of Victorian religious books—*The Harp and the Crown*, and suchlike. "But I'm not all that much goody-goody," she laughed, turning over their pages with scorn.

"But *Pilgrim's Progress* is a religious book, too?" I said.

"Ah, but that's different. There's something so *deep* about that book—I don't know what it is. I love that book. But these—ugh! A lot of sanctimonious nonsense, that's what they are. But there's one book here I think must have got into the bundle by mistake. Here, do you know this?"

She handed me a closely printed copy, scrubby and yellow-paged, of Smollett's *Humphrey Clinker*.

"But you haven't read all through that?" I asked, turning over the pages of infinitesimal print, made even more undecipherable by the fading of the paper.

"Indeed I have," came the prompt reply. "Every word of it. And there's nothing sanctimonious about that book!"

Smollett was just a name, like any other, to Mrs. Whillum. She had never had to read him for examination purposes. She had never had to read him so as not to feel "out of things." By an accident his book had come her way and she had sensed at once that here was something real, something drawn from life itself, with all its crudities and contradictions, all its sentiment, all its lack of fair play. Not for nothing had she been a sailor's wife! Living, he had led her a pretty dance—or so I gathered from some of the remarks she occasionally let fall; and dead, his basilisk eye still stared down at her out of the frame on the wall, while she sewed all the hours there were, to eke out her old age pension. But this much at least she had gained from him, a knowledge that life is hard for most people and a detestation of all that would pretend it was otherwise.

"Mind you," she said, as she took Smollett from me and put him back on the shelf, "I won't deny the book was a bit strong in places! But there, who's the worse for a bit of strong meat now and again?"

Smollett and Bunyan: it might seem at first sight that Mrs. Whillum's two favourites have little enough in common. And yet that would not be true. They have in common the one sure touch-stone of all great literature: their art is founded on the truth alone. Bunyan gives us the saints and Smollett the bawds; but both paint their pictures in hues of recognizable veracity. And Mrs. Whillum, sixty-five years away from the little village dame-school that was all her education, had at once sensed this fact. Not for her the cloud-cuckooland literature of the *Harp and the Crown*.

So while there are still Charlie Beslyns and Mrs. Whillums in our English villages, I do not think we have overmuch to fear from the taunts of those urban journalists who persist that in reality the countryside is the heart of darkness.

If they really wanted it, I could give them plenty of evidence to the contrary.

One piece of evidence springs to my mind immediately: not, it is true, from Larkfield itself, but from another village not many miles away.

I was living in a cottage next door to a gamekeeper. The gamekeeper's wife was a quiet, grey-haired woman who had lived all her life in cottages far out in the fields and woods, as game-keepers' cottages usually are. Their quietness seemed to have entered the secret core of her. When she spoke, it was like birds twittering in a thicket. When she laughed, and that was quite often, it was like a shallow stream in the woods, burbling among the stones. She had their quietness and she also had their strength. You may have had to listen close to hear what Mrs. Dickson was saying to you; but you minded it well, when you heard it.

She was the best the countryside can breed. Towns she had never known. "I never did live within sight of somebody else's chimney-pot," she said, when her children tried to persuade her to go and live among friends in the town, "and I'm sure I don't want to begin now." And all she knew she had taught herself. She knew almost as much about the wild life of the woods as her husband; and when it was so dark outside that I could not see my hand before my face, she would find her way across the fields by trees that to me were invisible.

But what I want to tell about her concerns quite another aspect of this true gentlewoman. Her daughter Bertha cooked for me and looked after my cottage. If I was away, her mother would come round and sit in my rooms while Bertha cleaned up the place. The sun shone on my cottage in the morning and on hers in the evening; and she liked to follow the sun.

One day I missed a copy of a book of my poems, and when I mentioned it, Bertha said: "I hope you don't mind, but mother's got it indoors." I supposed the old lady had borrowed it just out of curiosity, because she happened to know the man whose name was on the title-page, and I said no more about it. But that afternoon, when Bertha had left, Mrs. Dickson came knocking at my door and handed me my book.

"Here it is," she said. "I don't want it any more, thank you, because I've copied out the only poem I like."

"And which was that?" I asked.

Apparently it was the first poem in the book that had taken her fancy, a poem of about a hundred pentametre lines; and she had copied out every word of it.

"Wait a minute and I'll show it to you," she said, hurrying away. When she returned, she handed me a large, scrubby exercise book. "There it is," she said, and pointed to my poem written inside in pencil in large, honest script.

The end of the day

I turned over the pages. There were other entries, bits of poems, odds and ends of prose, little scraps of literature that had so pleased her that she wished always to have them handy.

"And you'll never guess," she went on, "what a comfort that old book has been to me. Nights I've lain abed, when Harry was out in the woods, never knowing what had happened, never even knowing if he'd come home alive or dead, and I've comforted myself with some of the things I've written down in these pages."

Charlie Beslyn, then, and Mrs. Whillum, Freddie the vicar and old Mrs. Dickson—such, it seems to me, are the props on which our village culture rests. Not on Mrs. Glow, with her itch to improve us all, nor on Mrs. Crosbie, with her library subscription ticket bringing the latest book hot from town, nor even (nay, here least of all) on the radio, with its chamber-music and its symphony concerts poured over us all like the rain, that falls on those who want it and on those who don't, in season and out.

Culture is worth nothing, and less than nothing, if it is not made part of one's own personal experience. Not all the odds and ends of Mrs. Dickson's scrap-book (my own poem included) were worthy to be ranked under the glorious banner of literature. But she had got from them all they had to give, and no author could wish for more from his readers. For my part, I know that it was one of the proudest moments of my life when I saw my poem included in that grubby, pencilled miscellany. "You'll never guess what a comfort that old book has been to me." Who could not be humble when he takes up his pen, if he realizes that such gentle spirits as Mrs. Dickson may chance to read his words and find solace in them?

And it is the same with Charlie Beslyn's hesitant tunes on his piano and Freddie's strident marches on his brass band: homely as they are, their true source is Helicon. As for advertised culture on the grand scale, we are content to leave that to others.

. . . . .

. . . On the outskirts of Larkfield stands a lonely old church, shut in a knoll of elms in whose swaying tops the rooks caw loudly at evening. A mere handful of people attend the occasional services that are still held there, for the church is too remote and inaccessible for the liking of an age that must have everything at its door. Architecturally it is a simple stone edifice erected in the fifteenth century: plain enough outside, now that the vandals of intervening generations have had their way with it, and even plainer inside. One thing, however, the vandals overlooked—and that, to me at least, makes all the difference.

On the north wall is a door, never used now, and moss growing over its step. Two corbel-heads once terminated the ribbed arch that spans it like a cruck. One is missing, smashed off by some zealot to whom all art was the devil's own handmaid. The other, unaccountably, he has left. One would like to think that even he, blinded with the light of his own puritanical convictions, could yet see enough to realize that here was something that must not be touched; though the true reason for his oversight is probably much more prosaic.

However this may be, there is the corbel-head to this day, a piece of sculpture to catch the breath with its beauty. It represents a boy's head, no bigger than a man's fist, and with its nose broken away and its whole face blackened from centuries of dripping rain.

How shall I tell you what that boy looks like? His lips are full, almost to pouting; and there is a hint of arrogance in his eyes, the arrogance of an aristocratic spirit. Eclectic even in youth, he is the destined conqueror. Passion is foreshadowed in those full lips and scorn in those thick-lidded eyes—a scorn that is echoed again in the very tilt of his wide-brimmed hat set above the deep fringe of his hair.

What anonymous artist wrought him there is no knowing; but certainly in this moment of creation the man touched genius, whatever else he achieved in his lifetime. This is no stylized face such as a master-sculptor, in his London workshop, might have reproduced by the dozen for the remote country churches he was commissioned to decorate. This is Somebody—as surely as Botticelli's "Portrait of a Young Man" is Somebody. Whatever else that sculptor produced, here at least he produced a work of perfection. And it decorates the unused doorway of an almost unused country church, where the rooks wheel in the wind and the long wheatfields roll up to the neglected graves.

I have never heard this corbel-head mentioned by anybody in the village, and most, I am sure, are unaware of its existence. And I am glad this is so. It lives in its own royal right now, vulnerable only to the wind and the rain. And chance will lead the feet of all who are destined to see it and to love it—as chance led Charlie Beslyn to his music and old Mrs. Whillum to her books. To advertise it for our improving, as Mrs. Glow might have done, would be to spoil both it and us. It is there for those to find who shall.

Chapter Seven

OVER the mantelpiece in my study is a mounted set of seventeen samples of local straw-plait. Their uneven ridges shine in the lamplight, flashing back a hint of summer into the wintered room. More than any picture, they tell the story of one of our most attractive cottage industries—an industry that thrived in Larkfield and the villages round about until the turn of the century.

James I worked better than he knew, perhaps, when, crossing the Border to succeed Elizabeth on the English throne, he brought a party of Scottish plaiters with him and settled them under the protection of the Napier family of Luton. In time Luton became the focus of an industry that spread so liberally into the neighbouring corn counties that, by 1875, as many as three thousand cottagers were engaged in it in North Essex alone.

Most Larkfield farm-hands could plait or braid, and it must have been one of the most characteristic scenes of the village to see them on summer evenings sitting before their doors or ambling along the lanes plaiting with quick fingers. They were one with Shakespeare's spinsters and knitters in the sun. The material they worked with was harsh and, one would have thought, intractable; but here are my samples to prove to what nimble patterns they could subdue it. From the plain and homely Shortcake to the scintillating Brilliant, all are beautiful and individual and woven with those minute variations which, although they are the bane of a machine-minded age, are one of hand-plaits' surest assets. They were plaited for me by Maria Bond, one of the few remaining old women in the village whose fingers have not forgotten their cunning in the practice of this precious craft. Maria is well over seventy years old, and when she dies, straw-plaiting, so far as this locality is concerned, will die with her. The more zealously, then, do I treasure my set of samples.

Maria lives in one of the council cottages that cluster, like a red scar, on the edge of the village. It is not exactly the sort of setting one would wish for the last of the straw-plaiters. If anybody should have a straw thatch over her head it is surely Maria; but the old cottage where she used to live, snug as a snail in its shell, was condemned by the authorities because its air-space did not conform with the regulations and because its sanitation depended upon the cleanly habits of the owner.

And so one day Maria's few belongings were piled on to a wagon (even a tin bath can look pathetic on such an occasion, much more so Maria's cane chair and bits of home-made rug), and she and they were transported to the new home. At seventy years and more an adequate air-space and an approved sanitation are no recompense for the loss of a home in which you have been born and bred: the most Maria could do, therefore, was so to arrange her belongings that the change might be as little apparent as possible. But even the furniture looked uneasy in such a brand-new setting; and four months after the move, when I asked her how she was getting on, the best she could find to say was, "Well, I'm getting *used* to it." Which means, of course, that she never will get used to it. Progress has carried her along with its relentless current and to the end she will remain still a little dazed by what has happened.

And what has happened to Maria herself has also happened to the homely craft of which she was such an adept. "You see," she says, "I couldn't possibly do it for a living now. Nobody would buy it." Then she adds, in the same resigned tone with which she might accept the inescapable chastisements of Providence itself: "Of course, it's the machines."

Exactly what those machines are, or why they have rendered useless the lovely work in which all her life she has excelled, is not her concern: she only knows that they have left her destitute in her old age and cancelled a life's ability.

Some little compensation there has been, it is true, and she is hardly to be blamed if perhaps she rates it higher than its value really is. The estimable organizers of the local Women's Institute got hold of her and on one or two occasions made her the star-turn of their handicraft exhibitions. Suddenly to become a centre of attraction like this was something Maria had never before experienced. She was taken to the county town in a motor-car. She was talked to by all and sundry. She was asked to demonstrate her craft in front of the assembly. She was photographed and her name appeared in a leaflet. And all this to-do, I suppose, must have seemed to her a sort of sunset splendour that somewhat compensated for past neglect. The machines may have taken away her livelihood but at least they had brought her fame.

I remember how, one day when she was explaining some of her patterns to me, she looked across the table, a little astonished that plaiting was apparently not entirely a mystery to me. "I suppose," she said, "you've been reading about me in the book," as though there were only one book and she its only theme.

In a corner cupboard near the fire, among her flowery china, Maria keeps the stock-in-trade of her craft. It is simple enough: a roller and board, worn thin and shiny with use, a bundle of straws, bleached and graded ready for plaiting, and a jumble of straw-splitters which, diminutive as they are, go by the pretentious name of "engines."

A comparatively few years ago such engines might have been seen in dozens of cottages in the village: now Maria's are perhaps the only ones remaining. Made either of bone or steel, they are no bigger than the kernel of a wild hazel-nut, and they consist simply of a needle-sharp prong round which radiate a number of blades, varying from three to ten, according to the grade of the straw which is to be split. A steam-hammer, weighing goodness knows how many tons and so delicately adjusted that it can fall on a pea without crushing it, is not more admirable to me than these minute instruments which, pressed between finger and thumb, into the pipe of the straw, cut the "splints" till they fall away in a whorl of golden ribbons.

"There used to be an old man," said Maria, "who lived in a cottage up by the chapel and made these engines for a living. He made them out of the leg-bone of a bullock—leastways, I think that's what it was."

Craftsmen were the salt and savour of village life, and I could not help being glad when even so minor a member of their brave community came alive for a moment in Maria's sketchy remembrance.

"I was never taught how to do plaiting," she said one day, as I sat watching her plait the thin straws with still agile fingers; "I just picked it up from my mother and sisters. Of course, mother had to go out into the fields to work, as well: all the same, she was one of the best plaiters in the village. Her Single Sevens were lovely! But then we could all plait in our home: even father."

Maria's own speciality was a complicated pattern called Brilliant. I remember the day when, with justifiable pride, she gave me the handsome samples that now glitter among my collection. She could not recall exactly how much a "score" she was paid for this queenly pattern, but it was much more than she was paid for the homelier kinds, such as Wisp or Satin, Diamond or Whipcord or Shortcake, which only fetched sevenpence or eightpence. Low as the price was, the women could often make more money from their straw-plaiting than the men could earn out in the fields. Once a week they took their coiled plaits down to the village shop, where they were inspected, measured, paid for, and finally dispatched to Luton.

Children call them the Keys of Heaven

Well, it is all ended now. The health of such crafts lay chiefly in the fact that they were indigenous to the locality. There was the corn in the fields; and in the village there was the manifold labour dependent upon that corn. In fact, corn was the fundamental reason for the very existence of the community; and if straw-plaiting was not perhaps so essential as milling or thatching or several other of the allied crafts and trades, at least it was as indigenous, and a very real part of the fabric of life in a cornland countryside. But it seems it had to go. At least—I look up again at my seventeen precious samples, eloquent in the lamplight, and wonder what progress really amounts to, after all.

Perhaps all the crafts had to go, and we waste our time when we regret their passing? I do not know: I only know that here in Larkfield even those that survive wear a dwindling, down-at-heel look.

Sam, for instance, was once an expert blacksmith as well as a farrier. There are iron window-catches and oven door-handles still in use here to show with what cunning he could contrive the delicate scrolls and spirals that were at once their use and their beauty. Yet to-day he rarely has occasion to practise even the simplest branches of his craft. And if you do find him some job to do he scarcely bothers himself to do it.

I wanted him to make me a hinge of a special sort. That was in spring. He came up to the house, produced a foot-rule from his ample hip-pocket, tapped here and measured there, and said yes, he would make me just the very thing I wanted. It did not occur to me at the time how much more interested he was in my apple-trees, then in full bloom, than in my hinge. Weeks went by and nothing happened. I called at the forge and spent many happy half-hours chatting with him over the roaring fire. What about the hinge? Yes, I should have it next week—but wouldn't I come round the back and look at his two baby pigs, "the little dears"?

Of course the hinge did not arrive. Sam, however, did arrive:

he had forgotten the measurements. Once again the foot-rule was produced. Once again the apple-trees, which by then showed fruit, were admired. So the weeks went by, and nothing happened. But Sam, *what* about my hinge? "Yes, midear, you really shall have it next week: you really shall. But just you come and see how fat my little old pigs are getting."

The summer passed, and my apple-trees were red with fruit when finally Sam came in the gateway one day, hiding the hinge behind his vast, sagging figure, like a guilty child.

"There you are, midear! Didn't I say you should have it?"

How could one possibly be angry with such a playful, guileless old man? Instead of my wrath, Sam took away with him a bunch of my flowers. I saw him shuffling down the road, sniffing his gaudy nosegay. "Mother won't half be pleased," he called back to me. And it was only when he was too far out of sight that I discovered the hinge did not fit as I intended after all.

But perhaps it is not quite fair to consider Sam as an example of the prevalent decay of craftsmanship in our villages. Last year he achieved his old age pension, and this little sense of security, after a life of heavy work, rather went to his head. If he more or less made his own time before, he certainly makes it now. Then again, despite his unquenchable good humour at his work, he would much rather have been a farmer or perhaps a smallholder than a blacksmith. Sam's vital interest is reserved entirely for his five-acre field.

I once said to him, as he stood blowing the "bellers" of his fire with one hand and mopping his forehead with the other: "If you had your choice over again, you'd never be anything but a blacksmith, would you?"

"I never had no choice," was his prompt reply. "Father was a blacksmith, and so I reckon I had to be a blacksmith, too."

Most craftsmen, upon inquiry, reveal the fact that they learned their craft from their fathers, and this is generally considered to be one of the reasons for the fine mastery they exhibit. The job comes as second nature to them: it is a knowledge in the blood as much as in the brain. Sam is no exception. A better farrier is not to be found for miles around; and, as I say, there are still plenty of extant examples of his admirable ironwork in the village. He has done his job to the top of his ability, because it was the job to which (as he considered) he was irrevocably called; but his heart is in the land.

And so, as work in the forge slacks off, and yearly there are fewer horses to be shod, he more and more gives himself over to a belated indulgence in the forbidden delights of farming. The village, it is true, is apt to laugh at his agricultural efforts. But Sam does not mind. And certainly there is nobody else in Lark-field who could wring more pleasure out of a skimpy five acres.

There is a child in Sam that all his bulk and years cannot hide, and I confess he rather toys with his field than farms it. Year after year, he has the greatest difficulty in getting it harvested. It is too much for him to do himself (though he used to mow it alone, often enough, working both by sun and moon) and casual labour is increasingly hard to find. Yet when, last year, Farmer Moore offered to plough, reap, and carry for him, if he would grant him permission to take his wagons through Sam's field on a short cut to some land of his own, Sam said no. That denial was a typical mixture of obstinacy and heroism. With Moore's wagons coming and going across his field, he would not feel that it was his and only his. All he actually said was: "They'd always be leaving my gate open, and I couldn't have that, now could I?"

At all costs, he feels, he must keep his field inviolate. It is the tangible symbol of a way of life that has been denied to him. It is his plot of dreams.

He can overlook it from the hatchway of his forge, and his eye is quite as vigilant over the barley waiting to be mown as over the horses waiting to be shod. Rain falls after a drought that had checked the crop. "That do look better by five bob a quarter a'ready," he says, appraising the freshened field from his hatch.

And when harvest comes at last, Sam just shuts up his forge altogether. If there are horses to be shod then, I don't know what happens to them: certainly no horsemen would be so foolish as to try to entice Sam away from his barley at such a time. The smile and the thunderous laugh disappear, and creases of anxiety take their place. Mrs. Merriman goes down the road at intervals during the day bearing trays (neatly covered with white napkins, for everything about Mrs. Merriman is neat and tidy) of food and drink; and Sam sits down behind his last year's stack, the gleaming scythe at his side, all his body sagging into the ground, to recover his spent strength.

Only when the last load is carried, does that endearing smile return. Once again Sam's mighty laugh is heard in Goose End, and once again he leans over his hatchway—there are two stacks to look at now—and dreams of what he will grow in his field next year. Perhaps he will plant it with trefolium—or "trepolium," as he calls it. Perhaps he will let it lie fallow. Perhaps . . . well, we shall see.

Yes, I agree it is not altogether fair to take Sam as an example of the decay of village crafts. Yet the decay is undeniable enough. Farming, like most else these days, is largely a matter of the smallest outlay and the quickest returns. The farmer knows well enough what he wants and it is part of his tradition to want only the best —the best thatching for his barns, the best gates for his fields, and so on. But the banks are pressing, and he can afford the best no longer, until at last he almost arrives at the stage of having persuaded himself that (for instance) the factory-made gates which he is compelled to set up in his fields are quite as good as any the local carpenter could make. At any rate, they are much cheaper and (so he is forced to argue) at least they will last out his time.

Thus consoled, he gets on with his job of forcing the land, instead of serving it. Never mind about layering the hedges in the good old-fashioned way: hack them down and stuff the gaps with brambles. Never mind about trimming the cornricks and decorating them with straw-cockerels: there is no time for such nonsense now. Never mind about resting the land after it has borne its best: a few sacks of artificial manure will serve just as well as a year's fallow and save a crop into the bargain.

So it goes on. To-day is all the farmer can afford to think about, who should really be thinking for his sons and his sons' sons after them. And in this general scramble to make ends meet, the craftsmen who served the farmer have been left behind. Their work may last longer, but it costs too much. It may be best suited to the peculiar needs of the locality, but it takes too long. And so, from being almost the most valuable men in the community, the craftsmen sink to the level of odd jobbers—men of a first-class ability for whom there is no longer any use.

Such a man is Josh Mengies, the carpenter. A few farmers in the parish still call on him to do little jobs for them. "I've worked on and off for him ever since I was a boy," he said of one local farmer; "he won't have strangers about the place." But for the most part he just potters about, doing nothing in particular.

Like his father before him, Josh is an excellent craftsman. His scorn for anything botched or shoddy is as strong as ever it was. I have seen a photograph of the shop in which he worked with his stern old father: the timber neatly piled for seasoning, the square-set stacks of planks, and the well-kept tools ranged above the benches. And the contrast with his own workshop to-day is less a criticism of Josh than of the way things have changed these last twenty-five years or so. One end of a double cottage serves him for workshop, and the rooms are so littered with junk that only by twisting this way and bending that can one progress from one room to another. Broken chairs, bits of window-frames, rusty iron, split sacks of cement and odds and ends of timber lie about in such confusion that even Josh himself can scarcely ever find what he is looking for.

Only the tools are still kept in order; and, although so many of them seldom get used to-day, Josh will not let anybody touch them but himself. He knows them like friends, their faults and their merits, and he cannot bear that they should be used by hands unfamiliar with their peculiar moods.

Then again, Josh is an inveterate collector of everything he can lay his hands on. Nothing must be thrown away because one day or other it may come in useful. The fact that it never does come in useful is beside the point, as is also the fact that he will soon be past using it anyway. He pulls down condemned houses and fills his yard with doors and windows and beams, and his workshop (where he can still find a corner for them) with locks and grates and oven-doors, all because he is convinced that one day they will come in useful.

One such oddment, I must confess, did come in useful—though I would perhaps have prevented it if I could. There is a small pond at the bottom of my garden which, if it is not exactly ornamental, at least serves to supply the garden with water in times of drought. The trouble is it shelves so steeply that every dip of the bucket is likely to send one plunging headlong in. So I asked Josh to come along one day and look at it. Couldn't he make me a landing-stage of some sort, so that I could stand a little way out over the water and dip my bucket without fear of falling in?

Josh paid me several visits and considered the matter very carefully. I explained how I thought the job might be done: a wooden girder here and a support against a tree there and so on. I should have known, of course, that Josh would never agree. He did not say so, outright, but I could see that he was not at all convinced. Suicide by drowning is rather a common occurrence in these parts and perhaps he wanted to be quite sure that I too did not come by a watery end. Anyway, he said he would look around: if I waited a little while he would be certain to find the very thing.

Then I went away for a holiday. When I came home the job was finished. Josh had indeed found the very thing. There is no danger now that I shall fall in when I dip my bucket, or that the landing-stage will give way under my weight. So long as iron endures I shall be safe, and those who come after me. Josh has laid the boards of the platform (themselves thick as railway-sleepers) on the discarded chassis of a motor-lorry.

"I knew it would come in useful for something," he said, proudly waiting for me to express my approval; "and there you are."

Two things you notice about Josh when you first meet him: the crystalline blue of his eyes and the lithe muscularity of his hands. Most craftsmen's hands are lean and well-shaped, trained in responsiveness, alive in every nerve; but I think Josh's hands are exceptionally fine. The whole craftsman lives in them. Age has done little to diminish either their strength or their sureness of purpose; but now they are mostly idle, their rare adaptability wasted on trivial ends.

As for his clear blue eyes, pale as ice, I sometimes wonder if they do not betoken in their unwitting owner the possession of something akin to occult sight. Perhaps I am being rather too fanciful here, but certainly Josh is proud of his prowess as a wart-charmer.

"Putting them away" is the expression he uses for this peculiar ability. I admit I have never verified his claims at first hand; but he says he has cured hundreds of warts in his time and is still ready to cure them on anybody who asks his help. He has no need even to see the person who wishes to be cured: it is apparently enough if Josh is informed of the number of warts.

Exactly what method he employs I have never been able to find out. I believe some charmers smear the warts with the slime of a snail and afterwards stick the snail on a thorn, whilst others rub them with a piece of old meat which they afterwards bury. Then there is what is known as "buying" warts. But Josh evidently favours quite other methods than these. Not only has he no need to see the warts but he also makes it a rule never to accept payment for his services. He did once own to me that he might perhaps use a certain formula of words; but on another occasion all he would admit was that "maybe I sometimes *think* about 'em, while I'm sittin' down, resting." Also, he insists that although he can "put them away" at any time, spring and summer, when the air is dry, are best.

Then, too, Josh has a more than usually happy knack in dealing with all sorts of plants and trees and animals. His fruit-trees, every one of which he has either planted or grafted himself, are some of the most bounteous in the parish; and trailing over a tumbledown shed at the back of his cottage is a grape-vine which, in defiance of all the accepted laws of nature, confronts the prevailing easterly winds with clusters of small black grapes, good for wine-making if not for eating.

Nothing appears to please him better than to be asked for advice in the matter of some fruit-trees one has planted in one's garden. It has become part of the ritual of the year that he shall come in and prune my trees for me; and I know he is convinced that, unless he does this, they will certainly not yield their best. He has told me the ancestry of most of the older trees (where they came from or who planted them) and if his names for them do not always correspond to the catalogues of nurserymen at least they are given promptly and with an authority I for one would not deny.

Like Sam, Josh rents a piece of land, though he has never bothered to plough and sow it. Instead, he allowed it to revert to grass and then he bought a colt and turned her loose in it.

It was Jessie the colt that first revealed Josh's tenderer side to me. He said there was Arab blood in her. Be that as it may, she was certainly a frisky creature. All day long she would stand about the meadow, nibbling at grass which she had long ago shorn of all its juicier blades. Then she would suddenly lift her delicate head, blow out her nostrils and neigh, and fly round the meadow in circles, kicking up a shower of turf with her slim, unshod hooves.

Mostly she was left alone all day, while John was out on some trivial job or other; and in her loneliness, she was glad of any attention. Children called to her as they came home from school, and passers-by stopped to stroke her and give her apples and lumps of sugar. If Jessie was glad enough of these attentions, Josh was torn between jealousy and pleasure: he liked to see her taken notice of, but at the same time he disliked to see any division of her allegiance. I don't think he need have worried. Jessie never neighed so loudly as when he arrived in the meadow every evening, bringing her hay which he stuck into the fence, or a bucket of well-water which she would empty without stopping, as if she were a suction-pump. And to attempt to entice her away, once he was anywhere within sight or sound, was a sheer waste of time.

Jessie endured all weathers and grew more tousled and more clogged with mud as the months went by. At last Josh decided she must be broken in. Night after night he encouraged her round and round, at the end of a length of stout rope. Her eyeballs shone, her young nostrils quivered. It was a game, the climax of every day's long waiting; and she never guessed that the end of it would be imprisonment between the shafts.

Josh had said he would never part with her, and I believed him. "Them old gippoes keep on botherin' me," he said. "They tell me I've only got to name my price; but I'm not selling her."

One day, however, he did sell her. What price tempted him away from his decision I do not know: or did some unvoiced necessity compel him? Jessie went. And no sooner had she gone, of course, than Josh repented of his bargain. No happy neighing greeted him now when he went up to the meadow in the evening. No use sticking armfuls of hay in the fence for her to pull at when she had finished her joyous canter. But regrets would not bring her back again; and if ever Josh thinks of replacing her, it will not be until after the war that he can do so now. Only a little while before the snow came, I saw him ambling round his meadow, nothing to do, nobody to talk to; and the peewits flying over with their melancholy wailing seemed the very voice of his loneliness.

Chapter Eight

IT may not warm the blood much, these bitter days, but at least it warms the mind, to turn over the pages of one's diary and read what one was doing in summer days gone by. What one was thinking and feeling is quite another matter and for quite another occasion. To read that I found a death's head moth in the lane on a certain July evening is far more interesting to me just now than to read of the psychological or emotional state I happened to be in at the time. Give me a bald and accurate diary of facts to read over and I am satisfied. The rest can look after itself. I was sad once and no doubt I shall be sad many times yet; but I may never again see a death's head moth in the lane by Penny Fields.

Not that only the more startling entries in such an objective diary are worth poring over. I have only to read such a simple record, for instance, as that which tells how, on March 6th last year, I saw five brimstone butterflies and a palm-willow full of honey-bees, oxlips in bud and coltsfoot in the fields by Bassetts Farm, for my mind to glow with the memory of a certain walk taken in the first flush of spring.

Such a memory almost gives the lie to present frost and snow. Almost, I say; for nothing will really gainsay this omniscient cold. Plants keep warm under snow; and even houses, it seems to me, should be warmer than they are just now for the generous white blanket with which the skies have covered them. But apparently there are no blankets that can keep out this cold. It penetrates to the very marrow. You sit over the fire (or even close inside the fire, if, as in my own case, you have an old open fireplace), and an illusion of warmth on your face at last breeds some sort of cheer in you; but your back tells the truth, and you have only to concentrate on that for a moment for the good cheer to vanish like a dream. I run my hand down the walls and discover that this north-east wind doesn't even need a cranny to enter in: defiant of mere matter, it penetrates and permeates all.

It is one of the minor irritations of a timbered room, that even in the depth of winter, when fire and lamp have made the air hot enough, bees and butterflies will tumble out of the crevices in the beams under the mistaken notion that spring has come and it is time for them to wake up. Dazed for awhile, they bask in the warmth, wash their wings free of clogging sleep, and then begin a frenzied dance of death round the lamp.

But this weather even the bees and butterflies hibernating in my beams have felt no premature urge to awaken. Pile the logs on as you will, they remain mercifully immune from any such temptation. Either that, or they are simply dead. And when I wake in the morning, to a house of unheated rooms, and see the breath rise from my mouth like steam from a singing kettle, and come downstairs to a fireplace full of dead ashes, and every blessed drop of water frozen to a block of ice—why, then I could very nearly agree that, in either case, the bees and the butterflies are better off than I!

But come, let me turn over the pages of my diary. They may perhaps help me to believe that once there were flowers in the garden and whistling thrushes in the trees and no news of wars in the papers. Call it escapist, if you like: I do not mind. Just now I would give my kingdom to escape from this annihilating cold (though of course in days to come I shall even be glad to recall it, if only as something endured and duly rewarded) and if the thought of bygone springs and summers can help me, then help me they certainly shall.

What, for instance, is this first entry for June of last year? "Went to the Essex Agricultural Show, at Braintree."

Goodness, yes, what a day of sunshine and brass bands and farmers in knee-breeches and white tents flapping in the breeze! As I sit here remembering, that day slowly comes alive for me, like a flower opening, petal by petal, in the sun.

It all began, I remember, down on the village green in the morning, where a small knot of us stood talking, while we waited for the 'bus. What the talk was all about I have now no idea; but my diary records how there were swallows "flossing" on the water, while we stood there, the sunshine lighting up the rich dark blue on their backs, as they dipped to meet their shadows and at each brief impact sent up a miniature fountain of glittering spray.

Then the 'bus arrived and off we went, stopping all along the road to pick up yet more passengers, till we could hold no more. For me, country 'buses are one of the very best contributions progress has made towards the amenities of country life, and rarely are they so attractive as on market days, when farmers and their wives, who used to spank along the road to market in their gigs, jostle and shout to one another till the conversation becomes a sort of distilled essence of all country talk. And the day we rode in to visit the Show was no exception. Small farmer, foreman, horseman, stockman—all were on holiday, shinily washed, and turned out by their wives much as they themselves, years ago, might have turned out their horses, combed and braided and cleaned to the last hair.

As for the Show itself, what I recall most vividly was watching certain events in the arena. The sun blazed and the music came in noisy gusts that made no sense so far away but were the only conceivable accompaniment to such a chatter and such a blue sky. A team of fine Suffolk horses entered close by the Grand Stand and began their slow progress round the course. Proud as the day itself, they walked in a string, announcing themselves with a chime of bells and a shifting gleam of brasses. Under their glossy chestnut skin the muscles rippled as they strained, gently and evenly, at the wagon behind them. With every lift of the foot, their long, combed fetlocks flounced like the skirts of a ballet dancer. Indeed, their whole progress round the course was like a slow pavan. By their sides trode three horsemen, trim in fawn coat and breeches, as full of pride in their charges (one of whom, I recollect, was called Stormer, and another Nelson) as we of pleasure at the sight of them. Little waves of cheering followed them round the arena till at last they drew into rank with the other entries before the judges.

Perhaps those thunderous Suffolk horses, plumed and braided, with golden moons dangling from their martingales, and sacks of corn piled so squarely in the varnished wagon behind them, have little enough to do with farming as it is practised to-day; but I know how glad I was to see them, even on a showground, and to know that there are still farmers willing to stock their farms with such noble creatures, and still farm-hands able to turn them out in this brave, traditional manner.

To see what farming actually is like to-day, and will be to-morrow, it was only necessary to walk across the field to the stand-holders' section, where every conceivable mechanical farm implement was being exhibited and explained by brisk and persuasive salesmen. Mostly, I noticed, it was the younger farmer, and farmers' sons, who showed the keenest interest here. Such older farmers as there were hovering around this shining, inhuman concourse, seemed to me to wear a sceptical mien as if to say no good could come of such devilish contrivances.

In fact, one of my plainest recollections of that afternoon is of a little group who came and sat next to me in the tea-tent. It consisted of an old white-whiskered farmer, frank and ruddy, and his two alert, well-built sons. Over the buns and the tea, thick and black as tar, the young men tried every way they knew to persuade their father to invest in a certain sugar-beet lifter that had taken their fancy among the exhibits outside. They ran over its points, but the old man looked as if he would rather they were discussing the points of a Punch or a Percheron. They demonstrated how in the end it would save time and money—but their father shook his head and seemed to imply that good husbandry was reckoned by other standards. And finally, in rising exasperation, they accused him banteringly of an obstinacy that would soon land them all in the bankruptcy court. "It's no use, Father," one of them said "if you don't mechanize, you'll go under."

I don't know whether these eager young men won their case; but in any event I don't think their old father would be convinced, however much the farm's turnover might improve.

So much for the Agricultural Show. Now what is this entry at the beginning of October? "Crab apples and sloes for jelly, gin and wine." Well, the jelly is all eaten and the wine all drunk, but something of their savour lives on in these few words recalling the dates they were gathered and made. Something, also, of the kindly atmosphere of those days—warm sunshine on newly ploughed fields, red leaves, and wasps in the fallen fruit.

Sloes are so plentiful here that it is only necessary to walk across the field at the back of my house to gather all I could possibly require. But crabs, although these also are fairly plentiful, are an adventure in themselves. Six trees in the middle of a balk that runs across a forty-acre field yielded me the fruit for my jelly that year; and clear as yesterday I remember the journey we made to fetch them in.

A flare of autumn colour ran along the hedges—maple and spindle and dogwood. Rooks and clouds were being blown pell-mell across the sky. And from a rickyard far away came the drone of a threshing-machine, the only sound in that mellow afternoon. The stubble had all been ploughed in, and the gleaming waves of the furrows still lay just as the share had turned them, shining with moisture, waiting till the wind and the frost should crumble them into a kindly tilth.

As we trudged over the heavy ploughlands to the crab-apple trees on the horizon, our boots gathered the clay in such quantities that their weight seemed like a magnet drawing us from the earth's centre. We were, as they say hereabouts, "all barmed up," but the fallen apples, speckling the clay with their blood-warm red, were a more than sufficient reward for our endeavour.

We had filled our baskets from the windfalls among the furrows, when somebody discovered that the best were in the ditch by the balk. And what I recall most of that afternoon's rich harvesting is the crunch of apples under my feet in the bottom of the ditch and the strong smell of water-mint as I picked them out. Who shall analyse why one detail of such an adventure is destined to stand out stronger than any other? At any rate, every time we opened the crab-apple jelly that year, I seemed to smell again the crushed mint under my feet; and now, when the jelly is all eaten, like a fume drifting across the mind that smell still remains.

Another entry in the diary, a week later, brings back that rich autumn mood even more vividly. "Medlars from 'Swallows,'" runs the record under October 18th: "apples and pears, bullaces and blackberries in quantities."

"Swallows" was once an outlying farm-house, though not even the foundations remain to prove its existence to-day. What does still remain, however, is a ruined close full of ancient, gnarled fruit-trees. How many years have passed since anybody pruned and tended them I do not know; but once now and then, in a year of plenty, they bear and litter the grass underneath with their unwanted fruit. Chiefly it is the medlars that draw me to "Swallows" about this time of the year; and if the jelly from them is somewhat harsh and certainly not to everybody's taste, well, there is a snobbery in jam-making as in everything else, and it is not everybody who can put medlar jelly on his table!

This particular season, however, every tree in "Swallows" close seemed to have surpassed itself. Pruning or no pruning, those old trees bore with a prodigality many a walled garden might have envied. The place was the very epitome of autumn's mellow fruitfulness. Bullaces, like peeled li-chee nuts, lay heaped in the grass. Fallen pears were so plentiful that wasp and bird had only bothered to take a brief nip out of one before passing on to another. Chestnuts had fallen, and, in falling, split and tumbled out "conkers" of a smoothness and redness and bigness that would have made any boy whoop with delight. There were plenty of medlars, rough-skinned and still as hard as stones. And trailing round the rim of the pond were bramble-bushes, heavy with their dark sprays of berries.

"Swallows" smelt of fermenting fruit, the whole of Keats' Ode concentrated in half an acre of neglected ground.

We gathered all we could carry and should have been satisfied. Instead, next day we returned for more. Perhaps it was foolish of us to expect to recapture the spirit of such a scene. Perhaps it was just one of life's little jokes—or a pertinent reminder that man cannot live by poetry alone. We pushed open the broken gate, eager to plunder the fruit a second time and to smell the winy air. A score of pigs stared at us, who had so unexpectedly interrupted them in their juicy meal. Still as stone, they glittered at us out of mean, beady eyes; and then, convinced that we were not worth their attention any further, suddenly began rootling among the fallen apples again. The final comment, I remember, seemed to me implied in the grunt of sensual satisfaction with which one of the biggest and nearest sows rubbed her scurfy buttocks up and down the bark of a tree.

Turning back the pages a month or two, I read: "July 14th. Clover cut and carted in Gilbert's Field," and a picture immediately presents itself of a high-piled wagon, its lower part just hidden beneath the dip of the hill, drifting across the horizon like a punt, with Jerry Gardiner guiding it, using his fork for a pole. I hear him calling to his brother, who leads a horse I cannot see, and sight and sound are one with the summery scent of clover drying in the sun.

But perhaps the entry of those summer months that stirs the most vivid remembrance in me is the one that reads: "August 9th.

Bankes' wheat, that has stood in traves ever since his son fell ill, is being carried at last."

Harvest is literally the crown of the year for us who live in the cornland belt: all the months lead up to it and upon its success or failure depends all we know of prosperity. No sooner is the stubble ploughed in, than the drill advances over the field, scattering the new seed, first the winter wheats, whose frail green straws now lie buried under the snow, and then the spring wheats and the barley. To casual eyes it all looks much the same throughout the spring and early summer; but as it ripens, the differences become obvious enough. Barley in ear is like fur, like a soft pelt, and it ripples like water as the wind blows over it. Gradually, as harvest-time draws nearer, the ails begin to bend over, till at last they point back to the earth instead of up at the sun. But to the very end, the wheat-heads remain erect, masculine and proud. Both fall at last, however, beneath the binder whose clatter is the best counterpart we have to-day to the sibilant scythe.

Perhaps that silvery whisper of the scythe was a fitter token of the heat and climax of the year, but the rackety-clack of the binder also has its appeal. Ears that were not trained on chamber-music find jazz the more appealing. Anyway, when the binders begin gyrating round the fields, scattering an untidy trail of sheaves with their fluttering, mechanical fingers, Larkfield touches the peak of its year's endeavour. Everybody then talks of corn. Everybody watches the weather. And everybody, from the farmer and the farm-hand himself to the visitor and week-ender, shares something of an excitement that has its origin away back in the days of the Open Field village, and even earlier, when the quantity and quality of the harvest was a measure not only of prosperity, but of existence itself.

The year of which my entry tells was the year of a bumper harvest. While plants in the gardens withered in a clay that was as hard as iron, the corn, loving such drought, flourished under the continual sun. "White unto harvest" was exactly the right

The village carpenter's handiwork

expression for those wide acres of barley and oats, whilst the wheat, burnished like copper, flashed the heat back at the sky.

All day long a series of minute explosions, like toy artillery, sounded in the wheatfields, and the farmers walked round the headlands, snatching an ear of corn and rubbing the husk away, to test the white starchy kernel between their teeth.

Of all the farms in the parish I do not think there could have been one more eagerly keyed up to the excitement of harvest than was Moat Farm, where young Bankes was taking over the management of the farm from his father. It was to be his first harvest; and with all the vigour of his twenty-one years, he prepared to greet the occasion. His binder was the first I heard in the fields in the morning and the last at night. The waking hours were not long enough to crowd in all the work he wanted to do. The sunny weather crowned his efforts, and I doubt if there was a happier young farmer in the county.

And then suddenly he collapsed and had to be carried off the field to his bed. Sickness had grabbed at him out of the skies and in a week he was dead.

Everywhere else the brisk work of harvest went on as usual: only at Moat Farm the stooks stood waiting in the fields, while their shadows wheeled around them through the empty day. The young man was buried and that afternoon the wagons came out into the field again and the interrupted harvest continued. In his black alpaca jacket Mr. Bankes loaded the sheaves: though the bottom had fallen out of his world, harvest must go on. Not a word passed between him and the farm-hand who forked up the sheaves, and the clink of the harness and the rumble of the wagon wheels only served to emphasize the silence which here replaced the laughter and banter immemorially attendant on such a task.

Slowly the loaded wagon was led into the rickyard, the black-coated farmer perched on top, like a mourning band on summer's golden sleeve.

. . . Coppery wheat-heads in the sunshine, loaded wagons

bumping over the stubble, heat, deep drinks out of bottles cooled under the hedges—yes, my diary of brief, factual entries certainly has its gift to make. To me, anyway. Sitting here in my study, turning over its pages, I had forgotten the deep snow outside and the chilly bedroom waiting for me upstairs. For an hour I have been back again in summer.

And, believe it or believe it not, where the heat of the lamp has warmed the beams, a hidden bee is buzzing, intermittently, half-heartedly, as if even he had partaken of my illusion and were wondering whether it was time to come out of his hiding-place to greet the sun.

Stay where you are, poor misguided creature! See, I turn down the light and prepare to face the arctic regions awaiting me upstairs, and soon it will be just as cold down here. So stay where you are. Go to sleep again and enjoy the merciful oblivion nature has so unfairly bequeathed to you and not to me. It is a long while yet to summer.

Chapter Nine

FARMER DEEPING has been taken to hospital. How the old man was carried from his farm out to the road I cannot imagine, for Brock's Hole is approachable only by half a mile of unmade road which, at the best of times, is no more than a churned-up ride between overgrown hedges and, just now, is an impenetrable and continuous drift of snow. But the Deepings, widowed father, son and daughter, are used to surmounting such difficulties. There are weeks on end when they cannot get their stock to market or carry grain to the mill, and even in the height of summer no tradesman will take his goods up that tangled lane.

So I suppose they carried the old man across the fields, out to the ambulance waiting in the road. And now he lies in hospital, who never was away from his farm so many days together, and whose illnesses, through all the long years of his strenuous life, have never before earned the attention of a doctor.

Farmer Deeping, so the report went round, was breaking up at last; but when we asked Priscilla Deeping how her father was, after her first visit to the hospital, she answered: "He says it's the best holiday he ever had!" The nurses, apparently, were delighted with him and could not do enough for him, so that when last Tuesday he shyly announced the fact that it was his eightieth birthday, "they made such a fuss of him [as Priscilla said] that it has quite gone to his head."

And I'm sure I don't wonder that he should be so popular, for he is one of those increasingly rare old countrymen whose characters are as sweet as a nut and as full of goodness. Honest, cheery, and old-fashioned, preferring always the generous comment to the critical, he is gentle in all he says and gentle in all he does.

There are few things I find more calculated to restore a wavering faith in human nature than a visit to Brock's Hole, the little isolated farmstead where he was born and bred and from whose familiar shelter he was carried away on a stretcher across the snowy fields.

Brock's Hole is a farm of about forty acres—a couple of meadows and the rest all good clay arable. Its very isolation compels it to be more or less self-supporting; but if Brock's Hole were on the main road, I think it would still be run on the same principle, so long as Farmer Deeping owned it. For he is a small cultivator of the old school, one of those farmers who are gradually being squeezed out of existence and yet who are indubitably the finest type of farmer this country produces. They truly may be said to serve the land. They know every inch of their farms, they waste nothing, and they abhor all that savours of the penny-in-the-slot methods by which the modern large-scale farmer, regardless alike of the past and of the future, forces his land to give the greatest possible yield in the smallest possible time. Yet such small cultivators, masters of a husbandry that has the sanction of hundreds of years behind it, will soon cease to exist in this country—unless the debacle into which the present-day system has thrown farming does not compel a complete revision of method.

Brock's Hole lies about a mile across the fields behind my house, and a walk there in April is a progress through tethered clouds of blackthorn. Over the fields where the young wheat is sprouting, larks sing against the clear blue sky, whose clouds all seem to have come to earth and are lodged in Farmer Deeping's hedges. The farm itself, sheltered by a few elms, stands islanded in the fields, a small orchard close by, whose last year's crop still sweetens in the

Coming home from the fields

farm-house's only attic, a rickyard, where the remnants of harvest still await the dealer, a pond, and an old timbered barn.

Deeping's son, Jack, has just brought the horses in from the fields; and while he goes into the stable, the harness trailing and clanking round his feet, Prince and Lady find their leisurely way to the pond. The moorhens fly before their heavy tread, with heads thrust away out before them, urgent with the red light of their beaks, like danger-signals. Fetlock deep in the cloudy water, Prince and Lady slowly drink their fill, then lift their drooling heads and stare contentedly around them. The day's work is done, and this playful drink at the pond, often as much out of habit as out of necessity, signals their release. Not until Jack calls from the stable door do they splash their way out of the water, clumsily, thunderously, and go leisurely home. . . . It is an evening ritual that has gone on for generations at Brock's Hole, other Princes and other Ladies splashing among the water and taking their slow, dripping way back to the stable at last.

Go inside and talk with Jack and you will find in him the ideal blend of the old and the new, the ancient way and the modern. Much of his day is spent with the tractor, the economical advantages of which he is well aware, but his affection is for his horses. To bed them down after their day's work in the fields is quite as much the completion of his day as of theirs; and admirable as he is in handling the tractor, I for one prefer to see him sitting up behind Lady on one of his frequent visits to the mill.

"A tractor's essential on a farm, even of this size," he says. "You can't get on without one. All the same, I wouldn't stay on a farm a fortnight where there wasn't a horse or two as well."

The fume of petrol and the warm breath of horses—somehow he reconciles the two: accepting innovation, he yet keeps his firm hold on tradition, a young farmer in whom the best of both worlds uncommonly unite. Gently his father chides him, remembering the day when his own father's two pedigree Punches were the pride of the parish. "Our Jack," he says; "well, he isn't as fond of horses as he should be." But Jack only smiles: persuasively, he knows the way to counteract his old father's innate conservatism, safe in the self-assurance of his own sense of balance. The past was good and must be listened to; but, after all, he lives in the present.

Jack's fondness for his horses was an old story for me long before I learned just how deep that fondness went. It was the evening when his father had said, "Our Jack; well, he isn't as fond of horses as he should be." We were standing in the barn, whose dim interior was stabbed with a golden shaft of sunlight coming through the high, open door. Jack winked at me from behind his father's back, as much as to say, "There goes Father again. The same old tale—but you know what these old men are like!" And when I had said good night to Farmer Deeping, and Jack and I were walking across the yard together, "I don't know about not liking horses as much as I *ought* to," he said, "but just come over to the stable a minute; there's something I'd like to show you."

Prince and Lady were in their stalls, chumbling and chewing in the warm aromatic dusk. Countrymen are notoriously brief of speech; and when they have "something to show you," they invariably like to keep you in a mystified silence and suspense while they prepare their surprise. Jack disappeared into the darkest corner of the stable and then, after a lot of fumbling among what sounded like a jumble of harness, came back to me in the doorway with his arms and hands loaded with gleaming brasses. There were swingers and bells, rosettes and elaborately studded hame-reins, and as handsome a martingale as I have ever seen. They flashed in the last red rays of the sun, zodiacal emblems such as were the pride and joy of horsemen and carters in the days when a man did not yet count it loss of time to rise in the dark of morning so that he might polish his horse-brasses ready for a journey to market.

"There!" said Jack, "I don't suppose you ever guessed there was anybody round about these parts who still had a complete set of brasses in his stable, did you? There's everything here; and it all belonged to Grandfather. Pretty, isn't it?"

And he held the swinger up before him, like a priest holding up the monstrance, and as the dying sun flashed back from its clear brass mirror, suspended in the shining ring, he flicked the tiny bells at the side with his finger-nail till they rang sweetly, briefly, like the bells of the ministrant. Indeed, in that moment there was something priestly in Jack's simple gesture: he was commemorating a race of countrymen whose like we may never see again.

"Sometimes," he said, "I wish I could take Lady out in the road, she looks so fine rigged up in her harness."

I had supposed they were no more than relics, kept in the stable for sentiment's sake; but now I discovered that Jack sometimes dressed Lady up in all her finery and paraded her up and down the green ride in front of the house. "Of course I only do it to amuse myself," he said, shy at the confession that had escaped him and perhaps afraid that I might think it daft of him; "but I can tell you she does look pretty, braided and plumed and all."

It was beginning to get dark, or I believe Jack would then and there have dressed up Lady and exhibited her for my benefit. The mood was on him and I had happily won his confidence. . . . And now it is too late. Lady was shot yesterday; and Prince, I remember Jack telling me, is not very amenable to such nonsense.

To find a young man, these days, able to plait and braid horses and the proud possessor of a complete set of bells and brasses, is a sort of discovery that can only be expected in small, off-the-map farms like Brock's Hole; and if the so-called progressive section of the English farming community gets its way, I suppose such small farms will soon be merged into vast collective farms (controlled, if not from Whitehall itself, then at least from some office in the towns), and agriculture will in general become so highly mechanized that horses will be as rare in our farms as golden orioles in our woods, and the Jacks of to-morrow will certainly have no chance to indulge such frivolous fancies as plaits and braids, bells and brasses.

Meanwhile, I may perhaps be allowed to take my fill of pleasure in Brock's Hole while it lasts. It is something if one can say one has enjoyed the savour of such things before they passed completely. Inside the farm-house itself much the same sort of unique atmosphere prevails. Perhaps Priscilla is less lenient than Jack in her attitude towards the way things are going to-day; for she is a woman, tenacious of the past, and almost idolatrously fond of her old father.

I saw her on the green this morning waiting for the 'bus which the recently cleared highroads now enable to run. The service is, to say the best of it, still highly erratic, and Priscilla, when I met her, had already been waiting the best part of an hour. But anybody who, even in normal times, must take so much trouble for the very simplest journey, is not likely to be much upset by a wait of a mere hour or so. She was going to the hospital to visit her father, and the number of parcels and baskets which accompanied her suggested that she was taking the best part of her storeroom with her by way of gratitude for the kind treatment he was receiving.

"One thing he told me to be sure and not forget," she said, "and that was his bread and butter. He says they feed him wonderfully—a lot better than I do!—but he misses my home-made bread and butter."

Priscilla's woollen-hooded face, pinched with cold and glazed with the shine of the reflected snow, creased into a smile of justifiable pride. Every week she bakes her own bread, and her father will eat no other. In fact, he never had eaten any other bread until he went into hospital, and it is one of his little grievances that, owing to the mysterious workings of the wheat quota, he can no longer have his bread made from flour that has been milled from his own home-grown wheat. Priscilla's butter, like her batches of bread, is made for home consumption only: it seems to them, up at Brock's Hole, just plain common sense that, if you farm the land, you should surely be able to get the best part of your food from what that land yields.

Thus it is a matter for continual amusement to Farmer Deeping (mixed, perhaps, with a little amazement) that his brother Paul, who is also a farmer, will insist on bringing his own white shop loaf in his pocket when he comes to pay them a visit. "He says he can't tackle our bread," says Mr. Deeping; "can't get on with it nohow. Which only shows, now doesn't it?"—though what exactly it shows he does not explain.

With her father away in hospital, and Jack, most evenings, somewhere down in the village, Priscilla has need not to be a timid woman. Nevertheless, even she confessed that, since this snowy spell, she has perhaps felt a little lonely at times. I can well believe her. The wind whines through the old house, the snow blows under the locked door, and outside not a single track remains identifiable to link her with the nearest cottage half a mile away.

"I'd have been all right, I think," she says, "if Lady hadn't been ill. I used to hear her coughing out there in the stable, and—well, it wasn't exactly pleasant. I told Jack a dozen times he ought to put an end to her misery; but he wouldn't. He made the excuse that if they shot her, they'd never get her out to the roadway, through all those snowdrifts; but I'm sure it was really because he always was so fond of Lady and couldn't bring himself to believe there wasn't any hope. Anyway, she had to be shot in the end. Yesterday it was; and they got her out into the road easily enough, after all. Dragged her over the snow with the tractor, and she hardly made a mark. Jack said she rode as soft as velvet."

There are days in spring when the sky can be ecstatic over Brock's Hole, so many are the larks that seem to prefer this spot for their special territory. It is as if invisible hands held a crown of singing light over the place: as if this little farm, worked almost entirely by an old father and his two willing children, were somehow preferred above its neighbours. Indeed, for me at any rate, Brock's Hole, while Farmer Deeping lives, is a place apart. I rarely pass that way, whether it is across the fields or between the blackthorn foam of that rutty-green ride, without I pause to lift the wooden bolt out of the barn door and see if the old farmer is pottering about somewhere inside. For the barn is where he seems to spend most of his time these days, as if his weak, narrowing eyes preferred the owlish dusk there to the sharp light in the fields outside. Through the chinks and knot-holes in the barn walls the light falls in soft pencil-rays, mote-filled, and subtly emphasizing the darkness of the interior. And like a shadow the old man dreams among his dusty relics and implements of yesterday.

Few talks have given me greater pleasure, or sent me home more certainly renewed in spirit, than those I have enjoyed with the old man as we sat on the sacks piled up near his threshing-floor. Perhaps "talks" is the wrong word to describe those rich, lazy half-hours; for Farmer Deeping is not much of a talker. He voices no pithy remarks, as Thurston, for instance, does; and if—but this is rare—he should attempt to illustrate his point with a story, the chances are he will either lose sight of the story before he has finished it or he will bring it to such a vague conclusion that you are still left wondering whether he has finished or not. And yet, in spite of this, something valuable is imparted, some fragrance of a life lived in quiet fullness and now drawing to its close. The whole of that life has been devoted, happily and unstintedly, to the land that was his father's before him and should be (but alas, probably will not be allowed to be) his son's after him; and from those forty acres the whole richness of his character springs.

The tractor may be working outside, in the fields, but here, in the barn, the past still holds precarious sway. I think that is perhaps why Farmer Deeping is so often to be found in here. Among the dust and cobwebs on the beams—so hardened with age that a nail will hardly penetrate them—hang such all-but-forgotten farm implements as flails ("frails," as everybody hereabouts calls them), barley hummelers, sickles, and scythes. If you want to unloose the old man's tongue, one almost infallible way is to invite his explanation of the use and practice of such pre-mechanical tools and properties as these. For him they have not yet been reduced to the unkindly status of "relics" or "bygones": indeed, he still occasionally threshes out some beans with a flail, and it is the pride of the year for him when, at the commencement of harvest, he takes down his scythe, hones it, and begins mowing down the corn around the difficult headlands or where it has been badly laid by the weather. The main work of the harvest is Jack's, with his spitting, snorting tractor; but there are still places where the binder is useless, and there the old man and his whistling scythe come into their own.

Over in one corner of the barn stands a dressing-machine, complete with every grade of sieve; and this, too, he contrives sometimes to find a use for. From an economic point of view it may be a waste of time; but the satisfaction it gives to Farmer Deeping to stand there turning the handle that shakes the sieves and rotates the fans and sets the whole box of tricks clattering is not to be measured in terms of economics. It is certainly a tiring job, and the most that can be dressed is about forty quarters a day. Jack laughs and calls it a waste of time, but he is wise enough to keep his laugh and his criticism to himself.

These old tools and implements are the farmer's tangible contact with a day when farming was less a trade than a way of life. Over in another dusty corner of the barn, for instance, stands a hand chaff-cutter. "When Father was alive," the old man said to me one day, as I stood by watching him feed the hay to the cumbersome blade, "there used to be a man come round regularly, with his own little chaff-cutter. He carried it on his back, and went about from place to place, putting in a morning's work here and an afternoon's work there. He didn't do anything else. There was always a meal for him when he came here and he brought us news of friends and farmers we hadn't seen for donkey's years. He used to be as interested in Father's horses and crops as if they were his own. I don't suppose he could have ever earned more than a shilling or two a day, but, oh, he was a happy old man. I can see him now, sitting in the kitchen with one of Mother's pies in front of him, and laughing and talking a good 'un. But now it wouldn't be worth his while, would it? They'd say he took too long; and, anyway, where's the horses to-day?"

Perhaps the thing I like most of all among Farmer Deeping's outmoded stock-in-trade is his winnowing-fan. Made of cane, it is fashioned like a vast scallop shell which, resting on the shoulder-blade, fits perfectly into the bend of the upraised arm when being carried. Its only use now is to collect the chaff, or "small stuff," and carry it away, either from the dressing-machine or from the wasteful heaps left behind by the threshers. Beautiful as a leaf, and as perfectly adapted to its own ends, it is for me the very symbol of that earlier husbandry which was the pride of the English countryside and the decay of which is now our loss and shame. Brock's Hole was just the place in which to find such a treasure; and who better than old Farmer Deeping to go striding across the rickyard with it pitched against his shoulder, laden with chaff that others would leave to rot or blow away?

Unhappy will be the day for England when such men are no longer to be found serving its willing acres!

Chapter Ten

IT is as if the whole round earth beneath our feet had gone dead: as if we were living now on another moon.

I look out of the window into the garden (or where the garden ought to be) and I see none of those comforting rings of bare earth in the snow, as if the plants' warm breath had melted a clearing round their living leaves. The wallflowers and Brompton stocks, which I planted in the autumn, stand out of the snow like grey rags tied to a stick; there is no warm breath in *those* leaves to melt away the snow. And that apple-tree, round whose base there should by now be showing the golden bubbs of the aconite—can such a filigree of iron ever break into a million down-flushed buds? As for the vegetable garden, that spade has not yet been invented which could dig up my leeks or parsnips, frozen into the earth like fossils in a rock. The whole universe has lost its breath; and in this arctic moment it seems to be touch and go whether it will ever find it again.

Mutz died last night, and the only way of burying him this morning was by thawing the ground a little with a bonfire. His death was itself something of a symbol—for me, at least—of the withering cold that has had us all in its grip these last few days. Eight months old, he was still not much more than midway between kitten and cat: a frolicking, irresponsible little creature one minute and already a not quite staid tom the next.

There had seemed nothing whatever wrong with him, no possible reason why he should die. And then yesterday afternoon he suddenly sickened. I made him a warm bed by the fire, and, since he refused all food and drink, left him to sleep. Sleep, I know, will cure most of the ills that cat-flesh is heir to, and so I did not worry. But the sickness increased. Nothing I could do seemed to relieve him; as soon as the bout was over, he would curl up in his rags again, look at me appealingly, and then bury his shivering head.

Once he dragged himself out of his bed, crawled across the floor on sagging legs, and made his way to the saucer in the kitchen where he always has his milk. When he failed to return, I went out to see what had happened, and there he lay in front of his saucer, his mouth inside it, and all the milk spilt over the floor. I warmed and diluted a little; but however much he may have desired it, he was unable to lap it up; and so I carried him back to his bed beside the fire.

I asked where I could for advice, but nobody knew what to suggest. Country cats are expected to look after themselves. "Let him sleep it off," was the general answer to my query; but as the evening advanced, and Mutz continued to lie there, questioning me every now and then, as I imagined, with his dulled eyes ("*Isn't* there anything you can do?"), I found it increasingly difficult to believe that sleep alone would mend all in the end.

To spend one's grief on a dying cat is usually considered a sentimental indulgence, and I admit I have seen instances all too many of people whose grief for suffering animals is only matched by their lack of grief for suffering mankind. "Animals have no souls," says one friend, a Catholic; "and so you do wrong to feel too strongly about the death of a cat." But I find myself preferring the words of another friend: "The virtue of non-attachment is demonstrated daily," he says, "but when creatures of living beauty attach themselves to one, one is willing to sin and take the consequences."

Certainly Mutz was no great beauty. He belonged to that vast,

The lane and the barn

harum-scarum race of country cats whose family tree is as rank as an elder and quite as ineradicable. But equally certainly he knew how to attach himself to one. All the wiles of the cat tribe who, of all living creatures, best know the art of retaining their independence while at the same time flattering the human desire for a show of complete submission, were his *in excelsis*. He gave, only in so far as it pleased him to give; and in return he got—all he wanted! It was impossible (at least in this household) to deny him. From the moment he crossed the threshold, deep in the safety of a jacket pocket, he ruled the place.

Clearly enough, I recall the occasion when we first brought Mutz home. I had asked the baker to try to find me a cat, knowing his own affection for all cats; and apparently all the mongrels of the parish were passed under review before Mutz was discovered and duly pronounced by him as just the cat for me.

It was Heinz's birthday—his first in England after being hounded out of a Nazified Vienna. With all the Austrian's love of animals and birds (did they not once charter an aeroplane to rescue the blizzard-caught swallows, stranded in the Alps, and carry them into the sunshine of the south?) he had asked me to get a kitten. At first I hesitated, remembering Sambo's depredations amongst the birds in my garden. With the skill of a tight-rope walker, Sambo would tread the top of the hedge and pick the naked wretches out of their nests. A family of yellow-hammers, flashing the gold nuggets of their heads in the sun of my garden, is as precious to me as rare flowers are in other gardens, and I did not relish the thought of a second Sambo nullifying my pleasure. And there was another thing. Sambo was a wanderer and had finally paid the price of his freedom by getting himself caught in a rabbit-snare, an end I was not anxious to have repeated.

But cats are not to be denied by mere humane considerations like these. Their persistence is almost psychic: they get themselves a home in spite of the stoutest denials. If there is somebody in the room who hates cats, it is just her lap and none other they will choose, and the unhappy recipient of their attentions has no alternative but to pretend she feels herself honoured. So with Mutz: in spite of all my determination, he arrived—as if the very stars in their courses had ordained it so.

One evening in July, therefore, we walked over to Nat Swift's to fetch him. The way home took us past Charlie Beslyn's cottage. From behind the leafy screen of his garden he must have been watching us; for that night a Woolworth envelope was handed in at my door, addressed in Charlie's clear, untutored hand. Inside were the following verses:

The primrose path of happiness
  Is walked in greatest measure
By those who seek, and find content
  In simple childlike pleasures.
This night I saw two men who found
  Delight, in simple treasure
By playing with a tiny pet
  To occupy their leisure.
Said Bertha who was with me then
  (I thought I'd better mention)
Just look at those two men out there
  And see how great attention
They're giving to that tiny thing
  A little ball of fluff
A kitten small and black and round
  And yet just big enough
To give them greater happiness
  Than tons and tons of pelf
Or all the pleasures gained by those
  Who pander to theirselves.

To set Charlie's verses down in a book, like this, in all the cool precision of print, is rather like setting a simple, stay-at-home girl in the glare of stage limelight: the original merit eludes the daze of publicity. I include them nevertheless, for they became part of our pleasure in Mutz henceforth.

Not many kittens have a poem sung over their christening. It is true that Mutz never showed any signs of wanting to live up to the dignity thus thrust upon him: to the end he remained plebeian, one of the masses, a cat whose manners were no better than they should have been, and whose name (bestowed impromptu, when his sex rendered irrelevant the original Mitsi) was the only unusual thing about him.

And now he is dead. Rightly or wrongly, proportionately or disproportionately, his dying affected me considerably. I believe now that the significance of the event was somehow rendered the more emphatic by (I know it sounds ridiculous) the weather. I found it impossible to get warm that night. Even when I sat inside the fireplace, logs and coals conspiring together for my comfort, I found the heat more an illusion than a reality. Somewhere inside me a core of cold persisted. And perhaps because of this, the sight of Mutz, incommunicable in his suffering, shivering his life away in that bundle of rags, bit itself the more keenly into my consciousness.

I tried to read, but the picture of a dying cat imposed itself between me and the words. At midnight, unable to do anything more to relieve him, I piled up the fire, tucked Mutz into his rags, and went upstairs to bed. I tried to sleep, but the thought of a dying cat came between me and the oblivion I sought. Finally, at about two-thirty, weary of the attempt to shut him out of my mind, I came downstairs again.

Never, in England, have I known such intentful cold. It seemed to squeeze the breath out of my body, as if I were being clamped in a relentless vice. Now, I felt, was the very zero hour of all this bitter spell of bad weather. In the fireplace was nothing but a heap of ashes. Mutz had crawled out of his bed and lay on the hearthrug a foot or so away. His eyes were open, but there was no meaning left in them. I lifted his paw. It was still warm, but it fell aimlessly out of my fingers.

I covered him over and went back to bed. And as I lay there, shivering, the fact of his death began to assume almost morbid proportions, until it seemed to focus the evil intensity of the cold. The force I had seen at work in the lane outside, piling up those malignant and yet lovely drifts of snow, so silently and so remorselessly, became for the moment identified for me with the death of my cat.

Uneasily at last I slept; and when I came down this morning, Mutz's body was frozen fast to the mat.

Chapter Eleven

LARKFIELD is typical of most English villages in that it possesses one fair-sized general stores, where you may buy anything from bacon to wine (the "rich, fruity port" beloved of cottagers), patent medicines to paraffin, or silk stockings to garden implements, and a number of small shops where, on the other hand, the selection is so limited and the service so casual that you may wonder how their owners manage to make a living out of such a twopenny-ha'penny turnover. As a matter of fact, I don't think the owners of most of these small shops, many of which are no more than converted front rooms of cottages, do make a living out of them. I don't think they ever really imagined they would.

Small farmers, whom these competitive times have squeezed out of their farms; craftsmen, who forsook their calling just in time to save some of the little capital it had brought them in better, more honest days; men and women on the look-out for some convenient means of eking out a more than modest income—such are the general run of owners of these little village shops. And if they welcome the pence that come trickling over the counter, it is certain they welcome even more the people who bring those pence. Trade is more an excuse for companionship than a means of livelihood.

If, for instance, you want the nearest Larkfield can give to an efficient, up-to-date service you must go to Mr. Mugridge's shop, where, with a modicum of good luck, you will get what you ask for; for Mr. Mugridge keeps the general stores, and serves the gentry, and draws the main custom of the parish. But if you go to Mrs. Wright's, or Mr. Ley's, or Mrs. Clark's, the goods you pay for over the counter will almost certainly be the least of what you will bring away with you. You buy a pound of sugar from Mrs. Wright —or Mr. Ley, or Mrs. Clark—and a pound of good fellowship is thrown in for make-weight.

Mrs. Wright, in fact, is an excellent example of this pleasant class of small village shopowners. "Shop" is almost too pretentious a word for the blue-washed room in her thatched cottage where she stocks sweets for the children, tobacco and fizzy drinks for the harvesters, and the less perishable groceries for their wives.

A visit to Mrs. Wright invariably entails an inspection of Bessie, the sow, sucking her curly tailed litter as she lies stretched out and snorting in her sty, or a stroll round the garden to see Mr. Wright's marrowfat peas or Mrs. Wright's cabbage roses, not to mention a conversation over the counter that may be productive of anything, from a forthright criticism of the newfangled methods being adopted over at Nortofts Farm to an unrecorded scrap of folk-song, sung in quavering and not-quite-unison by both Mr. and Mrs. Wright, or it may be productive of just nothing but the simple good feeling that accompanies a sincere inquiry after your health or an obvious pronouncement upon the state of the weather.

In days like these, when a knifing wind blows all day unhindered from the North Sea and the snow is a blinding weariness to the eyes, it is good to run into Mrs. Wright's for some trifle which you could probably very well do without. You hurry up the garden path to escape the wind as soon as possible, push open her door, and take shelter inside the friendly little shop.

Perhaps she will ask you through into the room beyond, where Mr. Wright, deaf and difficult, sits over the fire, lighting his pipe with a sere stick of hazel.

Such visits are sometimes productive of the most surprising

scraps of information, for the Wrights both come of farming stock and were themselves farmers long before they became shopkeepers. Photographs are taken out of a drawer, fading snapshots that still reflect a world that soon will be totally forgotten. Here is one of Mrs. Wright sitting up in her gig, neat and trim as a farmer's wife ought to be; and with shy, quiet pride she tells how she spanked along the road, coming home from market, overtaking all the other farmers and their wives on the way. And here is another of Mr. Wright, some fifty years ago, spruce in his suit of corduroy, whip in hand as he stands beside two proud horses hitched to a load of corn which he is taking to be milled. He looks the part all right, smiling out of the faded photograph; but there was evidently some sort of wanderlust calling him, for about this time he left his father's farm, intending to go to sea. With a friend, he somehow made his way to Liverpool.

"It was late at night when we got there," he told me, "and we paid for a room in a dutty ol' place—well, I dunno *who* hadn't slept there afore us. 'I ain't takin' no clothes off here, Jim,' I say, and I slept in all I'd got. Next morning, we were up early and went down to see the ships. I recollect the seat where we sat—one of them iron seats, you know, stuck in the pavement. I hadn't never sen the sea afore, and when I see them big ships on it, a-disappearin' out of sight, I say to Jim, 'Jim, come on! I'm going home. I don't think I want to go to sea after all!' "

When Mr. Wright married and took a farm of his own, I suspect it was mainly his wife who kept things going, just as she still does, when her husband is old and ailing and terribly temperamental. It is true that he has the lowest opinion of her abilities, but I notice he lets her do the work all the same.

"Clackety-clack," he says, "clackety-clack: it's all you ol' wimmen can do!"

And when Mrs. Wright has her sisters, or cousins, in to see her, he is generally to be found pottering around the garden. "You'll find her in there," he says, as I come up the path, and he jerks an impatient thumb over his shoulder, in the direction of the house. "I dessay you can' hear 'em," he adds, bitterly.

Yet I think, after all, it is largely his deafness which causes this impatience with his womenfolk. He suspects, and quite rightly, that they purposely don't let him hear all they are saying. And so he must needs find some way of counteracting this enforced inferiority. So he storms at his old wife on occasion, and, whilst letting her do the work, complains at the way she does it.

Only the other day they gave me an amusing instance of the fact that it is undoubtedly Mrs. Wright, herself white-haired and tottery with rheumatism, who "wears the trousers."

I found them both in the shop and still eager with the excitement of the nocturnal adventure that had befallen them.

"We heard such a thump and a bang in the night," said Mrs. Wright. "It sounded like——" and then, at a loss for the right illustration, she looked round the shop for something to bang with. But Mr. Wright, sensing her difficulty, got in first. He thumped his fist on the trestle counter, so that all the bottles of sweets jumped into the air. "Yes," Mrs. Wright affirmed, "it was even louder than that." "Well, I'm deaf," chimed in Mr. Wright, "but I heard it clear enough. We sat up in bed and Missus she lighted the candle. It was half-past two. 'Lawk-a-mussy,' I said, 'what's that?' " "I was sure there was somebody downstairs," said Mrs. Wright, taking up the thread of the story and holding it. "We listened and listened, but we couldn't hear anything. Then at half-past three we said we'd go downstairs and see what it was. Tom was all for getting his gun." "'I'll shoot 'un,' I said," Mr. Wright continued, the male in him seizing the opportunity for self-aggrandizement. "Of course, I wouldn't only a-shot 'un in the leg. But Missus, she said, 'No, don't shoot 'un; I'll take your stick with me.' And I followed her down the stairs." "We looked everywhere with the candle," said Mrs. Wright, claiming as hers the cadence and conclusion of the tale, "but we couldn't see anything anywhere. . . . And just now I found out what it was. A brick had fallen through the ceiling in the spare room: it must have come unlodged from the chimney-stack somewhere. But my, it did give us a jump!"

An hour they had sat there in the candlelight, still as mice, debating in whispers what to do; and then (I'm sure Mr. Wright in his excitement never guessed what confession had escaped him) it was Mrs. Wright, incapable, talkative female as she was, who led the way downstairs, stick in hand, to face the enemy.

Only in one matter will Mr. Wright never allow his wife to meddle. She may look after the shop, she may feed the fowls, she may even shift the fowls from one run to another (though, of course, she does so under a hail of criticism: "Drat the woman, she ain't got no more sense than a rabbit!"), she may attend to the garden, and she may gather in the plums and apples; but feed and tend the pig she may not.

If ever I see Mrs. Wright stumbling round the sty, in that bygone coat of hers, long-skirted and puff-sleeved, I know that Mr. Wright must be ill. For Bessie the sow is sacrosanct to her master's special care. She is child to him. She is everything to him.

When he is compelled to remain upstairs, he can overlook the sty from his bed, and Mrs. Wright knows, as she unbolts the gate and takes the pail of swill into the scared animal, that her every action is being closely watched. And when the doctor says he may get up again, and perhaps go out in the sun a little, the first thing he does is to wander down the garden to Bessie and commune with her over the fence.

If Bessie herself is ill, whatever the hour and whatever the expense, the vet must be fetched; and more than once I have had Mrs. Wright on my doorstep, coppers ready in hand, pleading for me to telephone to the town for help.

"Tell him he *must* come," she says. "Mr. Wright is in a rare state about Bessie. Tell him he *must* come."

And recently, when the shortage of animal foodstuff was at its worst and cottage pigs and hens were being killed off wholesale, because a short-sighted Government had failed to realize that in wartime it might be difficult to get supplies from abroad, Mrs. Wright must have spent many weeks' profits from sweets and sugar and ginger-beer in an endeavour to get food for the precious sow.

The reason for this almost religious attitude towards Bessie is written in bold white paint over the door. THOMAS WRIGHT. PORK BUTCHER. LICENSED SLAUGHTER-HOUSE FOR PIGS. Inside, there is more evidence of the reason. From the whitewashed beams of the ceiling hang a "spreader" and a couple of gigantic hooks. Over in one corner of the lean-to is a salting tub of immense proportions. And part of an elm-tree-trunk, four feet in diameter, stands in another corner. Spiders spin their webs from the "spreader" and the cutting-up block is used for a mere table, and the tub holds only Mrs. Wright's supply of soft washing water; but once they all had a nobler use.

For miles around Mr. Wright was famed for his sausages and his home-cured hams—particularly his sausages. People speak of them even to-day with a delight and longing that suggest their savour still lingers on the palate.

Village carpenters, as I have already suggested, are sometimes immortalized in the field-gates they made; blacksmiths in window-latches, oven doors, and the like; whilst many a thatcher's work is pointed to with pride long after he is dead. Mr. Wright's immortality will be in the memory of the sausages he made. So long as any man lives who once upon a time tasted them, he will not be forgotten.

His hams graced the table up at the Hall. Indeed, he still receives an occasional supply of pork from there to cure in his own inimitable fashion; but his criticism of the way it is cut and his chagrin that he can no longer do the whole business from A to Z combine to make the job no more than a half-hearted one—a sour reminder of past, irrevocable glories. And his pork-cheeses (nothing will induce him to call them brawn) were a delicacy enjoyed far beyond this parish. But his proper pride was in his sausages alone.

He knew their worth and he knows it still, and I verily believe he would think it neither immodest nor irreligious if the fact should be commemorated on his tombstone.

Meanwhile, that blistered bit of board over his door is a sufficient memorial. Mr. Wright has not killed a pig for years, but every March he still pays for his licence to be renewed. "Just in case," he says, in defence of the extravagance; but I have a shrewd idea it is solely that he may continue to keep that notice nailed over his doorway.

Pagan warriors treasure the scalps of their enemies and wealthy horticulturists point with pleasure to some rare gentian fetched from the High Alps; and why should not Mr. Wright be allowed the gesture of that bit of board over his door to commemorate the day he made sausages of such wide repute?

With such a reputation singing in his shiny old head, no wonder if he sits back now and lets the women do the work. Something may surely be allowed, even in this feminist age, for the dignity of manhood! *His* work is done. Things must go on, it is true; ordinary, everyday things like feeding fowls and serving fizzy drinks; but let the women look after these. . . . So he concentrates on Bessie and lets most of the rest go by. How long Mrs. Wright will continue to be able to cope with all the work that falls on to her sloping shoulders seems not to bother him: nor, if appearances are anything to go by, does it bother her. She has the blessed ability of taking everything as it comes.

To watch Mrs. Wright out in the garden these days of bitter weather, feeding the fowls, is scarcely to be set thinking of the village beauty. Her puff-sleeved coat is buttoned high round the neck. Her vast tam-o'-shanter flops over her white hair. And she treads as if her feet were bare to the spiky ice. Yet it is clear, on closer view and in rare moments of unmitigated health and happiness, that she could once have set men staring after her as she strode along. It does not need those faded photographs to assure one of the truth of this. I dared to say as much to her one day, as she paused in serving me, and some play of light from the window restored the beauty of her mobile face; but she only smiled a moment shyly, a little sadly, then looked away and said, "Maybe!"

I think her happiest days were when, together, they farmed Woodlands Farm and she drove home from market on Wednesday evenings, flicking her whip, and gaily calling out to the friends she overtook. Why they ever gave up the farm at all I have never rightly understood. The natives have their own ideas on the subject, but it is not always wise to accept their interpretation of private tragedies. From driving your own smart gig to market to driving a few old hens from one run to another is a long journey, and it has told heavily on Mrs. Wright. Her courage, however, has seen her through, and, to the outside world at least, she gives no hint of possible cankers eating at the heart of things.

It was one of the soldiers serving with the local searchlight unit who, the other day, set me pondering about the pride (he called it obstinacy and worse) of such small village shopkeepers as Mrs. Wright.

"There's no sense in it," he said. "You go into their shop and ask for something. They haven't got it and they won't be bothered to get it. They don't care whether they serve you or not. Dammit, what do they keep their shop for?"

It had happened to him, he said, times out of number during the five months he had been stationed in Larkfield, and he was reluctantly forced to the conclusion that, of all the inhabitants, and he hadn't a terribly high opinion of any of them, these small shopkeepers, petty tradesmen as he called them, were the laziest of the lot.

"You'd think they would be only too glad of the extra custom the war brings them—to say nothing of the fact that, after all, we did leave decent jobs and come here to defend 'em. But no, they don't give a tinker's cuss for extra custom; and when they do serve you with anything, they adopt a take-it-or-leave-it attitude that just gets my goat."

Wild Campion

But the soldier, I think, had got the matter a little bit askew. It is true enough that he left a good job, and all the comfort it implied, to do what he considered his duty; and it is also true that this duty has so far meant little else but almost unmitigated boredom in a camp that became waterlogged almost as soon as it was occupied and has been snowed under ever since. But what does that mean to Mrs. Wright?

Frankly, so far this war is something that is happening quite outside her ken. Certainly it will be a different matter when the bombs begin to fall; but at the moment she has not the faintest idea what it is all about.

The aeroplanes roar overhead, the searchlights fence the night sky with javelins of fire, there are a few soldiers in the village, there are ration-cards and black-outs and air-raid wardens; but these all belong to a scheme of things of which she has but the vaguest comprehension.

I stood in her garden with her the other day, while she was scattering corn to the fowls. A dispatch-rider flashed by on his motor-cycle, noisy and urgent on some errand of war. A bomber sped over the snow-blackened skies, returning—who knows?—from some deathly mission over the North Sea. Mrs. Wright heeded neither of them. She just went on scattering corn while the eager hens clustered round her feet. The dispatch-rider and the bomber meant next to nothing to her: they were totally outside the realities that have made up the seventy years of her quiet, courageous life.

And that night I happened to come upon a passage in Stephen Spender's *September Journal*. "Above all," the poet writes, "the world should be home, it should be somewhere where everyone has his place, is surrounded by the simple machinery, the task, the house, the furniture, the companion, the river, the trees or streets which assure him that he is loved. Everything should be rooted. This is the simplest thing in life, it is the cocoon that surrounds childhood, it is the simple security of the flesh and the kiss and the fireplace and the setting sun which brings him home.

"No one should want anything except to find his place in life, the centre of his potentiality to love and be loved. Yet if love is the essential thing in life, loss of it is the fiend which enters certain bodies and tears the life around them into shreds. The depredations of the loveless and the homeless who seek power over their fellow beings, can be seen everywhere to-day. The world suffers from the worst and least necessary of mental illnesses—homesickness. The papers are filled with photographs, and have been for years, of those who have been driven out of their homes—the endless rustle of shuffling peasant feet through the dust all night along the road outside Malaga, the family with their possessions piled up on a cart outside a burning Polish farm-house, the widow searching amongst the ruins of her house for a souvenir. They are driven from the little hole which surrounded and comforted them, into the elemental world of alien stones and light. Most homeless of all, little shreds of matter from distant countries that have nothing to do with them, are driven through their flesh. The whole universe of Outside enters their bodies—a fragment of a bomb, a bullet."

And I thought at once of Mrs. Wright, scattering her corn to the silly fowls, while the dispatch-rider flashed past and the bomber hurled through the clouds overhead. May that day never come when she, too, joins those nameless thousands of the homeless ones—a widow searching amongst the ruins of her house for a souvenir.

The soldier, however, was not only wrong in imputing to such as Mrs. Wright too vivid a perception of the war and what it entailed; he was also wrong in his estimate of what he called their obstinacy.

I did not tell him, but that same day I had seen an easy example of the kind of thing he complained about. Some threshers had been at work in a rickyard near by. Cold as it was, they had gone to Mrs. Wright for some of her fizzy drinks; but she had run out of them. In fact, crates of empty bottles have stood about the shop for weeks, waiting for the manufacturer's van to collect them. That afternoon she asked me to telephone and see what was the matter. Would they please explain why they had not been near the place for nearly two months and would they ask the van to call next Thursday, as it always used to? They promised; but of course on Thursday the van never arrived. I suggested to Mrs. Wright that she should send them an order by post: perhaps, with the order in front of them, they would remember to call.

"No," she replied, "I shan't do anything more about it. They'll turn up one day and then I'll let 'em see that I can be just as independent as they can. If they don't want to serve me, they needn't. I can quite well manage without."

And manage without she will. Never mind if there are a hundred and one reasons (illness, for instance, or shorthandedness, or what she calls "this war business") why the fizzy drinks never arrived. Never mind if she has to say no to all the thirsty threshers and roadmen and cyclists who may come panting into the shop. She will have lost her trade but she will have kept her pride.

And that, I think, is just the point which the soldier did not quite realize. At all costs Mrs. Wright will keep her pride. And it is the same with most small shopkeepers. Pride, we are told, is one of the deadly sins; but suppose it means pride in that little freedom which is all one has?

It is the job of shopkeepers to serve, and in serving they too often become servile. There is nothing servile about Mrs. Wright, however; and she, in common with Mr. Ley and Mrs. Clark and all the other cottage shopkeepers in the parish, does not sell you her freedom when she sells you her tobacco and groceries.

In this she differs from the larger shopkeepers. In the days before shopping by post and free delivery within a fifty-mile radius, the gentry did at least a fair proportion of their shopping in the village. Not to do so would have seemed to them unpatriotic. And so, when the Hall carriage drove up before the local general stores, there was a sudden commotion inside, and the grocer, hastily wiping his hands on his stiff white apron, flew out of the door, bowed, and, paper in hand, stood there in the wind and the cold, jotting down her ladyship's order. With a jingle the carriage drove away and the grocer returned to his duties, slightly flushed and confused from so near a contact with the great ones of this world. That sort of thing has gone on for generations until the whole race of large village shopkeepers has become tainted, however decreasingly, with the odour of servility. It is in their blood.

But it is not in the small shopkeeper's blood, since, as he did not benefit by her ladyship's patronage, neither did he have to pay for it in terms of servility.

Hence, therefore, Mrs. Wright's "obstinacy." She will sell you what she has got, but she will not necessarily go out of her way to sell you what she has not got. Particularly if you are a "foreigner." Half of her merchandise is good fellowship and, as such, only to be bought by those with whom she is truly familiar. What the soldier was up against was not so much obstinacy as the fact that he was, after all, a stranger.

Perhaps that day is not far off now when these small village shops will have gone the way of so much more that used to give the countryside its quiet, leisurely character and its sterling worth. Just as the big farms are swallowing up the small farms, so the big shops will swallow up the small shops. Rapidly we see the omnivorous mastication going on already. The war has delayed the process. We are learning to rely more on what we can get at home. And this isolating snow has even further centred us on the immediate community in which we dwell. But the process is only delayed, no more. We may have glimpses to-day of what village life was like when it was its own self-supporting entity; but they are no more than glimpses, soon to be lost again.

If I should be living in Larkfield when this process of mastication is completed, and Mrs. Wright's shop, and Mr. Ley's, and Mrs. Clark's, and all the rest of them have reverted to the domestic cottages they once were, I do not suppose there will be much compensation in the fact that I can remember the time when shopping could be as much a social visit as a commercial transaction.

Still, perhaps it is better to have shopped like this once than never to have shopped like this at all; and when efficiency rules, even in the remotest hamlets, it will perhaps be something to make the young folk goggle when one can tell of summer evenings when one went shopping at Mrs. Wright's, and found her sitting in the garden on an old form lodged against the plum-trees, the setting sun in her eyes and her hands quietly folded in her lap, and sat down beside her and listened to the idle talk, like a woodland stream lapping against the stones, till one forgot what one had come for and went home again, a full hour later, empty-handed (unless with a gift of fruit or new-laid eggs) but far from empty-hearted.

Chapter Twelve

OVER in High Wood the gamekeeper walks through the avenues of young spruces, bringing food to his pheasants. It is against the rules and regulations, in wartime, to feed partridges and pheasants, I believe, but in that case all I can say is Peel is not the only man whom this hard weather has forced into disobedience.

Out of the level whiteness, pocked with the dint of bird-prints and here and there a spatter of blood, melodramatic on the bright snow, the spruces rise in exact formation, less a wood than a regiment of trees. Hooded with snow, like the soldiers fighting in Finland, they thrust out white-gloved hands from which, every now and then, a snow-bomb falls, with an explosion that shatters the wood's intensified quiet.

These are hard days for Peel's birds and hard days for Peel himself. Though the pheasants are standing up to the weather fairly well, the partridges are dying off daily. It is true that he would be feeling their loss more than he does were it not for the fact that Squire only gave two shoots last season and therefore the birds could afford a bit of thinning out.

In the end war's effects are mainly considered in so far as they touch our own lives and our own work; and Peel's chief grudge against Hitler's precipitation of hostilities so far is that it has completely disorganized those shoots that are the aim and end of all his labour.

"I've got some wonderful birds," he says; "but what's the use? Squire says I'll have to shoot 'em myself: a pretty how-de-do, eh?"

Four thousand acres is the extent of the Squire's estate and to Peel this is all one gigantic sanctuary for his birds. Everything and anything that mitigates against a successful breeding season—foxes, wars, badgers, poachers, and so on—is his enemy. He almost seemed to take the view, last September, that Hitler might at least have waited until the shooting season was over before he began upsetting things as he did. In this, however, I must confess that he is only adopting the same point of view as many who had not even his excuse, namely, that gamekeeping, after all, was his livelihood. To many a hunting and shooting man and woman the Führer was a spoil-sport: is not their whole year little more than a crescendo of waiting until autumn announces the opening of the season?

Perhaps Peel was already a little spoiled the year before last, when suddenly Larkfield awoke to find itself the centre of Army manœuvres. The quiet lanes shook with the rattle of lorries, engineers overran gardens and fields with tangles of telephone wires, guns were fired on the green, blowing windows and ceilings down and frightening the sick and aged almost out of their wits. Only the Squire's breeding woods were immune from this harsh invasion. Large W.D. notices appeared, nailed to the trunks of convenient trees, forbidding the firing of guns or the intrusion of the Army in general. Old women might have their wits blown to pieces, apparently, but the Squire's birds must not be disturbed.

And although I never taxed Peel about it, I am confident he was in hearty agreement with such a privileged scheme of things, nor saw anything ironical in those W.D. notices so prominently displayed upon his trees.

And indeed, why should he? He served in the last war, and, as his frequent stories show, was given plenty of evidence of the sacrosanct status of the sportsman, whether in civvies or in uniform.

"Some of the officers in our battalion," he said, "bet as I wouldn't bring down a buzzard. It was when we were occupying the Rhineland. Well, I bought a gun from a German for 200 marks —and marks was 190 to the pound, then. And another thing: bullets were iron and not lead. Still, I got up early one morning and off I went down to the river with that old gun. I'd had my eye on a particular buzzard there for several days. I waited and then presently along she came—flying lovely she was, easy as a glider. I fired once, and missed. Now I've lost her, I thought. But I fired again, and brought her down. My, weren't they pleased when I took that buzzard into the mess after breakfast! Of course it was all against orders to shoot buzzards, but that was winked at all right. Still, there wasn't half a shindy when I took the bird into Cologne, later, to have it stuffed."

I have always detested gamekeepers—or, rather, I always used to detest them. Brought up in a woodland countryside, I looked upon them as the evil spirits of those haunted, delightful places.

As some people love the sea, so I loved, and always have continued to love, the woods. I would wander off alone and stay for hours in the depths of the woods, whether they were thickets of tangled brier and hazel, where the nightingale sings in the heat of noon—louder, finer, than he ever sings under cover of the velvet darkness of the night—or tall beechwoods, where the light was green, aqueous, like being under the sea. The woods were friendly to me, places where, if I kept still enough and had patience enough, I could come closer than anywhere else to the secret life of animal and bird. From the ant-hills among the hot drifts of sere pine-needles, where the myriad community hurried to and fro on its mysterious errands, to the birds in the tree-tops, whose songs seemed to my childish mind the very articulation of all that swinging, surging, sunny turbulence of green leaves, I loved the life of the woods.

And what incredible surprises they would suddenly spring at one! How should I ever forget, for instance, that morning when, straying into a woodland territory I had not hitherto explored, I dramatically found myself in an open stretch of first-year hazel and chestnut, where wild lilies of the valley, frailer than our garden species, grew in great quantities, hiding their white-and-green washed bells among the silken banners of their leaves? I had never seen wild lilies of the valley before. And, as if this were not enough, while I stood staring down at the flowers round my feet, nightingales broke into song near by, with those passionate alternations of indrawn breath, like a self-inflicted wound, and full, rapturous phrases, like a release after pain. Lilies and nightingales! Happily, I was too young to do more than accept it all just as it was, too young to moralize away the best part of what I was enjoying: I only knew it was good to be alive!

Yes, I loved the woods and there was only one thing that could overshadow my happiness as I walked in them: the gamekeeper. It was so then, and to a certain extent it has been so for years afterwards. The sight of the gamekeeper in his fawn jacket, long-skirted and bulging with who knows what dead creature, his gun over his shoulder, and his bright, suspicious eyes, seemed to me an intrusion of something very like evil in the last place where I might wish to encounter it.

Somewhere at the back of my mind, I suppose, every time I have come upon a gamekeeper, was the grim memory of a keeper's gibbet, or larder, in a wood at home, where stoats and weasels hung head downwards from an horizontal ash-pole, along with magpies and jays, their gay wings wet and broken and infested with the insects that batten upon decay. I knew this was the keeper's doing and I hated him for it. The picture of that senseless gibbet, as I first saw it, suddenly turning the corner of some sunny, green ride in the woods, printed itself indelibly on my child-mind and remained there to stigmatize all gamekeepers henceforth. The mere fact that they were gamekeepers was good enough for me: as such they were necessarily excluded from any possibility of being other than hateful men, destroyers, parasites on the idle rich, wanton killers, and so forth. I hated them all.

With glove and bill-hook

Until I met Peel. Peel taught me some sort of perspective in the matter; and if I am still not enamoured of gamekeepers as a race, I am at least prepared to accept the logic of their position and to believe that there are others besides Peel who occupy that position, admittedly a difficult one, with some dignity and a good deal of character.

In fact, gamekeepers, I have since decided, are a somewhat maligned and much-suffering people. Their job is about as difficult as any in the parish, since the natural inclination of everybody, short of the Squire himself and his friends, is to be against them. The village policeman's task is simple by comparison. He at least has right on his side, in so far as not even the most rebellious villagers would deny the usefulness of his purpose as the keeper of the peace. But the keeper of the Squire's pheasants and partridges, in most villagers' eyes, serves no such useful purpose.

In this hard winter, for instance, many cottagers have felt the pinch of cold and hunger; and nothing so sharpens a sense of injustice as an empty belly and a meagre grate. Yet these same hungry, cold cottagers must watch the Squire's pheasants impudently stroll about their gardens and allotments, nor lift a finger against them, since, if they do so, the keeper may have the law of them. It is an elementary point of justice but none the less cogent for that.

Mark Thurston put the matter neatly, according to his point of view, in the tap-room of the Wheatsheaf on the morning after the Squire's last shoot. Some of the men present in the pub had money in their pockets to burn: they had put in a day's beating. Moreover, they had obviously enjoyed themselves, though their part in the day's sport had been a menial one. Perhaps Mark, who in his younger days had also enjoyed the exhilaration of a day's beating with the guns, was a little envious that he should now be excluded. And yet I do not altogether think so. Age has bestowed on Mark somewhat of the philosophic mind, and he sees many things to-day in a light that was denied to him yesterday.

"I know the shoots up at tha Hall ain't what they used to be," he said. "Why, I can remember the day—and so can Ben here, if he's a mind to—when two wagons weren't enough to carry home all the birds they shot. Yet if you or me was to see an ol' cock pheasant a-peckin' at our peas one morning and put a bit of salt on his tail—never you mind how!—we could be fined for it, and heavy too. It wouldn't count for nothin' for you to plead that you was hungry (let alone the loss of your peas and all the blessed trouble you took over 'em). That bird ain't your'n, you'd soon be told; and like as not, it'll be the Squire hisself, or one of his pals up there on the bench, as would tell you so. I can't see it's right; I can't, and I never shall.

"Mind you," Mark continued, forestalling a criticism he no doubt sensed was forming itself behind the smiles of some of his audience; "mind you, I'd be a liar if I was to say I hadn't never tasted pheasant-pie meself. I have and I hope I'll live to taste it agen. But that ain't neither here nor there. If Peel was to catch me, I'd be for it; and that's what riles me."

"That's right enough," said Ben, anxious to add his mite to the argument, anxious, also, to share something of the limelight: "it's just like Mark says. I'll tell you what: if I was to set a trap for a rabbit—and they're varmin, ain't they?—and break off its leg an' leave it in the trap a-yellin' all the bloomin' night, folks as had a mind to could get the law on me. So they could. All right then; but if the gentry has a day's shootin', why is it I can't get the law on *them* for leavin' half-shot pheasants to crawl about the fields for days till they die at last in somebody's ditch? It ain't fair, and nobody in his senses can say it is."

Most of the farm-hands find it unfair. Whatever their feelings for the Squire as a person, they feel that in this matter of pheasants and partridges there is somehow one law for them and another for him.

Perhaps it isn't a very strong feeling to-day, and certainly it is stronger in the old men than in the young. Mark and Ben knew Larkfield in the days when the poverty of the farm-labourer (ten shillings a week if they were lucky, anything up to fourteen in a family, and bread and beer as the mainstay of their diet) was something the present generations can scarcely conceive; and stored in their canny old heads are memories of poaching exploits, undertaken out of a necessity which none but a brutal inhumanity could deny, and the cost of which, in fine or imprisonment, was out of all proportion to the offence.

And even these younger members of the community, to whom such exploits are in the main only hearsay, inherit something of the antagonism which colours Mark's and Ben's words. Like the inherited instincts that prompt the behaviour of a swarm of bees or a flock of migrant birds, these inherited memories of the war-to-the-death between poacher and gamekeeper dwell in the mass-mind of the village, prompting its attitude, even to-day.

The grievance against all keepers has its roots deep in our undemocratic past. Poor Peel must bear on his broad shoulders the hates and antagonisms of men long since dead and buried.

I remember very well the day I first had my eyes opened as to the possible humanity of this abhorred race of men. I had been walking through Squerry's Wood one day in spring, when the clearings, forsaken now by the wood-cutters whose faggots lay about in neat piles, were full of windflowers and oxlips and blue dog-violets. I sat against an oak, letting the warm sunlight seep through my pores. I was aware of nothing save the sunshine and the profusion of spring flowers which Dis had scattered round my feet. Such days are rare in the early year and this was the one place in which to spend them. War had not even been reckoned with as a possible solution to the accumulating problems that were vexing Europe: it was those days when we came as near to peace as we ever came between the cataclysm of one war and the next. And to the last speck of me I was happy.

Suddenly I heard feet approaching, snapping the dry twigs under nailed boots. I looked up and saw the familiar figure of the gamekeeper—the leather leggings, the long-skirted coat, the ash stick, and the sack-pockets swinging against the hips. If it had been anybody else, I should have taken no notice; but I suppose that old memory of the bird-hung larder sprang alive in me at the sight of the keeper coming towards me over the blue and white tapestry of the flowers. It acted like a button that sets an alarm bell ringing. I privately wished him to the devil.

"Good afternoon," he said: "I only wanted to say would you mind keeping to the paths and rides just now. You see, my birds are nesting and I don't want them disturbed."

I do not quite know how, but the reasonableness of his request and the hint of a smile that played over his austere features so triumphed over my mood of resentment that I somehow found myself offering him a cigarette!

Another keeper, perhaps, or another way of saying things, and I should almost certainly have made some foolishly sarcastic reply that referred to his precious, pampered birds. Instead, here we were, smoking cigarettes and talking, he leaning against a tree and me with my legs stretched out among the myriad waving flowers. And for that conversion to sweet reasonableness I shall always be grateful to Peel.

For he thereby not only cleared my mind of one of its more obstinate prejudices, but he also prepared the way for many a profitable and enjoyable walk and talk in the future. I came to see that the gamekeeper was not necessarily the evil spirit of the woods I had always imagined him to be. True, even Peel never quite completed my conversion, for not all keepers are Peels. We grow like the thing that most occupies our attention, it is said: butchers are often red-faced and bloody, bakers white as uncooked dough, a rabbit-fancier will look like a rabbit, and a horsy-minded person like a horse, whilst even a gardener imbibes a philosophic calm from his fruitful occupation. So with gamekeepers: as a rule, the animal is all too apparent in their faces. No, Peel has not wholly purged me of my prejudice, but he has at least taught me a measure of common sense in the matter.

Peel knows his woods like the palm of his hand. He knows the intricate paths and rides threading through them. He knows the favourite haunts of the animals that live in them, and he knows their calls and their prints. The woods are his world. To say that he is fond of them is to impute perhaps too conscious a feeling; but, at any rate, there is no other job for which he would exchange this dawn-to-dusk work in the woods and fields.

His knowledge is such as a trained naturalist might well envy; but it was his attitude towards his job that first intrigued me. I soon saw that it is not so much a matter of venom as I had supposed, but an exercise of deeply rooted sportsmanship. In trapping and shooting, he is pitting his cunning against the equal cunning of the birds and animals; and that is what gives him pleasure. His own birds may be pampered—he even admits as much—but his job is to safeguard them against their enemies—"strangers," as he calls them.

Badgers, for instance, may have all the virtues—and more—which the naturalists ascribe to them. They may be clean to the point of finickiness, they may clear the place of docks and beetles, they may be wonderful handy at scratching out bees' and wasps' nests, and their grease may be the sovereign remedy against the "old man"; but for all that they are strangers, they are the enemies of his birds, eating their eggs, and they must go.

Peel will spend days tracking a badger before he is able to spring it. I remember particularly his excitement at a kill last year. All that early spring he tracked the badger's pads, and by their size he knew that he was up against something worth reckoning with.

"She comes along Wally's Lane," he said, "across the field in front of Mill Cottage, over the road there, along the Bottoms, and then where do you think she goes? Somewhere through the orchard alongside my cottage: bloody cheek, eh? A full five miles' trek every night and goodness knows what she does it for. But I'll spring her yet."

And then one day he called me into his garden. Incongruous

and pathetic among the litter of Mrs. Peel's tin baths and pots and the children's broken toys, lay the badger—as stalwart a creature as ever padded over English fields. Her body lay limp along the cobbles, the black and white bristles dead and lustreless.

"I told you I'd spring her," Peel said; "and there she is! And it took pretty nigh an Atlantic cable to catch her, too."

He has the sportsman's admiration for a valiant enemy. Indeed, I suspect it is this rather than any very firm conviction that the badger is outrageously opposed to his own interests that gives him most pleasure in outwitting it.

"Father had a tame badger once, called Sally," he told me. "He kept her on a brace and she was as knowing a customer as ever you saw. Us kids used to think no end of Sally. Then I remember one day mother took ill and we had to send for the doctor. He was a sporting sort of a chap, very handy with a gun. When he came out of the house, after he'd been in to mother, he noticed Sally in the paddock. Father and he fell to talking about badgers as fighters and the doctor said he'd like to set his terrier on to Sally to see what'd happen. He thought a lot of his terrier, did the doctor. So next time he came along he brought the dog with him, and Joan, his daughter. He was dead set on seeing that fight. Father warned him what would happen but he only laughed: he was a rare one for a bit of sport. Go ahead then, father said; and that terrier was dead in a couple of minutes. Sally tore it to ribbons. My, the doctor was surprised—he thought his dog could stand up to anything. And Joan, I remember she cried like a baby."

We were walking through Lordship Wood when Peel told me this story. My inexpert eye had failed to notice a noose of wire among the brambles tangling over the path. It was a badger-trap. The noose was attached to a bent sapling, secured ready to spring at a touch. When Peel had explained the trap to me, he told me about Sally, and then went on to tell of how one moonlight night he had stood waiting against a tree close by a badger's hole. Soon two badgers came out and Peel saw the fight of his life, right there under his eyes, so still he stood in the moonlight, like a bough of the tree.

"They made enough noise to split your ear-drums," he said; "and then, when I'd seen all I wanted, I put a shot through one—but the other got away."

Every now and then, during the course of a walk, Peel will stoop down, without breaking the thread of his talk, rake a few sods away from a mole-trap, knock out a broken-backed mole with a click, and tuck the sleek-coated creature into the deep pockets of his coat.

I asked him if all woodland creatures were his enemies?

"Not by any manner of means," he replied. "Quite a lot of the small birds, for instance, are very useful to me in my job. I'll tell you for why. Say I hear a wren—and you know what a devil of a fuss a wren can kick up for such a small bird? Well, that's probably a cat on the prowl somewhere. Or maybe I hear a blackbird give that warning cry of his, and I know there's a stoat up to no good. I've only got to hear it making a certain cry—I know exactly how—and I go along and make a little whining noise, like so; then up comes the stoat, standing on its hind legs—and that's just the time to catch him! But perhaps the bird that helps most is the starling. It makes more pother than all the other birds put together; and ten to one that means a hawk. Probably a sparrow-hawk. And you know if there's one thing I like to take a pot at more than another it's a sparrow-hawk. They're proper brutes, they are: steal eggs by the hundred."

Peel's best friends, however, are apparently his ferrets.

"I treat my ferrets kind," he will say; "for they work hard for their keep, so the little beggars do. You could put one of my ferrets in your shirt and it wouldn't leave a scratch. Why, one day my youngest kid—she's four—went up the top of the garden and (I dunno how she managed it) but she opened the hutches and let all the ferrets out. And the next thing missus saw was our little Susie with them ferrets all round her legs, running about, and sniffing at her bare flesh; and they didn't leave a mark anywhere."

It was one of Peel's really unlucky days when his favourite ferret lost an eye. He put her in a hole, gave her a flick with his finger, and said, "Up you go!" There was a screaming inside the hole, and when the ferret came out she had one eyeball hanging by a sinew. A fox had bitten it clean out.

"So I got out my knife," said Peel, "and I cut the eyeball away; and there she is in her hutch now, good for many a day's work yet!"

Indeed, it's an odd mixture, the gamekeeper's life. More like a sport, perhaps, than a job of work. It is true that he still buys his pleasure at the expense of a certain ingrained animosity on the part of the rest of the villagers; but at least to-day he is immune from that degree of peril which old Mrs. Dickson referred to, when she told me how her scrapbook of verses had consoled her through long nights during which she had never known if her man would return alive or dead.

There is a lonely farm on the outskirts of Larkfield where, until recent years, a notice was nailed to a tree at the corner of the woodlands: Man Trap, Beware! And the grim engine itself hangs to-day on the farmer's outhouse wall. . . . But the use of such things is not within the memory of men still living: the present-day keeper knows nothing of the ferocity that was once integral with his work.

Even the gamekeeper's cottage, that stands with its back to the open pastures and its eyes to the thick dusk of the woods, is untenanted now, here as in many another parish. Peel's wife would not live in such a secretive place for twice his present earnings, and Peel himself doesn't much fancy it. Instead, he lives close by the highroad, like anybody else. Nevertheless, he is a man apart, even to day: he is in the parish and yet somehow hardly of it. . . .

"Do you want to see a pretty sight?" he asked me one day in May, when the crab-trees spilled their pink petals on the pasture and every roadside was frothing over with the bloom of kexes.

And in a remote corner of High Wood, where a sandy bank fronted the afternoon sun, we watched some fox cubs playing under the roots of an elm, six or seven of them, innocent as kittens, tumbling and rolling and jumping over one another, blinking in the sunlight, chasing dead leaves, lithe as panthers, and shy as shadows, while the dog and vixen watched from the thicket near by.

"Now if that ain't a pretty thing to see," said Peel, as we came away, "I dunno what is."

And his voice was a shade gentler than usual, his eyes a gleam brighter.

Chapter Thirteen

COUNTRY talk has a flavour of its own when it comes from the lips of men and women whose whole lives have been given in the service of the land. The smell of growing things is in it and the tang of air that blows out of unsullied skies. It is vulgar with the vulgarity of life itself and painted with the poetry of earth. Unless education has spoiled it, robbing it of the vitality that was its well-spring, it carries the history of ages and links this year of grace with the eras of Celt and Saxon long centuries dead.

And the countryside will be the poorer, by the loss of one of its most precious characteristics, when the printed word and the broadcast word, between them, have reduced all its rainbow colours to the common drab of schoolman's speech.

Indeed, it is beginning to be at a discount already. The bilingual Welsh and Irish are not more expert in the use of their two languages than are these Larkfield children speaking one tongue with their teachers and another with their parents at home. And that is not the worst. Wait until the children are a little older and you shall see them beginning to correct their parents as they are corrected by their teachers, until the rich dialect that should be their proud heritage becomes, instead, a cause for contention and even for shame.

It is so in dozens of cottages to-day. Proud of their new caps and coloured blazers, the scholarship children ride off to the County School, returning home one fine evening well on the way to becoming strangers in the house where they were born.

Well, I suppose it is all one with mechanization and all the other aids of standardization which are the prop and stay of our time, and we but waste our breath decrying it. Nevertheless, thank God, I say, for the untutored speech of such men as Ben and Mark, Sam and Jim Adams, with its firm hold on the things of everyday life, its sensuousness, born of the common clay in which all their days are rooted, and its transparent simplicity.

One of the best places in which to hear such speech is in Sam's forge. Flack the horseman brings one of his mares over from Sandy Ley to be shod; and while Sam is blowing up his fire, sprinkling the fine coal with little shovelfuls of water and raking the glowing heap to and fro, first one and then another look in to pass the time of day. It is warm in the forge and the pubs are not yet open; and anyway, Sam is always good company. Never mind if the place will be smoked out presently, when the red-hot shoe touches the horn of the hoof. Never mind if you will not be able to see a foot in front of you nor if the acrid stench will tickle your throat and lodge a long fortnight in the warp and weft of your clothes. Here is fellowship and talk, and what more can you wish for?

Sometimes Sam is included in the talk; and sometimes, as is befitting to one who bends over the mare's upturned hoof and gives only his broad backside to the company, he is excluded. But the main thing is, Sam or no Sam, the talk goes on.

A moment ago, for instance, Shadwell, the Sandy Ley foreman came in, perhaps to see how the shoeing was progressing, perhaps because he too loves a yarn. Anyway, there he is, leaning against the hatchway. Presently he is seen exhibiting the old broken-tipped spud which he never goes without and which is no small part of the reason why his fields are emptier of thistles than any others in the parish.

"Broke clean in two," I hear him say, between Sam's shouts of "Whoa there, you old b——r," and "Come up, do!": "and you'd never guess how it happened. That spud was given me by Willie Ganer, who was foreman up at Sandy Ley before me. He said he'd had it over forty years; and I've had it these twenty-five. That's sixty-five years old at least she is; and then the other day she went and broke in two, all along of an old bit of sugar-beet. A rum 'un, that was. I was walking through Long Acres, where they'd been taking up the beet, and I went to knock a lump of dirt off one, same as I've done thousands of times.

"Well, dirt weighs heavy, as anybody knows, but who'd expect it to break an iron spud in two? That's what happened, anyway. Just with knocking a lump of dirt off a sugar-beet my old spud broke clean in two. I walked away, thinking about Willie, and how long he'd had this 'ere spud, and how long I'd had it, and what a terrible many days it was since we'd heard a word of the old man.

"And as I went past the house, Miss Mary came running out with a letter flutterin' in her hand. 'Hi!' she called out to me: 'I want a word with you, Shadwell. I've just had a letter to say poor old Willie's dead.' There, wasn't that a queer coincidence?"

The surprise of coincidence may be an easy way of introducing drama into conversation, but it is nevertheless often effective; and certainly few devices of narrative are more favoured by the countryman in a tale-telling mood. One almost felt that there had indeed been some mysterious significance in the snapping of Shadwell's spud, some occult hint of its previous owner's passing. The broken tool, held up for us to inspect, was in some way a degree nearer to animism by reason of the odd coincidence in which it had shared.

Coincidence, then, and next to coincidence, suspense. The most ordinary incident, as an old countryman tells it, will gather interest by dint of nothing else than delay in the telling.

"I was peelin' me taters a-Sunday," said Ann Bright one morning, "same as I be now, and Ted, he was a-sittin' over there in his chair, when I see a motor-car goo past the window, sort of slow, and pull up with a bang. 'Denbys hev got a caller,' I says to Ted. Then Mrs. Banks went hurryin' by—you know how she do goo scanterin' along like a fussy ol' hen; and there was a scrapin' and grindin', and 'No,' I says, 'it's somebody lost their way.' I went to the winder and there was the car backin' right up to our door. I could see a soldier-chap sittin' inside, and 'What in goodness' name do *he* want?' says Ted. 'Why, if that ain't Wally,' I says. And who do you think it was? My gal Annie's boy as I ain't sen for nigh on eighteen years—not since he was no taller'n that ol' lavender-bush beside the door there. 'Granny, how are ye?' he shouts and puts his arms round me. And I cried, and he cried—but there, of course we was only cryin' for joy like. Fancy, now, after all them years!"

A tale of nothing; and yet, as Ann told it, leading up to her climax by repetition of fact after trivial fact, till the sheer intensity of her memory brought the tears again to her eyes, who could fail to share something of her very real pleasure?

But I think what delights me most about country conversation is not so much its dramatic devices, however effective they may be (as some might say) in making bricks without mortar, as in its general flavour.

Inch by inch, these men know the land on which they have worked. It is the main concern of their lives, and nothing about it is too trivial for their attention and consideration. The land—and the men who have worked with them to plough and till and reap it: this is the quiet drama with which they are as familiar as any scientist examining the tissues of life under his microscope.

The land! It decides the slow measure of their tread and it guides their hands, patient and unfumbling, in whatever task they undertake. It monopolizes their thoughts and it colours the words and phrases with which they express those thoughts. It gives their daily bread and takes in return their very lives. Such an absorption is hard for the townsman to understand whose days are spent in a more shifting and varied round of interests. But Jim Adams's "I wouldn't work in a town for all the money in kingdom-come: there's no *life* in the things you have to work with there," sums up almost all there is to say about the reason for this absorption; and no true countryman, with the living earth under his feet and the living fruit of it in his hands, but would wholeheartedly agree.

Larkfield has many an old man and woman whose talk is full of this happy flavour; but for me, from one cause or another, it is perhaps most consistently associated with the countless conversations I have enjoyed with Ben—some of them no more than a word or two thrown over the hedge in passing and others lasting through long lamplit evenings.

Unlike Mark, whose aptitude for drama would secure him an audience anywhere and anywhen, Ben has next to no dramatic sense. He does not seek, by the devices of coincidence or suspension or whatever else, to turn everything he has to say into a story. Indeed, when I first knew him, I thought him unusually shy and even unsociable. Then one evening, after we had been wandering more or less in silence round his garden, examining his crops of pears and plums and apples, he said: "Won't you come inside?" And as we sat round the fire (for Ben, in common with most old countrymen, loves to see at least a spark of fire in the grate even at midsummer) he began a narrative of his life that is now continually having fresh chapters added to it every time I see him.

If I had been wiser, I would have made notes, afterwards, of all those conversations; for Ben's life-story is essentially the life-story of many typical old farm-hands and countrymen hereabouts, and the gathered grain of his talk, threshed of its chaff and cavings, would have constituted a rich harvest. As it is, I must content myself with such scraps as I can remember at a throw, odds and ends which for some reason—a picture, maybe, or a phrase, or a piece of intrinsically interesting information—have defied the curse of an abominable memory.

The only instance I can recall of Ben's ever telling me a story for the story's sake refers to Nick Tyler, an old farm-hand who once occupied the larger of two cottages which, together, now comprise my home. Nick, who is a widower, lived here with his only son Josh, and, on those rare occasions when the sun has power enough to penetrate his rheumaticky bones, he still comes this way and leans over the gate, viewing in a stony silence from which I have never been able to rouse him, the transmogrified home of his earlier years.

"Nick never did much reg'lar wukk," said Ben: "he was what you might call a casual labourer, doing a bit of threshing here and a bit of scything there, everything by turns and nothing long. His son Josh was in the way of becoming much the same. Goodness knows how they did fare sometimes, and it was said, after Nick's old woman died, the cottage got into a rare dutty state. You wouldn't a-knowed it for the same place."

Ben was making his first tour of inspection of my house. He sat on the edge of his chair, a glass of beer in one hand and the worn, shiny handle of his thorn-stick in the other. His keen old eyes missed nothing, and just now he was concentrating their gaze on the big open fireplace to see what device I was employing to keep out the smoke.

"Nick used to do all his cooking—what there was of it!—at that old fireplace," said Ben. "And I recollect they had a little low form in front of it: I think they'd knocked it up for themselves.

"Well, as I was sayin', Nick an' Josh never 'xactly wore their-selves out with wukking; and, whether it were true or not, they had the reputation for putting their fingers on what wasn't their own. Leastways, once when they was doin' a job down at Moat Farm, sawing up some winter wood, the farmer said he'd 'ad about enough of their tricks and swore he'd soon put a stopper to 'em. So he hid in the barn a night or two an' watched where they stole the wood from.

"Then one day he bored a few holes in some likely bits, poured a little gunpowder in, and waited to see what would happen. Sure enough, they took the wood home. On the way they called at the butcher's shop for a bullock's head; and when they'd got indoors, they put it in a pot, laid the fire, and sat down on that old form of their'n to warm themselves. 'Course the gunpowder went off and blew the ol' bullock's head up the chimbley, and Nick and Josh fell back'ards on the floor. Nick was so scared he'd a-given you all the sovereigns 'twas said he'd got buried somewhere out in the fields!

"But the comical thing was that next morning, when he went down to Moat Farm to wukk, same as usual, he told 'em all what had happened and where he'd got the wood from! 'I wonder what could a-been the matter with that old wood?' he said to the chaps there."

Ben's father was one of the last of a grand old line of tenant-farmers, strict disciplinarians both in the house and in the field, mighty drinkers, and devotees of good husbandry. He farmed under the present Squire's father, and it was Ben himself who told me the three conditions which all applicants had to satisfy when one of the Hall farms fell vacant.

"First of all," said Ben, "you had to be a true blue Conservative. Don't, the old Squire wouldn't so much as look at you. Then you had to come of a reliable, churchgoing family. And last: if, you didn't hunt yourself, at least you had to swear you'd preserve all the foxes on the farm. And I wouldn't wonder," Ben slyly added, "if the last condition weren't reckoned the most important!"

"Maybe," Ben said on another occasion, "the old Squire *was* a bit of a tartar. He'd be down on you in a minute if he thought you was letting the farm run away. But I think that was a good system; and, anyway, a farmer fared better under the Squire than he does under the banks that are mostly his landlords these days. Rents were paid once a year, and a rare to-do that was, too! All the tenants 'ld troop up to the Hall and sit down to a feed that lasted half the night: there was pretty nigh anything on the table you could want. But it's all fallen out of fashion now. First it came down to a glass of port and a health to the Squire: now it's nothing at all—the tenants send in their rents by cheque."

Strict as Ben's father was with his children, working them like animals as soon as ever they could use a spade or a hoe, and paying them less than the lowest farm-hand, Ben nevertheless has happy memories of his childhood and early youth.

"I dunno what Tofts Farm looks like these days," he once said to me; "I ain't been that way for many's the year. But when we had it, there was a Glory de John rose rambling all over the front door and a great big ol' Marshy Neal round at the back. Full to everlasting o' roses, they used to be. I'd like to see 'em agen one day, but I don't suppose I ever shall.

"Then there was allus a tame jackdaw flappin' about the place somewheres: I don't remember the time when one or another of us boys hadn't got a tame jackdaw. When anybody called at the house, and stayed for a cup of tea, they used to sit on their heads and start peckin' away pretendin' they was lousy. And once I had a jackdaw that followed me everywhere I went. If I walked down the road, there she'd be, flying about over my head and following from tree to tree."

To children who anyway never went far beyond the parish bounds any stranger who happened to come along was a wonder; and most looked for of all were the visits, year after year, of such familiar characters as tinkers and organ-grinders and fairmen. It was one day when "London George" (as he is called) appeared in the village, pushing his antiquated organ down the street and calling out greetings to his friends, that Ben told me of a man who used to tramp through these villages when he was a lad.

"He was a big man," Ben said: "bigger an' taller than you, and he allus had a bear with him. He carried a long pole and used to make the old bear dance for us, tippety-tippeting about on its hind legs. He waved the stick and sang a little old bit of a song:

Broken windmill under the stars

Don-di-don, don-di-day,
How many eggs can a Jennifer lay?
Six in an hour, ten in a day,
Don-di-don, don-di-day!

"Nights, he used to lay rough anywheres he could get, and I recollect once he lay along o' his old bear in the straw of one of father's barns. I know I couldn't sleep that night for thinking of him out there in the barn.

"Oh, yes, we used to have a rummy lot of chaps call at the farm, one way and another. One night we were told a tramp had gone into one of our sheds. Father went out to look for him but he couldn't see him anywheres. 'If you don't say where you are,' he hollered through the doorway into the dark, 'time I count three I'll shoot.' 'Then shoot, you b——r!' the tramp answered. And then there was a deaf-mute who used to come round begging. He carried a slate with him—so's you could write your answers down. But one day when he came up to the back door, father suddenly shouted at him: 'Stick your tongue out, you!' And the old tramp was so scared he stuck it out there and then. My, and didn't father call him some names after that!"

Farmer Tripp's pride in his horses was a thing that has no counterpart in the farms of to-day. He went everywhere on horseback: he almost did everything on horseback. "He even used to broadcast seed sittin' up on the old mare's back," Ben said. "Eight acres a day was the least he'd do; and the mare would follow down the furrows as reg'lar as if she knew exactly what was expected of her. Father used to hand the mare over to me when he'd finished, so's I could bed her down for the night; and goodness, wasn't she in a pickle—her mane was all full of seeds!

"Father thought he knew all there was to know about a horse," Ben told me one day; "but I remember once when he got let down, nice and proper. He bought a stallion in the market and mighty proud he was when he brought it home. But very soon it began to ail: nobody knew why. 'Here, get up in that manger, boy,' father said to me, 'and pour some of this stuff down his gullet. Let's see if that'll put him to rights.' He handed me the medicine horn and I clambered up into the manger. I reckon I must have fumbled about a bit, for father got impatient and shouted at me: 'Get hold of his tongue, do!' But, dang me, I couldn't find no tongue. 'Come on down, you fool,' father said: 'don't run on so silly, don't.' But he couldn't find no tongue, neither. And what's more, there weren't no tongue to find! It was tore out—and father never knew.

"You see, it had been used as a stud horse before he bought it, and I suppose somebody had tied a bit of cord round its tongue, like they do, to hold it steady when it starts frisking about; and he must have left it there till the tongue withered. You can do anything with a horse if you tie a bit of cord round its tongue and give a tug. 'Course it wouldn't be allowed if the police was to get to hear of it.

"Well, father told me not to let on about it. 'We'll feed him up on some mash,' he said, 'and sell him as quick as we can.' And so he did."

A countryman's knowledge of the locality where he has lived and worked most, if not all, of his days, is so obvious to him that he tends to take it for granted that you must have the same knowledge. You ask somebody the way. "Keep right on as far as Dilly's Farm, then turn in by the old pollard oak there, and make your way over by Gilbert's Meadow"—and all this quite regardless of the fact that you are a total stranger in the place. Similarly, it is seldom the best way of obtaining information concerning the locality to fire off a series of direct questions. The only way of getting to know whatever you want to know is to wait until it comes out by chance in some narrative that probably has nothing to do with the matter you are immediately interested in. I have learned much, one way and another, from Ben; but it has seldom been the result of any direct questions I may have put to him.

"You say you've been all the way to Firkins?" I remember him saying one day; "and how did you get there?" I explained, until I was suddenly interrupted with, "Oh, yes, I know: you went by the dool and through Jesse's Farm."

Dool? I did not understand.

"That's what we allus called it, anyway," was all I could get from Ben, who immediately became confused and evasive directly I queried him about a word he had taken for granted all his life. At last I discovered what he was referring to: a grass path running sheer across an open ploughed field. And with that discovery I had lighted on a link with the days of open field cultivation, when "common balks" gave access to the separated strips, or "selions," which were the peasants' unassailable share in the land.

It was Ben, too, who convinced me that Pig and Whistle, the name by which an off-licence on the outskirts of the parish is known, is not its true name at all. Peggin Whistle he insisted on calling it, and I had to wait months before I learned that this was no mispronunciation. "Peg-in-Whistle" it was, because in former days beer was served in a sort of outhouse there and you had to call for service by means of a whistle which was always kept pegged into a hole in the wall.

A spirit of independence, inherited, it would seem, from his father, is still the most predominant of Ben's characteristics. It asserted itself early in life. At twenty-two, tired of the overwork and under-pay that was one of the major irritations he suffered under his father's strict régime, he ran away from home. It required courage and not a little craftiness, but he found the way. At that time he had a mare of his own and, somehow or other, he persuaded his father to buy her from him.

"Father gave me a cheque," is how Ben tells the tale, "and I went straight off to Melbury to cash it. But the day was Saturday, after the banks were shut; so I went to a lodging, showed the landlady my cheque, and said I'd pay her directly they opened a-Monday morning. As soon as I'd done that, I went up to the railway station and booked my fare to London. Sitting in my carriage, opposite to me, was a young gal name of Sally Pelham. I was so proud of myself, with all that money on me—they shovelled golden sovereigns out to you in the banks them days—that I was soon showing it to her. 'That's a lot of money,' she said, and we soon palled up. When we got out of the train at Liverpool Street, she asked me to come along home with her. But—well, I hadn't been in London afore, and I suppose I was a bit scared; so I never went. But she gave me her address and I remember it to this day: Number 9, Hammersmith Broadway. But I never went there."

His first job was in a carters' yard where he was put on carrying manure. It was easy enough to pick up work in those days. You strolled into a pub, got into conversation with a likely looking man, told him what you were after, and hey presto! there was the job. And of course nobody was more welcome in London in those days of horse-trams and carriers and carters than a well-set-up young man from the country.

What happened to Ben happened to others in this same parish, except that usually it was lack of employment on the land, during the slump of the last decade of the nineteenth century, that drove most of them into the towns. And other old men besides Ben have told me how their prowess with horses served them in such good stead in their new jobs that they often succeeded where others failed.

"I had an old hoss named Tiger," said Ben. "He weren't much to look at when I took him over. I expect that's why they gave him to me! But I soon got him shipshape, and on May Day and suchlike I used to braid and plait and comb him till he looked so fine the foreman said he was the best hoss in the yard."

Five years Ben stayed in London, his jobs ranging from sweeping up manure in the streets to fishmongering. He chummed up with another young countryman and between them they bought an old donkey and barrow in which to hawk their fish round the streets.

But long before the five years were passed, he wished he were back at Tofts Farm. He had neither written nor received any news from home. Fear of what his father would say, and do, if he returned, kept him in London until one day, in the heat of summer, the desire became so strong that he could not resist it. Whatever awaited him when he got home, he must smell again the clean country air and feel the good clay under his feet.

He fell out with his partner. Soon a few pence were all he had in the world. So there was nothing else to do but to tramp the sixty miles between London Bridge and the Glory de John roses at home.

"One would give me threepence here, and another fourpence there," he said. "I lay rough all the way. Mostly I slept out in the barley-fields. Time I got within sight of home, my boots were wore out and I hadn't got any collar round me neck. But oh, wasn't I glad when I caught sight of the old barn and the chimney-pots away across the fields! I saw my brothers carting clover and I went across to 'em and rode home on top of the load.

"I walked into the kitchen and there was father having his tea. He just looked at me over his cup and said, 'So you've come home agen, have you? Get some food inside you, do; and then go and give Tom a hand with that clover.' That was all he said!"

Ben stayed at home after that, married, and lived in one of the cottages on the farm.

If the sons worked hard, so did the father. "The old man never spared himself," said Ben, "I will say that for him!" His only wholehearted relaxation was cards, at which he had sometimes been known to win as much as twenty to thirty pounds.

"There was one farmer," Ben told me, "who lost a terrible lot of money to father, one time and another. He had been a rich man, and I dunno what happened, but I do remember he turned up at the farm one day without a pennypiece to his name. Well, you can tell from this how low down he'd come. Perhaps father felt a bit ashamed when he saw him: anyway, he went and shut hisself up in the stable out of the way. 'Go on, Ben,' he said; 'draw him a glass of beer. I can't bear to see him.' So I did, and when I took it out in the yard to him, 'Hold hard,' I said, 'there's some flies in it.' But he said that didn't matter. He just drank it straight down, flies and all: so you can tell how poor he was."

A game of nap and a bottle of port wine or whisky: these may have been the only pleasures the old farmer allowed himself, but he certainly made the most of them. He went through life with the strength and vitality of one of his own horses; and even the stroke that robbed him of the use of his legs seemed not to diminish him. His last three years were spent in bed, where, propped up against the pillows, he conducted the entire work of the farm with as close a knowledge and as keen an attention as if he were in the enjoyment of youth's own good health. Till the day of his death nobody dared do anything without first consulting him: somehow or other he would discover what was going on.

"He used to carry on cruel," said Ben, "stormin' and ragin' a good 'un. I've known when it's taken four of us, strong men all, to hold him down in his bed. And the night afore he died he asked for a bottle of port to be taken up to him and he drank best part of it himself—nothing would stop him!"

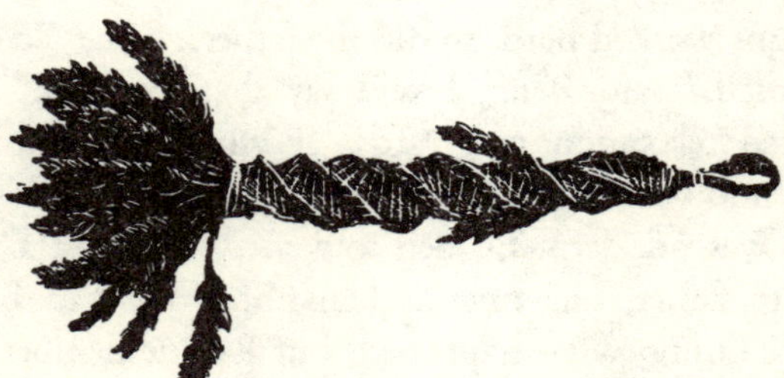

Chapter Fourteen

WE woke yesterday morning to find that the wind had veered round to the west overnight. It became the general topic of conversation: like prisoners released we all took new heart. Sam stopped short in the roadway and sniffed the benign air. "Don't it smell good, midear?" Not that there was any warmth in the wind as yet, for it blew across the whole width of an England buried deep in snow; but at least we could front it with pleasure as we walked down the road.

One of the first signs of this welcome change of temperature was the sudden appearance of icicles, hanging here and there from the thatch. Yesterday they were few and small, but by this morning they had multiplied and become the scenic feature of the village.

If cold weather brings anything more fantastically beautiful than the sight of frost ferns on your window when you wake in the morning, it is surely icicles dangling from the eaves of the thatch, rainbow-tinted in the sun.

Charlie Beslyn, as befits one whose sunflowers in summer are the biggest and whose hollyhocks are the tallest, claims to have the longest icicle of anybody: it hangs from a tiled gully in his thatch, a crystal pointer more than a couple of feet long. But if Charlie's icicles are the longest, then Widow Fields are the most unusual; for, where everybody else's are as erratic in size as in interval, hers hang along the eaves, exactly three inches apart, as if their precision had been achieved with the aid of a foot-rule. The reason is simple: Widow Fields' roof is made of corrugated iron.

Neither Widow Fields' icicles nor Charlie Beslyn's, however, are the ones the children favour. Their attention is solely directed to such as hang within reach of a running jump. The aim is to break off as long a piece as you can. This you proceed to suck, with simulated relish, until your fingers grow so cold that the icicle drops from their hold and breaks into splinters on the ground.

"Now we can look out for trouble," says Mark, voicing the general apprehension that lies behind everybody's smile. Thaw means floods; but before the floods and more dangerous to the traffic is the ice on the roads as the melting snow freezes with the treacherous alternations of temperature. If it was difficult for the tradesmen to get about before, it is even more difficult now, except perhaps in the middle of the day. Beneath the water, inches deep already on road and pathway, there is solid ice that will take days to thaw out of the earth.

Slowly the level beauty of the snow gives place to slush and filth: the ugliness of disintegration replaces the white perfection we have lived in for so long.

A fog lies over the fields, still white with snow, so that one gets the sensation of being at sea. There are no trees, only the sound of continual dripping water, as the icy twigs and branches, hidden from sight, thaw and pit with their quick drops the snow beneath. Birds (they can at least find water to drink now, if not worms to eat) hop about with wet bedraggled feathers, visible for a moment and then lost again in the enveloping fog. In places it is already possible to get a hint of the ruin that has overtaken hedges and stripling trees so long weighed down with the snow. And although that snowstill looks solid enough, in track and ride, you have only to put your foot on it and you will sink, suddenly, scrunchingly, up to the knees.

But perhaps the worst thing about this uncomfortable after-math is the extra strain it puts on people just when their powers of endurance, braced so long, are beginning to flag. It is much more noticeable to-day than it was yesterday, when the mere fact that the thaw had at last arrived was about all that anybody was aware of. To-day the thaw is already accepted and there is a realization that limbs and bodies are being asked to put forward more effort than they can well afford.

All through the thick of the snow Mrs. Swift, who serves her baker husband with a zeal and fidelity no paid hireling would ever dream of giving, has gone about her almost impossible tasks with a smile. Old socks covered her rubber boots, a couple of woollen scarves were tied round her head, and blue fingers stuck out of her mittens, and thus attired she delivered the bread in the village and in such of the cottages outside the village as she could reach on foot. She was forced to discard her trundling barrow, making innumerable trips back to the bakehouse, till goodness knows how many miles she laboured over the snow in the course of the day. Her jokes may have been a trifle heavy, but the merit of such pleasantries is not in their cleverness; and that she still had the heart to joke at all was for me one of the minor miracles of that unkindly season.

One little reward, however, always closed her heavy week.

"Ah, well," she would say, "to-morrow's Sunday, and then I can have a nice lay in. Father always brings me my breakfast in bed on Sunday, then turns on the wireless, so's I can listen to the morning service."

But to-day even Mrs. Swift wears a burdened look as if she had at last come to the end of her tether.

The Swifts' bakehouse stands under the shadow of Goose End windmill. It was a bakehouse when the mill still ground corn from the local fields; and Matthew Pierce, the miller, standing in his doorway overlooking the thatches, must often have shouted a greeting to the perspiring baker in his yard down below. To-day Matthew Pierce lies under the wall of the village chapel, but the baker still comes out into his yard to take a breather after he has put his morning's batch in the oven.

Standing in the bakehouse doorway, Mr. Swift lifts one corner of his white apron and mops the glistening beads from his forehead. His face is round and flabby, not unlike a lump of his own dough which someone has taken and pummelled into the likeness of a spoiled child. He smiles, while the sweat trickles off his eyebrows, but it is a smile that somehow looks more like crying—a misfortune that is emphasized now by the tears of sweat running down his cheeks. Once more he smudges his face with a corner of his apron and then calls out, "Mother! Is my breakfast ready?"

Indeed, to Mrs. Swift the baker is very much the child he looks. This has been her attitude for years, and it is even more so now that the Army has taken away her only son Jimmy.

When Jimmy received his calling-up papers, his father seemed at once to lose all grip on things. "Why should they want to take our Jimmy away?" he asked. "He's all we've got, and what *are* we going to do without him? Folk must have their bread, mustn't they? And I should have thought he was serving his country just as well by helping me and Mother with the bread as he will be kicking his heels in some camp or other."

The fact that Jimmy himself did not seem to mind at all, and that on his first leave home, fatter by many pounds and twice the man he was when he went away, he openly declared himself all in favour of a soldier's life, made no difference: Mr. Swift went on complaining about the unfair way in which these things are managed and the hard struggle it was, now, to keep the business going.

So far at least as the second part of his complaint goes, everybody agrees—and the more so since the snow came. A good deal has been said by our statesmen, since the war began, about the demands which will inevitably have to be made upon the civilian population; and, after the manner of statesmen in moments of stress, they have called upon the classics to bolster up their own inadequacy. Milton's "They also serve who only stand and wait" is an instance. Well, Mrs. Swift has not done much standing and waiting since Jimmy stepped into his uniform, but she has certainly done her share of serving. Even before the war, she was doing her share. If there was a cleaner bakehouse in the locality I cannot imagine it. Every week she scrubbed the troughs and peels and floor, and swept the ceiling, till the place was more like a dairy than a bakehouse.

But now such niceties must sometimes be neglected with the result that, to her annoyance, a cobweb is occasionally seen hanging from the whitewashed beams in the roof, and she may be heard complaining that ever things should have to come to such a pass.

To the scoured and tidy mind of Mrs. Swift a cobweb in her husband's bakehouse is a flag of war.

"There!" she exclaims, doing her best to hitch it off the beam on the end of a peel: "six months ago I'd have called you a liar if you'd said you ever saw a cobweb in our bakehouse. But what am I to do? I'm sure I'm on my poor feet all the hours there are, and even then I'm never finished."

The really distinguishing thing about the Swifts' bakehouse, however, is not so much its cleanliness as its brick oven. Mr. Swift belongs to the old school, and would as soon give up baking altogether as install a steam oven. It was almost as much as he could endure when he finally had to abandon stone-ground for roller-ground flour. He is old-fashioned enough to suppose that stone-milled flour, with all its life (and colour) still left in it, is better than roller-milled flour, white as his own apron the day it comes home from the wash; and that bread baked in a wood oven tastes far sweeter (and is better cooked into the bargain) than bread baked in a modern steam oven.

Leaving aside the question whether he is right or wrong, I for one am glad of his tenacity to the old ways. He is one of the few remaining links we have with those stout, individualistic days when almost every cottage in Larkfield had its own bread oven and almost every cottager baked her own fortnightly batch.

There are still such ovens to be seen in the village, with their close-fitting doors and their watch-stone let into the back wall, by whose glow the housewife could tell whether the heat was at the correct degree or not; but it is many years now since most of them shed an odour of newly baked bread. Like the oak and elm troughs ("trows" as we call them) which once held the family flour and on whose inverted lids the dough was thumped and pummelled into loaves, but which now have either been chopped up for firewood or are debased to such usages as chicken-food receptacles, these cottage ovens are a relic of the days when the self-supporting village was something more than a Utopian dream.

In a corn-producing countryside such as this, therefore, it at least assures some semblance of the continuity of tradition that Mr. Swift should cling to his wood oven. And, as with most traditional occupations, an element of poetry is present which one looks for in vain in modern usages.

I find few village "pictures" more fascinating, for instance, than the prospect of Mr. Swift flinging back the heavy iron door of his oven to see if it is ready for raking out. The whole expanse of the floor, as far as one can see through the open door, is covered with glowing, pulsating ash, a great nest of fiery feathers, throbbing and stirring with heat as if some invisible phoenix were being born out of the livid, flocculent ash, where it would spread its bright wings and issue from the oven door.

In just such a fiery furnace, as a boy, I had always pictured the miraculous adventures of Shadrach, Meshach, and Abednego; and something of the old childish wonder still stirs in me every time I see Mr. Swift fling back the door of his blazing oven. But "Another five minutes'll do the trick" is his only comment on this Biblical scene over which he presides every day. Then he slams the door again and goes out into the yard to get a breath of air.

Matthew Pierce, as I have said, is no longer alive to shout his greetings to the baker over the intervening thatch. Mr. Swift must go to the other side of the parish to get his flour these days, to Mr. Nayland's water-mill below Baldock Rise. It is not surprising the

By the mill-pool

two men should be friends: flour is the trade of both of them and, what is more, both are obstinately attached to the old ways.

If Mr. Swift's trade is no more extensive than it is, much of the reason is to be found in his conviction that, so far anyway as breadmaking is concerned, the old ways were best. If the villagers want their bread baked in the modern steam oven, let them get it from Beavers' bakery: they are welcome—and the implication is that their preference is little to their credit. So young Beavers, gay and noisy and modern, roars round the parish in his brightly painted tradesman's car, swift and capacious and fitted in the most up-to-date, accommodating fashion, mopping up the custom that Mr. Swift is too proud to solicit.

And so with Miller Nayland—or somewhat so. For it is true that he has installed roller-mills in his Doomsday water-mill; but for all that, he quite frankly admits he was happier with his mill-stones.

I remember his scorn one day when I was standing talking with him in the top story of his mill where the efficient-looking roller-mills stand in trim line. First he reached his hand down into one hopper and drew up a palmful of coarse, dun-coloured flour.

"Do you see those little yellow specks?" he asked. "They are bits of wheat germ. All the life and all the goodness of the grain is in them; but no, out they have to come! And for why? Because they spoil the colour. Did you ever hear such humbug? Never mind if all the best of the kernel is there: it spoils the colour, so out it has to come!

"And I'll tell you what makes me smile. When the goodness has been taken out of the flour, to keep it white, the manufacturers sell the germ again as a patent food—a sort of medicine to put right the wrong they did when they took it out of the flour originally. Did you ever?"

Then he dipped his hand into another hopper and pulled out a second palmful. This time the yellow specks were absent: the flour was white.

"That's how flour has to be to-day," the miller said; "else folk won't buy it. White as their own guts!"

Mr. Nayland's water-mill stands on the outskirts of the parish, where our humble river bends an arm round a small hillock crested with a windmill which also belongs to Mr. Nayland. The water-mill is still working, but the windmill stands as idle as old Matthew Pierce's in Goose End. Man and boy, these two mills, the windmill and the water-mill, have been the twin focus of this grand old miller's life. It tears his heartstrings to see that windmill stand idle on its green knoll, for this was his first love.

"They took me away from school when I was a nipper of fourteen," he said; "and at fourteen and a half I was running that mill myself. Yes, sir, fourteen and a half! Of course, father kept an eye on me from the water-mill down here; and if we were very busy I had another lad in to help me, but mostly I did everything myself—ran the whole blooming show. And I can tell you this: they were the happiest years of my life."

But then Mr. Nayland was, so to speak, very nearly born in a windmill. When he was a month-old baby, in long clothes, his father carried him up the mill one Sunday so that this should be the first mill he entered. No wonder he was ready, at fourteen and a half, to take charge of the mill on his own. The swish of these sails, responsive to his command, and the thunder and vibration of the whole massive framework of the mill, as he put on more feed and let the wind have its will with her, are a music that will haunt him to his dying day. "They were the happiest years in all my life."

Yet I realize I must not give the impression that Mr. Nayland is a nostalgic old miller with nothing but disgust for things as they are to-day. He has his memories, and they are happy ones; but he has his quiet pleasure in to-day no less. Indeed, the very fact that his windmill stands idle and his water-mill is seldom called upon to work at top pressure is in itself a sort of compensation. He can take things easily. He still has the satisfaction of being a practising miller, but he has time now to lean out of his dusty windows and watch the pigeons swirl over the mill-tail and settle, one by one, in the neat little cote he has set up for them among the willows. He has time to potter in his garden, time to prune the plums and apples in his orchard close that stands clouded with spring blossom by the river. And he has time to talk over old times when his cronies—Mr. Swift, for instance—come over to see him. Certainly there are compensations in such a 'diligent indolence' in old age, and Mr. Nayland is not one to let them slip by. As for his gruff criticism of things as they are to-day, is that in itself not a pleasurable indulgence? To see such folly going on all around him gives him a kind of superiority.

"Did you ever know such humbug?" he said to me one day as we sat on one of his idle mill-stones while his cats' yellow eyes gleamed at us from among the shadows. "They offered a prize at the County Agricultural Show two years ago for the best loaf made of all-English flour. Some of the women from the village came to me and asked me to mill 'em some home-grown wheat. One of them won first prize. But what tickled my fancy was this. English wheat is no good for bread-making, we are told: must have strong wheats, from abroad. Well, a year after the Show—a year to a day it was—I gave my daughter some of that very flour and told her to bake some bread from it. So she did, and better bread I never wish to eat. Did you ever know such a packet of humbug?

"Besides, if English wheats ain't no good for bread-making, how was it our fathers throve so mighty well on it?—working in the fields all day and eating precious little else."

Foreign wheat, when all the fields for miles around are full of corn, white flour, when common sense tells you that all the goodness was taken out with the colour—these are often the themes of Mr. Nayland's profitable chatter.

With his one eye he looks out on a world that has gone crazy. Since Doomsday, and earlier, a water-mill has always stood by the elbow of this little river; and, what is more, as far back as records go, there has always been a Nayland in charge of it. A thousand years of grand tradition lie behind the life and activities of this one-eyed miller: is it to be wondered at, therefore, if his thoughts are somewhat caustic to-day when he sees that long line of tradition broken?

Besides, when all due allowances are made for conservatism and old age, there is still so much sense in what he says. White flour and foreign wheat, these are themes that touch the very quick of modern civilization; and although Mr. Nayland is no economist to prove the mysteries of such matters as empire, importation, and high finance, and no scientist, to analyse the precise whys and wherefores of modern diatetic needs, he is wise enough to realize that there is something radically wrong with a world where wheat that is grown several thousand miles away is preferred to wheat that is grown at your own back door, and where flour will not sell until all the best part of it has been carefully extracted.

The heart of Mr. Nayland's mill is the second story, which is reached up a precipitous ladder. Peering through the cobwebs that curtain the windows with their natural lace, you look down on the willow-fringed mill-pond and the flurrying pigeons. The floor throbs under your feet as the mill-wheel turns in the darkness below. Through the centre of the mill rises the mighty wooden shaft on which all the ponderous machinery is geared.

"Yes," said Mr. Nayland, when he saw me fingering the silky surface of that shaft, and examining its intricate grain, "you'll have to go a long way, I'm thinking, before you find a better bit of pitch-pine than that. Have I ever told you where it came from? Although there's always been a water-mill here, it has been rebuilt three times, and the last to rebuild it was my great-grandfather. Somehow he heard of a ship that had been wrecked off the coast—about thirty miles from here. He went down to see her, bought the mast, and there it is!"

Well, from ship-mast to mill-post is not so odd a promotion

as perhaps at first sight might seem: ship's captain and miller have this at least in common—wind and water are the servants of both. Indeed, to run a mill in pre-mechanical days must have been very much like running a ship; and now I come to think of it there is quite a lot of the retired old sea-captain about Mr. Nayland as he lounges round his mill or leans over the mill-race with some friend, filling his pipe and telling of other days.

But it is not the great wooden shaft that makes this second story the heart and focus of the mill. It is the mill-stones, two pairs of them, cased in wooden coffins, with their dusty sleeves trailing over them, down which the grain dropped from the floor above, thence into the waiting hopper, and thence, by way of a continually vibrating "shoe," into the stones.

Have you ever examined a mill-stone at close quarters? Nowadays it is a little unusual to come upon one that is still intact: mostly they have been dismantled and converted into doorsteps, bird-fountain bases, and suchlike alien uses. But if by good chance you should come upon one in good preservation, you will notice at once what an extraordinary pattern has been cut all over its face. The stone (usually built up of slabs of French burr) is chiselled with innumerable sets of close parallel lines called "cracks," of which (at least in the case of the wheat-stone) there are some ten or twelve to the inch. Then there are deeper grooves, forming larger divisions, which go by the curious name of "harps." All told, there are many hundred grooves, large and small, in each wheat-stone.

Why they are arranged exactly as they are nobody knows. Their purpose is to keep the grain moving as the stones revolve, one over the other, and finally to distribute the flour at the periphery.

To keep these grooves chiselled clean to a proper depth was one of the most important jobs in the mill, and it was performed by a man called a "dresser" or "tramping miller." He was one of those itinerant craftsmen whose work, unpretentious and, to the general eye, unimportant, took them all over the countryside.

Sitting on the dismantled stone, with his left elbow cushioned on a bag of bran, the dresser cleaned out the cracks with his mill-bill. All day long the tap-tap-tap of his tool on the hard stone sounded through the idle mill, a strange substitute for the usual roar and under-thunder that accompanied the mill in action.

"Father always hated the tramping miller," Mr. Nayland once told me, "because of course it meant there couldn't be any work done till he was gone again. It took him about a day to dress each stone, and that meant working as long as there was light to see by. You'd think maybe it was a tedious job, tap-tapping all day with your face close up against the stones, to make sure the mill-bill always hit the grooves. But I never knew a dresser complain. In fact, if you wanted to take him off his work before he was finished, because it was getting dark and you wanted to shut up the mill, he only cursed you and just carried on till he *was* finished. That's mostly all a man wanted these days, to be allowed to get on with his job. He hadn't everlastingly got his eye on the clock like they have these days."

For good or bad, Mr. Nayland's mill-stones won't want dressing any more. And for all the handsome profits he makes out of his mill these days he might as well shut it up. The tradition is broken.

When the miller is dead the most probable fate of his mill will be that somebody will buy it and convert it into a domestic curiosity.

What an end to a thousand years of milling!

Chapter Fifteen

AFTER living for weeks in a white, muffled world, it is strange to hear again the sound of running water and to see the green of grass and young winter wheat.

"I saw wheat *growing* to-day for the first time since the snow," says Jim Adams, whose country eye is quick to detect the subtle difference between green and growing green.

But it is the sound of running water pouring off the fields and roaring through the dikes and land drains that announces our release most forcibly. It is as if we had been deaf, and suddenly, in a night, the gift of hearing had been miraculously restored. In mountainous regions, the spring thaw merely increases a water-music that never ceases all the year; but here, where the steepest rise is no more than three hundred feet above sea-level, this gush and splash of water has in it a note of genuine novelty. We lie abed listening to it, judging its rise by minute alterations of tone; children make themselves water-mills out of bits of planed wood and stick them in the balk under the flow from the drains; and as a subject for a passing word it quite outdoes the weather. Only in midsummer, when some sudden thunderstorm breaks the weeks of drought, and the rain falls too fast and heavy to penetrate the iron face of the clay, will this sound be heard again—and then only for a few hours. But now it accompanies our sleep at night, and by day induces a slight and quite unnecessary raising of voices as if in unconscious competition.

And see how the thaw is discovering the farmers' husbandry. In Rainbow Field the wringes of young wheat show clear and bright, but in Tolly's they point out of the water like rushes from a pond. The water stands in the furrows in narrow streams that reflect the sky like blue ribbons stretched across the fields. It cannot run away fast enough, though as you watch it spouting out of the drains and foaming through the ditches you might wonder where it all came from.

Dirty patches of snow are all that are left now in the pastures, whilst even those buttress drifts that flanked the roadside have been reduced to obstinate blocks of frozen snow no more than two or three feet high—waiting, as everybody insists, till the next fall.

The west wind is hurrying spring along as fast as it can: you can feel it already in the unaccustomed strength of the sunshine and you can hear it in the song of the birds. The skylarks are up over the fields around Brock's Hole, binding the clouds with silver chains. The blackbirds and the thrushes have been sadly depleted, but those that remain, veterans of a cruel winter, can be heard at dawn and sunset tuning their notes in the tree-tops. The rookeries are full of strange activity, and the peewits that have flown over the barren fields in flickering clouds are now beginning to separate off in preparation for that nuptial dance when they will call to their mates from the windy March skies and flash the white lining of their wings as they tumble and cry over the fields.

And in Cleavers' pastures, Hod's sheep, heavy with their lambs, kneel to nibble the welcome grass. They have regained a little of that fleecy whiteness which could not compete with the snow. In a week, or less, lambing will commence, and Hod is already putting up the trays and praying that this sunshine will continue so that his ewes may lamb in the open.

It is a crucial time for all shepherds, and most of all, perhaps, for Hod. This is his first season at Cleavers'. I fancy he rather feels he is on his mettle, though you might not guess as much from his stolid, unalterable behaviour. Shepherds are a lonely tribe,

A flock of peewits

whether they work on the high, open downs, far from human companionship, or among the scanty leys and pastures of a corn country. They walk apart from the rest of the men who work on the land, the yellow-eyed sheep their only concern.

And Hod is no exception. When the sheep were grazing in the meadow in front of my house, I used to see him arrive in the morning and stalk through the wet grass among his flock. With his hands in his pocket he went from one end of the meadow to the other, running his eye over all the sheep in turn, missing none, and pausing now and again as something unusual struck him. He knows all his sheep as surely as if the difference between one and another was as obvious as between a Norwegian and a Chinese; and they in their turn as surely know him.

Until Hod came to Larkfield he had never stirred from the village where he was born, fifteen miles away. He knows that all eyes are on him, for all "foreigners" are more or less suspect among countrymen until they have proved their worth. This is Hod's first season and much hangs on it. The more so, as sheep are something of a rarity in the parish to-day. Sheep are no longer folded by the hundred on these fields as they used to be. In a corn country they may be essential to good farming; but, under the present scheme of things, the farmer finds they do not pay; and so good husbandry, as far as sheep and roots are concerned, has to go by the board.

Once upon a time, every farmer hereabouts had his substantial flock. It was integral with his scheme of rotation, and a farm without its flock would have seemed like a garden without its potatoes. But now sheep are a thing to stare at, and those farmers who keep them in anything like numbers are talked of for miles around.

Over in the next parish, for instance, there is a flock of black faces that are as proud an asset to the place as its mythical monster is to Loch Ness. Go to the gate of the meadow where they are folded and see what happens when, for the moment, they mistake you at a distance for the shepherd and come charging over the rise towards you. With the setting sun behind them, each moves in an aura of light. So loud is their collective greeting that the bells of the parish church, a single field away, are not to be heard. And as they crest the rise, converging upon the gateway, it is like all the flocks of Israel being rounded up for a trek into the Promised Land.

Ever since January the shepherd of this Biblical flock has been tending his ewes through their lambing. Straw pens are erected round the stockyard, two deep, and there the puny lambs are first licked on to their feet, where they totter a moment, shaking a tail that is almost as fat as their bodies, and fall. Lambing in the open has been out of the question, with every field buried under the snow, and so the shepherd's hut, with his bottle hanging on a nail by the door and his crook lying against the shafts, stands near by the yard, ready for him to snatch an hour's sleep when he can.

That is shepherding on the grand old scale, such as Mark and others remember here in years gone by.

"But they don't hardly know what the smell of a sheep's like these days," says Mark. "Maybe you don't know it, but there's a power o' good in the smell of sheep. Same as if you've been ill now and was to go and stand up by the fold each morning, and hang about there a bit, the smell'd soon make a man of you again."

I don't know whether Hod has seen this fine flock over in the next parish. Perhaps not; for it seems either to have rained or snowed ever since he first arrived, and, anyway, Hod is a stay-at-home. He lives alone in his isolated cottage on the farm, and a journey across the fields to the pub or to Mrs. Wright's cottage for some tobacco is about as far as he goes.

The day Hod came to Larkfield, rain poured without let. A cottage move is a dismal affair at the best of times; but when there is such unremitting rain as fell that dark, November day, the furniture itself seems to cry aloud against the indignity of the whole procedure. To make matters even worse in this case, the cottage

Hod occupies is approached from the roadway by a narrow chase which that day was little better than a river.

"The places some people choose to live in!" said the lorry-driver, as if Hod were to blame for the cottage being erected where it was.

Hod merely grunted. He was too overwhelmed with the adventure of having moved at all to be aware of the townsman-quips that such a move inspired. Besides, the driver had alienated Hod's sympathy at the very outset: glancing over the shepherd's meagre belongings, before they started on the journey, he had said: "Are you sure you ain't forgettin' nothin'? I don't recollect seeing you put the arspidestra inside!"

And now Hod sat in silence. You would have thought, by the look on his face, that he fancied the prospect no more than the lorry-driver did. But it was not the mud or the rain or the inaccessibility of the cottage that was making him so downcast: it was the unfamiliarity of everything, the slow realization that he was a stranger in a strange land.

"Then it really is true," he seemed to be thinking, as he sat up there beside the driver, staring down the muddy lane to where his new home topped the uncut hedges: "it really is true that I've left the old place behind for good and all? And this is where I'm to live in future?"

"Well, now for it!" said the lorry-driver. "If we sit here much longer we'll be wanting a pair of oars to get you there."

And the lorry splashed its way to the cottage and pulled up before the garden gate. Hod clambered down. His new master was waiting for him in the shelter of the porch, penned in a shower of falling raindrops.

Carrying his crook with him—the symbol of his calling and age-old badge of all his tribe—Hod hurried up the path and shook the proffered hand. The shepherd had come to Cleavers.

That next afternoon his master said to me: "Come and make the acquaintance of a new neighbour of yours."

But Hod and I were already acquainted.

"In you come, sir," he said; and this time there was nothing downcast about him. The reason, once I was inside the cottage, was obvious. The place itself might be strange but the contents were familiar: Hod had spent the wet evening arranging his few belongings exactly as they had been in his old home, and, thus befriended and reassured, had lost something of his perplexity of yesterday.

All told, his possessions did not amount to much: a table, a couple of chairs, a bed, a few boxes knocked together to make cupboards, some bits of china, a radio set, a cat, and some brilliant oleographs. The radio set stood on an upturned orange-box in one corner, the focus of the little room, the Shekinah where dwelt the omnipotent Voice.

But it was the pictures on the walls which Hod pointed out to me with pride. The radio set might fill his cottage with symphonic orchestras and dance bands, but art for Hod was still represented in these homely, shining scenes. "Summer," with fields of ripe corn; "Winter," with sheep in the snow.

"But that one over there is my favourite," said Hod, pointing to a black and white print over the mantelpiece which depicted, with a lurid attention to detail, the heroic endeavour of Jack Cornwall, V.C. "That's a picture, that is," he said, and the glow in his eyes told what pleasure he had had in it as he sat alone before his evening fire.

He poured out a bottle of home-made wine and we sat round the fire, happy enough. And yet, when at length I got up to say good night and left him standing there in his lamplit doorway, some hint of the old perplexity seemed to return. He called his cat inside and shut the door. Who shall say what such a man feels, alone, at sixty, and uprooted for the first time from the village where he was born?

As I turned into the chase I could hear his radio loudly trying to set loneliness at bay.

That was six months ago. Now Hod has neither time nor need to seek comfort from that polished cabinet in the corner. He has his sheep. Few as they are, they represent something in the nature of rejuvenation in Larkfield: they are an attempt, on one farm anyway, to persuade husbandry back into the old healthy rotation. They are a banner stuck up in defiance of the chemicalized farm of the future.

Hod watches the weather in hopes of a good lambing. "Here's luck to you, Hod," I say.

Chapter Sixteen

"HI!" Sam shouts after me as I pass his forge. I cross over the slushy road, and there he stands, beckoning me with a smoky finger. "Hi! Jest you come round here, midear."

And he leads the way round to the shed at the back of the forge, silent and heavy with mystery. It is part of the technique of country conversation never to anticipate, never to show impatience with the slow prelude that will ultimately lead you to the point of the story. To travel hopefully is better than to arrive, says R. L. S., and this is certainly true of nine-tenths of the talk with which Sam and his kin beguile the lazy hours.

Sam unlocks the shed door and waits without comment for me to look inside. Piled on the earthen floor are bushels of potatoes, all spoiled with the frost. They exude a rank odour of fermentation. There must be at least half a dozen bushels—the total yield of Sam's well-tilled allotment.

"Ne'er a blessed tater left," he says. "Did you ever see the like? I had 'em all clamped up there in straw and sacks, till you'd a-thought they *must* be safe. And now look at 'em. I dunnow what we shall do"—and with his heavy boot he kicks the rotten tubers aside.

The action is expressive of his despair. Potatoes are the mainstay of his diet. He savours them as another man might savour his apples. He rubs his great thumb over their harsh coats, weighing them in his hand and appraising them like a judge at the local fruit and flower show. And here they are, the whole of his crop, rotten with the frost, fit only to be kicked aside with the foot.

"And we want 'em more'n ever now," Sam concludes, "seein' as everything is gettin' that dear it's like eating gold."

Others beside Sam are counting their losses now that the thaw has come. After one of the most prolific apple-crops within living memory, there is now a record shortage. In fact, only one thing consoles us as we survey the acrid-smelling mush that was once our apple store—the pigs, so hard to feed now that foodstuffs are almost unobtainable, will have plenty to eat at last.

It wouldn't have consoled Sam, but I, too, could have told him a tale of woe. With a rosy crop that weighed its boughs down to the grass, my favourite apple-tree stood in the sun those first weeks of war, like a rainbow in a stormy sky. Whatever else became difficult to procure, apples would certainly not fail till spring came round again. And friends, fingering them in their nest of straw on the shelves, prophesied that if I ate so many I should begin to look like an apple myself before the winter was out.

And then the other morning I went to examine them and when I had uncovered them I found, not apples, but balls of ice, glistening with frozen drops. I picked one out of the straw and my fingers slid over the sweaty ice. I cut one in half, and instead of the blade thrusting crisp and clean through the firm fruit it squashed into a mess of pulp. These were my apples that had made such a gallant show in the sun! For this my tree had crowned itself with flowers and triumphed over May frosts! I told a neighbour he could have the lot for his pigs and the sooner he fetched them away the better.

It is the same story everywhere. Down in the bar of the Wheatsheaf I hear variations on the same theme, including one on the best way of storing one's crop of apples or potatoes. Luke Negus is telling of somebody he knows who wraps each of his apples in specially prepared paper.

"Don't run on so silly, don't," says Mark; "as if a bit of tishoo paper could keep out the frost. There ain't only one safe way and it's nature's way: make a clamp of 'em in the garden, same as taters."

"Then I suppose your apples have come through the frost all right?" Luke retaliates, somewhat tartly.

"They have," replies Mark; "they have."

Luke is mystified. He passes Mark's garden every day on his way to work, but he has never seen any apple-clamp there.

"Then where did you store 'em?" he asks, anxious to prove his antagonist a liar.

"Where did I store 'em, you say?" Mark pauses a moment and then continues: "Well, I ain't got a tarrible lot of apples, as you know; only a couple of ol' trees and them nigh wore out. Still, they did uncommon well last year and I got 'em stored all right."

"But where?" Luke impatiently intervenes.

"In me belly, you fule!" says Mark over the rim of his glass of bitter; and it is perhaps an indication of the good humour we are all enjoying, now the thaw has released us at last, that this heavy humour wins approval all round.

Released—yes, that is the word. For weeks we have been largely shut off from the outside world, a community that resembled, as nearly as possible in England to-day, the early, self-contained village of our forefathers. We were like a ship in a bottle, and now the bottle has been smashed and the ship is free of the waters once again. Things we were learning to do without, because they were unobtainable, have suddenly become necessities again, now that supplies are renewed; and that contentment we were beginning to enjoy, because to stay at home was the only choice, has vanished now that there are buses and cars on the roads to carry us wherever we wish. In fact we are ourselves again.

Ann Bright stands in her open doorway, who all these weeks has viewed her narrow world from behind spotless curtains. She stands there taking the sun, faint and chill as it is, and will not let you pass. After so long an enforced silence she insists on the consolation of a talk. Whether you desire it also is neither here nor there. And the slightest excuse suffices.

"Go on, you," she says to the despondent ginger cat that rubs against her legs. "Go on, you; I ain't got your kittens." Then comes the story of how she compelled Bright to kill them this morning. "I couldn't stand 'em any longer," she says. "As fast as we carried the kittens out into the shed, the old cat carried 'em indoors agen. And you know, I can't bear to touch they little ol' things; no, I can't." And so Bright had been told to kill them. "Don't, I'll get somebody else to do it," she had said; and her husband, shamed before the taunt of cowardice, had complied. Now the cat is fussing and crying round her slippered feet. "Go away, do," Ann says. "I tell you I *ain't* got your kittens."

Nor is Ann alone in offering her simple salutation to the sun. Throughout the village, cottage doors are open, and here and there you may see men and women peering among the ruck and rubbish of their wintered gardens for the first sight of the forerunners of spring, frail green spears that were cased in ice a fortnight ago and now will soon break into flower. Charlie Beslyn is out in his garden as long as the light lasts, breaking the ground to a fine, crumbling tilth, and little children begin to search along the dikes and roadsides for the first celandines and wild white violets.

Away back in December we even dreaded the approach of spring. Better by far the bitterness of the winter weather than the fate that might befall us with the lengthening of the days. To think that man should ever arrive at such a sorry pass, we said, that he dreaded the coming of spring! But just now it almost seems as if we were wrong. The worst, and worse than the worst, may happen yet; but for all that we find ourselves welcoming the spring after all. Stronger than the dread of war, it appears, is man's happiness in the renewal of earth. The newspapers are full of rumours and the enemy is loud with threats; but the rumour of spring, as the snowdrops push through the thaw, is more insistent at this moment than all the newspapers, and the first thrush singing in the elm-tops is louder just now than all the threats of the enemy.

Later, when the first green rosettes garland the hedges, such optimism will no doubt forsake us—though it will not forsake the thrush. In the hedge by the roadside she will ride her little boat into which she can just fit, tail up at the prow and beak up at the stern, and she will watch you with her bright eye as you peer—not too closely, not too intently, but just for the pleasure of watching and because of the fascination of that brief, slender contact with life of another order, on another plane.

But, although the leaves are green on the thorn-bush and the crab-apple throws its shell-pink petals a few feet farther along the hedge, it will be a Maytime of war; and while the thrush sits there on her nest (her mate not far away somewhere, pulling a worm maybe, tug-tug-tug, out of my lawn and then cocking an ear this way and that, listening for another wriggling, succulent morsel to carry home), the War Department lorries will roar and rumble past, within three or four feet of her; the dispatch rider, with his leather case strapped importantly over his shoulder, will shoot by on his motor-cycle and she will not mind, because she only knows that, whatever they are up to, they are not worrying about her. Better by far, she thinks, the roaring lorry full of singing soldiers and the stinking motor-cycle of the dispatch rider, than nasty schoolboys creeping home along the hedges, looking for nests to rifle, eggs to blow, birds to shoot.

. . . . .

There are those who say we should all be glad to be living in this hour. The world is being shaped anew and it is a privilege to be alive while such high things are happening. Well may this be so; yet at this moment I think rather of those who have died already since the outbreak of war, shot down like birds or frozen to death in arctic snows, or cast upon the cold waters to die of exposure or plunged alive to the bottom of the sea, and I wonder what lasting good can come of such violence, such wanton refusal of the life so mysteriously given to us.

I look around me in this quiet village of Larkfield and all I see to-day speaks of life and hope—the spearing wheat in the fields, the audacious snowdrop buds in the gardens, the rising sap in the frail wands of the willow and the dog-wood, the mating birds and the busy farmers.

Only one thing seems in accord with the destruction that is silently piling up the other side of the North Sea.

Twice or thrice a day the timber-lorries splash down the road past my house, bearing the shorn trunks of oak and elm. They are felling trees on Arley Hall estate. Not one tree here and another tree there, but scores of them, massive trees that have breasted the winds of a century and more, bestowing health and beauty with their green turbulence of leaves.

Ever since the timber valuer arrived, weeks ago, these trees have borne on their trunks the earmark of destruction: like those crosses chalked on the doors of the houses of the Plague, they have proclaimed the pity of their approaching end. And now the end has come. First, their stout bases were hacked away, leaving a litter of bright chips scattered on the ground. Then the tree-fellers arrived, with rope and pulley and crane, and one day the mighty tree shivered and cracked and fell, with bleeding branch and twig.

Surely it should be decreed by law, in any civilized country, that for every tree which is felled another should be planted in its place? It is not enough that the Government should make belated amends by setting up trim forests of spruce, regardless of their suitability to the locality, and each planted in a dead straight line with all its neighbours. The glory of our trees (apart from their usefulness) is in their multitudinous dissimilarity, though indigenous to the district in which they grow. And every man whom chance, or ability, has made the owner of wooded acres should, if compelled to fell, have as much regard for the ultimate renewal of the beauty he has destroyed as he has for the cash with which such destruction has rewarded him. Felling trees to pay off debts which cannot otherwise be met is only robbing Peter to pay Paul; and no property can be said to be well-managed where the best of the timber has been felled to pay off debts, unless that timber is at least replaced with suitable and equivalent young trees.

One of the heartening things about the slaughter of trees on the Arley Hall estate is the almost general reaction of the villagers. Time and again, as the timber-wagons sway and rumble past, I have heard expressions of genuine regret that such denudation is necessary. These trees, we all feel, belong to every one of us and we are the poorer for their disappearance. Not even the fact that we shall be able to share in the spoil really consoles us. There will be "tops" at one and sixpence a time—enough wood to keep our fires burning through another winter, whatever hardships war may still bring; and even those of us who cannot afford so small an outlay will have chips by the bushel. But the trees will be gone. A loaf of bread is not always better than a poem, even to a starving man.

So the trees go past, bound for the railway station and thence for the timber-yard. Next to go, we hear, will be the spruce woods—"just the right size for pit-props." Once again the war is denuding the countryside, as it did a quarter of a century ago, of the trees that helped to give us health and sustain our spirits. These are war's scars on the body of the countryside—scars it will take years to heal, if ever.

Otherwise, there is still little enough in Larkfield to suggest approaching holocaust. More lads have gone into the Army to learn to endure their firm young flesh stretched upon the rack of war, and a few older men are volunteering while there is still time for them at least to choose in which of the Services they shall offer to die. Black-outs have all but hardened into a habit and, although we no longer carry our gas-masks, they lie ready to hand for the return of the day when we must. Squadrons of bombers have come back into our skies, but instead of rushing to the window to look at them we merely register the boom of their flight in the pauses of our conversation. Is it a lessening of fear or a gradual acceptance of fatalism? Or merely the sheer impossibility, here in the quiet, awakening countryside, of imagining the full horror of what may befall?

"I ain't goin' to wear no gas-masks," says Ann Bright; "no, that I ain't. There's a little ol' cupboard at the top of our stairs, and I shall hide in there till it's all over. And I 'ont come out for nobody."

Meanwhile, these green spears of life, these fattening buds on the trees—all the frail portents of the resurgence of spring—have an added poignancy this year, an added appeal to our sensibilities. Hod is busy with his lambing and the sight of him slouching through the mud, with a lamb under each arm, its long legs dangling awkwardly against his hips, is somehow sharpened in the mind by contrast with the dark thoughts against which it is set. He is leading his sheep into the fold for the night; dams, heavy with their undropped lambs, and day-old lambs that totter over the furrows on legs that have not yet found their native cunning. The baa of the anxious mothers and the answering bleat of the straying young is as much part of the music of spring as the tentative stanzas of that speckled cock-thrush perched against the sky, and both seem more precious now than ever before.

But most precious of all perhaps is the sight of Jim Adams ploughing in Humpback Field. I expect it is only my fancy but birds always seem to be more than usually plentiful in the fields where Jim is ploughing, as if they knew he liked their company and would do them no harm.

At any rate, all day he has been moving slowly across the field surrounded by a veritable cloud of seagulls blown in from the coast as if, all that distance away, the rumour had somehow reached them that Jim was at plough. There must be well over a hundred. They wheel and cry low over the field till Jim has crested the rise, and then they glide down to the newly turned furrows and settle

The setting sun that brings the labourer home

in thick clots of snowy white. Jim turns at the headland, advancing down the field again; and as the plough draws near they rise, some seeming to wait until the horses' hooves must trample them, and circle overhead, closing Jim in a flurry of gleaming wings.

Here and there among the flashing white horde are a crow or two, croaking mourners at a wedding feast.

"Them gulls are so tame," says Jim, "they just stand there as if it was *you* who'd got to get out of the way! But I recollect a chap once, when he was out ploughing somewhere, chucked a spanner or something at one and killed it—a seagull it was. Well, he never had no gulls following him after that. They stayed over the hedge in the next field and waited till he was out of the way."

Leaving Jim under his cloud of white wings I walk home towards the village.

There are moods of the spirit when the bright, particular things of everyday—houses, gates, the way a tree leans, the motion of a man at work in the fields—seem suddenly of more than ordinary beauty. They are like poems before the poet has spoiled them in the endeavour to chain them with the discipline of words.

I pass a villager pushing a tumbledown pram in which a child sits heaped over with kindling. The setting sun shines in the woman's eyes and something of the madonna shows through the weary lines of her peasant face. "Good night," she says; "good night," and the goodwill that prompts her words is part of the basis of that common understanding (would we but give it play) between person and person, village and village, nation and nation.

I pass lonely farm cottages set back from the road, to whose hearths the men will soon be returning across the evening fields. And they are fixed in my mind as the very type of all men's desire for the fulfilment of his "potentiality to love and to be loved." The faggots leaning against the chimney-stack, the grindstone under the apple-tree in the garden, the few chickens in their run, and the plot of garden waiting to be sown—I see it all as a promise of immense possibilities. Even the brick bungalows, and the staring red council cottages, seem suddenly endearing: homes, loved hearths, centres of that creative love which is the root of all our endeavour, however brief and small.

And as I loiter here and there, talking with first one and then another, I forget for the moment the misery that shadows all our lives in this first faint prelude of spring; I am only aware of the simple happiness that comes of innocent communion, man with man.

In all the shires of England, I think, such cottages wait in the fields and by the roadside, gilded with the setting sun that brings the men home from their work. This is England, though ninety per cent of her population dwells in the towns; for here the first condition of life is not gain but service—service of the land that feeds us and gathers us at last into its fecund darkness. Here men work creatively, ploughing, sowing, harvesting. Here, if anywhere, that goodwill may thrive, which, in spite of wars, shall at last bind the ends of the earth in the bonds of true fellowship.

CW01668099

THE ART OF LiFE

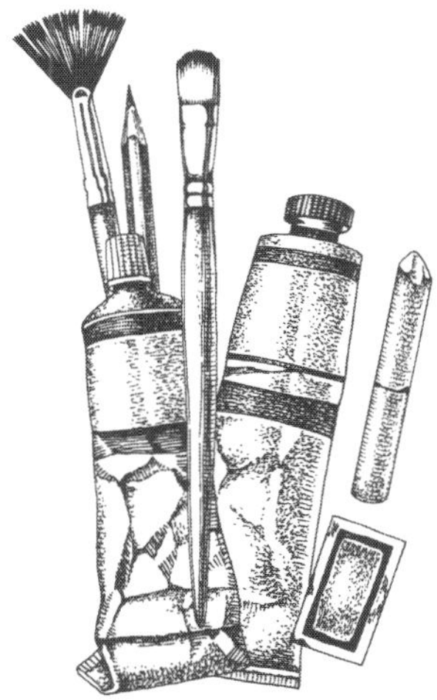

S. L. RUSSELL

Published by Resolute Books
www.resolutebooks.co.uk

RB
RESOLUTE
BOOKS

My warmest appreciation is due to my loyal and perceptive beta readers, my wise and patient book buddy, and my encouraging and supportive fellow authors at Resolute Books. Thank you all.

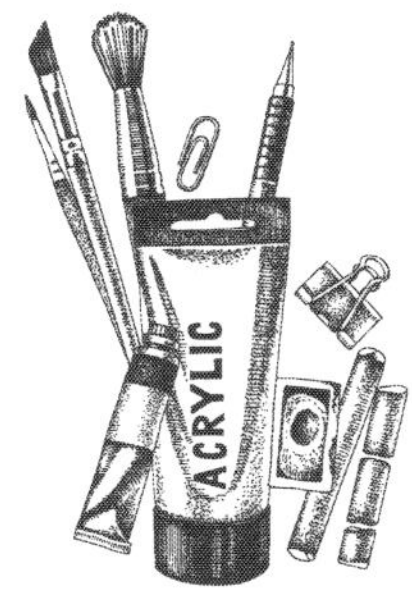

PART ONE

THAT AFTERNOON I was pedalling so hard I ran the risk of breaking my bike. When I hit a puddle left over from last night's rain and skidded, I knew I had to stop. I braked, breathing hard, and put a foot on the ground.

Stupid woman. Why are you going hell for leather anyway? Just because you're annoyed with Grace?

Grace is my closest friend, but that really isn't saying much. I don't have many friends, although after living in this place so long I know a lot of people. Maybe it's because I'm rubbish at small talk. Maybe people see my eyes glaze over when they are discussing the flowers for services, or falsely modest as they go on about their children's and grandchildren's achievements. I'm sure they're all geniuses, but it's odd there aren't any criminals or failures among them. You'd think there would be.

I sound sour, I know. And I am, especially this afternoon when I was hoping for a sympathetic ear from Grace. All she could do was defend John. I did try to tell her my husband needs no defending. He is fine. He has his life organised just as he likes it – except, perhaps, for the smiling, peaceable, compliant wife. But as I tried to explain to Grace, how I feel these days isn't about John. He's an important person in his own sphere, but in my current scenario he is simply irrelevant.

It's not about John – it's about me. I'm forty-one, but I feel as if I'm freewheeling gently down a barely perceptible slope to death.

About eight o'clock that evening the phone rang in the hall. I heard it from the spare bedroom where I kept my painting stuff. It was a cramped little space, but John had the garage, and the garden shed was full of mowers and bikes and flowerpots. He shouted up the stairs, 'That was Grace. Where are you?'

'Up here.'

I heard him on the stairs; then he was leaning on the door frame, a small frown creasing his eyebrows.

'She said she'd tried your mobile, but you didn't answer.'

I turned away from him. 'Yes, it's in my backpack. What did she want?'

'Reminding you about the art class tomorrow. I thought your class was Tuesday.'

'It is. I'm sure I mentioned it. We've got the famous, or possibly infamous, Ronnie Milburn coming to talk to us and look at our work. It's the only evening he could do.'

'Right.' He paused for a moment in the doorway, then realised I had no more to say and clumped back downstairs.

I was in the middle of trying to choose some of my paintings to take to the class, and I was probably over-sensitive about John seeing them. I am sure he regarded them as the trivial and talentless outpourings of an under-employed suburban housewife. Maybe I was doing him an injustice, but it was a part of my life I preferred to keep away from him.

I had a dozen spread out on the table in front of me, and I was unimpressed. They weren't uniformly bad; in fact, some of them were probably reasonably competent, and I had had my share of praise from our tutor, Phil. But somehow that evening I saw the modest collection of watercolours – scenes of the river at various times of day, the evening sun on the mudflats, silhouettes of fishermen bent over their rods, the odd distant sail – that sort of thing – as mediocre and insipid. I could imagine what someone of Ronnie Milburn's reputation would make of them, and I squirmed.

Then I unearthed something quite different, something I had almost forgotten, and tears sprang to my eyes. Why hadn't I thrown it away?

Compared to the river scenes, this was crude: strong, clashing colours, ugly brushstrokes. Yet somehow it had a vitality, an honesty that the other offerings lacked. It was a portrait of my cat Wesley, a big, rangy ginger with piercing green eyes, who'd gone missing a year ago. I remembered painting it furiously, in an hour of anguish, when John had made light of my worry at Wesley's prolonged absence. My cat never did come home, and we never found out what happened to him. On an impulse I put it into the folder with the other paintings. Ronnie Milburn could think what he liked.

I felt a pang of guilt at shutting John out with my increasing remoteness, so I went downstairs, made a pot of coffee and took him a cup. Usually he would be in his study, glued to his computer, but that evening he was watching sport on television. I realised I was foolish to imagine he'd even noticed I was barely present. I was doing what many people do by default: ascribing to others what we ourselves would feel in a particular situation. John was an intelligent man, successful in his work, but peculiarly blind and often carelessly negligent. Some things didn't appear on his mental radar at all. He looked fleetingly surprised when I gave him the cup of coffee.

With an inward sigh I went into the kitchen and started stacking the dishwasher. I'd almost finished washing the saucepans when I heard the sound of the TV cease, and John ambled in, empty cup in hand. He perched on a stool at the table.

'You've met this Milburn chap before, haven't you?' he said.

'Not really. I saw him across the room at that exhibition Grace and I went to a couple of years ago, but we've never spoken.'

'What's he like?'

I shrugged. 'Big. Tall, broad, starting to develop a paunch. Long hair, a bit unkempt. Bearded. Loud voiced. Waves his arms about when talking.'

'A good artist, though?'

'That's certainly his reputation among those who like to think they know. From what I've seen his stuff is big and brash like him, almost off-putting. But then—'

'What?'

'Well, then you see something you hadn't noticed at first, and you realise he has an amazing eye. The… the structure of the piece. The small details. It's hard to explain.'

John got up and put his cup in the dishwasher. 'Seems it always is.' I felt he was patronising me, but maybe I was over-sensitive. I bristled but kept my counsel. He stretched. 'I'm going to my study for a while. Got a few emails to reply to.'

It was June, warm and sultry, with that faded light that heralds the approach of inevitable darkness. I wandered into the garden, sat on the terrace wall and soaked in the scent of the big pink rose bush that climbed up from below, pinned to the wall with hooks and wires. Shadow was creeping up the lawn, round the base of the shed, wrapping its fingers round the bushes as it slid nearer. The garden was my other palette, and I felt deep pleasure contemplating it. Every shrub, every tree I had planted, nurtured, pruned and fed. John cut the grass and trimmed the hedges, a job he considered more important than looking after plants. I went down the steps onto the lawn and pulled off my shoes, feeling the warm springy grass between my toes. I saw a small dandelion sprouting half-hidden under a purple euphorbia, and I stretched out my hand almost automatically to tug it out, but then I hesitated, smiling to myself. *Let it be. At least for now.*

The shadows were lengthening, draining the garden of colour, and a small breeze sprang up. The scarlet willow wafted gracefully about, its slender branches waving, as if dancing. I thought of the other gardens I had the care of, in particular one I was due to see to the following day. Over the past five years or so I'd built up a little business gardening for others, mainly elderly ladies whose bodily state prevented them from mowing and weeding and hedge-trimming, and who found a female gardener a less alarming prospect than some brawny man. Besides, I was quite brawny enough myself for such tasks and I loved being outside. More and more the city stifled me, physically and metaphorically. It wasn't just the congestion, the noise, and the traffic fumes of the centre, or the endless roar of cars on the ring road. These I could mostly avoid.

It was the crammed, cramped, clogging sensation of so many bodies and souls in choking proximity. I would probably have felt the same in any city, but Brant seemed peculiarly repulsive. I'd never wanted to move here, but John got his dream job, and in those days my feelings were less strong and I didn't want to stand in his way. Now, at least, we no longer lived in the buzzing hive of the close-packed southern suburbs. John worked hard and prospered, and we moved to a wide and leafy road. Even so, it was a long way from the open hills and valleys of my youth.

ON THE DAY of the art class I made some salad and put it in the fridge, leaving a note for John, who had a late meeting. My unremarkable pile of paintings was strapped securely into a small portfolio which I'd bought cheaply online and customised so it could be worn on my back for cycling. I set off into the early evening, pedalling against a brisk headwind. There'd been a brief squall of rain earlier, just as I was finishing up in Elsie's garden, and the air was fresher.

As I approached the city centre, with the college visible above the rooftops two streets away, I came to a road closure. Beyond the barriers I saw workmen gathered round a large hole in the road. There was no way I could skirt round it, so I followed the diversion signs, weaving in and out of crawling traffic, until I came to the covered market. Closed now, it offered a short cut for two wheels. I rode down the cracked paving, avoiding slicks of standing water where stallholders had hosed down their pitches earlier in the day. Mingled smells wrinkled my nose – fish, blood, flowers, over-ripe fruit. It was one of the few places I liked in this city, reminiscent of a past that was being eroded. It was a good place to people-watch, if you could find a quiet pavement café: the colours were blinding, the noise relentless, the restless tide of humanity bewildering, but for a short time, before the desire for peace became overwhelming, it supplied many an image that could be brought to life on paper or canvas.

The diversion had cost me minutes, and I was only just in time for the evening's meeting. I padlocked my bike to a rack under a shelter and made for the stairs. The art room takes up a whole floor at the top pf the building and is flooded with light during the day. Now, with heavy clouds gathering and threatening more rain, the evening seemed more advanced than it really was. I took the stairs two at a time, my portfolio banging on my back, and arrived breathless.

I pushed open the swing doors and stood, momentarily nonplussed, staring into the room, which was thronged with people. Then I remembered we had another group with us that normally met on a Friday and had invited us along. There were faces I knew vaguely, others not at all, as well as the familiar ones I saw every Tuesday.

I shed my jacket and sidled into the room, making for the back of the crowd that faced the podium. There were chairs set out, and some people were sitting, but most were standing around in uneasy clumps, talking. I wanted to lurk out of sight, but that was always a problem. At five foot ten I was one of the tallest in the room, apart from Dave who topped me by several inches and was as thin and transparent as tracing paper.

Grace saw me enter and came to stand by me. 'I thought you'd be here earlier.'

'There was a diversion,' I said. 'A big hole seems to have appeared in Milton Road.'

'Good grief,' she muttered. 'This place is falling to pieces. I suppose it'll make other people late as well, especially those coming in cars.' She took my elbow. 'Don't you want to sit down? The great man'll be here in a minute. Someone said he's going to give us a talk about how he got to where he is today. Then we can ask questions.'

'Hm. An opportunity for our fellow creatives who like the sound of their own voices.'

Grace smiled. 'From the little I know about Ronnie Milburn, he's well able to shut down the garrulous. He's known for a lack of courteous charm.'

We found two vacant chairs to the side and rear of the rows. I put my portfolio down by my feet, noticing the splashes of mud on my trainers.

'What was it he's supposed to have said? Something about every artist needing a streak of ruthlessness?'

'Yes, it was in an interview in the Herald, wasn't it?'

I looked sideways at her, seeing the grey curl that had escaped her tied-back hair and lay wispily along her weathered cheek. 'So, are you ruthless, Grace?'

She chuckled and shook her head. 'I'm just an amateurish dabbler, we all know that. No need for ruthlessness. What about you? Do you have what it takes?'

I found a loose fingernail and gnawed it. 'Yet to be seen, I think. Anyway, he's here.'

Phil, our tutor, was dwarfed by the man who preceded him through the swing doors. Ronnie Milburn walked with a swagger, oozing self-belief. His shaggy brown hair fell to the collar of a brown jumper flecked and splashed with paint; clearly he didn't think the evening merited careful dressing. He hopped up onto the podium and bellowed above the buzz and hum of chat, 'Ladies and gentlemen! Good evening!' People shuffled into seats, and as the room came to order I observed him, noticing his narrowed eyes, the satirical twist to his mouth. He rubbed his hands together – big, rough hands with blunt fingers. 'I've been asked by Phil here to give you a bit of my background. That won't take long. After that I'll look at your work, if you want me to, and you can ask me any questions you may have.' He paused and cleared his throat. 'You know what, I'm probably not your typical artist, even if such a creature exists. I didn't go to a posh college, I've got no qualifications, and until the last few years nobody in the great world of art thought much of what I did. But I'm a lucky bloke – I have a wife who believes in me and goes out to work to support me. It's a great arrangement, and one I can recommend.' He grinned, his eyes sparking wicked humour under bushy brows. 'Plus, I come from a family who let me get on with it, even though I must have been a trial to them. You probably know I'm a triplet – my brothers are highly respectable – one lectures in physics right here in this college, the other manages other people's money in London and makes plenty of his own at the same time. Plus, my sister's a barrister. Where I came from nobody knows. Anyway, when I was about fifteen, I developed an obsession with Hieronymus Bosch. Wouldn't answer to any other name. I was christened Patrick, but my family compromised with Ronnie, and here I am. I grew out of the Bosch thing, though you can probably see his influence in some of my older work. I was an idle student; never did my homework, always in trouble, gave my dad, who was a teacher, many a headache. All I wanted to do was draw, and paint when I could get my hands on materials. But we weren't well off. As soon as I could leave school, I got a job in a greengrocer's and spent all my wages on art materials. Our little house was covered in my stuff – my poor mother.

'Anyway, I hadn't passed any exams, except in art, and I had no hope of getting a place in some posh art school. I wouldn't have felt at home there anyway. But then – and I'm not sure how it happened – my dad came across this place in Yorkshire that seemed different. Much freer. You had to pay to go there, and for your own materials, which meant I would have to find a job. My dad said, "Ron, if you're serious about this, you're going to have to support yourself. Pay your own way. It'll be hard. You'll get some teaching, but you'll have the freedom to develop your ideas and see where it takes you. This is an opportunity that won't come your way twice. I've spoken to Mrs Chibley, and she's willing to give you a chance. Don't waste it." I tell you, I went to Yorkshire like a shot. Dad was right – it was hard. But I loved it. I worked for local farmers, the blacksmith, the farrier, anyone who would take me, and when I could I painted. Martha Chibley, who owned the place, was an inspiration – tough as granite, wouldn't take nonsense from anyone, certainly not a raw teenager too big for his boots. But I suppose she thought I was worth the effort – maybe she saw something in me that no one else had – anyway, she taught me a lot, as did the peripatetic teachers who just somehow came and went. To this day I don't know how it all worked. But after three years suddenly it was over. I had to buckle down and make something of myself if I could. I came back to Brant, not knowing what I would do next. For a while it was odd jobs and painting in my dad's garage. Then I decided I needed to widen my horizons and travel.

I was a young, strong bloke, up for anything. Travelled all over Europe, all the usual things; hitch-hiking, sleeping under the stars, treading grapes for the harvest, working mending roads, a stint as a waiter – you name it. I was working for a fisherman in Greece when I met Tanya – my wife. The rest is history.' He grinned. 'Right. Enough about me. If you want to know anything about my painting, what I'm doing at the moment, you can ask. Let's look at some of the stuff you've been doing. If there's anything I can advise you about I'll be glad to. But I'll be honest – I don't think I know much that'll be of use!'

There were tables set up round the perimeter of the large room, and people got up, retrieved bags and portfolios and started to lay out their work. I chose a table at the far end, hoping we'd run out of time. My little pieces were an embarrassment. I said as much to Grace, and she fixed me with one of her scowls. 'Don't talk such garbage, Fen. You've got more talent than the rest of us put together. You just need some kind of direction.'

'Well, thanks. That's kind of you. Anyway, I'm not too bothered about him seeing my stuff, but I do want to ask him about this place in Yorkshire – if it's still going.'

She frowned. 'Why? Do you want to go there?'

I shook my head. 'I don't know. Like him, I don't have any qualifications. I don't have a great body of work. Not much more than these flaccid little offerings.' I waved a dismissive hand over my paintings. 'I've thrown a lot away. Hidden other things. All I know is I want to try something different. Something to stretch my imagination. Something big.'

She looked at me, her head on one side, and gave me a knowing look. 'Remember that Bible study group a month or two back? The one where you freaked everybody out, including our beloved rector?'

I groaned. 'Don't remind me. John had a real go at me about that when we got home. Said I embarrassed him. Why?'

'I just thought about you suggesting our next study should be on Revelation. There's a nice big subject for you – angels, fire, judgment, all that stuff.'

I stared at her, feeling a shiver run down my arms. 'Grace, you are a genius.'

'Fen, I was joking!'

'No matter. It's an astonishing idea. Huge canvases, huge subjects, brilliant colour – the opposite of these nice little views.' She stared at me, her mouth open. 'I don't know if I can actually do it, Grace. I don't even know if I can afford it – think of the materials! But it would be something, wouldn't it? Just to try.'

'I don't know what to say to you, Fen. But anyway, here's our famous artist.'

Ronnie Milburn approached us. He dwarfed Grace, but his eyes were on a level with mine. I remembered fleetingly how my height had been a burden to me in my teens, as I outstripped the lads my own age. Now it had its uses; even if I was quailing inside, I could use it to feign confidence.

Ronnie was shaking hands with Grace. 'Who are you?'

'Grace Fellowes. I have no pretensions. This is my friend, Fen Bailey. She doesn't either, but maybe she should have. I think she's talented.'

Ronnie turned to me and offered his hand. I shook it, feeling its dry, cracked skin. His eyes had a penetrating look that made me want to step back. 'Talent is overrated,' he said. 'Your best bet is hard work and refusing to give up.'

I said nothing as he turned to Grace's paintings laid out on the table next to mine.

I didn't listen to what they were saying, because I was thinking. No, properly speaking, I was plotting. After a few minutes their subdued voices turned to laughter, and Ronnie Milburn took a step sideways to my table. He looked at my watercolours, then he looked at me, a small smile on his lips. 'This is nice,' he said, his voice low. I felt a blush rise hot from my neck and cursed inwardly. He picked up one of my pieces by the corner as if he planned to point something out to me, but in doing so he exposed the rough, amateurish daub of Wesley. 'Hello – what's this?'

'Ah. That.' I was finding it hard to articulate. I cleared my throat. He smoothed out the paper, scrutinising my shamefully childish work. 'That's Wesley. My cat. Named after, of course, the great evangelist and writer of famous hymns.'

'It's not a polished piece, is it? Most people seem to have brought their best work along. Why a portrait of your cat? And done, I would guess, at great speed and in a state of strong feeling.'

'How do you know that?'

'It's chock full of passion. Maybe even grief.' He frowned. 'Is he dead, your Wesley?'

I fought back tears. I wanted to be composed in front of this man, not thought of as some middle-aged hysteric. 'I don't know. Maybe. He disappeared a year ago.' He said nothing, just looked at me steadily, and I battled on. 'But I don't want to talk about my feeble efforts. I want to know more about this art school you went to. Is it still functional?'

'Yes, but I don't know how,' he said sombrely. 'There must be money somewhere, maybe a trust. But it's fallen on hard times. I speak to Martha on the phone once in a while, and she's not a well woman. Painfully arthritic these days. Sometimes I go up there and give her a hand, but I can't stay long. It's a shame – the art world has got very mainstream, and places like Chibley are a great rarity, more's the pity.' He looked at me keenly. 'Why do you ask? Do you feel a yen to study there?'

'I hardly know what I feel, except there's something, some huge thing like a monster, battling inside me, screaming to get out. Anyway, enough of my nonsense. It's not your concern.'

Thankfully, by this point Grace had moved away and was talking to someone else. I felt an acute discomfort that I had said so much. But Ronnie shook his head. 'I have to go soon,' he said. 'Why don't you come by my studio, and I'll tell you about Chibley. It's quite a story. Tomorrow?'

'I can't. We're at the airport seeing my son off. He's flying out to America to his dream job – theatre design. He's hugely excited, can't wait to go. My daughter's coming home from university for the weekend especially to wave her brother off.'

'Sunday?'

'I'll be at church in the morning. Then I'll be making Sunday lunch for Alice – I'm sure she doesn't cook for herself.'

'Church, eh? I look forward to finding out about that. But yes, I was too poor to feed myself, all those years at Chibley. Lived on cornflakes, came home every so often for my mother's cooking. The afternoon, then? Do you know where I am?'

I hadn't even said I would go, but this seemed to have passed him by. Without waiting for an answer, he fished in his back pocket and pulled out a handful of crumpled business cards. He put one in my unresisting hand. 'Come about three.' He must have seen my look of doubt, because suddenly he laughed, so loudly that people stopped talking and looked round. 'Don't worry,' he said in a stage whisper. 'It's not a case of the amoral opportunist artist luring a lady to his lair. Tanya'll be around, and she'd flay me if I so much as thought of straying.'

He was beginning to annoy me. 'I assure you,' I said coolly, 'I am not in the market for adultery. But I would like to know more about Chibley, and to look at what you're working on, if you'll let me.'

'Excellent.' He patted my arm. 'See you on Sunday. I have a notion we have a lot to talk about, Fen Bailey.' He made to go, then turned back. 'What's it short for? Your unusual name?'

I winced. 'Fennel. By the time I arrived my parents had immersed themselves uncompromisingly in the ethos of the bohemian sixties. They were very into growing herbs. Not so bad for me, but they called my brother Juniper. You can imagine how that went down among the boys at school. He calls himself Nigel these days, after a motor-racing hero.'

'So many stories! I must run. Till Sunday.'

I watched him have a brief word with Phil and wave carelessly to a few people. He was grinning to himself as he went.

I decided to say nothing to John, not then, beyond a bland reply to his equally bland question as to how the evening had gone. After my visit to Ronnie Milburn's studio there might be more to tell – or there might not. Besides, there was something on the horizon that dwarfed these concerns: saying goodbye to our son. Daniel, my first-born, was now twenty-two, born to a green nineteen-year-old living in a tiny two-up, two-down in central Brant in the maze of streets at the back of the Abbey. From school he'd loved everything to do with the theatre, and after a getting a first in his bachelor's degree had just finished an MA in Collaborative Theatre Production and Design. We knew how hard he'd worked, not only on his degrees but in all sorts of part-time jobs, funding himself as far as he could, because he knew how ruinous it would be for us to put two children through university one after the other. Now he had landed a job in New York, starting very low down and on a pittance of a salary (by American standards). At some point during his time in London he'd met Rafe, doing an MA in something like Ecological Studies – I was never quite sure what this entailed. Rafe was American, from a wealthy family. His uncle had offered the two young men the use of a basement flat where both could travel to work – though at this point Rafe had no job to go to. He'd spent part of a day with us some months ago and seemed quite unconcerned. 'I'll find something when I get back home,' he'd said. 'And if all else fails I can always work for my dad.' He'd pulled a comical face and burst out laughing. You couldn't dislike Rafe, but privately I wondered about his friendship with Dan. I said nothing of my thoughts to John. Anyway, our son was an adult, if a rather naïve one, and how he lived his life was his choice.

We were due to meet Alice at the airport in plenty of time to have a leisurely meal with Daniel before his flight. The Saturday traffic was dire, and we were late arriving, so John was a trifle tetchy. We found both our offspring in a bar, talking and laughing, though Dan seemed to be constantly looking around. Rafe, it transpired, hadn't yet shown up. Dan sighed. 'Typical.'

We ordered food and sat at a cramped little table, banging elbows, watching the crowds flow by like the tides of a restless sea. I observed my children, wondering about how different they were: Daniel is tall like me, thin as a reed, but strong, with thick chestnut hair worn collar-length and dark-brown eyes. Alice is blonde, which must be some kind of throwback, with a serious mien behind square glasses.

Dan finished his food as if he hadn't eaten in weeks. 'Where's that fool got to?' he muttered. He checked the time on his phone. 'He's so laid back he's practically asleep.' Ten minutes later, breathless and full of good humour, Rafe showed up, throwing a huge backpack on the floor and greeting everyone with a hug, including John, who was visibly taken aback. Rafe had been to the barber's – his bright red hair was so short you could see the freckled scalp beneath. 'What's this, convict chic?' Dan demanded.

The little time left flew by. The young people dominated the conversation, with the two lads in a state of euphoria. John and I gave up trying to contribute.

'We have to go, mate,' Daniel said to Rafe. 'It's probably at least a mile to the gate. Mum, Dad, Ally – I'll be in touch.' He hugged us all, and as I held him in my arms I remembered the stages of his life: the fuzzy-headed baby, the daring toddler, the sweet-natured schoolboy; confiding, helpful, easily hurt. But he was a man now, I reminded myself, hoping he had grown a thicker skin against life's inevitable knocks. 'No weeping, now, Mum.' (I was dry-eyed.) 'I'll be home for Christmas.'

Rafe yelled his enthusiastic goodbyes, and then they were gone, lost in the departing crowds.

THE SATURDAY AFTERNOON traffic made the journey home long and weary. John muttered, I stared out of the window at nothing, and Alice fell asleep on the back seat, her mouth slightly open, her glasses endearingly askew. Awake, Alice rarely merited being described as endearing: she was often cross, moody and spiky. I had always tried to show no favouritism between my children, but things were usually more rewarding with Daniel. Alice, on the other hand, was a daddy's girl almost from birth.

As we pulled up on the drive Alice woke with a start and sat upright. Her glasses fell on the floor, and I heard her swear as she scrabbled to retrieve them. As soon as we were inside the front door, she muttered something about taking a shower and disappeared upstairs. Heaving a sigh, I went through to the kitchen and put the kettle on. John was in his study, reading what looked like a work report on his laptop, and acknowledged the cup of tea I brought him with a graceless grunt. Shaking my head, I reflected, not for the first time, what hard work my family was. The only member with whom I had an easy and uncritical relationship was already far away, somewhere high above the Atlantic.

Things improved later, helped by cake (a present from Grace) and more tea. From the open door of John's study, I heard a lively debate on the merits and otherwise of leaving the European Union and remembered that the referendum was just days away. I was thoroughly sick of the meaningless rhetoric on both sides but had privately determined to vote to stay in. I simply couldn't believe in the nonsense about Britain's golden destiny in a liberated future.

I was washing salad at the kitchen sink when Alice ambled in and perched on a corner of the worktop. She helped herself to a stick of cucumber and nibbled at it. She glanced up at me, wiping her fingers on her jeans. 'Anything I can do to help?'

'You can grate these carrots if you like.'

As she grated, she said, 'I decided on a topic for my end-of-year paper.'

'Oh, what?'

'You know I've been doing a module on American Studies, don't you? I've decided to write about the role of students in the civil rights movement.'

'Sounds interesting. When do you have to submit it?'

'By the end of the first week of term – October. So I'll be working on it during the summer.'

'Will you be at home?' I asked mildly.

'Maybe not that much. I'll need to be near the library. I might try to find a job nearby. But I'll pop home the odd weekend. Might look up some old school friends.'

'Well, keep us in the loop.'

She frowned. 'You and Dad going anywhere?'

'No, nothing planned. He's cooking something big up for next year, I think. His fiftieth, our twenty-fifth. Probably a cruise.' I grimaced.

'You don't like cruises.'

'So I've tried to tell him.'

Suddenly she smiled, and it transformed her unremarkable features. 'I remember what you did on that cruise he persuaded you to go on – when was it? Two years ago? Didn't the ship almost sail without you?'

'No! that's absolutely not true,' I protested. I turned to face her, seeing her for once animated, a flush of pink in her pale cheeks. 'All I did was to make ten days of torment a bit more bearable. And I got back to the ship with twenty minutes to spare. It would have been longer, but I took an expensive taxi to make sure I wasn't late, and we were held up by a traffic accident half a mile from the port. I'd have been better off walking. Your father was extremely annoyed.'

'And he still wants to do it again?'

'He's welcome. I shall not be going.'

She handed me the bowl of grated carrot. 'Want some dressing on this?'

'OK. There's some made in the fridge.'

I remembered that day – a day I'd planned almost from the beginning. We'd booked a shore excursion in Valencia, but I slipped away from the rest of the tour. I sent John a text: 'Don't worry, but I'm headed elsewhere. I'll see you back on the ship this evening.' I boarded a fast train to Madrid and spent many hours very happily in the Prado. Part of the time was given over to a favourite painting – the fabulous *Descent from the Cross* by Rogier van der Weyden. Stylised to a degree, with an emphasis on composition and the figures cramped together into an improbably tiny space, the artist nevertheless portrayed the anguish of the onlookers with a realism I hadn't expected from a fifteenth-century work. Just examining it in minute detail and at leisure filled me with joy.

Needless to say, John was furious. I doubt he was worried, as he claimed – he was well aware I could look after myself; he was embarrassed at my defection and even more so by his inability to explain my absence. When we docked at Barcelona I had to swear not to repeat my little adventure, but with the prospect of taking in so much of the work of Gaudi I was content to stay with the party.

Alice drifted away, and as I put supper together I thought about the imbalance in the family, each one of whom would regale me with pet projects, work, ambitions, news, yet rarely ask me anything about my own interests. It was as if, in their eyes, consciously or not, I had no life beyond these walls. Alice remembered my escapade but took no apparent interest in why I had done it. Why was my passion for art of so little moment? Perhaps it was because I rarely said anything about it. The fact was my husband and children were all much better educated than the foolish girl who bunked off school whenever she could, and that was when her parents stayed in one place for any length of time. Always on the move, finding work where they could, teaching their children whatever came to hand that they thought was fascinating; a systematic education was not a priority. I remember John saying, not long after we met, that it was a miracle I could read and write. A huge exaggeration, of course. I have tried to make up for it since, reading voraciously in any spare moment, but for many years I had huge gaps in my knowledge.

ALICE TOOK HERSELF to bed early, and John as usual disappeared back into his study. I took him a cup of coffee around nine and perched on the edge of his desk. 'Has Alice told you when she wants to go back?'

He didn't look up from his screen. 'No. Why?'

'Depending on the time, you might need to take her to the station. I'll get lunch ready earlyish. I'm going out before three.'

Now he looked up, trying to focus on me, a small frown knitting his brows. 'You don't normally have mysterious appointments on a Sunday.'

'It's not mysterious. You remember we had a visit from Ronnie Milburn at art class on Friday? Well, we got talking and he invited me to his studio.'

Now I had his attention. 'What for?'

'To see what he's working on, among other things.'

'But why you? Did he like what you were showing him?'

'Why should that surprise you? He did, actually. But it wasn't just about that. He told us about a very unusual art school he studied at. I wanted to know more about it, but there wasn't time then.'

He looked astonished. 'Don't tell me you want to go there!'

'I don't know yet. I'll let you know when I know more.'

'Where is it, anyway? And what's wrong with going on a course here, if that's what you want?'

'Yorkshire somewhere; I don't know exactly. As for taking a course here, I absolutely don't want that. This city chokes the life out of me. It's not about "going on a course". It's about having the freedom to make what's in me to make.'

'Well. You're a dark horse!'

'You've only just realised that? Anyway, at the moment it's just a visit to Ronnie Milburn's studio. I didn't say I was going anywhere.' I slid off the desk. 'Don't let your coffee go cold.'

FIRST, THOUGH, THERE was church: the ten o'clock service at St Swithin's. This was where we started to attend when we first moved to the suburbs. In the early years, before John's rapid promotion gave us the chance to relocate, we went to the Abbey, because it was nearest. John was never comfortable there, but I, a very new Christian, loved the colour and ritual, the beauty of the building with its graceful proportions, soaring columns and stained-glass windows, and it was a friendlier place than I might have anticipated. As an added benefit it had a children's ministry and a baby and toddler group which I helped with on a rota, so that there were Sundays when for an hour I was child-free. John, on the other hand, felt he had no role in such a big place with so many people to do the necessary jobs. John needed to feel important, and at St Swithin's he was treasurer; in most churches a role hard to fill. I once said to him that if you met for worship in a forest or a field there would be no need for the counting and banking of money or the balancing of books, but he snorted and told me I was naïve.

St Swithin's is small, conservative, and to my mind dull and timid. Our rector, Gilbert, is near to retirement and in no mood for great innovations, which seems to suit an ageing congregation. To be fair, he is a decent, hard-working man and likeable in a bumbling, hesitant way, and he tries to serve his flock faithfully. The occasion when I caused John embarrassment was the first of a proposed series of home-based Bible studies, attended not only by the usual older people but – by some miracle – a young couple new to the parish whom Gilbert was keen to encourage. He'd suggested we introduce ourselves to each other and the newcomers with an icebreaker (where on earth had he found that idea? It was so unlike him) that involved describing ourselves in one word. I was fed up with the repetitive, well-meaning tedium of these things and in a sour mood. As it happened, we were hosting the evening so it fell to me to make refreshments, and I was sick of that side of things as well. When it came to my turn I saw them looking at me – their not-so-gracious hostess – expectantly. 'One word? I can think of many words,' I said. 'But here's one word: Unfulfilled.' I was probably actually glaring. 'Now, who's for tea and coffee?'

Of course, there was an awkward silence and a titter or two before Gilbert laughed, a bit too heartily, and moved on.

Later in the evening I made it worse when Gilbert asked people what they would like to study. Various suggestions were made, all (probably quite rightly) intended to ease our young couple in gently. But I was not in a merciful mood. 'Revelation,' I said. 'It's hardly ever done. That's what I'd like to look at.'

And of course, dear Gilbert tried to be fair and kind and made all the right noises about it being perhaps a little too challenging. I left them chatting and went into the kitchen where I made a lot of noise with cups and plates.

When they had all gone, John rounded on me. I had shown him up, as well as myself. I had behaved like a brat, a badly-brought-up infant. This was a favourite accusation when I annoyed him, based on the eight-year age gap and his disapproval of my parents' way with their children. This disproportionate (in my view) fury sounded to me like a doom-laden hammering of nails in the coffin of our marriage. Because I too was angry – that he unthinkingly expected me to fall in with his worldview and the tiresome need for simpering politeness so prevalent in some church circles. That evening I shed tears, not because of his nastiness so much as at the recognition that he had killed the last vestiges of my idiotic hero-worship.

When I first met John, I was an almost-fifteen-year-old hoyden; ignorant, precocious, hedonistic, probably amoral. My parents let me and my brother run wild and learn what we needed to in order to survive and be free. We knew a great deal about trees, plants, animals, the countryside, the farming year, the weather, and quite a bit about people; we could read, write and do simple arithmetic. We knew little, according to John, of how to behave. At that point he was twenty-two, serious, hard-working, judgemental and easily shocked. In a strange way he had fewer defences against me than I had against him, because I was a knowing little witch, still a child in mind but a woman in body, and I used every trick I knew with blithe insouciance – whereas he was bound by the code of his faith and his sense of honour and propriety. I thought he was handsome, grown-up and unbelievably knowledgeable; I also thought it would be fun to seduce him. What I hadn't counted on was that he would resist me. I hadn't had any such problems before with the callow lads of my fleeting acquaintance. On his part he set about civilising me, from the great heights of his adult wisdom. With barely restrained lust thrown into the mix, it was no surprise that we fell into something like love. It was certainly intense and exclusive.

I was remembering these things as I sat in the pews at St Swithin's and probably should have been listening to Gilbert's sermon, but after the first few sentences I realised it was one I had heard before, or one very like it. I drifted away, smiling to myself, remembering John's concentrated efforts to educate me into his Christian faith, and perhaps it was not so remarkable that he succeeded. Whatever might become of us, I would always be grateful to John for introducing me to Jesus, even if before long his notion of what it meant to be a Christian diverged so sharply from mine. I didn't know if he was ever fully aware of how wide that chasm had grown. My smile grew wider. If only he knew! He would probably feel the need to educate me all over again.

After the service we gathered at the back of the church for watery coffee, and I did my best to be kind and charming to some old ladies whom I actually really liked and who had been in that Bible study group where I had misbehaved. I had long since repented of my immoderate ways and sent Gilbert an apologetic e mail.

When we got home, I was in haste to get lunch ready. I put a chicken in the oven and set to with vegetables. Alice appeared yawning, with wet hair hanging stringily round her shoulders.

'How was church?' she asked sleepily.

'Riveting,' I said, catching a sharp look from John.

'Do you need a hand?' Alice asked, more from duty than conviction.

'It's all done,' I said briskly. 'I've got somewhere to go before three. If you need a lift to the station before I get back your dad will oblige.'

By two thirty the dishes were washed and draining. When I looked outside, I saw it had started to drizzle. I put on a waterproof and got my bike out of the garage. 'I might see you later, Alice,' I said, hugging her briefly. 'But if not, keep us updated with your plans, won't you?'

'Yeah, OK, Mum.'

I reckoned it would take me about twenty minutes to cross the city out into the almost-rural belt beyond the river and Thripp's Ford where Ronnie Milburn lived and worked. By the time I arrived the rain was heavier; my waterproof, jeans, and bike helmet were wet. I wheeled my bike across the gravel forecourt and pounded on the door with my free hand. The Milburns lived in a clapboard farmhouse, once painted white. Now it had an air of dilapidation made worse by the rain. After a moment the door opened, and a tall, striking woman stood in the doorway. Her almost-black hair, streaked with grey, hung down her back. Her dark green eyes looked me up and down, but she was smiling. 'You must be Fennel,' she said. 'Great name, by the way. I'm Tanya. Come on in – you look soaked. The bike will be fine there.'

I followed her inside. Her long, cotton skirt, in shades of purple and black, skimmed the flagged floor. 'Here, use this.' She threw me a towel, and I took off my helmet and rubbed my hair. 'Ronnie's in the studio,' she said. 'I'll take you over.' She looked at me. 'Do you need something dry to change into?'

'It's fine,' I said. 'I'll dry off soon enough, thanks.'

'Right, I'll show you the way.'

We left the kitchen by a side door and crossed the yard to a large outbuilding. The rain had stopped quite suddenly. Tanya pushed open the door. 'Ron, your visitor's here.' She turned to me. 'I'll leave you to it. I'll bring you a cup of tea later if you're still around. Don't let the old bear bully you.'

Ronnie Milburn appeared at the far end of the room. He was wearing an enormous old shirt that once had been striped blue and white but which was now faded almost colourless, spattered with variously-coloured paint. He had a brush in one hand and a rag in the other. 'What was that about a bullying old bear?' he demanded. 'Hello, Fen Bailey. I wondered if you might chicken out.'

'Why would I do that?' I countered.

'I'm going back indoors,' Tanya said. 'See you later.'

The space I found myself in was enormous, lit by huge windows back and front.

'This used to be a barn,' Ronnie said. 'I had these windows put in when we bought the place. Anyway, come upstairs. That's where the action is.'

He led me across the room to an open staircase. The floor of the upper level was bare wood, splashed with paint. To one side, between the windows, the wooden wall was partly covered by a huge print of Hieronymus Bosch's famous painting, *The Garden of Earthly Delights*. He grinned as I went over for a closer look. 'I keep that there to remind me of the follies of my youth. You might see one or two references in my later work. I still have a soft spot for my old hero.'

Ronnie and I walked around the room, looking, barely speaking. There were stacks and racks of works leaning against the walls, but here were paintings he'd chosen to display, and they were varied. In some I recognised his current style, exuberant and gloomy by turns, thick with paint, often disturbing. But on another wall there were quite different pieces. I exclaimed aloud as we stood before a huge reclining nude, the flesh slabbed in unexpected colours – yet when I stepped back, they blended naturalistically. The subject was a statuesque woman, green-eyed, with heavy black hair cascading over her chest and back, a bold face that stared out of the canvas. 'It's Tanya,' I whispered, 'isn't it?' Ronnie said nothing, simply nodded. 'Does she mind?'

'Oh, very few people come here,' he said. 'And she's made me swear never to exhibit it. It's quite an old piece – about fifteen years, I guess.'

'It reminds me of Lucian Freud.'

'It's meant to. I was trying to reproduce some of his techniques. What do you think of it?'

'I'm not sure,' I murmured. 'It's like a challenge to the onlooker – both by you the artist and the subject herself.'

'The essence of Tanya,' he said. 'She's an extraordinary woman. You know she's worked for nearly twenty years so I don't have to?'

'I'd heard,' I said. 'She must believe in you. It's a lot to live up to. What does Tanya do?'

'She lectures in art history,' Ronnie said. 'But not here in Brant. Seen enough? Want to move on?'

We went through an arch to a smaller room. Here on the walls, to my great surprise, were portraits – some of them of Ronnie himself, and in an almost classical style. 'I wasn't expecting this!' I said. 'These are completely different.'

Ronnie nodded. 'It's my latest phase,' he said. 'I'm experimenting. I've got an exhibition lined up, did you know? Next spring. I don't know what they'll make of these, if I decide to include them. At least it shows I can actually draw.'

'This one,' I pointed, 'reminds me of the work of Frida Kahlo. Didn't she do a number of self-portraits?'

'The great thing with self-portraits,' Ronnie said, 'is an instantly available subject who doesn't need paying. I reckon you should try it.'

'Me?'

'Why not?'

I didn't know what to say. 'I've always felt sorry for Frida Kahlo,' I said, covering my confusion. 'She had a horrible life. Full of ill-health, pain, betrayal. But her paintings are vivid. The kind some snobs call *primitive*.'

There was a loud bang from downstairs, and then Tanya's voice. 'Two teas down here. Come and get it while it's hot.' The door banged again.

'Shall we?' Ronnie said with a flourish. I preceded him down the staircase, my hand on a rail that swayed alarmingly. 'I must get someone to fix that,' he muttered. 'Probably a death-trap. One day Tanya'll come in here and find me on the deck with my neck broken.' He grinned. 'Ah well. At least she can sell some of the paintings.'

Tanya had left two mugs of very strong-looking tea and a plate of biscuits on an upturned crate. Ronnie set up two camping chairs, and we sat down.

'So,' he said, blowing on his tea. 'You wanted to know about Chibley Farm. I know a bit about its history, but the best person to tell you all that is Martha herself. You should meet her. Amazing woman.'

'Where is it exactly?' I asked. 'Yorkshire's a big place. I know there's a sort of artists' colony of sorts, somewhere in those parts.'

'No, no,' Ronnie said. 'That's further south, much more… shall we say, eclectic, quite well known by some types of tourists. Some interesting characters there, though. I met a few. No, Chibley's well off the beaten track. I'll show you.' He got up, almost upsetting the crate and spilling his tea. He rummaged in the half-open drawer of a chest, pulled out a battered road map and thumbed the curling pages with an oily thumb. 'Here we are.' He spread the map out as he sat down again. He pointed. 'It's on this tiny road, not far from the river, but set back. There are a fair few acres attached, and the road up is not for the faint-hearted.'

'Good heavens.' I looked where he indicated, my eyes widening. 'I know it. Not the place itself, not even that road, but the area. From when I was in my teens. For once we stayed put for almost a year – both my parents found work and my brother and I actually went to school. Not that I was a regular pupil. I bunked off as often as I could and helped on a farm. I was quite the shepherdess at one time, but that was on the other side of the main road, north-west of the town. How extraordinary. I never heard of Chibley, though.'

'That doesn't surprise me,' Ronnie said. 'But you do, a bit, Fen.'

I glanced at him. 'Do I? What, outwardly respectable but with hints of a dodgy past?'

He laughed. 'Not exactly. But tell me more about that time – if you care to.'

'Well, for one thing, it's where I met John. My husband.'

'You were a teenager?'

'Yes, but he was older. He was doing an MChem here at Brant and was on a year out in industry. He was working at Hawkes Chemical.'

Ronnie made a face. 'That terrible place. They closed it down, did you know? For polluting the river.'

I nodded. 'We didn't know that at the time, but John always said it was badly-run with no thought for the environment – just profit.'

'What does he do now?'

'Oh, he's at Brant Pharmaceuticals, worked his way up, doesn't do much actual chemistry or research now. More on the management side.'

'Going to tell me how you met?' Ronnie asked with a quirk of his bushy eyebrows.

'You really want to know? It's all rather a long time ago.'

'Maybe, but what an intriguing combination – the serious, ambitious student and the school-refusing free spirit with no shoes.'

I laughed. 'It may sound intriguing, but that's not how I'd describe us now. And how did you know I went barefoot?'

'Of course you did. So you're – what? Fifteen? And he's—?'

'Twenty-two. Well, if you're really interested, we met at a Young Farmers' social in the church hall.'

Ronnie chuckled. 'I can picture the scene. Straw-chewing yokels with muddy boots propping up the bar. A bored young hoyden in a patchwork dress, probably a bit of a peach. And in comes the handsome young student with horn-rimmed glasses.'

'It wasn't quite like that. For one thing, there was no bar. The church hall didn't have a licence, and most of us were underage anyway. Some of the lads would have sneaked in a flagon of cider, but that's all. And John didn't need glasses then. But well, yes, in essence, you're not far off the mark, even if you've made it a bit of a caricature.'

'A bit of a tendency I have,' Ronnie said. 'Flights of fancy. Goes with the territory. But do go on.'

'I really don't know why I'm telling you all this. But you're right – I was indeed bored. Bored and restless. The locals were on the stolid side. And John, though it seems strange to say so now, was almost exotic in that milieu.' I paused, wondering how much to say. But I sensed Ronnie Milburn wouldn't judge me for my youthful errors. 'The fact is,' I said slowly, choosing my words, 'despite my general lack of education, in some ways I was quite precocious. There wasn't a lot of parental guidance going on. They loved us, I don't doubt that, and they did their best, but they were rather extreme products of their generation and very keen on personal freedom. We did have a few visits from the truancy officer, I remember. These days someone might have alerted social workers, but we were well cared for, after a fashion. You know, I don't think they'd have minded much if I'd come home with a baby. It would just have been added to the family. Anyway, that didn't happen. Despite my thirteen-year-old fling with a traveller lad called Samuel, among others.' I looked at Ronnie. 'I did say I was precocious.'

'And look at you now,' Ronnie said thoughtfully. 'But would I be way off the mark if I wondered whether that girl is still around, locked away, keen to escape?'

I shook my head. 'Not that girl. She's changed fundamentally. It wasn't just because John resisted my attempts at seduction – that was a shock in itself. He held me at arm's length for an excruciating length of time, partly because, of course, I was jailbait and he had no wish to go to prison, but also because of his beliefs.'

'Ah. I was going to ask you about that, ever since you mentioned going to church. Was John instrumental in converting you?'

'Yes,' I said. 'And for that I am thankful. Apart from the children, it's his best gift to me. In case you were wondering, it wasn't a case of bringing the young pagan to heel. I had a mind of my own, even if it was ill-furnished with knowledge. No. He made me see two things – that in my love of the natural world I was worshipping created things instead of the Creator himself. And that there's really no such thing as freedom. If you aren't governed by a beneficent being – God, in other words – however idealistically you might start out, you'll be ruled by your own desires. Inevitably, humans being what they are, much worse influences will eventually dominate.'

Ronnie finished his tea and put the mug down. 'That's certainly a point of view. And I can't disagree about the shady ways of human beings. Weak, selfish, so easily dragged down into wanting what will destroy them. Interesting, though, don't you think?'

'Always.'

'So, tell me,' Ronnie said. 'What do you want to do, now, with your art?'

I bit my lip. Would he laugh? Did it matter? 'It was something Grace said,' I told him. 'You remember my friend Grace? A throwaway remark, not intended at all seriously. I said I wanted to do something really big, and she said I should take inspiration from the book of Revelation.'

Ronnie slapped his great hands down on his thighs. 'You and many others!'

'I know. But should that stop me? Anyway, I may never do it. It's probably too big a challenge.'

He turned to me, his eyes gleaming with humour. 'Even my old chum Bosch painted St John on Patmos, did you know? It's got a few of his usual peculiarities, but for him I find it strangely subdued. No, somehow I don't think it's for me. But maybe you could do it – or if not that, then something equally challenging, inspired, dramatic. Let your imagination run wild. More and more I think you should meet Martha. Maybe nothing will come of it. Maybe you're too fond of your nice life. But you should definitely meet, just once. See what happens. I could phone her, if you like.'

I held up my hands. 'No. Thank you, but no – or at least not yet. There are others involved. I don't live in a vacuum. I'll admit, what you say about Chibley, about Martha, has stirred something up. And I'd love to go back to the Dales. I could see my old friends the Hipkins – we've lost touch a bit lately.' Ronnie raised an enquiring eyebrow. 'They're the farmers I worked for. I loved it – dealing with the sheep, running with the dogs, out in that amazing landscape in all weathers. I miss it. Never did like city life. We kept up with them for years – they used to rent out a couple of farm cottages for extra income, and when my children were young we stayed there several years running. John didn't care for it that much, but it was a cheap holiday when we didn't have a lot of money, and it was fun for the children. They liked being with the animals, and all that fresh air was good for them. I think the last time we went there was when my daughter was about eleven.'

'You kept in touch afterwards?'

'Just Christmas cards, a bit of news, but even that's dwindled the last few years.' I fell silent, remembering. 'It would be lovely to see Mary and Peter again. And their fabulous dogs. But I guess Old Joe's long gone. Maybe they're running one of his descendants these days.'

'Seems to me,' Ronnie said, 'you need to take a trip up north. But that's your call. If you want me to ring Martha and introduce you, just let me know.'

I stood up. 'Thank you,' I said, looking down at him. 'For showing me your work, for taking an interest. I don't know why, on such flimsy evidence.'

'Let's say it's instinct,' Ronnie said, serious for once. 'A feeling. I know I don't really know you, but I've learned to trust my instincts. Like the first time I saw Tanya. And see how that turned out!'

'I must go,' I said. 'You'll be wanting to get on. And I've probably missed saying goodbye to my daughter, so I'll be in trouble.'

'Remember, though,' Ronnie said as he followed me to the door, 'just send me a text if you want to meet Martha.'

I turned to him, tentatively stretched out my hand, and he shook it.

'Whatever else,' I said, 'you've made me think. Maybe I *can* do something. Make something of myself. Maybe it's not too late. Thank you.'

As I put my helmet back on and picked up my bike it started to rain again. The door was open, and I called through to the kitchen. 'Thanks for the tea!' I heard a distant answering hail.

I rode home through strengthening sheets of rain, pedalling far too fast, but luckily for once there was little traffic on the roads. I felt a peculiar mixture of excitement and apprehension – what to decide? Was this a foolish pipe dream? How to explain it? I arrived back utterly soaked, and once I'd put the bike away I ran upstairs, peeled off all my clothes and stepped into a hot bath. As I wallowed, John found me and sat on the edge of the toilet. 'There you are.' He was frowning.

'I got soaked and chilled,' I said. 'It was raining, in case you didn't notice.'

'Of course I noticed. I had to drive Alice to the station.'

'Ah.' I heaved myself into a sitting position. 'She's gone, then.'

'Yes. Pity you couldn't have been here to say goodbye.'

'We'll see her before too long, I expect. Can you hand me that green towel?'

He stretched over and put the towel in my hand. 'You can manage to see Daniel off but can't get home to say cheerio to Alice. You see why I say you favour him.'

'I don't.' I stood up and started to towel myself down. 'But there's a difference. He's gone to America, and we won't see him until Christmas at the soonest. Alice is less than a hundred miles away and will almost certainly be home some weekends over the summer. Excuse me – I need to get out.'

He stood aside but followed me out of the bathroom and into the bedroom, watching me as I perched on the bed, dried my feet and pulled on socks, underwear, T shirt, and loose trousers. 'Is something on your mind, John?'

'You could say so. But hadn't you better tell me what you've been doing all afternoon?'

'I did tell you. I went over to Ronnie Milburn's studio. I met his wife.'

'And?'

'What's this – an interrogation?'

He let out an exasperated sigh. 'You never tell me anything. How can I know what you've been up to?'

'For goodness' sake, John! I haven't been "up to" anything! If I don't tell you what I've been doing, it's because you take so little interest. If you'd like to know, we talked about art, we drank tea, he showed me some of his work. And we talked about the art school I mentioned.' Now I looked up at him, my annoyance at his attitude dissolving for a moment as I recalled my excitement at knowing – more or less – where it was, and the prospect – perhaps – of visiting. 'You'll never guess where it is! Just a few miles from where we first met. Remember that?'

'How could I forget?' He spoke grumpily, but I could see that his ill humour was receding. 'It was something of a defining moment.'

'John, I want to go up there. Soon. Just for a visit, a couple of days at most. Talking about it to Ronnie has stirred up so many memories. I want to see the old place again, drop in on Mary and Peter, meet this woman Martha Chibley who owns and runs the school. According to Ronnie she's quite a character.'

He looked at me, his eyes wide. 'You really are thinking about going there to study, aren't you?'

'No. At least, not yet. I need to see it first, find out exactly what it entails. Nothing is decided. Of course I would discuss it with you.'

'Well, I suppose that's something.' He sounded exactly like a cross adolescent.

'I don't know why you are taking this attitude,' I said quietly. 'You should be pleased for me, shouldn't you? What's really worrying you?' Of course I had a pretty good idea, and even though I was irritated I also felt sorry for him. But he merely shrugged and turned away. I left him to brood.

Later I made us some supper and no more was said. We watched the late news together, then I went to bed with a book and he disappeared back into his study to look at work reports or disappear down rabbit-holes on the internet – I didn't know. He often stayed up till the small hours, so I was surprised when he came to bed, in his pyjamas, while I was still reading. Without saying a word, he took the book from my unresisting fingers and put it on the bedside table. After twenty-four years, of course I understood. I wound my arms around his neck and pulled him towards me.

For John, sex answers all questions, cures all ills, softens all disagreements. I know better: things are just the same after as before. But I wasn't about to argue. Even if I was approaching middle age, I remembered how it was when we first met, the torment of waiting till it was legal, and even his staunch principles fell to smithereens, because at first he said we should wait till we were married. That didn't happen. But no doubt it explained our unseemly haste, because this foolish child was married at seventeen. What did I really know? Next to nothing. At least, nothing that would be of much use in the succeeding years.

As he lay in my arms, half asleep, I recalled the afternoon when – at his instigation – we took my parents to meet his father. His mother had died from cancer when he was twelve, and his dad, who was a charming and cultured man, had done his best to bring up John and his sister. It can't have been easy. The meeting was awkward but in hindsight hilarious – my tweed-wearing academic father-in-law and my bohemian parents, dressed in their best brightly-coloured cheesecloth and tie-dye, trying to find common ground.

'Fen,' John muttered sleepily, 'I can feel you grinning.'

'I was remembering the day my parents and your dad first met. I was embarrassed, you were uncomfortable, and your poor father couldn't quite grasp why his well-educated and normally sensible son wanted to marry a sex-starved adolescent gypsy. Bless him, he was very polite, but you could see he was aghast. What on earth did he say to you after we'd gone?'

'Not much. He demurred a bit. But he could see I was determined, if a little deranged. And you and he hit it off eventually.'

'We did. He was a dear man.'

He fell silent, and I thought he had gone to sleep. But a few moments later he resurfaced. 'Fen.'

'What?'

'Do you think Daniel might be gay?'

I blinked, startled. 'What on earth's brought this on?'

I heard him take a deep breath. 'I don't know. Seeing him with Rafe, I suppose.'

'Well, he hasn't told me. But would it matter? Whatever he is, he's still the son we love.'

'I suppose. But it doesn't sit well with me.'

'Look, love. If you want to talk about Dan, can we leave it to the morning? It's gone midnight, and you should get off me. You're heavy, and I need to go to the bathroom.'

'OK.'

A few minutes later he was gently snoring.

I, however, was alert, and I knew I wouldn't sleep until I had tied up some ends floating loose in my brain. I got up quietly, wrapped a bathrobe round me and crept downstairs. I located my phone and texted Ronnie Milburn: 'I'm going to Yorkshire. Please contact Martha and ask when's a good time to call.' I could easily have left it till the morning, but within ten minutes I had a text back: 'I jumped the gun. Martha says come any time – just let her know.' He'd added a phone number. I was surprised to hear from him at half past midnight, but I guessed he carried on working whenever he wanted. Unlike most people his working day – and night – wasn't dependent on any clock. I thought for a moment, a sense of unfinished business fuelling my restlessness. Before the moment passed, I composed an email to Mary Hipkin: 'Hoping to come to Yorkshire soon and would love to catch up with you and Peter. Any chance the cottage is free for a couple of days?' After a moment's hesitation I pressed 'send'. For an answer to this I was content to wait till morning. I had a sense that something irrevocable had been set in motion, and I shivered, though it was a warm night. There was excitement and anticipation, certainly, but also a twinge of fear. What was I doing? Could I cope with any fallout? I recalled Ronnie Milburn's rather disdainful reference to my 'nice life'. Yes, I had a nice life, one that many might envy; but the question remained, for now, unanswered – was that nice life what I wanted?

I had a reply from Mary the next morning.

> Dear Fen,
>
> How nice to hear from you. Yes, the cottage is available. Just let me know when you plan to come. I can get bed linen and towels up to the little cottage but may not be able to get out to the shop for supplies. If you're coming by train, you'll probably need to get something on the way. The shops in town will be shut.
>
> I'll leave the key under the mat as usual.
>
> Looking forward to seeing you,
>
> Mary
>
> PS You'll find things a bit different round here.

I wondered momentarily what she meant but thought it likely that she was simply referring to the eight years we hadn't seen each other and the changes that inevitably happen. Now that I had somewhere to stay it was time to contact Martha Chibley. I tried to suppress a shiver of apprehension: if I felt myself to be a fraud, what would she make of me? I waited till nine-thirty, hoping it wasn't too early. John had long since got up, showered, had a cup of coffee and a bowl of cereal and gone to work. He seemed cheerful enough.

I curled up on the sofa in the conservatory and dialled the number Ronnie Millburn had given me. After many rings it was answered by someone out of breath. 'Chibley Farm.' The voice was deep, throaty, even a little harsh, with an odd mixture of accents – Yorkshire, of course, but with hints of an American twang.

'Ms Chibley? My name's Fen Bailey. I wondered if—'

'Mrs Bailey, I am aware of you. Via that dreadful man Ronnie Milburn. I hear you are hoping to visit?'

'Yes, please. When would be a good time?'

There was a pause. 'Can you come on Thursday? Better then – there are some works going on here after that, which may be difficult to negotiate. Thursday, mid-morning. I'll expect you.'

'Thank you—' I began, but then stopped, realising she had rung off. I shook my head – I hadn't even agreed to her proposal. Evidently, she was someone used to getting her own way and not wasting words. But I hardly cared. Now apprehension gave way to anticipation. In a few days I would be back in Yorkshire, riding down the little roads with the wind in my face.

That day I had no gardening commitments, but I would have to tell two clients I wouldn't be around that week. I spent some time making travel arrangements online, choosing a few drawings and paintings for my portfolio and deciding what else to take. Since I would be carrying it on my back, I would have to make do with a bare minimum. I emailed Mary again with dates and times, but she didn't reply.

By the time John came home, everything was in order. I made a particularly nice meal and opened a bottle of wine.

He raised his eyebrows. 'Is it a special occasion?'

'Not exactly,' I said. 'But I am going away for a couple of days, if that's something to celebrate.' I gave him no time to answer but rushed on. 'I spoke to Martha Chibley. I'm going up there on Wednesday, back on Friday. I'll leave some meals for you in the freezer.'

He looked at me across the table, his face serious, almost forbidding. 'No need. I can cater for myself. So how are you getting up there? And where will you stay?'

'I'm going to take my bike on the train. Brant to London, London to Leeds, then the Settle to Carlisle line. It's a long way, so I'm going early. Staying in one of the cottages on the Hipkins' farm, like we used to.'

'You've been busy.' He picked up his glass and said no more.

ON WEDNESDAY MORNING, before he left for work, looking, I thought, a bit washed out, the lines round his mouth more deeply etched than usual, John managed to say goodbye. 'Let me know you've arrived safely,' he said. 'It's wild up there.'

'The forecast is good,' I said. 'I'll text. I don't suppose there's much of a signal where I'm going. But I'll be back before you've realised I've gone.' I phoned Grace, but her answerphone cut in, so I left a brief message telling her I would be away for a couple of days.

It was a long journey, and by the time I boarded the local train the afternoon was waning. I gazed out of the window at the landscape I had once known well, taking in the vast sweep of its hills, the clouds that gathered on its summits, the streams that flowed down into its valleys, and knew in some unfathomable way that I had come home. Brant to the Yorkshire Dales is three hundred and fifty miles, more or less, with two changes, and I'd had to manoeuvre my bike across two crowded city stations. I missed my connection at Leeds because of some issue on the line and had to wait more than an hour. When we'd travelled as a family to stay with the Hipkins for a week or two we'd always come by car, a quite different and more stressful journey with two children impatient and squabbling in the back seat, so this train journey was at once exciting and restful.

At last, with the summer evening fading, draining colour from the hills and fields, the train rumbled to a halt. I shouldered my pack and manhandled my bike onto the platform. The air smelled as different from London and Leeds as it possibly could have, and I took deep lungfuls. Before I left the station I remembered the story of Ruswarp, the elderly border collie who as a paying passenger had been permitted to sign with his pawprint the petition to save the line when it was threatened with closure. Subsequently, the story of his extraordinary fidelity in staying with the body of his master for eleven winter weeks on a Welsh mountain had been instrumental in bringing the line to public attention and raising the funds to make the necessary, and challenging, repairs. As I mounted my bike and started on the road down to the farm, six miles distant, I wondered what dog the Hipkins would have now. I vaguely remembered drawing Old Joe, along with other animals they kept: the Swaledale sheep when they came down for shearing, a shaggy piebald pony called Humbert, and litters of varicoloured cats.

There was little traffic on the road as I swooped down into the valley and took the narrow lane to the Hipkins' farm. I halted on the track above the farmhouse and looked down. It was already getting dark, and the first stars were appearing faintly in the vast deep-blue sky. Just one light showed from the upper floor of the farmhouse, and I decided I would leave seeing Mary and Peter till the morning. I rode gently down the rutted track, pushing my bike through a gate to one side of the cattle grid that marked their boundary and closing it after me with a hank of baling twine. The cottages, two of them, separated by a rough paddock, stood on a low ridge above the farmhouse. I walked up to the nearer, smaller, one and left my bike in the lee of a rickety lean-to with a corrugated roof. True to her word, Mary had left the key under the door mat, and I let myself in.

The smell of the interior brought back instantly the memories of those family holidays, but also of a time even further back when I'd worked on the farm as a teenager. Slightly damp, with the lingering scent of burning wood and dust, it was the smell of another life, almost the life of another person. Was she lost for ever? I wondered. Or could something of those days be retrieved? Perhaps some faint wisp of the past with its uncertainties and frustrations, but also of remembered summers and winters, sunshine on the hilltops and shadow in the valleys, never-ending rain that filled the hollows and seeped into the barns, ferocious winds that scoured the peaks and snow that covered every hummock, fence and gate with a soft quilt of untouched white.

I was enlivened, but also tired physically after the long day and the ride. I saw that Mary had put a pile of linen on the chest, so before I put the kettle on I made up the bed and covered it with a woollen patchwork in many colours. I'd managed to buy some basic supplies on my journey, and I cut a thick slice of bread, slathered it with butter and ate it sitting at the kitchen table with a wedge of cheese and a pot of tea – simple but tasting better than many a meal I'd eaten at restaurants in the city. I remembered to text John briefly.

Despite the warm day the little bathroom on the cottage's north side was chilly, and I had the briefest of washes before going to bed. As I padded over to the window to close the curtains, I noticed a green plastic folder on the scratched and scarred wooden chest of drawers, and I opened it. Mary had obviously left it there when she came to deliver the linen. Inside was a sheaf of papers of different sizes: my childish, almost-forgotten artwork. I hadn't realised she'd kept them, and I turned each one over, remembering, a tight feeling in my throat. Here were drawings from life – Mary at the kitchen sink, peeling potatoes, looking out of the window at the yard deep in mud; a mother cat in a basket on the hearth with three sleeping kittens; Old Joe lying at the foot of an empty chair, his nose on his paws, his liquid eyes open, waiting for Peter's return; five black-and-white-faced sheep in a pen. One or two of these drawings were dated, and I could see that I was about thirteen or fourteen when I drew them. I was astonished at how good they were, by any standards; I hadn't remembered being so accomplished. The lifelikeness and detail spoke of observation I would never have given myself credit for if I hadn't seen them with my own eyes, and a surprising maturity. Perhaps this was what Ronnie Milburn had seen in my sad little watercolours. Thoughtfully, I set them aside and considered that I could perhaps take them with me when I went to see Martha Chibley. They might serve as some kind of credentials, boosting my confidence.

I stretched out in bed with a book open, the bedside lamp making a pool of light on its pages, but before I'd read even a paragraph the deep silence of the valley, broken only by the soft soughing of the wind, plunged me into sleep.

MAYBE IT WAS the quiet, or my long journey the day before, or even being alone without a restless hot body beside me making my sleep shallow and fractured. Whatever it was I slept deeply and long, waking to sunshine softened by the curtains that sucked gently in and out with the breeze. I sat up with an exclamation – I never slept this long. By the time I'd showered and made some tea and toast it was time to ride down to Chibley Farm. I would have to leave seeing the Hipkins till later. I sent a brief text to Mary: *Arrived rather late! The cottage is as lovely as I remember – thank you. I always wanted to stay in this smaller one, especially when John was grumpy and the children noisy! Hope to see you this afternoon if that's OK with you.* Before I set off, she replied: *Looking forward to seeing you.* As I wheeled my bike onto the track, I saw her below me in the farmyard and waved, but she didn't see me.

It was another fine day of strong sun, but with a cool breeze that followed me down the lane to the main road. This I followed for a mile or so, past the road that led into the town, before turning south down another small lane, edged with drystone walls. To my right the river shimmered, a light haze over its surface, and on either side the fields, sloping down to the river or up into the hills, where sheep grazed – the familiar sheep of my youth, sturdy, with curling horns and black and white faces. As I whizzed past, some of the nearer ones looked up from their grazing, but not for long. The lane narrowed, making it difficult to see round corners, but I met no other traffic. I came to a track on the left, winding up into the hillside. Nailed to the post of the inevitable cattle grid was a weathered wooden sign: Chibley Farm. I bumped across the grid because there was no other gate and carried on up a stony track. The grid was redundant: there were no sheep in these fields, which were tussocky and rough with thistles. At the top of the rise there was a cluster of buildings typical of the area: a stone farmhouse surrounded by barns. But as I came closer I saw there was a difference: at the open end of the farmyard another building rose, taller and newer than the rest. It had several skylights in its roof from which the sun flashed as it appeared from behind the passing clouds.

As I approached the farmyard I dismounted and found a wall to prop my bike against. There were several doors in the main house and no one in sight. What was I expecting? A buzzing hive of artistic activity? I shook my head – the place seemed deserted, and a closer look revealed a level of dilapidation. One of the skylights in the building I took to be a studio was cracked; the flagstones of the farmyard were overgrown with weeds; and in one of the smaller barns the roof was partially collapsed. I took my small portfolio off my back, slinging it over one arm, and rapped on the door that looked most like a front door. No one answered, I pushed it gingerly, and it creaked ajar. I put my head round and called out, 'Hello! Anyone home?'

From some distance a voice answered me, but I couldn't make out any words. Eventually I heard a slow gait and a tapping, and the door was pulled wide.

'Well now! Don't stand in the doorway. Come in.'

I stuck out my hand. 'Fen Bailey.'

Instead of shaking it she patted my arm. 'Yes, yes, I know who you are.' She led me further into the room, a huge farm kitchen with a flagged floor, none too clean, a vast range and pots and pans hanging on hooks from the rafters. She waved towards the table and two long bench seats. 'Do sit.'

As I did so she looked down at me. 'I'm Martha Chibley, obviously. Probably not quite what you were expecting. Though who knows what Ronnie would have said about me.'

'I don't really know what I was expecting,' I said. 'But it's good to meet you, Ms Chibley.'

She grunted. 'Martha will do. Would you like tea?'

I said that I would, and I watched her as she made her way to the sink.

She was above middle height, perhaps as tall as me, but bowed. Her walk looked painful, and she leaned on a stick. Her face was not old – I took her to be somewhere in her sixties – but her body had grown heavy and slow, and I saw that her hands were bent. She was dressed entirely in black – a long skirt, a loose shirt and a shawl draped round her shoulders, despite the warmth of the day. Admittedly, it was cool in this great stone kitchen, and perhaps she rarely went outside. With apparent difficulty she filled a kettle and set it to boil, then with an audible hiss of pain came back to the table and manoeuvred herself into a wide wooden chair padded with cushions.

'Would you mind, my dear? I'm very stiff today. It'd be so much quicker if you did it. Milk's in the fridge. Tea and cups in that cupboard.' She waved a hand in the general direction, momentarily closing her eyes.

'Sure.'

I managed to locate everything, including a teapot, and brought it to the table on a tray.

'Thank you.' She looked at me. Her eyes were almost as dark as her clothes, and her hair, cut short, had also obviously once been black but was now streaked with grey. Her skin was pale and barely weathered, but what intrigued me most about this woman was her voice: deep and slightly hoarse, with a local accent that was overlaid with something altogether other. I remembered her American forebears and wondered if perhaps she still had relatives on the other side of the Atlantic. 'You see I am not as able as I would like. Arthritis, of course. Some days are better than others, and today is not a good day.'

'I'm sorry to hear it,' I said, hefting the great teapot and pouring its contents into two china mugs. 'That must make daily life difficult.'

'Well, I can more or less take care of myself,' she said, 'which is just as well, since there's no one else to do it. But can't paint much any more. My hands won't hold a brush for any length of time, and that's surely a curse. But on better days I can still get around. And I still know plenty.' She tapped her temple with a long-nailed finger. 'I can still teach. And I can still tell if someone has any ability.' She picked up her cup in both hands and sipped, looking at me across the rim, her eyes bright with intelligence and, I thought, a hint of malicious humour. 'So, tell me, what brings you to this scene of decay?'

'Ronnie Milburn. I don't exactly know why he said I should come, but he seemed to think I should meet you.' I leaned forward. 'I want to learn,' I said with some urgency. 'I want to find out if I can draw and paint the things that are in my head. But I am surprised. You're right – it's different here. I don't know what I thought it would be like, but not like this.'

'Oh?'

'Yes, I thought there would be people – students, artists – maybe teachers. I imagined a busy, active place.'

'Mm. And I guess,' she said thoughtfully, 'you didn't expect to see weeds and broken windows and holes in the roof.'

'I suppose not.'

'Well, Chibley Farm isn't what it used to be. There's no money to speak of. My solicitor likes to send me letters telling me how bad things are with the accounts, as if I didn't know. Yes, there used to be students, a few of them, back in the day. I'm surprised Ronnie didn't warn you.'

'He kind of did,' I said. 'But I think he hasn't been here for a while. And that makes me wonder what he thought I could do here.'

'I'll tell you.' She fixed me with her bright black stare. 'It's what you make of it, like most things. I can help you. And this place still has resources. A great barn of a studio full of stuff – canvases of all sizes, frames, paint, brushes of every kind you can think of. It's not free – the deal always was, if you use it you pay for it. That's how Chibley paid for itself even before the original money ran out.'

I looked around. 'Where is all this stuff?'

'Ah, you must have seen the big building, the newer one, up on the east side. Take no mind to the broken skylight – a man's coming tomorrow to fix it. It'll cost me, but it has to be done. Besides, it was me that broke it, trying to open it. That building is in good shape. It's this one, my living quarters, that's gone downhill. I'll show you later, if you're interested.'

'I am, of course,' I said. 'But puzzled too. Would I be the only student? That's if I decide to come, if I can afford to, if I can organise it.'

'No. At least not all the time. People come and go. People who've been coming and going over a number of years – there aren't too many new ones nowadays. They come for their own reasons, stay for a week or a month or a summer, do some work, put some money into the account, keep the place ticking over for a while. Once in a while someone comes to teach and pay their dues that way. My friend Audley is one of them. But the art world has changed. I guess Ronnie might have alluded to that. He's done well, but he's canny, and he has a wife who supports him. He's not the only one of my former students who's made a name for himself, though – a few here and there, both sides of the pond.' She named a sculptor I had heard of, and I was startled. 'Oh, yes, there are a few Chibley alumni who've made a mark,' she said, a hint of fierce pride in her voice.

Distinctly unsettled by the reality of Chibley Farm, I was nevertheless intrigued. I lifted the teapot with a querying look, Martha nodded, and I refilled her cup and my own. 'Ronnie said you'd tell me how this place came to be. It seems an unusual choice of site for a school of art.'

'Ah, well, there are reasons.' Martha sipped her tea. 'About fifteen miles away from here, north of the road, there was a remote farm, sheep farmers time out of mind. I say *was* – when the original family died out the farm passed to someone else – it was only ever rented. Anyhow, that was the Chibleys. My grandfather Robert was born in 1880, married a local woman and raised four sons. They had many acres of unforgiving land and ran maybe a thousand sheep. They thought their boys, and their grandchildren and great-grandchildren right down the line, would carry on working the land into the future, breeding prizewinners and establishing a grand reputation. Three of the sons did indeed carry on the family tradition but son number three, Alfred, had other ideas. At twenty-one he emigrated to America, slaved away in some terrible jobs, finally worked his way up to a position of responsibility in a company making and selling shoes, made himself indispensable and earned serious money. The old man who owned the business had no heirs and he left it to Alfred, who could now afford to move in polite society. At the age of forty he married the only daughter of another very successful businessman who'd despaired of ever finding a husband for his daughter, who was in her thirties, considered to be on the shelf as well as a little peculiar. This woman was a painter and – shall we say – a bit of a bohemian. From what I can gather she didn't do anything very scandalous, but her habit of outspokenness, her eccentric clothing and so on, gained her something of a reputation among the starchier matrons. "Thank heavens," they thought, "safely married at last to that respectable man Alfred Chibley. We don't know where he sprang from, but he's extremely rich and very well-mannered so his forebears can remain a mystery. What he sees in her we can't think. Nobody would call her a beauty."'

I had to smile at Martha's rendition of the respectable matrons' speech, and she smiled back, obviously enjoying her story.

'Fact is, though, Alfred adored her – Georgina. They had two sons, Robert and William, and seemed happy. There came a time when Georgina persuaded Alfred to take a trip back to the Old Country. She wanted to see where he'd grown up. From the minute she got here, Georgina fell in love with the Dales. The light was perfect for her painting, and she spent many hours out in all weathers with the easel and her little stool, drawing, painting, taking it all in. The boys meanwhile ran wild, and Alfred visited his surviving brother who was still on the original farm – Northend. The old folks had long since died, one brother was running his own sheep elsewhere, and the other had drunk himself to death. So the story goes.

'Year after year Georgina wanted to come back to Yorkshire, and Alfred indulged her. Eventually he bought a plot of land with a couple of buildings on it, and he improved them and expanded and built the studio – far too big for Georgina, but that was Alfred. It was quite something back then – I have photos – not like you see it now. Well, to cut this garbled yarn short, one of the Chibley lads shared his mother's fondness for this place and when they all went back to the States he stayed, married a local girl and worked it as a farm for a while. That was

William, my father. Then old Alfred died, and one of the stipulations of his will was that Chibley Farm should be run as an art school. It was Georgina's dying wish, and he was ever the fond husband. My dad was no artist, but the gene passed to me, and here I am, the sole survivor, hanging on and remembering a more glorious past.' She spoke ironically, but I detected both pride and sorrow in her voice. Then she sighed. 'Well, I guess it'll all get sold one of these days. I don't have anyone to leave it to, and there are debts to pay. I have an idea I might want to go back to the States to visit my family there – a few cousins – before I get too crippled. Meanwhile we totter along, the farm and me, as best we can.' She looked over at me, her gaze keen. 'So, tell me, what's burning in you?'

I was startled. 'Burning?'

'Well, isn't it?'

I thought. 'Not so much burning, more battering,' I said. 'Needing to get out and breathe. Just being here in Yorkshire feels like a liberation. If I could paint as well…' I let the words hang unfinished.

She nodded towards my little folder. 'You got something to show me?'

'Uh, nothing of any weight.' I squirmed a little; my work, such as it was, seemed so flimsy next to an internationally recognised sculptor, not to mention Ronnie Milburn.

She stretched out one clawed hand, and I pushed the folder towards her. 'The watercolours are the most recent,' I said. 'There's a painting of my cat. And then these drawings – I did them when I was a teenager.'

She spread them out on the table. 'You kept them? Why?'

'No, I'd forgotten all about them. I'm staying with some people I used to know, way back. Because this whole area is familiar to me. When I arrived late yesterday evening, I found these left for me. She must have kept them all these years.'

'Where are you staying?'

'One of the cottages at Whitepost Farm. We used to have holidays there, year after year, when my children were young. But I go back further than that with the Hipkins.'

Her head jerked up. 'Mary Hipkin?'

'Yes. You know her?'

'To say hello to. Not well. I know of her.' She went back to her silent study of my drawings. I wondered at her words – what did she mean, she knew 'of' Mary?

After what seemed a long silence, she looked up. 'You were – what? – fourteen? When you did these? They're good, full of promise.' Her hand fell on my adult work. 'A promise not yet fulfilled, I'd say.' A tiny smile lightened her features. 'Maybe there's more to come. Maybe that's why you've come all this way.'

'That's what I'm hoping.'

'So,' she said, 'what's this thing inside you that's trying to escape?'

I felt my face heat up. 'It seems childish to describe it that way,' I said. 'Melodramatic.' I took a deep breath. 'The book of Revelation. I'd like to try something big. Angels, books, horses, elders, mountains, fiery stars, apocalyptic creatures. That sort of thing.'

'There's no need to sound so apologetic,' she said. 'No shame in thinking big. But you know it's all been done before.'

I laughed. 'Endlessly, past and present. But not by me.'

She smiled. 'Well, as to that, I guess everything's been done before, and the Bible sure is a fabulous source of ideas. See that laptop? Can you push it over to me?' I did so, and with some difficulty she opened it up. 'I should warn you, if you do decide to come here and you bring your own device, the signal can be very patchy. You'd probably be OK here, but up at the Hipkins' it'll be next to nothing. The hills get in the way.' She tapped at the keyboard awkwardly with her stiff fingers, muttering and cursing. 'Come and see.' I got up and stood behind her, leaning on the back of her chair. She had pulled up image after image of artwork based on scenes from Revelation. Some of them were familiar to me from my own hesitant forays. Together in silence we studied them, scrolling down to more and more interpretations.

'Which ones do you like?' she asked.

'The older ones,' I said. 'Medieval wall paintings, for example. The ones that set out to instruct rather than dazzle or horrify. The ones where you sense they sprang from awe, from faith, from a momentary vision of God's purposes, maybe even a desire to warn. Some of these more modern ones seem to glory in the weirdness, the gruesomeness, the shock element. They seem almost pagan. I realise Revelation is difficult, but I don't like to see Scripture used like that. It's dishonest, cynical.'

'And is that what you want? To instruct, to warn?'

I shook my head. 'I don't know. I don't even know if I am capable of making it work. Maybe it's just a pipe dream.'

'Persistence and hard work. If there's any recipe for achievement, that's it. You'll only find out if you try.' Her eyes narrowed. 'I assume you've actually *read* Revelation?'

'I'm rereading it now. Not everyone's idea of a bedtime story.'

She gave a little throaty chuckle. 'Indeed not. Enough to give you nightmares, some of it.' Abruptly, using the stick and the chair arm, she heaved herself up. 'Would you like to see the studio now? Then I'm afraid you'll have to go. I have an appointment this afternoon.' She blew out her breath. 'Not one I relish.'

She led me out of the door and slowly, painfully across the farmyard and up a gravelled path. She took a bunch of keys out of her capacious skirt pocket and slid one into the lock of the studio's main door. 'There's a lot of capital outlay in here,' she said. 'Things I can't afford to replace. And even here in this pleasant place there are thieves with eyes and ears everywhere.' She pushed the door open and gestured for me to enter.

It was an enormous space, lit from above by four huge skylights, one of which was cracked. Under it on the floor was a stain left by rain. There were also windows high up in the long walls, running along the length of the building on both sides. The room was empty except for a stack of easels leaning up against the far wall and a few paint-stained rags on the floor. At the far end there were two tall doors. 'Materials in there,' Martha said. 'Shelves, cupboards. Most things most people want. If it's something a bit unusual you bring it with you. Sometimes I can order stuff in. What do you think?'

'It's a wonderful space,' I murmured. 'No partitions? If there are other people you work together?'

'Partitions would ruin the light. Anyway, like I told you, these days not too many people come here.'

I was silent, imagining having this enormous place to myself, the light pouring in, no sound but the sounds of the natural world. The prospect made the hairs on my arms prickle.

It was almost as if Martha had read my mind. 'If you found yourself in here,' she said quietly, 'with a nice stretched canvas, blank and waiting, what would be the first thing you'd do?'

I smiled. 'Before I got to that point I'd have made some drawings. Otherwise, I might ruin that pristine canvas with my first blob of paint. I think what I'd do would be St John on Patmos, looking up and seeing an angel there. That's the beginning – and it anchors the visions to the ordinary world.'

She nodded. 'I get it.'

'Look, Martha,' I said. 'I should go. I'm grateful for your time – and your stories. I've got a lot to think about. Whatever I decide to do, I'll be in touch.'

'You've come a long way,' she said. 'I hope you don't feel it's been wasted.' We left the building, and she locked the door, pocketing the keys.

'No, I don't. I'm very glad to have met you.' And I meant it.

I kept pace with her as we returned to the house to pick up my bike.

'I guess,' she said slowly, 'you haven't caught up with the Hipkins yet.'

'No, I slept unusually late.'

She nodded and heaved a deep sigh. 'Well, if you haven't seen them for a while you'll find some changes. But it's not for me to go on about that.' She turned to face me. 'Thank you for coming, Fen Bailey. Or is it Fennel Mayne?'

I blinked – but then I realised she'd seen the signature on my early drawings.

'I suppose I'm both of those people,' I said.

'Maybe you'll find out,' she said cryptically. 'Have a good journey back. I hope we meet again.'

As I RODE back to Whitepost the air seemed to thicken and close in, and I saw clouds building up on the hills to the north – just where I was headed. I hastened my pace as I pedalled along the main road, through the town, then upwards to the lane that led, finally, to Whitepost Farm. I was still a mile away, most of it uphill, when the first splashes of rain pattered down, growing in strength and helped along by a wind that came in random gusts. With the wind and rain in my face I slogged up to the next crest and down the other side. As suddenly as it had begun the rain stopped and a weak sun filtered through the escaping cloud. The wind had changed direction and now gave me speed, but of course by now I was thoroughly wet.

As I rode up the last incline and looked down at the farm I saw Mary, sitting outside at a small table. I raised a hand in greeting and freewheeled down the last slope. She'd been peeling potatoes into an enamel bowl; now she jumped up and came to greet me. I threw my bike down and hugged her, a small shock shivering through me as I felt how small she was, how thin she had become.

'Fen, dear! Lovely to see you! But why are you so wet?'

'It rained on my way back. You've not had any rain?'

'Not a drop. But I'll not be surprised to see those clouds back again by nightfall.' She looked me up and down. 'You look well. And I swear you've grown.'

I laughed. 'I don't think so. Maybe you've shrunk.'

'More than likely. Why don't you pop up to the cottage and get out of those wet things, and I'll make us some lunch.'

'That sounds great. I'm ravenous after all that pedalling uphill. I guess Peter's out on the farm somewhere?'

I saw her expression change and felt a passing unease. 'No, he's indoors. See you in a moment.' She went into the house and closed the door.

I picked up my bike and pushed it up to the cottage. Inside, I peeled off my wet clothes and draped them over the shower rail. As I dressed in dry things I wondered: something seemed amiss. All the hints about things having changed from both Mary and Martha, but no details; the look on Mary's face when Peter was mentioned. And why was he indoors on a fine June day, not in some far field somewhere fixing a fence?

As I approached the house Mary reappeared. She laid a hand on my arm. 'Fen, wait. There's something I need to tell you before you come in.'

Now I was worried. 'Mary, what on earth is it?' I looked at her more closely, seeing the pallor of her face, the deep lines, the hollow look in her eyes. Yes, it had been eight years – but this was not the hearty countrywoman I remembered, full of wry humour, strong in the face of any disaster.

'It's Peter. He is very bad. Just after Christmas it was, snow on the ground, about six inches, with more to come, and he went up into the high field to find some ewes he wanted to bring down. Old Joe was with him, of course. When it got dusky and they didn't come back I wasn't unduly concerned; Pete knows this place inside out. But when it got properly dark I did start to worry, and then I saw flashing lights way up on the hilltops, and the next thing I know old Will Wharton from Tubside comes haring down on his quad bike all of a lather. Seems he was coming home when he came across the dog, knew something must be wrong if Pete wasn't with him. Followed Joe and there was Peter, collapsed by a hedge. It was a mercy Will found him when he did, or he'd have died of exposure. As it was Will by some miracle managed to get a signal and call an ambulance. The weather didn't help, of course, but they got to him, and did whatever they do before taking him down to the hospital. He'd had a stroke, Fen, right out of the blue.' She bit her lip, and a tear trickled down her cheek. 'Trouble was, he'd been there goodness knows how long before they found him, and the damage was done. He's in a poorly way, you'll see.'

Horrified, I squeezed her shoulder. 'Oh, Mary. I'm so sorry. Poor Peter, poor you.' I remembered Peter Hipkin the last time we'd been here, in his sixties but hale and vigorous, running his sheep and working his farm, bluff and ruddy.

'Well, I didn't know what to say when you emailed,' Mary said. 'But I had to warn you now. He's not the man he was. Needs a lot of help just to do ordinary things. He can walk, but he spends most of his time in his old armchair with Joe at his feet. And Joe's old now too, of course. Never leaves Peter's side unless the nurse is here and we've got Pete in the bathroom.'

'You have some help?'

'Just once a week. She's very good, but sometimes she can't get here when the weather's bad.'

I was aghast. 'And then what?'

Mary smiled faintly. 'Ah, well, I manage. I keep him warm and fed and watered, build up the fire, put some music on when he's fretful, talk to him though he hardly answers. He's a big man – I can't get him in the shower by myself, but a bit of dirt never hurt anyone, and he's not going anywhere to get muddy. But come in.'

I followed her, a feeling of dread leaden in my gut. 'Will he know me, Mary?'

'I don't know. He recognises Diane, the nurse, and the odd neighbour that comes. Folk have been good – people bring me what I need, and I get deliveries from the supermarket in town.'

I paused in the doorway. 'What about the farm?'

'I'll tell you all that later. And you must tell me about yourself and those children of yours.'

I followed her indoors. Here was the homely kitchen I remembered, barely changed, the big, well-worn table taking up the middle with pots and jars and ladles ranged in rows. 'I've been bottling,' Mary said. 'Remember that old cherry tree on the south side? It's fruited well this year.'

'I can smell it,' I said. 'Unmistakable.'

Against the far wall, not far from the hearth, Peter sat in an enormous armchair, swaddled in blankets. 'He feels the cold, just sitting there,' Mary said. At his feet lay his dog, the most recent in a long line of Old Joes, old himself now, his muzzle grey, his eyes rheumy. As we came in Peter didn't stir, but the dog lifted his head from his paws and his tail twitched. I had a heavy feeling in my chest as I went up to Peter, first greeting the dog with a scratch behind his feathery ears. 'Remember me, Joe?' I took Peter's heavy hand in mine. 'Hello, Peter.'

For a moment he seemed to be asleep; then to my surprise his eyes – dark brown, bloodshot – flew open. 'Little Fennel Mayne – is it you?' His voice was unexpectedly strong, and hearing it the years unravelled. I hadn't thought he would know me, and to have this instant recognition brought tears to my eyes. But then he seemed to withdraw, moved restlessly in his chair and dropped my hand; a moment later his eyes closed.

'That happens sometimes,' Mary said, her voice low. 'He has moments when he seems almost normal, like his old self. Then it goes again. It breaks my heart.' She came to stand by me, looking down at her husband. 'Still, that was a surprise, wasn't it? How long has it been? Ten years?'

'Eight, I think.'

'Well, it's long enough. And he knew you.'

'Yes,' I said shakily. 'I didn't think he would.'

'Well now,' Mary said briskly. 'Come and have something to eat. I'll warm some soup up for Peter when he wakes.'

We sat at the table, and Mary cut slices of her own bread and handed me cheese and ham and chutney. There was a jug of apple juice on the table, and Mary poured it into two glasses. 'I've a friend in town with apple trees in her garden and a nice sheltering wall,' she said. 'She says she always has too much for herself, so she brings me gallons of it.'

As we ate and drank she asked after the family, and I told her about Dan going to America and Alice studying history and John in a managerial position these days. Then she looked up at me, a small frown between her brows. 'So tell me, if you care to, what's brought you back, all the way up here, for just two days? And bringing your bicycle on a train! Surely too short for a holiday, all on your own. I can't think you have just come to see Peter and me, not after all these years.'

'No,' I admitted. 'I had a purpose, and of course I'll tell you. But I did want to see you and Peter, very much, and I'm glad I have, especially seeing him as he is. You never said a word, Mary. A Christmas card as ever this year, and no hint.'

She shrugged. 'I didn't see the point. What could you do? But you were going to tell me why you're here.'

I took a sip of sweet juice. 'I've been to see a woman called Martha Chibley.'

'Ah.'

'You know her? She said she knew you – actually she said she knew *of* you. I didn't quite get what she meant by that. Now maybe I do.'

'This is a small place. She probably knows something of our situation. And sometimes she comes to our church.'

This was a surprise. 'Really? St James's? Or is it the chapel you go to?'

'No, the church in town, when I can. And she's not always there. She's not very mobile, is she? But we'll say hello, how are you, and talk about the weather. She asks after Peter.' Suddenly her eyes widened. 'It's that art place, isn't it? That's why you're here. But word is it's very run down.'

I nodded. 'It is. On its last legs, according to Martha. Running out of money, hardly any students.' I told her about Ronnie Milburn. 'But Mary, you must have second sight or something. You left those old drawings of mine for me to find.'

Mary smiled. 'Nothing mysterious about that,' she said. 'When I knew you were coming I looked them out. Thought you'd like to have them.'

'Funnily enough, Martha liked them.' I sighed. 'I came to see if I might study here. But I don't think there's much teaching going on – apart from Martha herself. On the other hand, to be here again would be wonderful. I can breathe here. Maybe I can even make something here, who knows what, but I want to try. I don't know, Mary. It's a big decision.'

Frail as she seemed to have become, Mary had lost none of her perceptiveness. 'What about your husband?'

I felt heat rise in my face. 'What about him?'

'Would you be coming here all by yourself?'

'Yes, of course. He has his job. But it wouldn't be for ever. Maybe a year – and I'd go back once in a while.'

'Hm. What does he think?'

'He doesn't know. Because I don't know myself – not yet.'

Mary fell silent, her lips pursed. I knew better than to say how her situation, and Peter's, might sway my decision. 'Well,' she said at last, 'I may have my thoughts, but I'll not share them. It's not my place to advise you.'

'Mary, that's nonsense!' I said. I reached over the table, squeezed her work-roughened hand. 'You and Peter were more parents to me than my blood-kin. Especially at a time when I needed guidance, and they were never strong on that. If I know anything about right and wrong, how to behave with people, so many things, it's down to you two. I'd say you have every right.'

'I suppose so. They were lovable people, your mum and dad, but a bit away with the fairies, weren't they? And you were running wild. Pete and I could see you'd end up in trouble.'

'If I didn't it was thanks to you.'

'I don't know about that,' Mary said modestly. She got up from her chair and started to gather our empty plates, then she paused. 'So, is all not well with you and John?'

I groaned. 'On the nail as ever!' I pushed my chair back, collected the jug and glasses. We went together to the sink. As the water ran into the bowl, I took a deep breath. 'I guess we've just diverged,' I said. 'Running in parallel, like a lot of married people do after a while. No real connection. We have very little in common except the children, and they're at an age when they'll soon fly the nest. He likes the city – I hate it. It stifles me. He likes glamorous holidays – I don't. We even have different ideas about what worship should be like! He's an intelligent man, but I don't think he has the first clue what goes on in my head. He thinks my art is a nice little hobby. He often finds me embarrassing.' I tailed off; perhaps I had said too much.

Mary was silent as she put on a pair of pink rubber gloves and started to wash the dishes. I stood by, a tea towel in my hand. 'So if you came here,' she said quietly, 'would it be running away?'

'Maybe it would. I haven't thought long-term. I probably couldn't afford to stay for ever anyway. I've got a little pot of money saved from my gardening job, but it'll soon run out. And then what?'

Mary stacked the dishes, wet and steaming, on the draining-board. 'What indeed?'

She seemed to have nothing more to say on the subject, and I gratefully let it lie.

'I have to go home tomorrow,' I said. 'I'll take the early train. But I'm here for the rest of today. There must be something I can do to help.' I finished stacking the plates, now dry, and folded the tea towel.

Mary was drying her hands. 'There may be something.' She smiled. 'That's if you remember anything of your shepherding days.'

'I'm not at all sure about that,' I said, alarmed. 'I wouldn't want too big a responsibility.'

Her smile faded. 'Big doesn't come into it, not any more. When I saw that Pete wasn't ever going to be able to run the farm, I had to make some decisions. I could have done it, just about, but I have to look after him and it's a full-time job. So I sold the machinery, most of it. Just a few bits left now, and I kept the quad bike. It's the only thing that'll cope when the weather's bad. And I sold the sheep too.'

I was shocked. 'All of them? But you had so many!'

She nodded. 'Almost nine hundred, yes. But no, not all of them. Peter was so anxious about the farm, especially at first. I had to keep him on an even keel. I kept eighteen sheep, old ewes, not much use for anything, but it meant I could tell him we still had a flock and not lie. Plus, I needed something for Sadie to do.'

'Sadie?'

For a moment her face lit up. 'Sadie is my dog. I trained her myself, and she is a first-class sheepdog. You can't have a sheepdog and no sheep. I'd have to sell her, and I can't bear to do that. She's four years old, small, very fast, very clever. Some people say she's the best dog around these parts.' Her pride rang in her voice. 'I could sell her, and she'd fetch a good price. But I won't, not if I can help it. Sadie is my friend and my comfort, just as Old Joe is for Peter. The eighteen ewes are her job, and she takes it very seriously. Of course it's not enough, so sometimes I lend her to a trusted friend who needs an extra dog. That's where she is now, helping Will Wharton, our neighbour. He should be bringing her back any time.'

I shook my head. 'Eighteen ewes, Mary. After nine hundred.'

She nodded. 'I know. But it's where we are. And at least selling the flock's put a bit of money in the bank, which will give me options when I need them.'

'So what's this shepherding job you have in mind for me?'

She patted my arm. 'Nice and easy. Sadie'll do all the work. I can remind you about the calls, and you'll have my whistle in case she gets out of earshot. You'll enjoy a brisk walk up onto the high field – or wherever those ewes have got to. I want them back down here so I can check them over before shearing time.'

'Are you sure I'm up to it?' I said doubtfully.

For the first time I heard her laugh, and it took me back to the old Mary. 'I don't suppose you are. But Sadie is. Think of it as keeping Sadie company and being on hand in case of anything happening a dog can't cope with.'

'Such as?' I said, frowning.

'One of those daft ewes falling in the river.' At my look of horror she chuckled, her eyes gleaming. 'Go on with you, it won't happen. Sadie knows what to do with her eighteen old ladies. Come and sit back down. I'll make us a pot of tea while we wait for Will to come back with Sadie. And you can tell me what those parents of yours are up to.'

I sat back at the table while she filled the kettle. 'They're still out there,' I said. 'In New Zealand. It amazes me they've made a go of their orchard, them being so very impractical. Maybe I've misjudged them all these years – my mother at least had the sense to do something positive with what her father left her. And they were as generous as ever, you know – they shared it with Nigel and me. It allowed Nigel to set up in business and helped John and me get a bigger house.'

Mary brought the teapot to the table. 'Have you ever been out there to see them?'

I shook my head. 'I never have. We write to each other once in a while, so I know they're well, and have friends. They'd be happy wherever they were, I think.'

'Hm,' Mary said. 'That's not something you can say of many folk.'

We sipped our tea in silence, busy with our own thoughts.

As I SAT on the train, I was almost grateful for the torrents of rain that fell in sheets from a glowering sky, washing down the train windows, obscuring the landscape. Especially after my hours on the hills with Sadie the previous afternoon I knew I would miss the eye-stretching views, even after so short a visit. My heart leaned towards these sweeping hills, their summits crowned with gleams of sun and clouds swept along unresisting before the wind, and the valleys dark and secret, hiding fast-flowing streams. Whether I succeeded or not in producing anything approaching art, much as I wanted to, I knew beyond doubt that this was home. But how could I reasonably achieve it – this escape, this homecoming? There was so much in the way, not least twenty-four years of marriage, and all the life that had grown up around us; an encrustation of habit.

The train rumbled into the station at Leeds. I had forty-five minutes before my connection, and I sat on the station, my bike at my side, and in my hands a sandwich and a paper cup of almost-drinkable coffee purchased from a café on the platform. The further south I travelled, or so it seemed, the heavier became the weight that had settled inside me as soon as I'd boarded the train.

I wiped my buttery fingers on the paper napkin supplied by the café and looked up at the crowds of people swarming in every direction, their expressions intent, perhaps focusing on their destination and what awaited them, just as I was. Were any of them as full of conflict? Of a wearisome mixture of anger, longing, guilt and mournful repentance? I would never know.

I thought back to the previous day, and it seemed like another time altogether, existing almost apart from my current universe. Mary and I were on our second cup of tea when we heard an engine approaching, the squeal of brakes, the clanging of a door and a loud halloo.

Mary got up, smoothing down her skirt. 'That'll be Will now.'

I followed her out into the farmyard.

'Hello, Will. All done, all well?'

A large man with a red face and a much-patched jacket on top of muddy overalls was leaning on a beaten-up four-by-four towing a small trailer. 'Yes, all good, Mary, and thanks for the loan of your dog. She runs well with my Meg – they make a good team.' He glanced at me, and for a moment he frowned, as if in recognition, but then his face cleared. I had no memory of him. Mary introduced us, and we shook hands.

'Well, we'd better let her out,' Will said. 'She's a bit mucky. We had a bit of a squall half an hour ago.' He went to the trailer and unlatched the tailgate. A black-and-white dog sprang out and trotted to sit at Mary's feet, but then something happened that gave me gooseflesh. Sadie turned her head and fixed her dark brown eyes on me, unblinking, her gaze penetrating. I felt a strong, unmistakable moment of profound connection with this creature I had never met before, and a shudder passed through me. I tried to tell myself I was being fanciful, that my imagination was running away with me, but the sensation was so powerful that these arguments seemed as flimsy as wet straw.

'Are you all right, Fen?' Mary said. 'You look a bit peculiar.'

'I'm not sure,' I mumbled. 'It was something about the way Sadie looked at me. Weird!' I forced a laugh. 'Take no notice, I'm probably seeing things.' Then Sadie surprised us both; she got up, walked over to me and put her nose in my hand.

'That's really unusual,' Mary said. 'She's normally quite wary of strangers, isn't she, Will?'

'That she is,' Will agreed. 'I must be off, Mary. Bess will be wondering where I've got to. It all took longer than I expected. I'll see you soon. Don't hesitate to call if there's anything you need.' He nodded affably to me and climbed back into his car. A moment later after some crunching of the gears he was rocking down the track, waving his hand out of the window.

Sadie was still sitting at my feet; I leaned down and stroked her silky head, and she thumped her tail on the ground.

'She must have a drink before she goes out again,' Mary said. 'I doubt she stopped long enough to drink out of a stream. Come, girl.'

I was wearing trainers suitable for cycling. 'You'll ruin those,' Mary said. 'Especially if it's a bit wet up there. I'll get a pair of Peter's boots for you and some thick socks to pad them out a bit. I think my boots will be too small. And you'll need a coat up on the hilltops. I've got something you can borrow.'

Twenty minutes later, we'd gone through some of the commands for the dog and I was kitted out against the weather. 'It seems all very peaceful now,' Mary said, 'But you know how fast it can change.' She opened the door, and Sadie stood waiting, ready to spring away, her ears pricked, her tongue lolling. 'She'll know where to go, but I expect the ewes to be up on the high field, maybe a bit scattered. I'll see you in an hour or two. Enjoy your freedom while it lasts.'

THE TIME I spent with Sadie out on the hills reminded me that it was, after all, possible to feel pure joy. The June sun was warm, the breeze cool and scented with crushed grass and growing things. The shadows of the clouds slid across the slanting fields, bringing a chill as they momentarily obscured the sun, and I remembered that this place could be unforgiving in November or February – but the beauty of it was still there, if bleaker. Sadie ran before me, stopping every so often to make sure I was following. I felt a pleasant ache in my calves as we trudged uphill; the jacket grew too warm and I took it off, knotting the sleeves round my waist. I breathed deeply, feeling the freshness enter my lungs together with a sense of liberty that I'd almost forgotten existed. Sadie seemed to know exactly where she was going, but from time to time she stopped, lifted her head and scented the air. The going was rough: there were walls that had partly fallen, and small swift streams, and I was glad of the stick Mary had lent me.

It took us half an hour to reach the crest of a ridge from which we could see down into valleys that stretched away to the north. We had seen no sign of life on our way up except for a few high hovering birds of prey, but now sheep were visible, dotted about some way below us. Sadie looked at me. 'Are those your eighteen old ladies?' I said. The sense of connection with the dog I had felt earlier was still strong.

As if I had uttered some command, Sadie sprang away, her speed astonishing, a low, black-and-white blur against the green. I watched in admiration as she gathered the scattered ewes, patiently circling, persuading the stragglers to join their fellows, until they formed a tight, tidy mass with the dog behind them, sometimes dashing, sometimes trotting, sometimes down on her belly inching forward, but always intent. They came closer, saw me and began to shy away, skittering apart. I stood to one side; Sadie gathered them in again, and together we turned, climbed the ridge and unhurriedly descended the long hillside. Sadie took us on an oblique path this time, passing a stout barn with an open stone-walled enclosure to one side. Here she stopped by a low trough and drank. Then on we went, me trudging along beside the sheep, but at a respectful distance, Sadie focused on keeping them moving all together without haste or panic, until the farm and its outbuildings came back in sight. She looked at me, and I knew she wanted me to open and close the necessary gates. It was all the work that was required of me, a humbled and useless shepherd. I had no doubt she could have done it all without me, except perhaps for the gates. In minutes the sheep were penned in a paddock by the barn, and Mary was there with hay.

'You were right,' I said. 'This dog of yours is a wonder.'

Now the London train was sliding into the station, and with a sigh I climbed on and found a place for my bike. The train was crowded, but I managed to slip into a seat; luckily I had no bulky luggage, just my backpack. For some miles I looked out of the window, then I set myself to try and prepare what I would say to John, but eventually the tedium of the journey sent me to sleep. By the time I'd found the right platform and waited for my connection back to Brant, it was early evening before I wheeled my bike up our drive and put it away in the shed.

I'd expected to find John either in his study or not at home at all; sometimes he stopped off at a local bar with colleagues on a Friday evening. To my surprise he was mowing the back lawn, his work shirt open at the neck and sleeves rolled up. I watched him for a while as he pushed the mower down the grass, his back to me, noticing for the first time that he was getting a bit of a bald patch on the crown of his head. He'd always had a good head of hair and was even a bit vain about it. I felt a twinge then – of sadness, perhaps of guilt – that I was going to disturb his peace, and wondered what exactly I should say. Then he turned the mower to retrace his steps and saw me, and for a moment he had the strangest look on his face, as if he didn't know who I was. I walked over to him.

'You're back, then,' he said. 'Was it worth it?'

'Yes,' I said. 'I'll tell you about it later. Have you thought about anything for dinner?'

He shook his head. 'I thought I'd get a takeaway.'

'Good idea. Shall I order something? Then by the time you finish the lawn it'll be here.'

He nodded, and I turned and went into the house. I had the sense that the evening was not going to be easy.

We ate our meal with little talk. I opened a bottle of wine, thinking it might make conversation easier – hoping at the same time that the emotional temperature might not be unduly raised. John raised an eyebrow but accepted a glass without comment. He answered my questions about work, and I asked him if he'd heard from Alice – he hadn't. 'You've only been away two days,' he said.

I fiddled with my fork, staring down at the tablecloth. 'It seems longer.'

'So, tell me about it. You want to go there, don't you? It's what you've wanted all along, isn't it?'

I took a deep breath and looked up at him. He was holding something in, something powerful. 'No, because I didn't know what I would find when I got there. I admit I wanted something, but I couldn't have said what. But now that I know, at least a bit, yes, I want to go and learn. But it's not just that.' I told him about the situation with the Hipkins: Peter's illness, the difficulties Mary was experiencing, the break-up of the farm. 'I didn't know any of this before I went. And I can help them, I want to help. I'm strong, I've done farm work before, and yes, I know it was a long time ago.'

John made an impatient sound. 'Why do you have to go to Yorkshire? Can't you do good works in Brant, if that's what you want?'

'*Good works?* Whatever are you talking about? Peter and Mary aren't *good works*, they're old friends, people I owe a lot to.'

After a moment of baleful staring he said, 'When would you want to go? And how long for?'

'Soon. As soon as I can make arrangements, tidy things up here. I don't know how long for – maybe a year in the first instance. I want to learn, John. And I think Martha can teach me. But I'd come home, of course. At least for Christmas.'

'Why now? What's the hurry?'

'Chibley Farm is on its uppers as a business. I don't know the details. Martha may decide to sell up, go to the States to be with family. She's not a well woman. If I don't go now, I may have lost the only opportunity.' Getting slightly desperate now, I ploughed on. 'And I've got my own money. I wouldn't be needing any financial support. I've saved up every penny from my gardening work, five or six years' worth.'

He made a dismissive gesture. 'It's not a question of money. You've never lacked for anything, have you?'

'No, of course not, but—'

He cut me off. 'Fen, let's be honest – for once. Are you leaving me?'

'What? Um, no – that is, as far as I have a plan at all, that isn't in it.'

He laughed, a brief, humourless bark. 'Seems to me I'm not in your plan at all.'

I had nothing to say to this, because he had, probably unknowingly, spoken the truth, and it was frightening. After almost a quarter of a century the man I had seen almost as a saviour, whom in the beginning I had adored without question, had somehow, quietly and imperceptibly, become irrelevant.

'Look,' I said, trying to be calm, keeping my voice low. 'It's what I want, what I need. I have to go, and if not with your blessing then at least it would be nice to have a measure of understanding.' A cynical thought struck me, and I spoke without thinking. 'You can explain my absence as a kind of sabbatical, to which you've generously agreed. You'll look very noble and self-sacrificing.'

He threw down his napkin. 'I've had enough of this conversation. You'll do whatever you want, I have no doubt. Perhaps at some point you can let me know what you have in mind for my birthday and our anniversary. On the other hand, they are probably of no interest to you.'

He got up abruptly, scraping his chair on the floor.

'John, that's ridiculous! You're over-reacting—'

The door banged; I was speaking to myself.

Unsurprisingly, there was no conciliatory sex that night. John remained cloistered in his study till the small hours. We saw one another briefly at breakfast in an atmosphere of tense politeness. He told me he was going to play golf and would get his meals at the club, with friends. He didn't say who, deliberately excluding me, and while I had no wish to be with his golfing friends it made me sad to think he felt the need to wound. I spent the day sorting out any drawings and paintings I would take with me, and phoning my gardening clients, promising I would find someone to take over for me. I already had someone in mind, a friendly rival. I emailed Martha and Mary just to tell them I had made up my mind; any details could be ironed out later. Mary replied saying I could have the cottage indefinitely, naming a ludicrously low rent. I told myself I would help on the farm in lieu. If that involved working with Sadie it would be a privilege and a pleasure; even if not, I would happily haul bales and clean out animals and collect eggs, whatever she needed.

I wondered what, if anything, I should say to Alice; but I had no need. In the afternoon my phone rang.

'Mum! What on earth is going on?'

'Hello, Alice. How are you?' I said mildly.

'Fine. But I've had Dad on the line saying you're decamping to Yorkshire.'

'That's the plan.'

'But why?' Her voice rose to a squeak.

'Well, there's this art school—'

'Yes, yes, he said – but I don't understand! What about Dad?'

'Your father is a capable man, Alice, well able to take care of himself. He is not in his dotage, nor is he some potentate needing a slave.' I spoke more sharply than I meant and heard a loud sniff at the other end.

'But he'll be lonely! I'll have to come home at weekends—'

'You'll do no such thing. Neither he nor I would want you to neglect your own life, your uni work. You mustn't think of yourself as his keeper, Alice. Besides, I'll be back at Christmas.'

Now she sounded like a truculent five-year-old. 'Maybe, but that'll just be to see Dan.'

I was beginning to lose patience. 'No, it'll be to see all of you. You, Dan, and your dad. And to cook Christmas dinner, I dare say.'

She must have heard the edge in my voice, because her next question was larded with false innocence. 'Mum, don't you love Dad any more?'

If I hadn't felt so annoyed I might have laughed. 'My dear Alice, even though you are the result of it, my relationship with your father is strictly our business, not yours.'

All soppiness and infantility vanished like the dew in the morning. 'God, Mum, you're such a cow.' She rang off.

⁂

On an impulse I got my bike out and pedalled down into town to see Grace. I found her in a hammock in the garden of her bungalow, half asleep, an open book resting face down on her stomach.

'Hello, queen of idleness.'

She sat up with a start and almost fell out of the hammock, which was swinging wildly. 'Fen! You nearly gave me a heart attack.' She fanned her flushed face with the book. 'You're back then. How did it go?'

'Lots to tell you. But I'm going back again, as soon as I can get things sorted here. I'm going to ask Tracy and her team to cover my garden customers. But I'll go and see all of them first, explain the situation and get every garden immaculate before I go.'

'Crikey. Big changes afoot. I never thought a visit to Ronnie Milburn's studio would set all this in motion. Anyway, tell me all. But let's go indoors – I'm baking out here. I'll get the kettle on.'

In her kitchen, sitting at the table, I told her about Martha and Chibley Farm, and how things were with Mary and Peter.

'And is this what you really want?' she asked sharply. 'Or are you just a bored housewife fed up with her old man?'

I swallowed a retort, remembering her enduring bitterness at her own divorce. She wasn't likely to sympathise with anyone willing to desert a perfectly acceptable husband.

I shrugged. 'I don't know, Grace. I'll keep you posted.'

I could see she regretted her question, because her voice softened. 'I imagine Alice won't like it.'

'She doesn't. I already had her on the phone earlier.'

'Well, she's very close to her dad. Look, I'll keep an eye on them both, far as I can, if you like.'

'Thank you.'

⁂

THE NEXT DAY, Sunday, I made an effort. Instead of cycling to church in trainers and jeans as I usually did, I put on a dress and suffered to be driven. It was a strained journey, blessedly brief. John barely said hello to anyone before he disappeared into the vestry, probably to do something with the safe. I drew on a mantle of civility and chose to sit with two elderly ladies I liked, because beneath the archetypal outfits and softly permed hairdos they had a bit of spark. They had even been known to giggle like schoolgirls at some private joke during the sermon. 'Morning, Ellen, morning, Margaret,' I murmured. 'All right if I come and sit in the back row with the naughty set?'

'Oh, do, dear,' Margaret said. 'Just don't lead us astray.'

I snorted. 'Much more likely to be the other way round.'

They were still suppressing titters when the organ music came to a close and Gilbert stood before us, his surplice beautifully starched, his white fluffy tonsure like a halo. John slipped out of the vestry during the first hymn and came to rest on the end of our pew. Margaret and Ellen nudged each other and looked sideways at me. 'Such a handsome chap, your husband,' Ellen whispered. I smiled painfully.

After the service people gathered at the back of the church where there was a short counter with cups laid out. Someone whose turn it was made tea and coffee and put biscuits on plates. I accepted a cup of coffee and chatted idly with a few people, the usual subjects: the warm weather, the referendum. Then Gilbert appeared, no longer robed but in his Sunday white shirt, black trousers straining at the waistband, a narrow blue tie. People gathered round him like chicks round a hen, each chirping their various concerns. Normally by this time I would be chafing to go home, but today I wanted to put off being indoors with a surly, resentful man. I leaned against the cool stone wall and watched the congregation, feeling unusually benevolent. Now that I was leaving, now that I wouldn't be in attendance every Sunday feeling like a stranded fish, I admitted that there were excellent people here, some of whom I was even quite fond – though more the fondness of familiarity than anything else, if I was honest.

I saw Gilbert replace his empty cup on the kitchen counter. Then, to my surprise, he turned and came purposefully towards me.

He had to lean back a little to speak to me – he was a short man. 'Fen, I have something for you. Will you come to the vestry for a moment?'

Intrigued, I followed him up the central nave and into the vestry. He closed the carved wooden door with care.

'You see, I thought about what you said at that Bible study meeting we had a few weeks back, how you wanted to study Revelation, and I thought if that was a serious request I should help you. I didn't feel it was the best choice for the group at the moment because of the need to nurture the new members – it's a difficult book, quite obscure to many. But I thought if you're reading it by yourself you might need some guidance – the background, the symbology.' He reached over to the table and picked up a book. 'It's a commentary,' he said. 'I hoped it might help you understand.'

I took the book from him. It had a shiny yellow cover. I was touched – I hadn't thought he was at all interested in my opinions and choices. 'That's very kind of you, Gilbert. I appreciate it, truly. But I'm going away. I won't be able to give it back to you any time soon.'

He nodded calmly, as if this was not news. 'Keep it as long as you need to. I have others – there's no hurry.'

I thanked him again and went back into the body of the church clutching the book, feeling I had misjudged him.

The clusters of worshippers were breaking up as people began to drift off to their Sunday meals. I knew John would be some time yet, organising the collection, making various arrangements. I told him I would walk the mile and a half home, and he looked surprised but said nothing. I made my farewells and stepped out into the churchyard, into the hazy sunshine. It occurred to me that Gilbert, ever tactful, had made no comment when I'd said I was going away. I wondered what he'd thought. Would he, ever so gently, ask John if all was well?

As I walked home, I thought about the great gulf between John's idea of God – so it appeared – and mine. Yes, he had been instrumental in drawing me into the church, for which I was grateful, but our paths had parted company. He seemed more concerned with the nuts and bolts, the tasks made necessary by buildings and their upkeep. No doubt that was how he thought of his service, and I respected it, but it made my spirit feel leaden. I remembered the wide-open landscape I had just left behind, to which I was about to return. It seemed to me that the great Creator of the universe, its mysteries and glories, could not be tidied into petty human arrangements but was calling his followers to an unknowable, indescribable adventure, at once thrilling and terrifying. There was little of any sense of adventure here at St Swithin's. I wondered if I would find it anywhere else.

AND NOW ONCE again I sat on a northbound train, my bike and a rather larger backpack safely stowed, the commentary Gilbert had lent me on my lap. Tying up my life in Brant, even temporarily, had taken longer than I'd anticipated: two weeks had gone by since I'd promised to return to Yorkshire, two weeks of working on clients' gardens and assuring them that Tracy and her team would take over and do a good job, informing those who needed to be informed, and leaving things at home to make it all easier for John. He watched these preparations, when he was around, without comment, and Alice too was unusually silent – at least as far as I was concerned. I'd emailed Daniel about my movements, and he had replied typically: *Sounds great, Mum – I almost envy you – but not quite! All well here.*

A few miles out of Leeds I decided to use the train toilet to avoid the problem of what to do with bike and backpack on a station. I left the book on my seat and made my way along the aisle. The facilities were a couple of carriages away, and the train was crowded with people who clearly hadn't found room for their baggage, which stuck out into the gangway from between the seats. Intent on not tripping I almost bumped into someone coming the other way. A hand on my elbow briefly steadied me, and I looked up into the dark-blue eyes of a very good-looking man.

'Excuse me,' he said with a smile. 'My big feet.'

I smiled back. 'A problem I also have.'

Back in my seat I found myself inwardly grinning at my response to an attractive man whom I would never see again. The old Fen was still lurking somewhere in my psyche, it seemed. But then of course John marched into my thoughts, and I sighed. I'd been, as I thought, so reasonable, so pleasant, trying to bring him alongside, to be a willing partner in my plans, if not an enthusiastic one. At one point I'd said, after assuring him again I'd be home for Christmas, 'You know, I'm only going to Yorkshire, not the moon. You could come and visit.' But even as I said it I knew he wouldn't come. It came to me that, whether he was consciously aware of it or not, in his eyes he had rescued me from my old louche life and I was now disloyally hurrying back to it. Perhaps cynically I saw that he would never leave the circle of his dominance and enter one where I held the reins. He was taking my defection personally, and maybe, to a degree, he was right, although there was much more to it than he cared to acknowledge. I'd made one last attempt to appeal to his good nature, and tacitly also to our years together, as I'd wheeled my bike out of the shed on my way to the station. He was standing at the front door, his arms folded, watching me. I leaned the bike against the wall, went up to where he stood and brushed his cheek with my lips. 'You're not an ungracious man, John. At least wish me well.'

He grunted. 'How can I, when I think you should be here?' He shrugged. 'At least let me know you're safe.'

'Of course.' And that was it.

I STARED OUT of the window of the train, barely registering the countryside flying past, backward, always backward. I turned the book with the yellow cover over and over in my hands. The bookmark stuck out two thirds of the way through. In spare moments, the past two weeks had seen me delve into it, my Bible beside me, and now my imagination was crowded with the bewildering images it had thrown up. Was I closer to understanding its contents? Probably not. But I was beginning to understand how naïve I had been to think I could mine its riches for art – not only naïve but somehow presumptuous. A hazy realisation was beginning to dawn: there was far more here than I had bargained for. It wasn't my first reading of Revelation, but I'd never before read it with an erudite guide, and I was learning, with some discomfort, how shallow my past understanding had been. This complex wisdom couldn't be reduced to a series of dramatic images. Somehow, I had to convey its spiritual significance as well, as far as I was capable; and I doubted my ability. Just as I needed help to assimilate the meaning of Revelation, so too I needed someone to help me with the practical task of putting my ideas into visual form. Coming back to the daily world with a jolt as the train slowed into a station, I heaved a sigh. I was pinning a lot on the willingness and expertise of Martha.

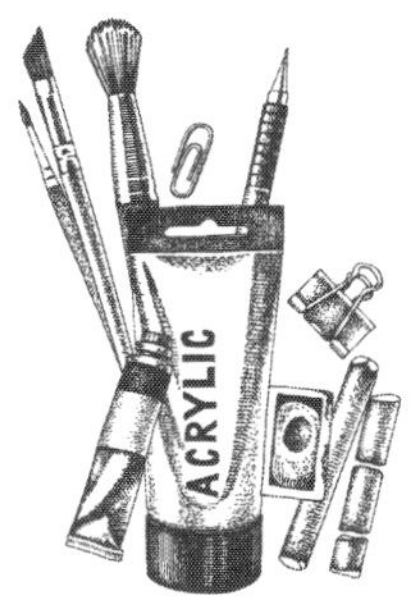

PART TWO

I finally made it down to Chibley at two o'clock and found Martha sitting outside her front door on a rickety camp chair, doing nothing, her eyes closed, her face turned up to the hazy sun, her hands loose in her lap. When I skidded to a stop, out of breath, she opened her eyes.

'There you are.'

I propped my bike against the wall. 'I've been Peter-sitting,' I said. 'Least I can do when Mary charges me the smallest rent you can think of.' I sighed. 'Most times I'll pick up any shopping she needs on my way through town, but sometimes she feels the need to get out herself. She must be stir-crazy, stuck inside the farmhouse day in, day out with a sick man.'

Martha nodded. 'Especially this time of year, when she can see everyone around out harvesting. How's it going at Whitepost?'

I shrugged. 'There's not much to do these days. She's down to a couple of fields now, and even those are being harvested by neighbours.'

'So you're not helping on the farm?' Martha asked, her eyes narrowed against the sun.

'I'd like to be. You know me, I love to be out of doors. But there's barely any farm to work on, and I'm too much of a greenhorn to be of any use to other farmers. All I managed today was a bit of weeding in Mary's little kitchen garden while Peter was asleep. Anyway, my work's here. Not that I seem to be getting on too well.'

'You're still doing drawings, aren't you?' Martha said, her tone sharp.

'Endlessly. But I'm daunted. It's such a huge subject. Maybe I've given myself too massive a job.'

She heaved herself out of the chair, which wobbled alarmingly, and reached for her stick, propped against the wall next to my bike.

'Come inside,' she said. 'Let's think about it. And take a look at your drawings. Maybe we can see where you might begin.' She hobbled indoors, and I followed. 'Put the kettle on, Fen. We'll need coffee for this.'

Ten minutes later, mugs at our elbows, we sat at the great kitchen table, my drawings spread out in front of us.

'I've been thinking, trying to reduce it to something manageable,' I said. 'There's no way I can do everything. And I want it to be accessible to someone now, in the twenty-first century. That, to me, is the point. My interpretation. I'm a creature of my time, and I want to speak to others in the same boat. So I want to start where it all began, with St John and his vision. From what I've been reading in that commentary Gilbert lent me, Revelation isn't really an apocalypse like the others. John himself regarded it as a prophecy, and his purpose was moral – all those calls to repentance.'

Martha looked at me, her expression inscrutable. 'You want to call modern people to repentance? Do most of them even know what it is?'

'That's just it,' I said. 'Most probably don't, or don't see the need of it. There was a time I didn't see it myself. I don't know, Martha. Do you think I'm attempting the impossible?'

'No,' she said. 'It's a matter of expressing what you know, what you've seen, translating it. Just like St John himself. He wrote down what he saw – you're going to paint it.'

I was beginning to feel slightly desperate. 'Maybe it won't be any good.'

'Maybe it won't,' she said with some asperity. 'But unless you get something done we can see, no one will ever know. And that's what you're here for, isn't it? Anyway, don't you need to have something to show for your time here, for when your husband comes to visit?'

'Yes, or he'll think I'm on some kind of holiday,' I said, wincing at the thought. 'But I've got till October. He said he'd come then, when Alice has gone back to uni. To be honest, I'm amazed he even wants to come at all.'

'Why wouldn't he? Didn't you tell me it's where you met?'

'That's just it. I don't think he likes to remember me as I was then. Wayward, untutored, unpredictable.' I thought for a moment. 'Maybe that's why he was always reluctant to come back here for holidays. Never as keen as I was. Maybe it reminds him of how lust wrecked his judgement.'

Martha chuckled. 'If that never happened the human race would have died out long ago.'

'A bit extreme in our case, though. And now I guess he'll think of this as the place that stole me from him.'

'Are you sure you're not seeing more than is there?'

'Probably. No wonder he can't understand my thought processes.'

'You don't surprise me. OK. So, let's think about this project of yours – what other artists have done for a start. What research have you done?'

'Well, I've looked at work online – a big range – from Bosch to Titian, Botticelli, Orrente, Dolci, Poussin, Durer – and others – and in every case I've learned a lot, but I want to do something quite different, like I said, a work for our own time. Also, I've finished reading Revelation itself, and the commentary, and made notes. I've decided to stop before the bit with the seven trumpets. The material before that is more than enough for three panels, even big ones.'

'Three panels?' Martha said, frowning. 'A triptych? Is that what you have in mind?'

'I suppose. If I get that far.'

'Did you come across the John Martin triptych?'

I nodded. 'So big! Each panel more than six feet by ten! I don't think I want to be quite that ambitious.'

Martha grunted, settling into her chair, her shoulders hunched. 'I saw those paintings, you know. Went down to London specially.'

'Really? When was that?'

'Tate Britain did an exhibition of his work in, um, 2011. I think it was then.' Her brows contracted. 'Yes, it was – I remember it because it was the same year I had that first operation on my hip – which wasn't a big success. Anyway, that triptych was the basis of the whole exhibition. Martin wasn't always appreciated, of course. The public liked him, but the art critics were sniffy. As they so often can be. And by the early twentieth century he was regarded with some disdain: too Victorian, too religious. He did a lot of dramatic biblical scenes, did you know? *The Destruction of Sodom and Gomorrah*, *Belshazzar's Feast*, for example.'

'You know a lot about him,' I said, wondering at this woman who kept so much knowledge. No wonder Ronnie Milburn held her in such regard.

'Well, I don't care about fashion, in life or in art,' Martha said with her cryptic smile. 'And I like his stuff. I like that triptych, especially *The Great Day of His Wrath* – marvellous. He was prolific in a lot of genres, small stuff as well. The big over-the-top biblical scenes aren't everyone's cup of tea, but I like them, and I think he was brave to paint things like that when it wasn't fashionable. As it isn't now, of course.'

'I don't care about fashion either,' I said. 'I'm just doubting my ability. Not only to paint it, but to communicate.'

'I can help you up to a point,' Martha said. 'What I think you need to do now is condense it, all your research, your thoughts, these drawings.' She waved a hand at my bits of paper. 'Get it down to what you want to put in each of the panels. Plan it out. You're right, you can't do it all. Pare it down. You'll still have a mass of material. Make it manageable so you can start. We'll need to talk about materials.'

'Martin did his with oil on canvas.'

'I know, but oil takes a long time to dry. Anyway, acrylic hadn't been invented in the 1850s.' She paused for a moment, thinking. 'Someone's coming soon, someone I think might be able to help you. An old friend. I don't know why I call him old when he's only thirty-something, but I've known him a few years. I mentioned him before – Liam Audley. He'll be here in a week or two, and I'm hoping he'll stay a while. Get yourself as prepared as you can, and then we'll see.' She looked up at me, one gnarled hand resting on my drawings. 'In the studio, in the room at the end where all the stuff is, there's a bookshelf. You might find something of interest there, something to give you some ideas. Histories of art, that sort of thing. Even if you're familiar with some of it, it won't hurt to look.'

I got up from my chair. 'Thanks, Martha. I'll go now. Feast my eyes, if nothing else.'

A WEEK LATER I was there, sitting on the studio floor with the rain pounding down noisily on the skylights, open books spread out around me. I had my A3 sketchpad by me and a couple of pencils and was trying to copy some of the images from the books. I knew something was weighing on me, but I didn't know what; whatever it was seemed to be holding me up, preventing me from making a beginning. I had ideas, but they were too many and too fluid; I couldn't pin them down. The thought of a big, expensive canvas filled me with anxiety: what if I made a mess of it? As it was, my money would run out long before I was in sight of the finishing post. The gardening had never earned me much, and art materials were costly. I sighed, pulled myself to my feet and went into the back room where everything was stored. There was my canvas, stretched, primed, innocent of any marks. Martha had helped me to get it ready the day before, and she'd given me many meaningful looks, but had said nothing. Was I imagining it, or did her heavier-than-ever tread, the staccato tapping of her stick, tell me what she was thinking, if not saying? 'Get on with it, Fen, for heaven's sake.' Perhaps it was my own irritated voice I was hearing. I looked again at the bookshelf and noticed something I hadn't seen before: a sheaf of paper clumsily bound in brown card. I pulled it off the shelf and smoothed a fine film of white dust from its cover. I opened it, and on the title page read: 'Materials and techniques of European art: An overview,' and at the bottom of the page the author, L.P. Audley. With a soft exclamation I realised this must be Martha's friend Liam. There was a date: 2004. Twelve years ago – so was this some sort of university dissertation? I had no idea. I put it on the table in the back room, opened it up and started to read. It was ill-typed and poorly edited, but I soon ceased to notice. As soon as I began the introduction, I was intrigued. The premise seemed to be that the history of art, in Europe at least, hinged on the techniques that rested on the availability of particular materials at any given time. For instance, before Van Eyck, artists would have been working largely in fresco or tempera, unable to produce a smooth, glossy surface. The invention of oils in the fifteenth century revolutionised their working. Earlier works would often have been produced on wood panels, first sized, then sometimes covered with linen strips to hide any knots, before two applications of 'gesso', made from gypsum and animal glue, were applied – first a rough coat, then a smooth one. The replacement of these panels with canvas meant that work could be rolled up and transported, allowing the artist to work outside if he wished, or to work in a studio rather than in the home of the commissioning patron. Studio work led to a greater use of models and a more lifelike treatment of human anatomy, as well as a mastery of light and shade.

I took another book from the shelf and turned to a favourite image, *Supper at Emmaus*. Staring at it, I marvelled at the details: the wicker basket, the rotting apples, so immaculately realised, but also the big things; the deep shadows, the true-to-life faces, not at all idealised, and the clever illusion of something immediate, something extraordinary, happening before one's eyes at that very moment in time. 'The trouble is,' I said to myself aloud, 'I want to paint like Caravaggio.'

'Don't we all.' The voice came from the doorway, and I flinched, sucking in my breath; I hadn't heard anyone come in. No one came except, rarely, Martha, and her tapping stick and shuffling tread always preceded her. But this was not Martha.

'Apologies! Did I startle you?' A man pushed himself off the door frame and came towards me, his hand outstretched.

I gaped stupidly. 'Oh! It's you – the man from the train!'

For a moment he frowned, obviously puzzled, then light dawned. 'Of course! I remember – I almost tripped you up. Liam Audley.'

I shook the proffered hand, feeling slightly dazed. 'Fen Bailey.' I laid a hand on his open monograph. 'I've been reading your book.'

He looked slightly pained. 'It hardly merits that description.'

'No, it's really interesting. I haven't got very far yet, but I'd like to read more, if you don't object.'

'You're welcome to. I doubt it will tell you much.' He shrugged. 'When I wrote it there was a lot of nonsense talked in the art world. So much emphasis on social influences on what painters could produce. The idea of being hamstrung by your colours or your working space was too ordinary, too practical. But the fact is the greatest genius ever born was limited by what he had to work with. We're lucky these days – so many colours, for instance – all in nice tidy tubes. No need for a bunch of minions mixing difficult pigments.'

'Yes,' I said slowly, thinking. 'Things have changed a lot. Back then the studio would have been full of people, buzzing with activity. Now we all work alone.'

'Do you regret that?' he asked, a quizzical expression on his face.

'Kind of. It's a big, quiet space, this great building.'

'And possibly a bit dreary on a day like today. Look, I've been sent by Martha. She says you should come down to the house for a cup of tea so we can get properly acquainted. It's still raining, but I brought an umbrella. I took the liberty of looking at your drawings – they're good, really good. But why so many sheep?'

I laughed, feeling heat bloom in my face. 'Ah, well, maybe Martha said something to you about my plans – as yet unrealised. I'm hoping to do some big canvases based on the book of Revelation. The Lamb of God features quite frequently, as you might imagine. Standing on thrones, and such. And I am currently living on a farm, so I have plenty of subjects.'

We left the studio, hastily closing the door behind us, and Liam put the umbrella up and held it high above our heads, managing to douse us both in cold drips.

He smiled. 'Lovely Yorkshire weather! Are you used to it yet? I hear you're a city dweller down south.'

I bristled slightly. 'Not by choice. And a bit of rain is no bother.'

We squelched down to the yard, where now a putty-coloured car, rusting round the door frames, was parked on the streaming cobbles.

'Yours?' I asked.

'No, it's borrowed,' Liam said. 'But yes, it's what I arrived in yesterday evening. When I saw you on the train, I was going to catch up with friends south of here. They were keeping some work of mine as they've got more space for storage. They lent me the car to bring the paintings up here. I'm supposed to be doing an exhibition. Nothing too grand, just the town library. I don't suppose anyone will take much notice, but it's a lot better than nothing. Martha's influence, not for the first time.'

He pushed open the farmhouse door, collapsed the umbrella and shook it free of rain. 'Take a seat – I'll make some coffee.' Humming under his breath, he filled the kettle and set it to boil then went to the door that led to the stairs. 'Martha!' he called. 'We're here.' A distant voice answered him, but I couldn't make out the words.

Liam busied himself with mugs, milk, and cafetière, bringing things to the table in random order, and I found myself watching him, covertly I hoped, noting the odd combination of clumsiness and grace that marked his gait, the fluid motion of his hips as he walked, his sudden jerky movements. He would have made an intriguing subject for a life class, I reflected, then suppressed a smile at my train of thought, imagining him posing on a pedestal or draped over a chair, barely clothed. As he came to the table clutching a handful of spoons, he caught my look. 'What's funny?'

'Nothing. Just a passing bunch of images,' I said. 'So, how do you know Martha?'

He slid onto the bench opposite me. 'Long story,' he said. He flicked an errant lock of hair from his forehead, but it flopped straight back down. 'I was a destitute would-be student. No money, no prospects, plenty of airy ambition and cheek.' He chuckled. 'I ask myself what's changed! No, Martha was a saviour, took me under her wing, no idea why. She let me stay here, camping in one of the barns. I still do when I'm here, though nowadays it's a bit more salubrious, a proper little rustic flat. In return I did jobs round the place and, in between, I painted.' He paused. 'I've done all right, really, I suppose, better than some. I've had a few exhibitions, nothing major; sometimes I even sell a piece of work. There are people who like what I do, one or two in the States, and I do a bit of teaching. But I always find my way back here. Martha's a good friend.'

'Seems she's been instrumental in a few careers,' I commented. 'Did you meet Ronnie Milburn?'

Liam shook his head. 'I've heard Martha speak of him, but we've never coincided. He was here, I know, but it was a few years before my time. I've seen some of his work, though. He's doing well.'

For a moment we were both silent, then with a sudden gesture Liam hefted the pot and rather erratically poured coffee into three mugs. 'I wonder where Martha's got to. She's getting less mobile: every time I come I see a change in her. Slower, stiffer.'

The door creaked open, and Martha came in. For once I hadn't heard her approach; her soft leather slippers made little sound on the flagged floor. Frowning fiercely, she cuffed Liam round the ear. 'Cheeky boy!' she growled. 'There's life in this old hag yet, I'll have you know.'

She sat heavily in the chair at the head of the table and pulled a shawl round her shoulders. 'It's freezing in here,' she said. 'You'll have to get me some more logs from the store. Make yourself useful.'

Liam slid a mug of coffee towards her. 'Yes, ma'am.'

'So,' Martha said, looking from me to Liam. 'Have you two been getting acquainted? Had any more thoughts, Fen?'

'I've been looking at Liam's – what? Treatise? Dissertation? Interesting ideas.'

'Ah, yes,' Martha said, nodding. 'The boy pretends to be an airhead, but he actually has brains.'

Liam grinned and got up, finishing his coffee in one gulp. 'I love your backhanded compliments, Martha. They do so much for my self-esteem. I'll go and get those logs.' He went out, and the door banged behind him.

Martha sipped her coffee. 'What do you make of him?' she asked abruptly.

I made a face. 'I hardly know. We only just met. No, actually we met on the train – almost fell over each other. But I didn't know who he was then.'

'Hm. He's got a good heart, talented too. But a bit of a lost soul, I always think.'

'How come? He has an air of confidence.'

Martha shook her head. 'That's a front. He has no one – which is unusual. Oh, plenty of friends, but no family. I don't know all the details, but he was in a children's home for years. He doesn't speak about his parents. I think there was a sister who died – no, maybe I'm mixing him up with someone else. Ignore me. He's done all right, and I've helped him where I could. I think there've been women too, but no one that's stuck. Not sure why – he has plenty of charm. Handsome too.' She gave me a knowing look, one black eyebrow raised. 'Don't tell me you haven't noticed.'

I shook my head. 'Martha, I'm a married woman.'

'When did that ever stop anyone?' Martha grunted. 'You have eyes, I dare say.'

'Yes, and they're all for art these days,' I said firmly.

She laughed quietly, a throaty rumble. 'Speaking of husbands, have you heard from yours recently?'

'He's supposed to be ringing me this evening. Sent me a text yesterday. Something he wants to talk about, he said.'

'You still haven't started on that canvas, have you?' Martha said.

'No, but I've done some more drawings.' I heard a note of desperation in my own voice.

'What of?' Martha challenged. 'More sheep? That dog of Mary's?'

'Sadie? I have the merest scribbles of her. She never stays still long enough. No, actually – buildings, from memory.'

'Buildings?'

'Blocks of flats, multi-storey car parks, department stores. I'm thinking of putting them in among the scenes of the seven churches, side by side with the temples.'

Martha nodded. 'The message of Revelation is for now.'

'I believe it is.'

JOHN RANG LATE that evening, after nine-thirty, when I'd almost given up on him.

Brushing aside his apologies, I said, 'Were you at the golf club?'

'On a weekday? No, I was still at work.'

I frowned. 'Why so late? Did you get any dinner?'

'I picked up a takeaway on my way home. That Chinese place on the corner of Deller Road. Surprisingly good. I've only just demolished it – mucky cartons everywhere. As to why so late, it's what I wanted to talk to you about.'

'Go on,' I said cautiously.

I heard him clear his throat. 'Thing is, I'm afraid I won't be able to come up and visit after all. Do you remember there was all that talk at work a couple of years ago about a merger?'

'It all died a death, didn't it?' I said.

'Yes, well, it's been resurrected. And it seems to be going ahead at a great pace. I've been given a schedule of meetings you wouldn't believe, and obviously every one of them involves a lot of preparation, then reporting and documentation, and more meetings… I may have to go to America. I'll be lucky if it's all sorted by Christmas.'

'Good heavens! And it all has to be you?'

'No, of course not. The whole senior management team's involved. It'll be a massive step up for the company. Anyone with a holiday booked can forget it. So I'm sorry, but a trip to Yorkshire, even for a few days, is not going to happen.'

'That's a shame. I hope you don't get too exhausted.'

'Yes. Well, I'll try to pace myself.' He sounded more complacent than worried or disappointed, and I felt certain he was looking forward to all the novel activity and the feeling of being an important part of the process.

'So, what have you been up to?' he asked politely.

'Planning my Great Work,' I said. 'Learning a lot about art. Cycling in all weathers. Egg-collecting, stable-mucking-out, Peter-sitting. At this moment I'm like you, ignoring dirty dishes. But mine was a humble bowl of soup, not a Chinese blowout. And I've been studying my Revelation commentary again.'

I heard him snort. 'Sounds riveting.'

'It is,' I said. 'There are things I never really realised.'

'Such as?'

'Well, the idea that St John wasn't talking about the fall of any particular city, but of the collapse of what we call civilisation. And it comes close to home – we're all inclined to be too comfortable, those of us with a nice lifestyle. What would we do, people like you and me, if we were faced with persecution? And even without that, aren't we tempted – I'm talking about Christians here, not the general population – to collude, to slide into worldly thinking, to turn a blind eye to wrong things, to pretend we haven't noticed, just because we want comfort and security? He's warning us – because we're all so prone to bend God to the shape of our own desires, the trends of our times. It's all too easy to be corrupted.'

'So do you feel in danger of corruption?' John said. I heard the smile in his voice and knew he was patronising me. But somehow, I no longer cared.

'I might have to get a job,' I said suddenly. I hadn't planned to say this, and as soon as the words left my mouth I regretted them.

'What? Why? Are you running out of funds?'

I took a breath, thinking. 'Not yet. But I've chosen to do something big. Materials are expensive. And part of the deal is a contribution to the running of Chibley. But you knew that.'

'You should let me help.'

I bit my lip. 'I wanted to be independent, to do this under my own steam. It's not as if you wanted me to do it, so why should you foot the bill?'

'No, no, that's wrong,' he said. 'It's not a question of me footing the bill. It's your right to use our joint resources.'

'Which I didn't earn.'

'Of course you did. Keeping the house going, looking after the children. Supporting me.'

'Which I'm not doing right now,' I said, feeling I was losing the argument. 'Four hundred miles away.'

'Not quite that far, I think,' he said. I felt a spurt of familiar irritation. 'Anyway, I live in hope you'll be back. For Christmas, and eventually for good. You don't begrudge me my membership of the golf club, do you? That's pretty expensive. No, Fen, if you want to do this you shouldn't be hamstrung by lack of money. I'll put something in your account as soon as we hang up, and you have to promise me you'll say if you start to run out.'

Momentarily I closed my eyes. 'Thank you. It's kind of you.'

'No, it isn't. Any money we have is yours as much as mine. It's part of the deal. "All my worldly goods" – remember?'

After we said goodbye I sat for a while, my phone in my hand. Something about our conversation made me realise, with a certainty I couldn't at that moment have explained, that our paths, John's and mine, had diverged so far that any coming back would be almost impossible. I had no problem acknowledging that he had been reasonable and generous. But that was no surprise – John was a decent human being, trying, within his limitations, to do his best. Perversely, I would have preferred it if he'd been angry, disappointed, pleading, accusing – anything but this calm acceptance. An uncharitable thought crossed my mind – uncharitable and mean, but it was there. Was John perhaps having an affair? My paid-off absence would be welcome, wouldn't it? Then I berated myself for the unworthy thought. I'd been gone barely six weeks, and besides, it would be completely against all his avowed beliefs and principles. Once the thought was acknowledged, though, it took on life. Would I mind? Of course, in a way, I would mind. He'd been mine for a long time, and I'd selfishly assumed he always would be, whatever I did, even if I was pulling away. Naïve, no doubt. Unthinking, definitely. He was human, after all. Maybe lonely and bored, probably not short of admiring female company. What did I know of the people he consorted with at work, at the golf club? Not much. Yes, I would mind, and there'd be sadness at what had been lost, and I had myself to blame for that as well. But there was no real pain involved; it was survivable, and that said a lot. Thoughtfully I got up, took my dishes to the sink and started to wash them. Through the uncurtained window the night, now clear of rainclouds, was bright with stars. My thinking was almost certainly wrong, I told myself. He'd be far too busy with work commitments to think of straying. And even if he did, I could hardly complain. I wondered whether I would feel freer now, knowing he wasn't coming, that he wouldn't be sitting in judgment on my lack of achievement, my feeble efforts. I hoped that would be the result, because it was the only freedom I wanted – freedom to work, to create, unhindered by doubt, or guilt, or regret. Was I kidding myself? Was that even possible?

At three in the morning, I woke blearily from a disordered dream and stumbled to the bathroom, shivering, aware suddenly that autumn was waiting in the wings, closer here in the north. As I climbed back into bed and pulled the covers up over my shoulders, I recalled my thoughts of the previous evening and realised I had indeed been kidding myself. Of course I couldn't go forward without the usual weight of encumbrances: all those things – self-doubt, memories of every shade, that vague sense of not being good enough (for what?) – they would all have to go with me into whatever work I made, a work created by a flawed being for other flawed beings, riddled through with every worry, regret and struggle – and with every moment of illumination, every delight. Suddenly I was wide awake, before my eyes a clear idea of the shape of my first panel. I got up, put on a warm fleecy jacket and took pad and pencil to the kitchen table. By the light of a table lamp with an inadequate bulb I sketched out the plan – at last, something that looked right. And another thought came to me: at the same time as the big painting I would do some smaller ones, for Mary. Somewhere among my adolescent drawings I remembered a sketch of Peter, younger and healthy, leaning up against a gatepost, looking out over his land, Old Joe at his feet. Perhaps all those drawings I had done of Sadie and sheep might prove useful too. As I laid down my pencil and went back to bed I was smiling – whatever became of the big work, the small ones would be a labour of love.

THAT WINTER, so they said, was drier and milder than most, taking the whole country overall. Locally, it rained relentlessly towards the end of November, and there was flooding in some of the valleys. I spent one long morning with a stiff broom, sweeping dark brown water out of the animal pens at Whitepost farm, when I was, at last, fired up to work on my Revelation canvas. That was frustrating, but I couldn't leave Mary to deal with it on her own. She was already grey with weariness as she dealt with Peter and broken nights. Every day I arrived at Chibley late and wet, desperate to make progress while there was light in the studio.

The morning of the flood I leaned my bike up against the wall and went inside, pulling off my waterproof and brushing rainwater out of my eyes. I was surprised to find Martha sitting on a stool in front of my outsize easel, dressed in her usual voluminous black, leaning on her stick and staring at my painting. The sheet I had draped over it was lying crumpled on the floor. I picked up a towel from a chair and rubbed my wet face and the hair that was sticking to my forehead. Clearly, she hadn't heard me come in, and jumped visibly when she became aware of me standing unspeaking at her side.

'Oh! Fen, there you are. I thought you wouldn't make it today.'

'I nearly didn't,' I said. 'Some of Mary's outbuildings were awash.'

She turned on the stool, trying to hide a grimace of pain. 'I see I've been caught out. Do you mind me looking? Some people hate the idea of their work being scrutinised before it's finished.'

I shrugged. 'No, I don't mind. Maybe you can tell me if I'm doing something wrong.'

She shook her head. 'No. I see where you are going with it, and I like the drama. You haven't started on the central figure yet.'

I smiled, amused at her perceptiveness. 'St John isn't the hero, then, according to you?'

'Of course he isn't. Anyway, I can see he's more or less done, all but the details. No, I'm talking about that great blank gap left and centre.' She waved a hand in the direction of the canvas.

I walked up close, studying my work of the previous day. 'That's going to be a challenge,' I murmured. 'It has to be dazzling, eye-hurtingly bright, lots of gold and highlights, a complete contrast to the gloom of the rocks behind the saint and the earthly buildings.'

'Nothing too subtle, then,' she said with one raised eyebrow.

'I don't see the subject as having much room for subtlety,' I said. 'Except in those details you mentioned.'

She fixed me with that dark stare of hers. 'Changing the subject completely, I haven't seen you at St James's in many weeks. I can see the painting is going on quite nicely, and you can tell me to mind my own business if you like, but I thought maybe you've been neglecting your spiritual being, and I wondered why.'

Inwardly, for a moment, I bristled – but then I relented. Martha took liberties all the time, but I guessed she felt that was what friends did. Certainly, over the months I'd been at Chibley she was more of a friend than the owner of the place where I worked and studied. Liam came and went, sometimes there was a visitor for a few days or a week, but for the most part Martha and I were alone, thrown on each other's company. I returned her gaze. 'A few Sundays I've been keeping an eye on Peter so Mary can get to church. Her spiritual being is more depleted than mine.'

'Ha, I'm not sure about that!' Martha barked. 'And yes, I know you've been doing that. Good for you. But doesn't Bess Wharton sometimes spell Mary?'

'She does, when she's not up to her floury elbows baking.'

'So where were you? When Bess was doing her neighbourly duty and you weren't in church? Feel free to tell me to butt out.'

I ignored this invitation. 'Out on the hills, sometimes sketching, sometimes keeping an eye out for stray sheep, mostly just looking. Looking at the light on the hills when the clouds part. This place is an endless source of wonder to me. It changes all the time. I could spend hours just watching the clouds whip across the sky, casting their shadows on the hillsides. So perhaps,' I said, glancing sideways at Martha, 'I am attending to my spiritual being. Just not singing hymns and making small talk with farmers' wives.'

'That's as may be,' Martha said, relentless as ever. 'I'd never downplay the value of solitude. But you need nourishing as well, and you're alone a lot.'

'I sit in my little cottage late at night,' I said. 'Wrapped up in blankets. That's when I read and pray, because most evenings I am spending with Mary. If anyone needs company she does, not me. So, you don't need to worry about my spiritual state.'

'Hm.' Martha didn't sound convinced, and perhaps she was right. 'There's a point to my nosy quizzing,' she said abruptly. 'Have you given any thought to what you might do with this great monster of a work when it's finished? If it ever is.'

I sighed. 'Yes, but got no answers. Why?'

She turned back to contemplate the painting. 'Because I had a word with Steve.'

'Steve the very tall vicar?'

She nodded. 'I mentioned what you were working on. Yes, yes, I know I take liberties. But you did say you wanted to communicate with people through it, and that won't happen if it's stuck in here under a sheet.' She prodded my crumpled cover with her toe. 'I told him it might be a great thing to have it in church.'

I was astonished. 'What did he say to that?'

'Well, he didn't say "Not on your life, Martha." I'd say he was receptive. Cautiously positive, in fact. Of course he'd have to see it, and that means you have to finish it. But it wouldn't hurt meanwhile for you to show your face in church and get to know Steve and the good folk there and generally be pleasant. Otherwise, they'll be thinking of you as a moody egocentric recluse, concerned with nothing but your art. And maybe posterity.' She gave a quiet chuckle.

'Very funny, Martha. I don't think posterity is high on my list. And you really are a terrible busybody, but I guess I should thank you. You were instrumental in getting that exhibition for Liam as well, weren't you? It seemed to attract quite a bit of interest, I thought.'

She heaved herself off the stool. 'I have to keep Chibley in people's sights,' she said, serious now. 'Even if it's just locally. There's a very strong possibility of this place folding up, you know.'

I nodded. 'Yes, I know,' I said soberly.

She walked stiffly towards the door. 'Do you want to come down to the house for coffee?'

'No, thanks. I think I'll crack on while the light lasts.'

'Good. Just don't perish in the cold.'

An hour later I realised I was frozen. My hair was sticking up from my forehead in damp spikes, and my fingers were stiff from holding one paintbrush after another. Above me the skylight told me the light was going from the day. I stood back from my work and let my eyes roam across the canvas, planning my next move. I knew I could go on, but it was good to stop – to ease my body, to give my mind time to rest and regroup. Sometimes these pauses were the most fruitful part of the process. I took palette and brushes to the sink, ran water and found myself humming quietly – some tuneless thing.

The door creaked open, and I half-turned to see Liam enter. He raised a hand in greeting as he let the door close behind him. He came to stand beside me as I ran my brushes under a warm stream, letting the water run over my hand. 'Hey.'

'Hello,' I said. 'We haven't seen you in a while.'

'I've been with my friends in Theasby. They needed their car back.'

I dried my brushes and palette and left them to air on the draining board. 'I'm done for today. It's getting dark.'

'Can I look at what you've done?'

'Sure.'

We stood together in front of the painting, and I saw how the paint that had been thickly applied was still wet and shiny. Liam said nothing for a while. Then he turned to me with a smile. 'Tell me what you have in mind next.'

'OK. But it may change.'

'It probably will.'

I waved a hand. 'Up here, and down the left side, you see I've pencilled it in. This is where I'm going to put something to represent each of the seven churches – what each one was known for – maybe a great temple, or a centre of commerce, or a famous library. I'm going to label them: Ephesus, Laodicea, Sardis, and so on.' I saw his raised eyebrows. 'Yes, I know it's unconventional. But I'm going to label my saint as well. Because I love how he introduces himself: "I am John, your brother." It brings his message close to us. That's what I want, to make it accessible. Even for people who read their Bible regularly, Revelation is a daunting book. I want to give people of today a way in.'

He took a deep breath. 'Martha said she's trying to get the local church interested. Because I guess this is for Christians, isn't it? Anyone else will surely find it baffling.'

'I guess so,' I said. 'But then, a lot of art is baffling. Even to those of us who make it. If it makes people think, I'll feel I've done what I intended. Anyway, believers also need help and support and encouragement.'

He studied the canvas in silence for several minutes. 'It's well done, very well.'

'Thanks.'

'Obviously you've had experience.'

'Some. I started going to classes when my daughter went to secondary school. So about eight years. I've mucked about with different mediums over the years: oil, pastel, watercolour. I even had a spell of making clay models – not too successfully. I thought acrylics would work best, but I prepped the canvas very thoroughly – I thought it needed it being so big – layers of gesso and then a brownish wash.'

'Do you mind if I offer you a bit of advice? I don't want to seem presumptuous.'

'Go ahead. All help is gratefully received.'

He pointed. 'This big, blank space. What's going in there?'

'It's John's vision of the risen Christ. I've left it blank because it's so important to get it right. He's glorified and bright. His arm's outstretched, the seven stars flying from his hand. Ranged behind him the seven gold lampstands.'

'How bright are we talking about? Because that will determine how you paint it.'

'Yes, I've been thinking about that. I want it to dazzle, but not blind. Because it's the light that overcomes us, that strikes us with awe, of course, but it's also the light we see by.'

Liam nodded. 'I get it. I think you should do it with a palette knife. It makes the paint go on differently, so your figure will stand out, not just because of the size and colour but because of the texture.'

I turned to him. 'Thanks, that's a great idea.'

He sketched a little bow. Then he said a little diffidently, 'Do you have any plans? I wondered if you felt like finding something to eat in town.'

I thought. 'OK, yes. But I can't be long. I want to drop in on Mary before I go indoors for the evening, so not too late. You know about the Hipkins, don't you?'

He nodded. 'I've not met them, but Martha mentioned their situation. You've known them for years, so she said.'

'Since I was a teenager.'

'A year or two ago, then.'

'Ha, ha. I don't think so. I have a twenty-two-year-old son.'

Liam grinned. 'Impossible.'

A thought struck me. 'How are you going to get into town? I have my bike.'

'I'll borrow Martha's car. She won't mind. Especially if I offer to bring her a takeaway back. I don't think she'll want to come – it's a big effort for her these days, just getting out of the house.'

Half an hour later we were comfortably settled in an Indian restaurant just off the high street, glasses of chilled beer in front of us, waiting for our food. There were few other diners so early and on a weekday; the place was warm and the servers attentive.

'This beats soup and a sandwich in my draughty cottage,' I said. 'It was great in July, but now…'

Liam took a gulp and wiped his mouth. 'Sounds similar to my so-called flat above the stable here,' he said. 'I've got a broken window plugged with newspaper. But Martha keeps it for me, and I pay my rent in jobs around the house. Of which there are plenty – the place is crumbling away.'

'How does she manage when there's no one here?' I wondered.

'I don't know. It must be difficult. But she won't think of living anywhere else.' He turned in his seat as a waiter approached, carrying a tray loaded with steaming dishes. 'Ah, great! I could eat a horse.'

'I'm afraid, sir,' the waiter answered, deadpan but with a quirk of his lips, 'we don't serve horse.'

'Yes, I know. Much too chewy.'

My eyebrows were raised, but both men seemed to be enjoying their schoolboyish banter. Moments later the dishes were organised and our plates full of aromatic food, which we proceeded to demolish with few comments.

'Tell me,' Liam said as he put down his fork, 'are you going to be around here for Christmas?'

I had the idea he already knew the answer; Martha would undoubtedly have told him. I didn't understand their relationship, but they seemed close.

'No, I'm going home. To Brant. I promised I would, to be with my family. And, I suppose, to cook vast quantities of turkey, roast potatoes, mince pies and pudding.'

'Will it be a big party?'

I shook my head. 'Just the four of us. I always invite my good friend Grace, but she never accepts. This year I believe she is going to her cousin in London. My son will be home from the States, but he probably won't be with us for long. There are lots of friends he'll want to see. My daughter will be home from university but again probably won't be at our house much. And I expect my husband will be itching to get back to work as soon as New Year's over. So, I'll return here as soon as I can. Two weeks away, maximum. Less if I can manage it.'

He looked at me intently. 'Don't you miss them?'

'Not really, though I'll be pleased to see them. We do speak, you know! On the phone sometimes, texts, emails. What about you?'

He didn't answer for a while, and I thought I might have strayed into sensitive territory.

'I'm going down to see my friends,' he said finally. 'The ones who lent me the car. But I won't stay long, unless the weather closes in. There's supposed to be storms coming, but that's nothing new. I know Martha is going to her friend in town, but only for a couple of days. I want to be back here to keep an eye on her. I don't tell her that, of course.'

'You've known each other a long time, I gather.'

Liam stared at the tablecloth, seeming suddenly moody. 'Yeah. Martha's been good to me. A lot better than my actual mother.' I didn't know what to say to this, and I let the silence gather. Then he sighed and raised his head. 'She gave me away, you know.'

'I didn't know. When was that?'

'When I was two. Put me in a children's home.'

'At two? Good heavens – why?'

'She was an alcoholic. Couldn't cope. I was neglected. It wasn't so much that she gave me away, more like I was taken away and she let them. Oh, she moaned and cried and carried on. But she didn't really want me.'

'What about your father?'

Liam laughed, a grim little sound. 'Who's he?'

'Ah. How long were you in care?'

'Till I was sixteen. I had foster carers from time to time, but they never lasted. I was a bad boy – stole things, got into fights, sold drugs, ran away… the whole nasty predictable scene.'

I took a deep breath, imagining a lost teenager. 'So how did things change?'

'Who's to say they have?' Liam said, attempting a flippant grin.

'Don't be daft.'

'Someone new came to work at the home. A bloke called Tony. He noticed I used to draw, all the time. He bought me some things, out of his own pocket – brushes, paint. He wasn't soft, though. He told me to get a job and pay him back out of my first wages, and meanwhile to practise drawing and painting and if I worked hard he'd help me when I had to leave.'

'That was a turning-point?'

Liam shrugged. 'I suppose it was, looking back. But it didn't work out, not straight away. I thought Tony would be like all the others, giving up on me when I didn't improve. I suppose I was testing him. No one had ever believed in me before, and of course I didn't believe in myself. But he persevered – I don't know why. He was hard on me if I started to slip back into my old ways. And in the end I got good at art, and that's what made the difference. But I wouldn't have done it except for him. He did something else too – he found my mum.'

'Found her?'

'Yeah. She used to come and see me in the home sometimes, not very often, when I was little, when she had money or a new bloke in her life. Dressed up to the nines, smelling of cheap perfume to cover the stink of booze, she was all over me, but it wasn't for real. I hated her visits – bad as I was myself, she made me ashamed. The other kids used to take her off, and there were a few fights. In the end social services told her not to come till she'd dried out. As if that was going to happen! So I didn't see her for years. Then when Tony came, he got the story out of me one night. I had my sixteenth birthday, I had to leave the home, but between them all they found me a job, on a farm, funnily enough, and I had a room there. It was hard, lonely work; the old farmer was a tough nut and his wife was worse, but at least they fed me and I liked the animals. I used to draw at night. I'd been there a few months when Tony came to see me out of the blue. He was in the farmhouse talking to the farmer for a long time, then he came to me and said he'd tracked my mum down. She was in hospital, he said, very sick. Her liver'd finally packed up, I guess. I don't know how he found her, and to this day I don't understand why. Perhaps he thought I needed to forgive her! I can tell you, there was no way I was going to do that. I was a very angry young man. There's something about mothers, isn't there – instinctively you expect so much of them, even when you're just a kid that knows nothing, so when they fail you it's worse, a lot worse, than someone else dropping you in it.' Suddenly he stopped dead, swallowed, and smiled. 'But hark at me, telling you this horrible story! What am I thinking of? It's all water under the bridge, and here I am, almost a respectable citizen.'

The waiter had been hovering for some minutes, waiting to collect our empty plates; now he approached discreetly. 'Do you want dessert?' Liam asked.

'No thanks. I couldn't eat another thing,' I said. 'And much as I love Indian food, I'm not a great fan of their puddings. I'll have coffee, though.'

We sat in silence for a while, until our coffee arrived. Then he said, 'I'm sorry. I shouldn't have loaded you with all that.'

I shook my head. 'Please, there's no need to apologise. But you can't leave me hanging. What happened? Did you see your mother? And then what?'

He stared at me. 'You really want to know?'

'Yes, if you're OK to tell me.'

He thought about this for a moment. 'Tony said my mum was dying. She wanted to make her peace with me. She'd dried out, but the damage was done, and her life had been very hard the last few years. I was adamant; I didn't want to see her. But Tony knew me well enough to suspect that under that sneering façade was a hurting heart. And he's a persuasive bloke. But he also bribed me. He said if I went to the hospital with him and saw my mum, just once, he'd get me out of the farm to a place where I could draw and paint to my heart's content.'

'So you went?'

'Under protest, yes. It wasn't a good experience. I barely recognised her – she was in a very bad way. I hardly said anything. She said she knew she'd been a terrible mother, and she was sorry. She didn't expect me to forgive her, but she just wanted to see me one more time before she died. And that's what happened. I went with Tony to the funeral, and to my great surprise I cried my eyes out all the way through. It was a sad little ceremony, barely anyone there, but I don't think I was crying for my mother. More like for myself, all the wasted years of my miserable childhood.' He looked up, and now his smile was unfeigned. 'Of course, as you must have guessed, my reward was three years at Chibley, and Martha. Paid for by Tony. What a hero.'

'How did Tony get to know Martha?' I asked.

He shook his head. 'I never found out. It's possible he already knew her – they're of an age. Who knows? Anyway, here I am, a graduate of Chibley and just about making a meagre living from art.' He grinned broadly. 'Or perhaps I should say living from hand to mouth, with no fixed abode and borrowing other people's cars. I've got no career prospects and not a lot of money, but hey! The world could end tomorrow and none of that stuff would be any use. And at least I'm doing what I love and I'm freer than most. Shall we get the bill?'

'Yes – and we'll split it.'

'No, let me. I sold a painting the day before yesterday – just a small one, but it's a sale. Don't protest – think of it as payback, my penance for subjecting you to the story of my sad life!'

'I hope it's not too sad any more,' I said as I got up and put on my coat. 'At least you have your friends who loaned you the car. And Martha and Tony.'

I saw his face change, from insouciance to regret in a moment.

'Ah, yes, Tony. Poor old chap's in a nursing home, I'm afraid. Nasty accident on a motorbike two years ago. Affected his brain. I go to see him when I can, but he's in Edinburgh, because it's near his sister.'

Liam paid our bill, and we made our way to the door. 'Does he know you?' I wondered.

'I think so,' Liam said. 'He seems happy enough, but it brings me down to see him like he is.'

I unlocked my bike and fastened my jacket. The wind was getting up. 'Seems you've had a lot of trouble and sadness in your life,' I murmured. 'Let's hope it gets better.'

'I hope so too,' he said. 'You must tell me about your life one day. I guess it's a bit more serene than mine.'

I smiled. 'It's had its moments. But that'll have to wait. I must get back to Whitepost. See you back at Chibley, and thanks for dinner!' I mounted my bike and sprinted away. There was little traffic on this cold, wet evening. As I rounded the corner of the high street, I looked back to see him still standing, rather forlornly, in the restaurant car park, waving goodbye.

I HEARD THE rumble of tyres and looked up from my sketch pad. With the first panel well under way, I was thinking about the second – what to put in it, what to leave out? There was so much, and I still had no clear idea how long I had. I'd vaguely mentioned a year to John, but what if it needed to be longer? I pushed aside the feeling of dread at having to leave this place at all. Thinking about that would have to wait. I glanced over at Peter, but he was asleep, comfortable enough, I hoped, despite the odd little moan and sigh that escaped him. I heard voices outside and got up to open the door. Mary was waving off Will Wharton as he careered up the track in his battered pickup.

'Ah, good, you've kept the fire going,' Mary said as she came into the kitchen. 'It was chilly in church this morning, and Will's old rattletrap has a window that won't shut.'

'Shall I make you some coffee?' I asked.

'Yes, please.' She peeled off her gloves and put them in her coat pocket, unwound her scarf and hung it up behind the door. 'How's Peter been?'

'Fine. Quiet. I made him some tea an hour ago, and he drank that OK. Sleeping pretty much since.' I busied myself with kettle and cups.

'It's good of you, Fen, looking after him,' Mary said quietly. 'But you know, you should be getting to church too. Quite apart from anything else, Steve's been saying he'd like a chat.'

I smiled as I brought two mugs to the table. 'Martha's been talking. But you're right. Next time Bess Wharton offers to sit with Peter, I'll come with you.'

Mary sipped her coffee, seeming deep in thought. 'They've decorated the church beautifully for Christmas,' she said at last. 'Holly wreaths, children's pictures, a tree all lit up.' She put her cup down and looked around her kitchen. 'I wonder,' she murmured. 'Maybe this will be my last Christmas at Whitepost.'

I frowned. 'Then what? Won't you hate to leave? What will you do?'

'Maybe you didn't realise,' Mary said. 'We've only ever rented the farm. The land, the buildings, all belong to the Whartons. They've been such good landlords – neighbours, friends – for so long. They could be working this land, but they let us stay here. But you know, Fen, now that Peter is as he is, and he's bound to deteriorate, I'm afraid, we can't stay. If we'd had children, it might have been different. As it is, I'm just waiting for a place to become vacant at the nursing home in town. I know the woman who runs it. Then I'll move into town as well, maybe stay with my friend Anne till I can get somewhere permanent.'

'It's so sad, Mary.'

She shrugged. 'I'd have hoped for something different – maybe seeing grandchildren by now, perhaps with one of them interested in the farm – but that's the way it is and I have to make the best of it.'

'What about Sadie?'

She heaved a deep sigh. 'Aye, well, I can't decide. She's my dog, my company, but she's a sheepdog, she needs to work, and those eighteen old girls aren't enough. Which is why she's at the Whartons' now. I don't want to give her up…' Her voice trailed to silence, and the lines in her face seemed etched more deeply.

'How do you tell if a pup is going to be a good worker?' I asked, hoping to distract her from things that couldn't be changed. 'You must have chosen her when she was very young.'

Mary brightened as she thought back. 'It's an instinct. Even when they're little you get an idea. Of course, at eight weeks old they're like any other puppy: bundles of energy, friendly, play-fighting with their brothers and sisters. There was something about Sadie, though. She wasn't the prettiest, still isn't, a bit on the skinny side, odd ears, but there was something… I was looking for potential, for speed and persistence, the desire to please, concentration… turns out I was right, eh.'

'She's an incredible dog, for sure.'

'But then, her bloodline was good. We could trace that back for generations.'

I stood up, stretching to unkink my back, and gathered up the cups. 'Even so, it must have taken a lot of work to train her.'

Mary pursed her lips. 'It was more a case of building her confidence. She was very quick to learn. And there's no meanness in Sadie. With some dogs you're using the instinct to hunt and kill, and that has to be controlled. Sadie is small – she has to use her brains, not her brawn.'

'Brains she has aplenty,' I said.

'Yes, but she had to gain experience. There were times when she seemed a bit, I don't know, cowed by the sheep. They can be awkward, you know, sheep! Especially when she had to get them out of a corner or away from a fence. She had to learn how sheep behave. She had a good eye, and her speed helped.'

'I should get back to Chibley, Mary. Do you want me to give you a hand getting Peter to the bathroom?'

'No, I'll manage. Let's leave him while he's peaceful. Yes, you must get on with your painting.' She saw me gather up my pencils and sketchbook. 'I'm glad to see you've been working. I'm looking forward to seeing the finished article.' She smiled. 'Maybe even on the church wall.'

She followed me to the door, and I unhooked my coat and shoved my arms into the sleeves.

'You know, you should learn to ride the quad,' she said suddenly. 'Then you could go and help Will on the farm when he needs an extra hand.'

I wound my scarf round my neck and tucked it in. 'I don't know how much use I'd be,' I said doubtfully.

She patted my arm. 'You need experience. Just like Sadie did. And confidence. I can help you with the commands and the whistle, if you like. I know you love being out with Sadie.'

I strapped on my bike helmet. 'Yes, I do.' I hesitated. 'Mary, what about Christmas? Are you going to be all right, on your own with Peter?'

'I won't be on my own,' she said softly. 'Diane the nurse will come, as she always does. The neighbours will help.'

'And I'll be back, as soon as I can after New Year.'

I opened the door, and a gust of cold air flew in. Mary frowned. 'You mustn't think of cutting short your celebrations on our account, Fen.'

I laughed, and even to me it was a brittle sound. 'Celebrations? I wonder. Of course I'll be glad to see them again. But if I'm very honest I'd rather be here.' I pulled on my gloves and straddled my bike. 'Now, I must go to that lovely woollens shop in town and do a bit of Christmas shopping,' I said. 'Go inside, Mary. It's freezing out here. I'll see you soon.'

A COUPLE OF evenings later I was perched at the table in my cottage, sorting through sketches, mainly scenes of the high moors. I'd thought of lighting a fire – Mary had given me a basket of logs – but decided it was simpler just to fill a hot water bottle, put on warm socks and go to bed. It was only a quarter to ten, but I was cold. I was warming some milk, dressed in my pyjamas and dressing gown, when my phone trilled. Frowning, I answered cautiously.

'Mum!'

I was taken aback. 'Daniel?'

'That's my name,' he said, and I heard the chuckle in his familiar voice. 'How are you?'

'Fine, thanks. But what are you doing ringing me all the way from America? Isn't it costing you a fortune? Shall I call you back?'

'No, that's just it. It's costing me nothing. I just got a new phone and a new deal, and that includes free international calls. So I thought I'd have the pleasure of talking to my one and only mother.'

Of course he couldn't see, but I was beaming. 'I'll see you soon, won't I? You are still coming home for Christmas?'

'Of course. I even bought my ticket. But I thought you should have my new phone number, in case of any hitches.'

'Yes – hold on, something's boiling over.' I turned off the pan of milk. 'Better tell Dad as well.'

'He's next on my list. I'll ring him tomorrow.'

'Everything OK with you?'

There was a tiny pause. 'Yes. But my phone number's not the only thing that's new. I can fill you in when I see you, but I'm not at the same address. I can text it to you if you like.'

'What happened?'

I heard him take a breath, clear his throat. 'I'm not with Rafe any more. He's working for his father now. Another guy I know from work offered me a room in his apartment, much nearer to the city, cheaper too.'

'Oh. Is that working out?' I wanted to know more, but let it lie. He would tell me, or he wouldn't.

'It's fine. I'm fine. But I want to hear what you've been up to.'

'I was just going to bed. Mainly to keep warm. What's the time there?'

'Almost five. I'm thinking about what to do with my evening. But you haven't told me anything about what you've been doing. Go on, spill, or I'll imagine the worst.'

I found myself catching his mood, and laughed. 'You can imagine anything you like, but I'm not causing any scandals, I can promise you that. I'm in deepest rural Yorkshire, not New York. But I have been doing something quite exciting.'

'Go on, amaze me.'

'I've been learning to ride a quad bike. Under the tutelage of a sixteen-year-old boy, who, of course, is already expert.'

'That sounds like fun. Is it dangerous?'

'It could be, with all the hazards you find round here, but I've been practising on a nice flat field, there's no snow at the moment, and I go quite slowly. Maybe that will change!'

'Have you told Dad about this escapade?'

'Not yet. He'd probably be horrified. But I can ride a bike and drive a car, so this is just another vehicle.'

'Except, I guess, if you're out in a snowstorm and can't see the holes, walls, rivers and bogs.'

'Sounds like you remember what it's like.'

'I do. It was nice in the summer, but I bet the winter's a very different matter.'

'Yes. Which is why I've decided not to bring the bike when I come back for Christmas. I'll have a few presents to bring, and when I come back here I'll need a few warmer clothes, so I'm going to take the train.'

'Anything else I need to know?'

'Well, apart from the quad, I've been doing a very minor bit of helping out at the Whartons' farm, and learning quite a lot about sheep farming. Young Thom – that's the Whartons' grandson – has been regaling me with all sorts of fascinating information.'

That small pause again. 'But – I know you're interested in the life and all that, and it reminds you of your youth, but what will you do with all this knowledge? I thought you were there to paint.'

'Of course I am. And I am doing just that. As to the rest, I don't suppose I'll do anything with it. But it's nice to feel more a part of the way of life while I'm here.'

'Ah. For a moment I thought maybe you were thinking of decamping permanently.'

I took a breath. 'Do you know, Dan, I don't know what I'm thinking. Not about the future, anyway. I'm just taking the days as they come, and enjoying them.'

'I get it. I think.' His voice trailed off. 'Anyway, Ma, I must let you get to bed before you freeze. I'll see you very soon.'

'You will. Lovely to hear your voice, Dan. Lots of love.'

'Likewise. Goodnight, Mum.'

Later, lying in bed, the hot water bottle clamped to my chest, beginning to drift off, I wondered at Dan's question and what my answer might have sparked in his mind. He knew me better than most people; even at that distance perhaps he had intuited my indecision, my restlessness. Perhaps I was due some grilling when I got back to Brant, and not only from John.

CHRISTMAS FELL ON a Sunday that year. I knew I had to allow myself time to prepare, so I needed to be in Brant for a few days to shop and ready the house. I doubted that John would have put up decorations or thought about a tree. If I let him know when I was arriving he might clean up a bit, but he was busy at work, and Christmas had always been my job. I wanted to talk to Steve at St James's before I left, and the Sunday before Christmas seemed a good day. The carol service was due to take place at six, but there would be a morning service when he might be more available, provided he was not at one of the several outlying parishes which he served. I asked Mary, and she seemed to think he would be elsewhere for the first half of the service and turn up to deliver the sermon. Will Wharton arrived with the first flakes of snow, dropped off his wife Bess to sit with Peter, and picked up Mary and me. As we climbed into his pickup he looked up at the sky, rubbing his rough red hands against the cold. 'If it settles at all, it won't be much,' he said.

'You're usually right, Will,' Mary said as she strapped herself in.

'Aye. We can leave the yows where they are today.' He started the engine and pulled away from the farmyard, glancing over at me with his bright blue eyes. 'I hear you had a rare old time with young Thom.'

I smiled, remembering. 'He's a very knowledgeable young man,' I said. 'I know a lot more about hill farming than I did. And learning to drive the quad bike was quite an experience.'

'Our quad is a lot older and rattlier than Will's,' Mary said. 'I thought you should start on something newer. But you're right, Thom is a farmer in the making, isn't he, Will?'

Will grunted as he took the corner onto the road. 'Maybe. He's a good lad, doesn't mind what he does, but he's young. Could change his mind.'

'I don't think so,' I put in. 'He seemed pretty committed. Said he wants to go to college next year.'

'Aye, well, we'll see,' Will said.

By the time we arrived in town the snow had stopped, and there was nothing but a light dusting on the pavements. Already the sun was out and the roads were wet.

'I'll see you ladies about twelve,' Will said. 'Down in the car park. I guess you'll be staying for a brew after.'

MARY WAS RIGHT: there was no sign of Steve yet. The first half of the service was conducted by his wife Jane, competently playing the hymns on the keyboard by ear, accompanied by a tiny choir of enthusiastic girls. I liked this arrangement – it was homely, unpretentious, a family affair. There were younger children about, a play area in the corner, and parents of varying ages as well as older folk. An elderly man with a military bearing read the lesson, slowly and deliberately. More songs followed, and then Steve appeared, the shoulders of his jacket sprinkled with snow. As he passed the pew where we sat, he patted Mary's shoulder briefly, and she smiled up at him. Then he vanished into the vestry and came out without his coat. 'Good morning, everybody!' he called out. 'It's snowing up at Rack Falls. Is it going to settle?' A groan answered him from the congregation.

There was communion that morning, delivered with due solemnity but without fuss, and I remembered from previous Sundays how I had felt unexpectedly moved as Steve called for the children and the parents first. They trooped up in little family groups, and as Steve gave the bread and wine to the parents and blessed the children, I felt the palpable love that flowed between them. As I took my own place at the rail, Mary beside me, Steve looked down at me from his great height, a warm smile lighting his eyes behind his glasses – which, I remembered, were always slightly crooked on his bony nose.

Afterwards we milled about and chatted, a steaming coffee cup in one hand and a home-made mince pie in the other. Steve spoke unhurriedly to everyone that crossed his path, singling out the singing girls for particular praise, and then made his way over to us.

'Mary dear, how are you?'

'Well enough, thank you, Steve.'

'And Peter?'

'Much as ever.'

He nodded thoughtfully and turned to me. 'Fen, I think we need to talk about a certain painting.' His eyes twinkled.

'Ah. Martha has got to you, hasn't she?'

'I wouldn't put it quite like that,' he said with a mock-frown. 'She has certainly mentioned it to me. Mentioned you a few times too. Where shall we put it, this masterpiece of yours?'

I gaped. 'You want to put it here, in the church? I'd see that as a great privilege. But are you sure? Would everyone agree? You do know it's pretty big, don't you?'

Serious now, Steve said, 'I've spoken to a few people. If we can find the right spot, I think the privilege would be ours.'

'You're very kind. It's no masterpiece, and it isn't quite finished yet, but really I think you should see it before you commit yourself. You might actually hate it.'

He smiled broadly. 'I'd love to see it! May I bring Jane? When's a good time?'

'If you could come to Chibley tomorrow, that would be ideal. I have to go back to Brant to get Christmas organised for the family, so I need to take the train south soon. I doubt my freezer will have much in it.'

ON MONDAY MORNING I was at Chibley early. There had been a light flurry of snow in the night, and it was thinking about settling, but the sun was faintly visible through the cloud; it could go either way. I caught sight of Liam going into the farmhouse; we waved to one another as I leaned my bike up against the wall of the studio. Inside it was cold, and I turned on a small fan heater to take the chill off.

A little after ten I heard a car labouring up the track. As its engine stilled, I looked out of the door and saw Steve and Jane, well muffled in heavy coats, hats, scarves and gloves. They looked up and I waved, so that they knew where to go. They waved back and trudged up the path, the inch or so of snow crunching under their stout boots.

'Come in,' I said. 'It's a little warmer in here, but not much. Heating this great space is beyond the power of this little machine.' They stamped their feet outside, and snow flew off their boots. 'It doesn't matter about a bit of wet. Have you been here before?'

They shook their heads, gazing around in wonder at the huge height of the building, the winter light pouring in at the long windows. 'I had no idea,' Jane said.

'Have you got time for coffee?' I asked.

They said they had, and I busied myself in the little galley as they looked around at the space. Some of Liam's work was propped up against the wall, and there was one of my small studies on an easel, the one of Peter and Old Joe that I was planning to give Mary for Christmas, but the Revelation panel, balanced rather precariously on two easels, was shrouded in a sheet.

I brought in three mugs and handed them out. 'No biscuits, I'm afraid. We're not so well supplied as St James's.'

'What an extraordinary building,' Steve murmured.

'Yes, it is,' I said. 'We're fortunate.'

'You're not alone, then?' Steve asked.

'No, at the moment there's another artist working here, Liam Audley. He had an exhibition in the town library recently.' I indicated the far wall. 'That's some of his work drying there.'

'Ah, yes,' Jane said. 'I meant to go to that, but I just didn't seem to have time. Which reminds me, the children's library books are overdue.'

'Is that it?' Steve waved his half-full coffee mug at my panel. 'Can we see?'

'Of course.' I started to remove the sheet, taking care – one wrong tug and it would come crashing down. 'I've tried to do it so that it looks OK from a distance and up close.'

There was silence from Steve and Jane, and when I looked at them they seemed frozen in place, still clutching their mugs, their eyes and mouths wide. Jane approached the painting hesitantly, reaching out her free hand as if to touch it, then thinking better of it and dropping her hand to her side. She turned to me. 'It's quite amazing,' she whispered. 'I've never seen anything like it.'

I wondered what acquaintance she had with painting generally, but simply thanked her. Steve came up and joined us. 'You've made it so clear,' he said. 'Labelling the cities. And here, "I am John, your brother." It puts it on everyone's level.'

'That's the idea,' I said.

Their eyes roved all round the painting, taking in the small images: the temple, the pack of wolves, the library of scrolls, the serpent and the martyrs, all the things the cities were known for, and John himself seated under the rock, his arm outstretched, so that their gaze was directed to the empty space left and centre.

'What goes here?' Jane asked.

'I did warn you it wasn't finished,' I said. 'That's going to be the risen Christ, the seven stars, and so on. I'm still thinking how to pull it off – I keep having the feeling I'm not really up to it.'

Steve shook his head. 'Artistically or spiritually?'

I smiled at his perception. 'Both.'

'Maybe a lot of prayer is needed while you're away,' he said. 'But it's quite astonishing. Just the size, the conception, the colours. It's wonderful, Fen. It'd be an honour to have it in our little church, even if only for a while.'

'Thank you,' I said. 'I'm glad you like it. And the honour is mine.'

They handed me their empty mugs.

'Martha said you're hoping to do a triptych,' Steve said. 'What do you have in mind for the next one?'

I took a breath. 'I've thought and thought about this,' I said finally. 'There's too much in Revelation to squeeze it into three panels, however large, and there's also the question of how much time I'll have. I'm going to stop before the seven trumpets. There's still a huge amount of material to draw on. This first one deals with earthly realities, as you see. The second one I'm thinking will be more about heaven. John's quite reserved about the details, so I can let my imagination roam free, but it'll present even more of a challenge – painting the throne above all others is an overwhelming thought. But there are all sorts of great things going on for an artist, almost too much really – the open door, the rainbow, the thrones and the prostrate elders and the gold crowns, the sea of glass, the twelve tribes on the gates, the seven lamps blazing – dazzling, a bit bewildering. I'll have to do a lot of sketches beforehand to get it all straight in my mind. As a composition it'll be a huge undertaking.'

'But you've made a marvellous start.'

'I'm very glad you think so. If you like it maybe others will too.'

AFTER THEY'D GONE, I thought I'd try to begin on the figure of Christ, just blocking in as a preparation for doing the details when I got back in the new year. I heard the door creak open as I was mixing paint, and then Liam appeared.

'Hello, stranger,' I said.

He seemed subdued. 'Was that the local vicar?'

'Yes. And his wife. Come to inspect the goods.'

'What did they think?' He came to stand beside me and looked intently at the painting, even getting up close so his eyes were almost on the canvas. 'Is anything wet?'

'Not yet. I'm going to try to progress it a bit while we've still got decent light. And yes, they seemed to approve.'

He nodded slowly. 'That's good.' He heaved a sigh.

'Are you all right? You seem, I don't know, a bit down.'

'I'm going to put the kettle on. Do you want anything?'

I shook my head, and he went into the kitchen. Minutes later he emerged with a mug of tea. 'Don't let me hold you up.'

'OK.' I started to apply a wash.

'Do you ever feel you're wasting your time?' he asked abruptly.

Brush in hand, I raised my eyebrows. 'Right now, no, but generally, of course, all the time. Is that how you feel?'

He perched on a backless stool, hooking his feet round the crossbar. 'Trouble is,' he said moodily, 'I'm no good at anything else.'

I turned to him momentarily. 'Do you want to do anything else? Anyway, what's brought this on? I thought the exhibition went well.'

He shifted his feet restlessly. 'Yeah, it was OK, but you know so many people are doing stuff: painting, making pots, whatever. How do you rise above the rest, how do you make yourself seen? Anyway, it's not just the work. I don't seem to know where my life's heading at the moment. If I ever did.'

I shook my head. 'Do any of us?'

'I guess not. Look, you're trying to work. I'll leave you in peace.' He drained his mug. 'Ugh, that was awful. I can't even make tea.' He took his cup to the sink, then with a defeated little wave headed for the door.

I felt a pang of sympathy. 'Liam, wait.' He paused and turned. 'I'm heading south tomorrow, got to do Christmas with the family, but if you're not doing anything do you want to borrow Martha's car and bring a takeaway round to my cottage this evening? It can't be a late one because I need to pack.'

His expression changed, his eyes lighting up. 'That'd be great, thanks. Sevenish?'

'Perfect. Bring some beers as well. I'll pay this time.'

He was smiling as he left. I felt a sudden qualm, a shudder, wondering, without any real reason, whether I was letting myself in for something that might be difficult to control. I shook myself impatiently, suppressed it and turned back to my work.

Liam arrived in a better mood, carrying a fragrant brown paper bag and a six-pack. I heard the door of Martha's elderly Beetle slam and the crunch of boots on snowy gravel, and I opened the door to let him in.

'Let's get this door shut,' I said. 'It's freezing out there, and I've lit a fire in your honour.'

'Sheer luxury,' he said as he removed his coat and hung it up.

'Did you get horse?' I enquired.

'What? No, chicken and lamb. You didn't say what you wanted, so I improvised.'

'Fine. Let's eat while it's hot. Plates and glasses on the table.'

Liam opened a couple of cans and poured while I opened cartons. He looked around, taking in my tiny domain. 'This is cosy. Did you say you used to hire this cottage when your kids were young?'

'Not this one, the one next door. It's bigger. I don't think you could squeeze four people in here.'

Within minutes we were eating and drinking, mostly without speaking. When the cartons were almost empty Liam said, 'The last time we were having a meal together you said you'd tell me your story.'

I looked up. 'What's this, curry and confession?'

He smiled, lighting up his bright blue eyes. 'Why, have you got something to confess?'

'Plenty, I'm sure. So, what do you want to know?'

'You mentioned you had a rather unusual childhood.'

'Ah, yes. I think I'll need a refill. This could be thirsty work.'

Liam poured, and I scraped the last of the food onto our cooling plates. Replete, we threw the debris in the kitchen bin.

'Let's find a comfortable chair and hug the fire,' I said. 'I'll give you the short version. I still have to pack.'

We settled into the two armchairs, one on each side of the little fireplace. I opened up the fire and fed it another log.

'So, Charles and Fiona Mayne, my parents. They didn't call themselves that, of course – they had any number of names for themselves, all taken from nature – I called my father by the names of trees oftener than Dad or Charlie; my mother might have been Rosehip or Snipe on any given occasion. They're currently working apple and pear orchards in New Zealand, still hale and only in their sixties, having started their family young, though not as young as me. My father came from rather well-heeled and almost aristocratic stock, and my mother's family were all very respectable, so I think my grandparents, whom I hardly ever saw, were a bit taken aback at the ways of their children. Possibly aghast. Because my parents adopted a freewheeling bohemian lifestyle, the whole sixties shooting match. When I think about it, I'm surprised they bothered to go through a conventional marriage. Lots of people among their friends weren't bothering with such repressive arrangements, much to the horror of the older generation. I doubt that anything mercenary was in my father's mind – the thought, for instance, that he might not inherit if he didn't observe some of the conventions: he had a fine disregard for material wealth. They were also faithful to one another, which again wasn't always so among their free-loving friends. Anyway, we travelled round the country – mostly in the north – and they worked at whatever they could find, nothing very skilled: farm labouring when casual workers were needed, and in the winter they did craft work to sell… we managed to survive, and it was all I knew, but now I wonder how we did it at times. Moving around from place to place didn't help my education. I didn't like school, partly because I was so different from the other children, in the way I dressed and talked, among other things, and I went as rarely as I could. The authorities caught up with us sometimes and then my parents sent us for a while, but they thought it was all very oppressive and taught us lots of things themselves, which is why I knew how to weave and make corn dollies but couldn't have told you the whereabouts of Japan, for instance, or the currency of Greece.'

Liam drained his glass. 'It sounds quite idyllic! Do you want another?'

'No, thanks, and you'd better not either – you'll be driving on snowy roads later.'

'If you say so, Grandma. Go on, this is most enlightening.'

'What can I tell you? We settled around here for quite a while, almost a year. We were living in a caravan on a farm further up the valley, not far from Mary and Peter's. It's how I got to know them. My parents were busy, and I remember feeling a bit lost. I'd have been about thirteen then, an amoral adolescent with little idea how to behave. The Hipkins took me under their wing, fed me, taught me things my parents had neglected, and were suitably appalled at my precocious record of behaviour with traveller boys. They also encouraged my drawing and bought me materials. I owe them a lot. They're like my second parents.'

'That's how you got into the farming life.'

I nodded. 'I helped where I could, and I enjoyed the work and the landscape. The weather didn't bother me, and I especially loved the animals. I drew endless studies of horses, dogs, sheep…'

Liam nodded. 'You were talented even then.'

'Well, maybe. But it all changed that evening I met John at the Young Farmers' social. But that'll have to be a story for another day.' I glanced at the clock. 'I'm going to throw you out in a moment, Liam. It's getting late.'

He pulled a face. 'Must I? It's cold out there. And not much warmer in my barn.'

'I don't know what you're thinking of,' I said tartly, 'but you sure as heck can't stay here. Everyone knows everyone's business, even though they're all so remote and scattered. And whatever you may have speculated, as you probably have, about the state of my marriage, seeing as I am here and not with my husband, the fact remains that I am still married. And absolutely not in the market for adultery.'

Liam got up from his chair with a smile that would have melted a snowman. 'Well, that's told me. I have the reputation of being a bit of a chancer, and I thought I'd just see what you said. Can't say I'm surprised. Shame though! Thanks for the meal and the fire. I'll see you next year, I hope. Have a safe journey tomorrow and a happy time with your family.' He put on his coat and wrapped his eight-foot scarf many times round his neck.

'Take the rest of the cans with you.' I accompanied him to the door and opened it to a freezing blast.

He bent and brushed my cheek with his lips. 'Goodnight, virtuous one. Get this door shut before you turn into an icicle.'

THE NEXT MORNING found me striding up the track from the cottage, my boots creaking on the new snow. It was a glorious day, crisp and cold. For once my backpack wasn't heavy; it contained little but Christmas presents: sweaters in local wool for John, Dan, and Alice, and a soft shawl for Grace, from the woollens shop in town, in various combinations of colours – heathery purple, burnt gold, cloudy blue. I'd also, as an afterthought, bought some local cheese for Gilbert. I'd brought few clothes; I had plenty at home, and I planned to pack lots of warm things for my return.

I'd left plenty of time to catch the bus up to the station, but as I walked down the road towards the town, filling my lungs with clean air, I heard a clatter behind me and a squeal of brakes. I turned and saw an old and muddy Land Rover with someone's arm waving out of the window.

'Do you need a lift somewhere?' It was Steve the vicar from St James's.

I climbed in beside him. 'Thank you,' I said. 'I'm hoping to catch the bus up to the station.'

'Right, I'll drop you off at the market stop.' He set off again, taking the corners with practised speed, humming something hymn-like under his breath.

'You're out early,' I observed.

'Yes.' He smiled and jerked a thumb into the back of the car. 'Thought I'd take Henry out for a good walk on the moor.' I turned my head, and my gaze was met by that of a large black Labrador with lolling tongue. 'I guess you're away south for Christmas, is that it?'

'Yes. In time for a marathon of cooking, I suspect.'

'I expect your family will be pleased to see you,' Steve said. 'How long have you been away?'

'Hm, six months or so.'

'But planning to return here?'

I looked at him sideways. 'Of course. I have a painting to finish, and maybe two more to begin.'

'You don't miss your life in – where is it?'

'Brant. And no, I don't.'

He said no more; perhaps he thought he'd asked too many questions already.

I CAUGHT THE bus – in fact, with my early start and the lift I had time to spare, and spent it in one of the touristy little shops selling cards and prints, some of which I bought in case there was someone I'd forgotten needing a present. The little bus was full, and as it climbed the hill its windows steamed up with all the people breathing. Everyone got off at the station and spread out along the platform. Ten minutes later, as my feet were beginning to feel the cold striking up from the concrete, the train rumbled into the station. I found a seat, stowed my pack, and started to thaw out. The train was warm.

When I'd done this journey in the opposite direction, it was summer, the fields were splashed with colour, the trees in leaf. Now the scene was quite different, but to my eyes even more beautiful: the starkness of the high moors, the rushing torrents in the valleys, the grand sweep of the hillsides, and everything white with a thin layer of snow through which the earth showed brown and black. The sun was rising high; soon the snow would be gone and with it some of the sheer glamour of the scenery.

The train clattered on, gathering speed, until it plunged down a defile and into a long tunnel. Now there was nothing to see, and I looked around covertly at my fellow passengers: an elderly woman opposite passing a sandwich to her flat-capped husband, a younger woman with two dark-haired, bright-eyed little boys standing on the seat and staring at me. I gave them a wave and they giggled and disappeared. I heard their mother admonish them. Further down the carriage I heard the high-pitched excited chatter of a handful of teenage girls.

Then the train pulled up from underground into the sunlight, and started to climb, thundering over a long, dramatic viaduct high above the valley.

I sighed, deeply content. Something in this landscape spoke to me at a profound level, and I knew I had to be here, come what may. I couldn't think about the future, how I might pull it off, whether in the end I would have to compromise, to capitulate; for now it was enough to know I'd be back in a couple of weeks, and it would still be winter.

The part of the journey down into Leeds was less inspiring, and my mind wandered. I found myself thinking about Liam, and then John, even ranging back to the transient flings of my youth before marriage claimed me. They hardly counted as relationships, and I remembered Mary, in her quiet way, warning me against such shallow escapades. I was a wife at seventeen, a mother before I was twenty, and I had always been faithful. I'd only ever really known John, and I wondered what it would have been like if I'd had more experience. Not, I told myself sternly, that I was about to seek any. But although I had given Liam short shrift, and although I wasn't tempted in any real way to stray, it was probably because I had plenty to occupy my thoughts. Loneliness and boredom had much to answer for, I thought; and I was suffering from neither. I smiled to myself. I had no plans to succumb to any passing seducer, however handsome and charming; I had made promises and meant to keep them – but to be propositioned was not entirely unwelcome. I wondered about Liam: was I to take him at his own estimation, an opportunist with no serious intent, or were there depths that he guarded under that façade? Something about him, added to what he had told me about his past, gave me the impression of a lost soul. But I hardly knew him well enough to speculate.

My thoughts of John were altogether more subduing. I had no real idea how he would be towards me after our long separation. We'd talked on the phone, of course, and exchanged regular messages, but I'd had little hint of his state of mind. Would he keep his distance, subtly signalling his disapproval, resentment even, at my defection? I didn't know, and I thought I would need to see his face, gauge his reactions, study his body language, to get near the truth. Considering how I had left, how we had parted, I surprised myself by how much I cared what he might be thinking. I wriggled in my seat, trying to shake off my thoughts. The closer I got to Brant, the less comfortable I felt. 'It's only two weeks,' I told myself. 'I can ride it out, whatever happens.'

As IT TURNED out, looking back weeks later, nothing about that Christmas was as I expected. I had the feeling at times that the twists and turns of my life were designed to wrong-foot me, but perhaps I had simply developed the unhelpful habit of overthinking.

My journey back to Brant was unexpectedly smooth, and I was indoors by mid-afternoon. The house felt particularly big and echoing, quiet, with a patina of dust. John had obviously vacuumed the carpets and the kitchen sink was empty and clean. I glanced inside the freezer and the fridge and found them pretty much empty. I had planned anyway to shop for food the following day. I found a neglected pot of stew at the bottom of the freezer and put it in the microwave to start defrosting. That, and frozen vegetables, would have to do for the evening. I guessed there may be potatoes in the rack.

Upstairs it seemed quieter still, muffled by dense carpets, and spacious after my tiny cottage. I stowed the Christmas presents in my too-tidy art room and went into the bedroom to put away such clothes as I had brought. The curtains were closed, the air fusty. I opened both curtains and, for a while, the window to freshen the air, despite the gathering darkness in the street outside. Here in the south it was simply cloudy and mild, the pavements wet after rain. John had pulled back the quilt, but I thought he probably hadn't changed the sheets for a while, so I stripped the bed and threw the bed linen into the washing basket. I was stuffing a pillow into a clean case when I heard a car pull up on the gravel drive. A moment later there came the sound of a key in the lock and John's voice calling up the stairs. 'Fen! Where are you?'

Pillow in hand, I went to the top of the stairs. 'Hello! You're early.'

'I bunked off,' he said, his smile wide. 'Couldn't wait to see you.'

He shed his overcoat, and I trotted down the stairs and into his arms. After a moment I pulled back and looked up at him. 'You've lost weight, John. I swear I can feel bones.'

'Too busy for three squares a day,' he said. 'Almost no alcohol either! I've been waiting for you to feed me up.' He kissed me lingeringly, then nuzzled my neck, inhaling as if breathing in my scent. 'I've missed you,' he said, his voice husky. 'You've no idea.'

I disentangled myself. 'I've missed you too,' I said softly. I had to say it, but found I meant it more than I thought I would, and that was a surprise. Oddly, I felt startled by the solid reality of my husband, as if he had become, in my mind, more and more insubstantial during the months of my absence. 'I'll make some tea.'

'Oh,' he said. 'Is there any milk, or did I use the last drop on my cereal this morning? I'm afraid I haven't done any shopping to speak of.'

'So I saw,' I said. 'But I'll need to do a big shop tomorrow. Christmas is just days away, in case you haven't noticed.'

'So it is.' We went into the kitchen, his arm round my shoulders, as if he was afraid I'd disappear again. He parked himself in a chair as I filled the kettle. 'You look well, Fen. Bright-eyed and rosy-cheeked.'

I leaned back on the kitchen counter. 'I am well. All that cycling in the fresh air.'

He looked at me, his expression serious. 'So it was a good thing, this project? You're happy? It's going well?'

'Yes,' I said quietly. 'Pretty well, thanks.'

He seemed sunk in thought as I made the tea. I put a mug in front of him and slid into the chair opposite.

'I've been thinking,' he said. 'I didn't send you off in the best spirit – I see that now. It seemed, I don't know, to happen very quickly. But I've realised you needed to go, you had a right, to make something of yourself I suppose; to see where it led.' He paused and took a sip of his tea, and I waited. He looked up, his eyes seeking mine. 'I don't like it, obviously. It's no fun coming back to an empty house. No one to chew over the day with. But the fact is the last few months have been crazy – if I'm not at one airport or another I'm in endless meetings, and more often than not I've come home late and worn out with no thought in my mind but sleep, and the next day it all starts again! I would have been very poor company. But there have been times…' I raised an enquiring eyebrow and said nothing. 'Those few mornings when I could relax, when I just had paperwork to catch up on, when I didn't have to go into the office, that's when I missed you most – no warm body beside me to wake up to.'

'Well, we can do some catching up, I hope,' I said. 'Have you got time off now?'

'I finish the day before Christmas Eve. So I can pick Dan up from the airport, and Alice from wherever. But things are winding down, thankfully. For the moment, at least. With any luck we'll have a bit of time.'

'And after Christmas?'

He shook his head. 'I'll get a couple of days off for New Year. Other than that, it'll all be revving up again. Things are at a critical point, and they'll need me.' He leaned across the table and took my hand, stroking my work-roughened knuckles with his thumb. 'We'll have time. There are things I need to talk to you about.'

I finished my tea and got up. 'I found an elderly pot of casserole in the freezer. That'll have to do for tonight.' I smiled. 'We'll start that fattening-up process.'

'I'll open a bottle,' he said. 'Celebrate your homecoming.'

Hot food and a couple of glasses of wine later, we washed the dishes together and chatted about nothing much. I dried my hands. 'What was it you wanted to talk to me about?'

His eyes glinted. 'That can wait. I'm thinking an early night might be a good idea.'

'What, and miss the news?'

He slid his arm round my waist. 'I can do without the news for once. You'll see how much I missed you.'

Somehow this was a side of John that I'd forgotten, and it was faintly alarming, but I had no problem with the prospect of sex. In the event, loving and tender as he was, he was way too urgent and it was all over too soon. 'Sorry, sorry, sorry,' he groaned, pulling me into his arms so that I could scarcely breathe. 'I'm just so tired, and you feel so lovely, so warm, and you smell so good, I just couldn't…'

'Go to sleep, John,' I said quietly. 'Tomorrow's another day.'

'I'll make it up to you,' he murmured, already half asleep. 'Wake me up at six.'

'Don't be silly.'

Frustrated, watching him slide down into oblivion, I felt a pang of annoyance. I couldn't sleep for a couple of hours: the bed was too warm, I missed the cool room I'd left behind, and John tossed and muttered in his sleep. Somewhere around three in the morning I drifted off, and woke scratchy-eyed to find John fully dressed and smelling of toothpaste, leaning over me and planting a kiss on my forehead. 'Got to go,' he said. 'See you this evening. I won't be late.'

TRUE TO HIS prediction he was home by five and breezed in damp from the rain. He sat at the kitchen table where I was elbow deep in pastry, making a second batch of mince pies. 'They look good,' he said, eyeing up a trayful I'd just taken out of the oven.

'Have one if you like,' I said. 'If you don't mind a burned mouth.'

He folded his arms, rocked back in his chair. 'Things are slowing down a bit at work. Even the most dedicated are beginning to wind things up in time for the holiday. It won't last, but I plan to make the most of it. Tomorrow I might even take the afternoon off and do a bit of Christmas shopping. Not before time!'

'I haven't got much in the way of presents,' I said. 'Just for you, the children and Grace.'

'There's no need to go overboard, is there?' he said. 'So, what have you been up to today?'

I went to the sink to wash my floury hands. 'Busy. Did a huge supermarket shop and spent a lot of money. The freezer looks a bit healthier. I've cleaned the place a bit, and if you go into the lounge you'll see there are some decorations up, but we need more. Perhaps you can bring the tree in and see if the lights still work. I couldn't find the wreath for the front door. Do you know where it is?' He shook his head. 'Maybe we can get a new one. Oh yes, and on my way to the shops I called in on Grace.'

'How is she?'

'You haven't seen her while I've been away?'

'Hardly at all. I think she hibernates in winter. Oh, yes, thinking about it, she did call in a few weeks ago with a cake she'd made. But she didn't stop.'

'She promised me she'd keep an eye on you and Alice.'

John looked startled. 'Do we need supervising?'

'Of course not. Anyway, I thought she didn't look well. She does suffer with her chest, poor thing. She's had a nasty bout of something or other, said she was better, but she looked quite grey. Our climate doesn't suit her.'

'Is her daughter still on at her to emigrate? What's her name again?'

'Andrea. Yes, and I think Grace may be weakening. It's probably true that the weather in Western Australia would be a help to someone like her.'

'You'd miss her if she went.'

'Of course,' I said, putting the towel back on its hook. 'But if it was good for her health… I'm worn out with all this shopping, baking and decorating. You can make the tea.'

He got up and filled the kettle. 'Seems you need more sleep.'

'Hm. That didn't work out so well last time you suggested it.'

'All right, don't rub it in!' he protested. 'I told you I'd make it up to you, and I will.'

I narrowed my eyes. 'I'll believe that when it happens.'

He came to where I stood and grabbed me round the waist, putting on a frown that was supposed to look intimidating but succeeded only in being comical. 'Is that a challenge?'

I shrugged. 'Question is, are you up to it?'

'You'll find out, won't you, hussy? Now, my love. To be serious, let's make this tea and talk cruises.'

My gut clenched at this, but I didn't let him see. 'You want to go on another cruise? After last time?'

He released me and poured boiling water into two mugs. 'It'll be different. I have something in mind, something you might like.'

I sat at the table, still covered with flour and bits of pastry. 'Go on.'

After a moment he set a cup of tea in front of me. 'Are these pies cool yet?' He didn't wait for my answer, but picked one up and bit into it. 'Mm, good. This cruise,' he said, swallowing, 'goes to interesting places, historical sites you might just be interested in, places you might even want to sketch. And there are lectures on board, lots of subjects, even art. Wait, I'll get the brochure.'

Moments later he came back with a glossy publication.

'I'll wipe this table down,' I said. 'Otherwise it'll be covered in flour.'

'Do that later,' he said. 'Let's look at this in the lounge. Then I can admire your handiwork with the decorations at the same time.'

Side by side on the sofa, tea at our elbows, he took me through the delights of the ship, called *Athene Four*. Part of a fleet, I supposed. It was a glamorous floating casino and five-star hotel, everything I disliked. But the itinerary was enticing enough, and there were indeed some lectures of interest. I tried to be enthusiastic for John's sake; I could hardly complain when he was doing his best to be generous and reasonable. With an inward sigh I said, 'When were you thinking of booking?'

'September, I thought. Alice will be starting her final year around then, and the weather won't be too stifling. I've waited to consult you, but I'll need to book soon or lose out. What do you think?'

'Yes, it looks good,' I said. 'Go ahead.'

John turned to me. 'By the summer, with any luck things will be more settled at work. With two big companies merging there'll be a lot of stuff to sort out, different ways of working, new protocols to draft… I'll be busy most of next year. But after that we hope it'll be more or less plain sailing. And you'll be back, won't you? The project will be finished by then?'

Would it? Perhaps it would; but the idea of not having the triptych to work on gave a me a cold feeling of loss. I forced a smile. 'I hope so.'

'I was thinking,' John rushed on, 'we could have a little celebration for my birthday before the cruise. Nothing too fancy, perhaps a few friends?'

'Whatever you like,' I said. My smile was beginning to feel fixed. 'Yes, you go and book it. You don't want to be disappointed.'

He got up, beaming. 'I'll go to my study and do it right away. I'll try and get us a cabin with a view.'

Even if it's only a view of endless ocean, I thought, but said nothing.

I CLEANED UP in the kitchen, but my thoughts were elsewhere. I realised it wasn't the cruise that was making me feel leaden; after all, that would be just a matter of a couple of weeks, and I didn't begrudge John his pleasure. It was more his assumption that my time in Yorkshire would be over, the paintings done, with the need for it out of my system. And then what? Another forty years of comfortable housewifery, punctuated by the odd dabble in art? The prospect was as grim as it had ever been – worse now, having had a taste of the freedom to be my other, I believed truer, self.

I had to push these thoughts away, swallow them down, if this Christmas was not to be tainted by my resentment, my thoughts of escape. Perhaps I could make it work. Perhaps, after all, I had had my moment, and that was all there was. Besides, I didn't have to think about it yet. September was a long way off. I took a deep breath and resolved to behave as if all was well. Momentarily I faced the unpalatable possibility that, in the long run, my marriage was doomed. I didn't want to hurt John; I still felt love for him, but the life that seemed inevitable with him filled me with a sense of futility. But as I started to prepare our evening meal I set these thoughts aside. I'd given them attention, and now they must wait. Resolution was not to be hoped for, not yet.

For the rest of the evening John was buoyant. He'd succeeded in booking the cruise for the second half of September and took delight in showing me the kind of cabin we would occupy. Even the usual miseries of the world news didn't dampen his enthusiasm, and afterwards he made good on his promise – more than once. It was like, and unlike, old times; I remembered our early years, but now it simply made me sad. Was I facing a lifetime of endless pretence?

Stop, I told myself sternly. *This is what you have at this moment, and you need to make the best of it.*

THE FOLLOWING EVENING, I broached another subject that was bothering me. 'Has Alice been around much? While I've been away?'

John shook his head. 'One or two weekends, but even then she was meeting up with old friends. I didn't see much of her. Why?'

I sighed. 'I don't know. She worries me. We've had a few chats on the phone, but she doesn't really tell me anything. She seems unhappy.'

John frowned. 'She doesn't tell me much either. But I get the impression there's been some love interest that's not worked out, some boyfriend giving her grief… maybe you should sound her out. Ask her what's going on.'

'I can try, I suppose. She'll tell me about her work, but if anything more personal comes up she tends to withdraw. Does she talk to Dan?'

'No idea.'

'I don't want to stick my nose in; she'd tell me where to get off if I tried. I'd like to think she was happy, though. And I don't think I've ever been the sort of confiding, cosy mother who listens to her children's woes and dishes out sage advice.'

John laughed. 'Maybe not. But you're the mother they've got, and I am sure they know they're loved.' He looked at me meaningfully. 'Speaking of which…'

I pretended to be shocked. 'John, what are you like? Are you on some wonder drug? Haven't you had enough?'

'Never,' he said firmly. 'Anyway, in a week or two you'll be gone again, and I'll be forced to resume my monk-like existence. I don't want to alarm you, but I'm just getting into my stride.'

I laughed. 'All right, Casanova.' I got up from the sofa, took his hand and pulled him to his feet. 'I'm all yours. Convince me.'

ON THE MORNING of Christmas Eve, I had to wake John from a deep sleep.

'John, it's ten past seven.'

'What?'

'It's a good two-hour run to Heathrow.'

He sat bolt upright and ran his hand through his hair. 'Heathrow? Oh, yes, I'm picking Dan up, aren't I?'

'Look, if you don't feel up to it I'll do it.'

He groaned softly and put his feet on the floor. 'No, it's fine, I'll come to in a minute.'

'Why don't you have a quick shower while I make you some coffee, maybe a piece of toast?'

'Done.' He stumbled to the bathroom, and I flung on a dressing gown and ran downstairs. Fifteen minutes later he appeared, his hair damp, his eyes bleary. 'It's not Dan who's on the red-eye, it's me.'

I passed him his mug. 'Are you going to be OK to drive?'

He took a sip of his coffee. 'I reckon. This is strong enough to keep an elephant awake. Anyway, there won't be much on the road this early. I'll put the radio on, and then I'll have Dan to talk to.'

'I wouldn't count on that. He'll probably be asleep. He'll have had to get to the airport very early to catch his flight.'

'Don't worry – I'll go very sedately. And maybe I can catch a couple of hours this afternoon while you chew the fat with Daniel. Have we heard from Alice?'

'The briefest of messages – she'll be at the station around one.'

John finished his coffee and munched half a slice of toast. 'I'll probably have to wait for Dan to clear customs and find his baggage. I can stoke up on caffeine then.'

'Please go carefully.'

'Always.' He planted a kiss on my cheek and was gone.

THE CAR ROARED up the drive at midday. I'd managed to hang up some late-arriving cards, put sheets on the children's beds, make a batch of soup and have a bath.

The front door banged open. 'Mum! Where's my favourite mother?'

I'd almost forgotten how he sounded, my lovely son, even though we'd spoken on the phone a few weeks ago. Then there he was, his hair much longer, a scrub of beard on his chin, his eyes bleary, his clothes as crumpled as ever. He swept me into a tight hug.

'Sorry,' he said. 'I probably don't smell too fresh. Long day yesterday, bit of a rush getting ready.'

John appeared, and I saw how washed-out he looked. 'I'm knackered,' he said, his voice slurring slightly. 'I'm going to try and catch up on sleep.'

'Do you want anything?'

'Maybe later.'

Dan went to his father and put an arm round his shoulder. 'Dad's a hero,' he said. 'Getting up with the sparrows and braving the traffic. Go on, old man, get some sleep.'

'Ha! Old man indeed!' John protested. 'The only reason you're so chipper is because you slept all the way home. Right, yes, I'm going.'

Daniel perched on a stool at the table. 'My body clock's all over the place. I'm starving.'

'You look as if you haven't eaten in a month,' I said. 'D'you want some soup? A hunk of bread, perhaps? Cheese and ham?'

Dan sighed. 'You say the nicest things.'

I furnished him with his makeshift meal and sat opposite, watching him gulp soup and tear chunks off his bread. 'So, what's the latest?'

He looked up. 'Not much… very busy at work, had to get one thing finished, just made it. It's a lot easier now I'm closer to the centre. Less time travelling.'

'Tell me about your new place.'

Dan put down his spoon. 'It's not big. In fact, it's tiny. We have a minute bathroom, a kitchen that houses a sofa and a TV, a bedroom overlooking the street, and it's three floors up with no lift. No wonder I'm skinny.'

'What about the man you're sharing with?'

'Clyde. Yeah, him offering me a place to stay was a big deal. I couldn't have afforded the old flat on my own once Rafe moved out.'

'So, what happened with Rafe? If I'm not being too nosy.'

Dan laughed. 'No, Mum, it's fine. Give me some more soup and I'll tell all.'

I brought the saucepan to the table and ladled soup into his bowl. 'I'll settle for the expurgated version.'

'Rafe, yeah. Turns out he was a bit of a tart.' He looked up at me, serious now, his spoon halfway to his mouth, dripping soup back into the bowl. 'You know, don't you, Mum?' he said softly. 'You've always known.'

I shook my head. 'No, not always, love. And you didn't say anything, so I was never totally certain.'

'Well, here I am, coming out. Rafe and I were supposed to be an item, but he liked to play around.' He shrugged. 'Rafe's not a bad guy, but he's young, and I guess not ready for anything deeper. Whereas I'm an old man of twenty-three.' He grinned. 'I even found a grey hair the other day.'

'And Clyde?'

'Clyde's a very different sort of person. Quiet. Steady. But wickedly funny. Yeah,' he said softly, 'Clyde's all right.' He looked at me a little anxiously. 'But are you OK with it?'

'It's your life, Dan.'

'I know, but…'

'It's got to be preferable to finding your son makes bombs or mugs old ladies or steals from charities.'

'What? How did you know? Who's been talking?'

'Silly. Honestly, Dan, I don't have strong feelings about it. I'm more interested in you being healthy and happy.'

He scraped his bowl clean and then polished it with the last of his bread. 'Dad won't like it, though, will he?'

'Hm, no, I guess not. He's usually pretty reasonable, but some things seem to get to him at a gut level. I guess it's something to do with the way he was raised, the culture… I don't know, Dan. Do you want me to speak to him?'

'Kind of, but that seems a bit cowardly.'

'Let's just play it by ear, yeah?'

'If the opportunity arises, I'll talk to him myself. But I won't flaunt it.' He sighed. 'Anyway, I won't be around that much. Christmas, of course. But there are quite a few people I want to catch up with while I'm this side of the pond. And I already have something planned for New Year.'

'Of course you do.'

'What about you? Got some revelry in store?'

'Your father mentioned some vague thing about seeing some golfing chums of his. I can't say the prospect thrills.'

Dan laughed. 'I hear you've agreed to a cruise. Did he browbeat you into it?'

'Certainly not.' I looked up at the clock. 'Oops, time's flying, Dan. Your sister will be at the station any time now. I'm surprised she isn't on the phone demanding to know where her lift is.'

'I'll get her, Mum.' He got to his feet, stretching. 'Then I might just follow Dad's example. That early start's catching up with me.'

'Just don't crash the car. That would really land you in hot water.'

HALF AN HOUR later excited chatter and whoops of glee let me know both my children were in the house. They came into the kitchen pushing, shoving, complaining, and laughing as if they were small children again. Alice flew across the kitchen and gave me a hug. 'Hi, Mum.' She sounded breathless. 'Dan's misbehaving again, and honestly he stinks.'

Daniel's grin was broad. 'Miss Hygiene has ordered me to take a shower, so I'll oblige.' He gave us a mock-salute and disappeared upstairs.

'Where's Dad?' Alice said.

'Sleeping off his early start. That's if he can stay asleep with the racket you two make.' I studied my daughter and was agreeably surprised. She seemed to have put on a little weight, and it suited her. For once she wasn't pale, and her usually limp blonde hair seemed shinier. 'You look well, love.'

'So do you, Mum. All that fresh air and exercise?'

'Yep. What's your secret?'

She took a deep breath. 'If I'm going to tell you all my secrets I'll need sustenance. If Dan has left anything. That cheese looks nice.'

'Help yourself. There's soup if you like.'

I was beginning to think there was something in the air; to have both my children so forthcoming was a rarity. Perhaps it was something to do with my being away and less available; perhaps, astonishing though it was to contemplate, they had missed me.

'So,' Alice said between mouthfuls, 'what would you like to know?'

'Whatever you want to tell me,' I answered, perhaps a little cryptically. 'But specifically, why you look and sound so much better than the last time I saw you.'

She laughed. 'Well, that's an open field, for sure. But first,' she added, sobering, 'I should assure you I haven't neglected my studies even when things were at their most dire.' She took another chunk of Stilton. 'Mm, this is good.' She looked at me across the table where I was chopping up onions and peppers. 'What are you making?'

'Lasagne. Go on – don't keep me in suspense. It's bad for my blood pressure.'

She took a deep breath. 'Well, I suppose the bottom line is, I got rid of a toxic influence from my life. My closest friends, that's Lottie and Alex, had been on at me for ages, but I wouldn't listen. It was a bit like being in a cult.'

'What?' I looked up, alarmed.

'No, don't worry, I wasn't, it was just one person who was ruining my life, but it was my own fault, I let him do it. Until now.' I said nothing, simply raised my eyebrows and reached for the garlic press. 'Sebastian Ormerod. There's an aristocratic name for you! I don't even know if it was for real, but he claimed to be a genuine blueblood. Why didn't I see what a huge snob he was? Stupid virginal little Alice, so mousy, such a nerd, always getting her work in on time, didn't know how to have fun, then along comes Seb and pays her attention, and she's flattered! I was an idiot, Mum, I really was. But it was a bit overwhelming – the very handsome Seb Ormerod, charming when he chose to be, witty, popular, confident – I was a starry-eyed sitting duck. And at first it was all lovely: you know, trips on the river, flowers even! My friends said 'Don't trust him' but I just thought they were jealous. Their boyfriends seemed so dull by comparison. I did wonder why he was interested in me when he could have had any girl he wanted, but in the end I found that's exactly what he was doing – having any girl he wanted! But I refused to see it, and by then I was in too deep. Of course, his behaviour got worse, and the nastier he got the more I clung and cried and needed reassurance and the more he tried to shake me off. By that time, he'd got everything he wanted from me – I suppose it was all a power trip to him.' She fell silent, biting her lip.

'How long did all this last, Ally?'

'Oh, about eight months. I did keep a shred of sense, though. I managed not to get pregnant.'

'Thank goodness! What made you see through him in the end?'

'It was horrible. We were out with a group, mates of his, not very nice people, most of them, and they were all very drunk and loud, and I was sober because I was getting over a chest infection and I was feeling rotten and on antibiotics, and you know what it's like when everyone is drunk and you're not – they all seemed immature and annoying, laughing at things that weren't remotely funny. He was being very rude and abusive to me and finding it hilarious, and I said I felt unwell and wanted to go home, and he said, 'Well, go then,' and they all ran off laughing fit to burst and left me, and it was one o'clock in the morning, a long way from my hall, and I had no money. That was when I woke up and admitted he didn't care what happened to me. I walked home – it was only a couple of miles, but I was wearing stupid shoes and it was raining.'

'Good grief.'

'Yeah, well, a couple of days later he turned up at my door, holding a big bunch of flowers, full of apologies, totally insincere of course – perhaps he thought I was still that brainless weakling he could treat any way he liked and still take everything he wanted. I kept him on the doorstep and told him what I thought of him.' She grinned. 'I spoke very loudly, and he tried to shut me up, but people were coming out of their rooms to listen, so I told him – and them – what a louse he was and a total failure, and utterly useless in bed, and then I said his ego was ten times the size of his – well, that was the moment he threw the flowers down and ran off.' And people were standing in their doorways laughing and clapping. I think there were others he'd treated badly but they were too embarrassed to admit it.'

'What a vile experience. My blood is boiling, thinking of you ill, in the middle of the night, abandoned! Anything could have happened.'

'That's exactly what Alex and Lottie said, among all the "I told you sos".' She sighed. 'But when the sense of triumph evaporated, I got really down. All that glamour – gone! And where was I? Who was I? Just another foolish girl, taken in. I was ashamed and miserable. Anyway, I got my head down and worked, and did really well, which did my self-esteem some good, so things started to improve. And I went out with my real friends and did some silly, fun things, no pretence at sophistication, and that's when I met Rory.'

'You've had quite a roller-coaster year. I had no idea.'

'Yeah, well, I didn't say anything, did I? I didn't want to admit what a fool I'd been. So I was just miserable and bad-tempered.'

'I wish you had said something,' I murmured.

She shrugged. 'What could you have done? Anyway, you weren't there. When I came home for the odd weekend I didn't tell Dad anything either, but he must have known something was wrong. He was very kind to me. Made an effort to get my favourite meals, that sort of thing. I guess he didn't really know what to do.'

'I'm just sorry you had to go through that. Not just sorry – appalled.'

'It's taught me a lot – mostly about myself. Anyway, things are a million times better now.'

'So, are you going to tell me about Rory?'

She smiled. 'I went out with Lottie and her bloke Jay and a few others – we'd decided it might be a laugh to go ice-skating! None of us was any good and I fell over so many times, you wouldn't believe. We went to the café there afterwards, and Rory was working in the kitchens. He's a student, doing – what is it? Biochemistry and something – but he has no money so he has to work. Someone spilled their drink all over the floor, and Rory arrived with a mop and bucket. We got chatting, I thought he was nice, and that was it. But a week or so later we bumped into each other on campus and went for a coffee, and that was the start. A very slow start, too, nothing like dashing, smooth-talking Seb, because Rory is almost as much of a workaholic nerd as I am, and anyway I don't think he'd know how to sweep anyone off their feet! He's the opposite of Seb in practically every way I can think of – he's not handsome, he's a bit overweight, his hair is always unruly, and he wears terrible baggy clothes, but he's one of the kindest people I've ever met. He's also very Scottish and very funny and doesn't take himself too seriously. The only time I've seen him anything but calm is when I told him about Seb. He was so angry! When he is excited about something his Scottish accent gets thicker, and I fall about laughing because I can't understand a word!'

'Well, that's good news, love. He sounds nice.'

'Yeah, he is. He helped put me back together. One day you should meet him.'

'I shall look forward to it.' Privately I marvelled. This was a version of my daughter I hadn't seen for a long time, and I was thankful.

ONE AFTER THE other John and Dan came down, both red-eyed and bleary, and John with a greyish pallor I didn't like, but they both revived with food and a glass of wine and the meal was convivial, the children making each other laugh with their antics and John and I looking on and shaking our heads. I was still in a state of wonder and disbelief that things were going so well. Could it last?

As we always had, John and I drove down to St Swithin's for the midnight service, through the quiet streets wet from rain, the puddles reflecting the Christmas lights that festooned not only the houses but also their trees and hedges. In the lit-up festive darkness even Brant could look beautiful.

The service was as usual a quiet one. I took the opportunity of greeting a few people, and at the end everyone wished each other a happy Christmas and there was a real sense of solidarity – at least in part, I thought, because we were all out at almost one in the morning when most sensible people were asleep.

At the door I shook Gilbert's hand. 'Happy Christmas, Gilbert.'

'And to you, Fen. It's good to see you. Are you home for long?'

'Just a couple of weeks,' I said. 'But we'll be here tomorrow morning, as usual. Oh, and I've left you a little gift on the vestry table. A souvenir of Yorkshire. You need to keep it in the fridge.'

'How very kind! '

'It's just a bit of local cheese. I know you and Norma are fond of it. I didn't see her tonight – is she not well?'

Gilbert looked grave. 'No, I'm afraid she's had one of her spells. They seem to be happening more often these days.'

'I'm sorry, truly. Please give her my love.'

'I will, thank you.'

'Oh, and also, Gilbert, I've returned your book. It's been most helpful.'

He smiled, and his watery blue eyes lit up. 'Excellent. You must tell me how your work is going.'

'Tomorrow! Perhaps there'll be a moment.'

Then John was at my elbow, having done what needed to be done with the safe, and he wished Gilbert a happy Christmas and steered me through the door.

'We'll be back in the morning,' he said.

'As far as I'm concerned,' I said, 'you can sleep till ten fifteen. But I'll have to get up early. If you want Christmas dinner I'll need to see to food.'

He unlocked the car, yawning widely. 'I need more sleep. I can't understand how you're so wide awake.'

'It's because I'm so much younger,' I said.

'Ha, ha.'

On the way home I told him what Alice had told me – a short version.

'I thought something was up,' he said, frowning. 'If I'd known…'

'What, you'd have given Seb a thrashing?' I said. 'That, my love, would have been a very bad idea.'

'I suppose.'

'Anyway, I think Alice's revenge was probably more effective.'

His mouth quirked. 'It's good to see she's got spirit, as my old dad would have said. It's been in short supply the last few months.'

I sighed. 'It's a pity she had go to through that to learn who to trust, how to be wary.'

'I hope this Rory fellow is an improvement.'

'Well, whatever he is, it's up to her. Believe it or not, she's a grown-up. At her age I had a child and another on the way.'

'But you were grown up by the time you were ten.'

'Silly.'

THE CHRISTMAS MORNING service at St Swithin's was as it always was: calm, traditional, reassuring. I thought with an inward smile of the amiable mayhem at St James's, where half the congregation, adults as well as children, would be taking part in an barely-rehearsed interactive Nativity, draped in sheets and tea-towels, complete, so they hoped, with a local farmer and a sheep making a guest appearance – it was too early for a lamb. There were no children at St Swithin's, and the only Nativity was a little scene populated with knitted figures someone had made years before and that got taken out of the cupboard annually in time for the Carol Service.

Christmas Day and Boxing Day happened in our household with much noise and loud music from Dan and Alice, too much eating, unwrapping of presents, and on the children's part liberal drinking. Had my offspring always been this excitable? Or had I simply forgotten? At their instigation we played board games and cards, and there were several occasions when I caught John asleep in his chair. By the end of Boxing Day I had a headache, needing a long walk in fresh air. I suggested it for the following morning but was met with groans, so in the event I went by myself, and was reminded as I trudged the dreary winter streets of my dislike of the city. Eventually I found my way to Enson Park, where I encountered families with dogs, all getting very muddy. I was beginning to wish I'd brought my bike.

Having done their family duty, as they no doubt saw it, Dan and Alice disappeared for much of the time between Boxing Day and New Year, looking up friends, sometimes coming home to sleep, sometimes not. When they were at home, they spent hours on the phone to respective partners and constantly foraged for snacks. After days of rest and good food John began to perk up, but by this time the usual family gripes were starting to surface as small irritations, exacerbated by being cooped up together, led to sniping and minor outbursts. I seemed to spend a lot of time cooking, cleaning up and doing laundry, until I found myself wishing they would go back to America and university and leave us in peace.

Dutifully, though with a leaden heart, I went along with John to a New Year's party at the home of one of his golfing friends. In the past, obliged to attend such an occasion, dressed up in uncomfortable glamour, I might have sought relief in too many gins; now, buoyed up by the prospect of imminent escape, I was able to restrain myself.

On New Year's Day, 2017, I stood on the back terrace in my dressing gown, nursing a cup of tea and gazing down across the garden. It looked especially neglected, the lawn sodden and rank, the flowers still with shrivelled dead heads attached. Everyone else was asleep; John had gone straight to bed after the party, and the children came home much later but – under threat of severe repercussions – had managed to keep quiet and not wake us up.

For some reason the prospect of the wet, straggly garden, untended and unloved, made me think of my lost cat, Wesley, who had loved to lie under shrubs in the shade or bask on the terrace, stretched out in all his ginger glory. I wondered, not for the first time, what had become of him – was he dead, perhaps run over? No body had been found, and there'd been no sightings. Had he wandered off and found another home, someone who offered him tastier food? Had he – I shuddered at the thought – been stolen for his fur? He wasn't a special cat, except to me, with no hint of a pedigree; I'd got him as scrawny, leggy kitten from a local animal sanctuary. Had he, perhaps, gone for a snooze in the back of some tradesman's open-doored van and been driven far away? I supposed I would never know, and I felt a pang of loneliness. Wesley was too independent and wide-ranging to be anyone's cosy chum, but he was unchallenging company when I needed it, and he'd been the only pet I'd ever had. I'd grown up with animals, both farm and wild, but we moved around too much to look after pets, and my attempt to rear an abandoned baby wild rabbit was, inevitably, doomed.

For me, a life without animals in it was somehow impoverished, lacking in some important dimension that human friendship could not supply, but John wasn't keen, and when Wesley disappeared he made it clear he didn't want another cat, or a dog, especially since, so he said, Wesley's loss had hit me hard. I didn't believe he was trying to defend me from more sadness and worry – that was just an excuse. But at the time I didn't have the will to fight my cause, and besides, Wesley was irreplaceable. In Yorkshire, of course, I was now surrounded by animals

– sheep, cattle, horses, the occasional goat, chickens, moles, mice and rats, and other people's pets; but the only one close to my heart was Sadie, and although she seemed content in my company there was no doubt that she belonged to Mary.

I spent the next couple of days making freezer meals for John, and then he went back to work, and Dan to America, and Alice back to Rory before term began. Much as I loved them, I was ready to go. John was in a strange mood, by turns tired, surly and resentful, then apologetic and loving, almost clingy; and after a few days he was needed back in Boston, so this was my cue to leave. We parted friends, but there was a hollowness about it; I asked him when the merger would be completed and he was vague, merely saying that he hoped by February he wouldn't need to travel but could work from the UK office. I suggested again that he might like to visit me in Yorkshire when things eased up, and he said he would, but I sensed his polite lack of enthusiasm. I wondered if perhaps he felt he'd made enough concessions and would wait till I stopped being selfish and flighty and come back where – according to him – I belonged. Perhaps I was doing him an injustice, but whatever the case, our ideas of the future were as sundered as they had ever been. He, it seemed obvious, had no idea of the conflict I was feeling.

Sitting in an overcrowded train full of damp coats and bulging bags, I thought with longing of the clean hills of Yorkshire. I hoped to find snow as soon as I left Leeds. There was a heaviness within me I couldn't escape; I'd tried to banish all thoughts of the future from my mind, except what was immediately ahead, but the idea of leaving my new life, temporary as I'd agreed it must be, and returning to Brant permanently, made me think of a prison door, heavy and metallic, clanging shut and leaving me, once again, in the dark.

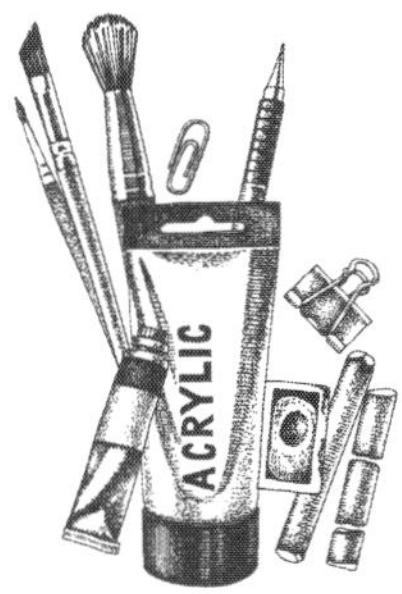

PART THREE

JANUARY CAN BE bleak anywhere, but for a week or so it stayed fine. Snow met me when I arrived back, with clean blue skies, and overnight frost adding an extra crunch under my boots. The freezing cold failed to dent my spirits. Cycling was hazardous everywhere except on the A-road through the town, and even that froze overnight in the corners the gritter had missed, which was exactly where a bike had to go. I was careful but had a few heart-stopping slithers nevertheless. The weather didn't seem to keep people indoors; well-muffled and padded they went to the shops and pubs full of cheer simply because the sun was shining, and of course they were natives well used to what winter might deliver.

For that week I hardly saw anyone. I'd checked in with Mary and found things much as I'd left them. I spoke briefly to Martha through her bedroom door. She had a cold, adding to the misery of her painful joints, and told me to stay away. I made sure she had what she needed and did as I was told. Liam was nowhere to be seen.

All this suited me well. With renewed energy I tackled the last, and most important, part of the first panel, taking my time to mix the precise colours and use the right brushes. I followed Liam's suggestion and applied some of the paint with a palette knife, smoothing off the thick swathes of Christ's white robes so they flowed like water, contrasting with the glowing gold of his belt. I had a few puzzled moments of knowing there was something wrong with his outstretched arm, but I managed to alter it so that the seven stars appeared to fly from his hand. His face and head I left till last, going back to Revelation to recapture its images, but it was not difficult to do: I had only to open the door of the studio to see the drifts of snow for his hair, and the sun sparkling on its unbroken surface to see it shining in his face; and as I'd ridden home the previous evening there was the sunset, sinking down above the hills, blazing crimson and orange for the fire of his eyes.

I'd lowered the panel off its rickety supports onto the floor, leaning it up against the wall and holding it in place at its base by lengths of timber I'd found in the back room. Now I could perch on a low stool and get close up to the small area I was working on. Every so often I got up and walked around, partly to ease my stiff limbs but also to step back and make sure the perspective was right. I felt my stomach growl and decided it was time for a warming coffee and a couple of biscuits left over from Christmas and now getting stale.

As I munched, waiting for the kettle to boil, my thoughts entirely absorbed in my work and for once feeling no shadow of uncertainty or doubt, I heard the door of the studio open, and felt a little frisson of pleasure that Liam was back – who else could it be? Productive though they were, my long days and nights were lonely, and I welcomed the thought of talking shop. Then I heard voices, his and another's, as the door closed, and I went to the doorway into the studio, the steaming kettle in my hand.

Liam was there, and preceding him a woman. She had her back to me, so all I saw was an ankle-length black coat, a matching hat shaped like a turban, and a sky-blue scarf wrapped round her neck and trailing down her back.

Liam looked up and saw me, and his eyes lit up. 'Fen, you're back!'

His companion turned then, and I saw a face so pale it was almost ghostly. From under her hat straggled hair that could have been described as blonde if I was being polite. Everything about her seemed washed out, including her light green eyes. She was tall, too, as tall as me in her high-heeled boots, and willow-thin. She looked at me, a frown between her eyebrows, and then she looked at my huge, uncovered painting, and the frown deepened.

'Ah, er, Fen,' Liam stammered, clearing his throat. 'Let me introduce you. This is Oliv—' The woman glared at him. 'Sorry, Olivia Wastwell.'

I put the kettle on the work surface and went towards them, smiling, my hand outstretched. She hesitated a moment, then shook it briefly without removing her gloves. 'Fen Bailey,' I said. 'Glad to meet you, Olivia.'

She mumbled something barely audible, then looked over again at my painting. 'Is that yours?' she asked.

'Yes,' I said. 'Almost finished, but not quite.'

She gazed at it for several seconds. 'I see.' She turned to Liam. 'You didn't tell me there was someone else here.'

Liam gave a weak smile. 'There's plenty of room for us all, I think.'

I was trying to fathom what was going on, and failing. 'I've just boiled the kettle,' I said. 'Can I make anyone some coffee?'

Olivia made a face. 'Not for me, thank you.'

'I'll have some,' Liam said. He followed me into the back room, leaving Olivia Wastwell wandering round the studio, looking at the paintings – mostly Liam's – that were stacked up there, some against the walls, some on easels.

I raised my eyebrows enquiringly as I poured hot water into two mugs. Liam gave a little shake of his head and mouthed, 'Tell you later.'

We took our coffee back into the main body of the studio and found Olivia standing up close to my panel. Too close, I thought, feeling a small spurt of protectiveness. Perhaps she was short-sighted.

'Be careful,' I said. 'That bit's still wet.' I saw her recoil and take two steps back.

'What is it?' she said. The frown hadn't left her face.

I found myself reluctant to explain my work to this woman. I prevaricated. 'Are you familiar with the book of Revelation?'

'Hardly.' She turned to Liam, and her attitude changed. Suddenly she was smiling, but it was a sly smile without warmth, I thought. 'Don't be too long with your coffee, Liam darling. The taxi's waiting with the meter running. I only came to see Martha for a moment, but I need to get to my hotel and warm up.'

'Right.' Liam drained his mug and put it on the floor. 'See you later, Fen. I'll come back as soon I've dropped Olivia off in town. Will you still be here?'

'I expect so.'

By this time Olivia was waiting by the door. She had a strange way of walking, almost a glide. 'Come along, Liam. I'm frozen.' She glanced over at me. 'Nice to meet you, er, Fen, is it? Will you be staying long at Chibley?'

I found myself irked by her lack of civility. Who on earth was she, anyway? I lifted my chin and looked down my nose at her. 'Oh, yes,' I said. 'I've still got a lot of work to do.'

She didn't respond but turned to Liam. 'I'll need help with my luggage. I've brought far too much stuff, as usual.' She shivered. 'It's so cold! I hope the hotel is warm. Get me settled, will you, Liam darling. You can use the taxi to get back here.'

In the doorway Liam shot me an apologetic look, and then they were gone.

IT WAS AN hour and a half before Liam reappeared, even though the journey into town would have taken five minutes in a taxi. In that time, I'd blocked in most of Christ's face and wanted to ask Liam's advice before I applied any highlights. I was in the back room, eating a sandwich for my lunch, when he put his head round the door.

'It's snowing again,' he said, rubbing his hands together.

'I can see that from the delicate peppering in your hair. Do you want a sandwich? I've made plenty.'

'Yes, please.' He came and sat beside me at the small table. 'I left Olive deciding to have lunch in the hotel. She did ask me to join her, but I made my excuses.' He grimaced and bit into his sandwich.

'Olive? Or Olivia?'

Now he grinned. 'Her given name is Olive, but she insists on being called Olivia. She thinks it sounds less pedestrian, I suppose. Classier somehow. I keep forgetting, and then I get the glare. But that's Olive all over. Absolutely dyed-in-the-wool snob. Shall I make some tea?'

I dusted the crumbs from my fingers. 'Good idea. So, what's the story with Ms Wastwell?'

Liam busied himself with the kettle. 'She's been coming to Chibley, on and off, for years. I'm not sure why. Maybe because Martha and I are nice to her. She has pretensions to art, and actually is a quite reasonable watercolourist, but definitely not as accomplished as she thinks she is. And as you may have noticed, she's rude, entitled, and demanding. Not an easy person to get on with.'

I pondered this for a moment. 'The question occurs to me, especially as Martha in particular doesn't waste time and energy where she doesn't have to, is why do you put up with her?'

Liam poured boiling water into two mugs and stirred vigorously, spilling splashes of tea onto the work surface. 'Good question, and easily answered.' He brought the tea to the table. 'You don't take sugar, do you?' I shook my head as he sat down. 'Any more of those sandwiches?'

I pushed the packet towards him. 'Help yourself.'

'The thing is,' he said between mouthfuls, 'as you know, Chibley, as a business, is on its uppers. Not many people come here now, so very little gets put into the coffers. It's a vicious circle – the place is run down, other places have better facilities, fewer people come, so less money, and round it goes. But Olive, bless her considerable bank balance, is rich. She never stays on site; I don't think she would even if there was a nice cosy flat for her, no, she likes to be in town at the George, though she complains about it all the time – terrible food, worse service, lumpy beds – you get the picture. She hasn't been here for a couple of years; she's been ill, apparently. She says she has a heart condition and is basically an invalid. So we all run round her in circles because she puts money into the account.' He paused, his expression glum. 'She really is very wealthy, and open-handed with it, providing we fulfil her every whim.'

I was intrigued despite myself. 'Where does this great fortune come from, do you know?'

'Nobody does, not really,' Liam said. 'Olive claims to have inherited it from blue-blooded forebears. She's even hinted there's an ancestral seat somewhere, inhabited by distant cousins. But Martha is convinced she won it. And then cannily invested the proceeds.'

I shook my head. 'A woman of mystery.'

'Well, she likes to give that impression. She can be positively coy. You hardly ever get a straight answer. I guess the truth is probably a lot duller, but there's a lot that's bogus about Olive, I think.'

'How long is she likely to be around?'

Liam sighed. 'Who knows?' He turned to me, his face the picture of gloom. 'The worst of it is, and please don't laugh, but Martha is convinced that Olive is pursuing me.'

'What? In a romantic sense? Sorry, Liam, but it is quite funny.'

'Huh, not for me it's not. Martha is a terrible tease. She says, "Now Liam, how far would you go to save Chibley from its creditors and complete ruin? Perhaps you'll have to marry Olive." She thinks it's funny too.' He shuddered. 'Can you imagine? It'd be a fate worse than death.'

My grin was very broad. 'I'm sure it won't come to that.'

'You've only seen her wrapped up for winter,' he said. 'She's skinny and bony, no colour to her at all, her hair is long, yellow and ratty, and she has a pointed nose like a witch.'

Now I laughed aloud. 'Oh, Liam! I'm sorry, but you sound about six years old.'

He allowed himself a reluctant smile. 'I know.' He heaved a huge, doleful sigh. 'Oh, Fen, if only you could see the contrast!'

'Between what and what?'

'You and Olive. Her so feeble and limp and pale, so self-important and full of falsehood! And you so strong and healthy and, I don't know, *real*.'

'Maybe she really is ill. In which case we should be more compassionate, shouldn't we?'

'I suppose so. But she doesn't make it easy.'

'I see that. But as to my health and strength, that's hardly a virtue. I'm very blessed.'

Liam plucked at a loose thread on his jeans. He looked up, his face serious, his eyes wide. 'Did I cause offence, Fen? You know, before Christmas, when we had that takeaway at your cottage? Should I apologise?'

I patted his arm. 'Don't let it bother you. I could even consider it a kind of compliment.' I mock-frowned. 'But don't let that give you any ideas.'

Now his smile was unfeigned. 'I'll try to remember you have a jailer, I mean husband.' He offered his hand. 'Friends?'

I shook his hand, warm and paint stained. 'Of course.'

WE SAW NOTHING of Olive for several days, and it provided a spell of peace that both Liam and I used to full advantage. We were mostly alone; Martha was still nursing her cold and keeping warm, and needed little attention, although we kept an eye on her between us and took her hot drinks and small meals.

Liam was working on a series of landscapes that kept him busy in and out of the studio. He regularly arrived, flushed and frozen, with sketches in a backpack after a morning out on the hills.

When he was there, I picked his brains. I'd applied the highlights and done some touching up, and now the first panel was finished, but I knew there was still work to do.

'You need to leave it to cure,' Liam said. 'Probably a month, if impatience doesn't get the better of you.'

I shrugged. I don't think Steve at St James's is in any great hurry.'

'Good. Anyway, you've got plenty to be getting on with. How are your ideas for the second panel coming along?'

'I've done a lot of reading and thinking,' I said. 'And I've made some sketches. Doing the first one has taught me a lot. So, I wait a month. And then what?'

'You use a spray or a special brush, and you coat it at least twice with polycrylic. There should be some here – I'll go and look.'

He went into the back room, and I heard him rummaging and muttering. He returned with a scabby looking can. 'There's a bit here, but someone didn't close the can up properly. We'll have to order some in. But you've got plenty of time.' He joined me in front of my panel and nodded slowly. 'So, you put on at least two careful coats, leave two hours between each coat, wash your brush out thoroughly, and it'll be all dry in 24 hours.'

'And then it's ready? I can think about getting someone to frame it and take it down to St James's?'

'Yes, though that'll need thinking about. It's a big beast, this work of yours.'

'OK, we'll cross that bridge when we come to it. Thanks for your input, Liam. Now, I must let you get on with your own work before Olive – excuse me, *Olivia* – returns and showers you with her attentions.'

He pulled a face. 'Stop it, please.'

'Sorry. But why has she come to Yorkshire in January if she feels the cold so much?'

'Ah, well, apparently she's escaping from difficult conditions at home.' I raised an enquiring eyebrow. 'She inhabits some huge mansion flat in London, so she told me,' Liam said. 'A stately, but crumbling, Edwardian pile. There's going to be work done, major stuff. And it's already begun. Olive said the noise the workmen made was "*insupportable,* darling." She says at least it's quiet here, even if, in her words, we are rather primitive.'

'The George looks very comfortable to me,' I said. 'Not in the least primitive.'

'Ah, but,' Liam said, 'your standards are probably not as exacting as hers.'

I laughed. 'I guess not, since my residence is a tiny chilly cottage on a hillside. Anyway, if the poor soul really does suffer from ill health, she's likely to be more sensitive than most.'

Liam scowled. 'When you get to know her a bit better, I think you might not be quite so charitable. Olive is sensitive all right, but only as concerns herself. To others she's hard as flint.'

I couldn't resist an innocent tease. 'Surely not to you, Liam.'

He shuddered. 'Don't. It's horrific. Frankly, I can't wait for her to be gone.'

IT WAS ALMOST a week before we saw Olive again. By that time heavy rain had washed away the snow, revealing sodden squelching ground under leaden skies that had none of the deceiving glamour of a crisp snowscape. My bike ride from Whitepost to Chibley took me through puddles that splashed my legs and feet so I arrived soaked and cold. It was supposed to be a few degrees warmer, but it didn't feel it; the air was raw.

I was making a cup of coffee in the chilly studio back room when I heard the rumble of wheels approaching up the track and looked out of the door to see a large black taxi coming to a halt in the yard. I caught sight of Liam, bare-chested and yawning, gazing out of the window of his flat above the barn, and for a moment we both looked down as Olive, swathed in a vast fur coat, climbed out of the taxi. She paused for a moment to talk to the driver, then as the taxi turned with a grinding of gears, she started up the path to the studio, leaning on a stick. She carried a large flat bag over one arm.

I held the door open for her, and she nodded her thanks. 'Ah, this weather!' she wailed. 'I can't work in the hotel – it's far too cramped. My flat in London is uninhabitable with workmen sawing and shouting and I don't know what, and here it's positively Arctic. I don't usually come here in the winter – isn't there any heating at all?'

'There are a couple of fan heaters, but they don't make much impact in this space. Still, you could put them each side of you, wherever you want to work. Meanwhile, would you like a cup of coffee?'

She looked at me down her nose, its tip pink from cold. 'If I remember rightly, the brew here is some ghastly cheap instant that gives me indigestion. I shall bring my own. So no, thank you.' She looked around. 'Where's Liam?'

I shrugged. 'As you see, not here. If you'll excuse me, I should get on. The light doesn't last long these days.'

She frowned. 'Can't you set those heaters up for me?' I paused, looking at her with my eyebrows raised. 'If you would be so kind, *please*.'

Without a word I went into the kitchen area, retrieved the heaters, took them back into the studio and plugged them in. 'You can move them where you want them,' I said shortly.

Her eyes narrowed. 'What about you?'

'I'm well layered up.'

'Good, because I can't possibly work in this coat.' She took the coat off and draped it carefully over a chair, and I saw that under it she was wearing just a long, clinging jersey dress, which showed her bony form to no advantage and could do little to keep her warm. Was this perhaps her idea of tempting Liam? For a moment then I saw the whole ludicrous scenario from his point of view, and no longer felt inclined to laugh. I also felt a pang of sympathy for Olive, despite her incivility.

She now unzipped her bag and started to take out several small watercolours that she laid out, slowly and reverently, on one of the nearby tables. 'This table is dirty,' she said, frowning. 'I hope these paint stains are dry.'

'Ages old, I think,' I said, then, out of politeness, 'May I see?'

She stepped back, and I took in her work. The scenes seemed to be largely of urban parks, streets and buildings. They were rather pedestrian for my taste, but were, as far as I could see, quite well executed.

I turned to her, smiling. 'These are charming.'

I saw her bristle. Did she find me patronising? That hadn't been my intention. 'It's what I can see from my balcony,' she said sullenly. 'I can't always get out, not as much as I'd like. I'm in poor health.'

'That must be difficult.'

She shrugged, as if my opinion was neither important nor interesting. Her gaze wandered round the space. 'That's yours, isn't it?' she said abruptly, indicating my canvas stretched across its frame, leaning against the far wall – even though she knew perfectly well whose it was. 'You're doing some vast biblical scene, so Liam told me. I wouldn't have thought there was much call for that sort of thing.'

'Perhaps there isn't,' I said.

She frowned. 'What is it actually *about*?'

'As you said, it's a scene from the Bible, specifically Revelation.' She was silent. 'I gather you don't care for such things.'

'Well, it's… it's…' she floundered. 'All that drama, that passion! And those colours! It makes me tired! All very well if you like things brash and primitive, I suppose.'

I was saved from having to make any further comment, because at that moment the door opened and Liam sidled in, wearing a ratty sheepskin coat and a bedraggled brown woollen scarf. 'Morning, ladies. Wow, Olivia, aren't you frozen?' He didn't wait for her answer but strode over to the table where her paintings lay. 'Are these what you were telling me about?'

She stood beside him, smiling, but rather spoiling the image by shivering. I had to admire her aplomb, although I feared her attempt at impressing was way off. 'Yes, some of them,' she said breathlessly. 'There are more back at the hotel. What do you think?'

Liam said nothing for a moment. Then he turned to her. 'Yeah, these are nice. I see you've taken some of my advice.'

This very faint praise seemed to go to her head; she positively beamed, and for all her lack of social graces I felt sorry for her. Something told me, though, that it wouldn't be long before some remark of hers drove away any shreds of charitable feeling in me.

Liam looked at me, then at Olive, and back at me. 'Look,' he said to Olive, 'why don't you go down to the house? Martha's up and about now. I'm sure there are things you need to talk about. And there's not much you can do here while it's so cold. Maybe you need to put a few more layers on if you're thinking of working for any length of time. I'll be down in a few minutes to bring some logs in and make up the fire.'

Olive looked at me and frowned, and I began to see how the land lay. Somewhere in her warped way of thinking it seemed I was a rival – and may become an enemy. I wanted none of it.

I shrugged. 'You know what, Liam, you're right. This place is an icebox. I think I'll be better employed up at Whitepost. Mary always needs something doing.' Liam gave me an almost imperceptible nod. I collected my coat, and I saw him hold up Olive's heavy fur so she could put her arms in the sleeves.

I saluted them both as I put on hat and gloves. 'See you when it warms up,' I said. Out in the cold sunlit morning I picked up my bike and pedalled away down the track, breathing in the sharp air through the wool of my scarf. *For what it's worth, you can have him all to yourself,* I thought. *And with Martha around as well, I won't be throwing him to the wolves. But why should I worry? You're both adults. And the last thing I want is any part in a stupid little triangle. You're not my responsibility.*

I STAYED AWAY for several days. Since Olive's arrival at Chibley I'd felt a sense almost of suffocation. I wanted to recapture my freedom – to walk on the hills, to paint, not to become embroiled in insoluble human tangles that were none of my making. Besides, I felt a need to see how Mary and Peter were doing. Whitepost had become, it seemed, my bedrock, from where I could explore the unknown.

Leaving my bike propped up against my cottage wall, I went indoors to change out of my wet clothes. Then I walked down to the farmhouse, opened the door a crack and called out: 'Can I come in?' Although Mary had said I was welcome any time, I didn't want to barge in on delicate operations.

'Yes, Fen, of course! Can you bring that box of logs by the door?'

I picked up the box, which was heavy and not very stable, and shouldered my way inside. I dropped the box by the fire. 'Shall I put a couple of logs on?' I paused to stroke Sadie, who was curled up at the fireside.

Mary was at the table, swathed in an apron, cutting up leeks on a huge wooden board. 'Yes, do. You might put the kettle on too.'

I did as she asked and came back to join her. 'What are you making?'

'Soup. It's sometimes the only way I can get nourishment into Peter.'

I looked around; Peter's chair was empty, and there was no sign of his dog. 'Where is he?'

Mary sighed. 'He seemed very tired this morning. Didn't want to get up. I left him dozing; at least he's warm. This kitchen gets draughty, and it's still cold out there, even though the snow's gone.'

'I noticed. The studio is freezing. It's such a huge space.'

'How's the painting coming along?' Mary asked.

'The first panel is finished,' I said. 'Now I have to leave it for about a month, to cure. And then it has to be sealed. I've never done anything this big before – Liam's helping me with the technical side.' The kettle clicked off. 'I'll make a pot of tea, shall I?'

'So, what now?' Mary wanted to know.

'Now I plan the second panel – and maybe start thinking about the third as well.' I made a face. 'I don't think I realised, before I started, just what a massive project this would be. Do you know, Revelation has twenty-two chapters? And these three panels, if I get to finish them, will cover just the first six.'

Mary looked up at me, frowning. 'But of course you must finish them, Fen. Just seeing the small ones you've done makes me keen to see the big panel. That one you did of Peter and Old Joe brought tears to my eyes – it was so lifelike.'

I carried the tea pot to the table. 'Where is it?'

'I've hung it in our bedroom, so it's the first thing Peter sees when he opens his eyes.'

I gathered cups, spoons, milk, and sat opposite her. 'Did you show it to him? Did he react?'

'Not at first,' Mary said slowly. 'He was puzzled, didn't seem to understand what it was. But then, a few days later, he was propped up in bed, and I was tidying the room up a bit because we were expecting the nurse, and suddenly his arm shot out, and he pointed at the wall, and he said, sort of wonderingly, "That's me, isn't it? And oh! – there's Joe as well." Just like that.'

I lifted the heavy pot and poured tea into our cups. 'It's strange, isn't it, how sometimes he seems to come out of his dreamlike state, like waking up. I wonder why.'

Mary sipped her tea and shook her head. 'I'm sure I don't know, Fen. The brain is a mystery. So, you're preparing for the second panel. That's great progress, I'm sure. Will you do your sketches at the cottage? You can always come down here if it gets too cold. There's plenty of room for both of us on this table.'

'You're very kind, Mary. I might just do that.' I paused for a moment, drinking my tea, watching her cut the leeks into small chunks and throw the pieces into a huge black cast-iron saucepan that looked as if it had been her grandmother's. 'Once I start to paint I'll have to be at the studio, of course. But it's not just the cold that's keeping me away. Someone's come that seems to upset the balance and make everything awkward. She's perfectly entitled to be there, obviously. But I'm keeping a low profile.' A thought struck me. 'Maybe you know her, since you seem to know everyone round here. She's been to Chibley before, though not for a year or two. Olive Wastwell, though she calls herself Olivia.'

'Ah! Yes,' Mary said. 'We've never met, but I've heard of her.'

'Has she had exhibitions here, then?'

'Possibly, but that's not why I know about her. She stays at the George, I think.'

'She does.'

'Will and Bess's daughter-in-law Vicky, young Thom's mother, works up there, part-time behind the bar. Says the lady can be difficult. Demanding and complaining. Insisting they call the doctor out late at night, that sort of thing.'

'I can imagine. She's taken against me, I'm afraid, though I've done nothing to deserve it as far as I'm aware. Apparently, Martha is convinced she's got a crush on Liam. Martha finds it all very funny, but Liam definitely doesn't.'

'I expect she's jealous,' Mary said.

'No reason for that,' I said, feeling heat bloom in my face. 'Liam's a friend, that's all.'

'So I should hope,' Mary said with a touch of asperity, but also with a barely-suppressed smile. 'Which reminds me, how's your family? Heard from them recently?'

'Yes, I talk with John every week at least, but he's fiendishly busy and often in the USA. Dan drops me the odd e mail. And Alice is tons more forthcoming since she hooked up with Rory, who I'm looking forward to meeting. Maybe after Easter.'

Mary nodded. 'Good.'

I finished my tea. 'Now, Mary. It's still early. There must be something I can do to help. To be honest I can't wait to get back up on the hills, and if you can spare Sadie all the better.'

'Yes, there is something. Look, let me get this soup on then I'll make you a sandwich. You can't go stomping about in all this weather with an empty stomach. And if you like come and share some dinner with me this evening. I'll be glad of the company. I won't keep you late – I'm sure you're keen to get on with your drawing.'

'That'd be great, thank you. So, what is it you want me to do?'

Mary heaved the saucepan to the hob. 'The Whartons, bless them, saw to our yows while the snow was on the ground. Now it's gone there's some pasture for them, but it won't be the best. They need some hay, but Will's gone down with a bug and Thom's back at school. If you could take the quad and Sadie and find the old ladies and give them some of the hay that's stored in the barn, the one just over the ridge, that'd be a load off my mind. You can't take a hay bale to them on the quad without a trailer, and I don't think you'd feel confident enough for that yet, so get Sadie to bring the yows to you, give them some hay and send them back out.'

'Done. I'll try not to fall off.'

Mary smiled. 'Well, at least now you can see where you're going, even if it is all mud.'

THAT AFTERNOON I felt like a prisoner released. It took me a while to get used to the Whitepost quad, and Mary insisted I ride it round the farmyard a few times before setting out. The weather was horrible, wet gusts blowing in our faces as I carefully negotiated rutted tracks, open hillsides and temporary streams. Sadie rode up with me, so I went slowly, afraid of losing control of Whitepost's rackety quad and injuring the dog. I left the engine running when I needed to open and close gates, but in a short while we crested the brow of the hill and the barn was in sight. Sadie leapt off as soon as we came to a halt and looked at me, waiting for orders.

'Off you go, Sadie. Fetch the old ladies for their supper.' This was definitely not the sort of command a sheepdog would be accustomed to, but Sadie knew and off she raced like a monochrome missile. I watched her go till she was out of sight, marvelling anew at her speed, racing low to the ground and sure-footed even on the tricky terrain. I turned back to the barn, always kept well-maintained, as were most of the barns hereabouts thanks to government grants, and noticed that the door hung askew, attached by only one hinge – a casualty, I supposed, of the recent snow and high winds. Bracing my gloved hands along its length I managed to heave it back into position, but it would need something more permanent. I opened the door gingerly, keeping it aligned, and went inside. The winter light was fading, but I was able to see hay bales on wooden pallets against one wall, and a shelf on which rested a box with various useful items – a torch in a plastic bag, a bowl for a dog, and a couple of rough blankets. I glanced upwards to see if the roof had survived the recent weather, and saw bats up there, hanging by their feet from the rafters, fast asleep.

Fifteen minutes later I heard bleating and went outside. The sheep were milling about, but were kept in a bunch by Sadie, who lay panting behind them.

'Good girl, Sadie.' The bales were too heavy for me to pull down, but one was already broken into, and I pulled out huge handfuls, as much as I could, and scattered them among the ewes who fell to with enthusiasm. This I repeated several times until I thought they'd had enough, though I couldn't really tell. I counted them, of course; all eighteen were there, and as far as I could see with my untrained eye they looked well enough.

'Right, ladies, that's your lot. It's getting dark, and Sadie and I want our supper too.' I clapped my hands, and hay dust flew into the darkening air. Sadie got up, stretched, yawned and shooed them off, scattering them down the hillside away from the farm. One or two looked back, perhaps hoping for a second helping, but then they disappeared into the dusk.

'Come on, dog, we've done our bit now.' I started up the quad, found the lights after a moment or two of fiddling, and set off back to the farm, first up, then down, the barn disappearing from view. Sadie, clearly realising she could easily keep up with my slow speed, ran alongside until the lights of the farmhouse came into view.

MARY HAD MADE a huge pot of chicken and vegetables, which both smelled and tasted delicious, served with a still-warm loaf she had baked. She'd also dusted off a bottle of plum wine, which she said a friend had given her at Christmas a few years ago.

'Are we celebrating?' I asked, savouring its clear red sweetness.

'Not really,' Mary said with her slightly sad smile. 'Still being alive, I suppose.'

'I'll drink to that,' I said, and did. 'Mary, that was the best meal I've had in ages.'

She stood up and took our plates to the sink. 'I'm not surprised – I'm sure you live on sandwiches and coffee.'

I stretched and yawned. 'I do all the cooking when I'm in Brant. It's a blessed relief not to think about catering.'

'We can do the dishes later,' Mary said. 'Throw a log on, Fen – let's sit by the fire for a while.'

'That sounds like a plan,' I said. 'But before I forget, someone needs to fix the barn door – it's attached by only one hinge.'

Mary nodded. 'I'll ask Will to see to it once he's back on his feet.'

We settled into ancient armchairs on each side of the fire, and Sadie crept between us and stretched out, basking in the warmth. 'Now, Fen,' Mary said, 'tell me about these paintings of yours.'

I described the finished panel. 'I guess I was kind of feeling my way at the beginning,' I said. 'But now I've got a clearer idea of where I'm going. That first panel is about earthly things – St John himself in exile, his visions leading directly to the messages to the seven churches, which were real places in his time. That's why I've put things of today among the cities – a multi-storey car park, a shopping mall, a children's playground. Real places that people of today can recognise, so they understand that Revelation has truths for them as well. There are still heavenly things in there too, of course: the risen Christ with the stars in his hand and the sword of his mouth. So that's the first panel. In the second panel I'm going to move on to heaven itself, as he sees it.'

Mary's eyes were wide. 'That seems quite a challenge.'

I nodded. 'It will be. Much prayer needed! But John is not all that forthcoming with details, so I'll have to supplement the vision with bits of Ezekiel, plus a lot of imagination. It'll be a sort of composite. Maybe more of a mishmash, if I'm honest! Anyway, this is the idea: on each side, top to bottom, the edges of the doors to the Most Holy Place, engraved with figures in relief and covered with gold. I want it to seem that St John, and we, are looking through the open door into heaven. Right at the top, as if far away, the throne above all others. Somehow I want to draw the eye there, even though it will be quite small, so maybe bright colours will be the answer. Then the rainbow that soars above it, reminding us of God's promise never to flood the earth again. In front of the throne the twenty-four elders, robed in white and crowned with gold, and their thrones. And on each side of the throne itself the four living creatures, with their faces of a bull, an eagle, a lion and a man, and their fabulous wings all covered with eyes. As we move down the panel things get bigger, nearer: the sea of shining glass, which will be quite difficult to paint – maybe I'll need some help with that. The seven lighted torches blazing away, and of course great throngs of angels. And an inscription: "Holy, holy, holy is the Lord God Almighty, who was, who is, and who is to come." I haven't decided yet where that will go.'

Mary shook her head. 'That sounds quite extraordinary, Fen.'

I sighed. 'If I can pull it off. I am very aware of my own limitations, my lack of experience. And the visions aren't mine, of course. I'm just interpreting them as best I can, hoping that somehow they'll resonate with other people.'

'I can see that'll keep you busy for quite a while.'

'Yes, and I want to do a third panel as well, a triptych. But maybe I'll run out of time.'

'You have a deadline?'

I shrugged. 'Not as such. But I think John expects this project, this escapade, to last a year and no more. He's booked a cruise for September. I'm sure he sees me being here as a sort of escape from reality. But to be honest with you, Mary, it's this life that seems most real to me.'

She was silent for a moment, staring into the fire. 'I suppose you can see it from his point of view,' she said. 'Maybe it seems to him like you're living out a fantasy.'

'I'm sure he does think just that. And I know I'm very privileged to be able to do it. But it's not just painting. I want to be more involved with the life here. Do you think Will Wharton will let me help with lambing in the spring?'

Mary smiled. 'You'll have to ask him. But won't you be going home some time then?'

I heaved a sigh. 'Yes, after Easter. First I have to get the first painting sealed and framed and hung in church. I need to talk to Steve again. He said something about me doing a question-and-answer session with members of the congregation once the panel is hung. He said they'll want to know what it all means. I'd better come to church with you this Sunday.' I glanced up at the clock on the mantel. 'Shall I start on the dishes? You stay there, Mary – let me do it.'

Mary settled back in her chair with a sigh and closed her eyes. At rest, she looked exhausted. As quietly as I could I cleared the table and filled the sink with steaming soapy water, thinking to myself it was a pity Mary and Peter had never installed a dishwasher; but perhaps they didn't think it was worth it with only two of them, and old habits aren't easily put aside.

I was drying my hands when Mary came to with a start. 'Fen, I can hear a phone ringing.'

'Oh! Yes, that sounds like mine. It's in my coat pocket.' I crossed the room and retrieved the phone. To my surprise it was Liam.

'Fen, hey.'

'What's up?'

'We need you at Chibley. When are you coming back?'

I frowned. 'Who's "we", Liam?'

'Martha and me.' There was a note of desperation in his voice.

'You'd better unpack that. I'm not too crazy about hanging out with Olive. I think she's got it into her head that I'm some kind of rival for your attention.'

'I know. But it's Olive we need to talk about, as well as other things. Martha wants a meeting – herself, you and me.'

'I don't see what I've got to do with anything. I don't even know how long I'll be able to stay at Chibley.'

I heard him grunt. 'Well, Martha seems to think you have a contribution to make. And apart from that, Olive is driving me nuts. I was trying to persuade her to stay at the hotel while the weather's so cold, but then Martha pulled the rug out by saying she could work in her kitchen – it's big enough. And you know why Martha wants to keep Olive on side. But she, Olive that is, keeps on popping into the studio when I'm trying to work, and I can't concentrate, thinking of her turning up out of the blue. She even climbed up that rickety staircase to my flat and banged on the door, just to offer me a cup of coffee, so she said. I'm feeling harried, Fen.'

'I'm sorry for you,' I said with barely suppressed impatience. 'But that's just what I don't want – to be dragged into some idiotic love-triangle that exists only in Olive's imagination.'

'I get that. But maybe you, me and Martha can come up with a strategy so we can all get on. Please come soon.'

'OK, look, I'll think about it and get back to you.'

'All right.' He sounded dejected but rang off without saying more.

Mary looked up from her chair. 'Trouble?'

'When isn't there, with people? To think I'd hoped to get free of all that.' I flopped down into the chair opposite. 'Olive, I guess, is lonely. She's persuaded herself that she's pining after Liam, who really couldn't do her any good, nice guy though he is. Martha needs Olive for her financial contributions. She wants me to go down there for some kind of strategy meeting. I don't want anything to do with it. Am I wrong, Mary? Is this a case of having to be my brother's keeper? All I want to do is get on with my work while I've got the chance.'

Mary pursed her lips. 'I don't know, Fen. I don't think we can ever be free of other people's troubles, and we're certainly called to shoulder their burdens when we can. Maybe you should try to befriend Olive. It sounds like she needs a friend.'

'Hm. Honestly, Mary, I don't think it's my friendship she wants. Quite the reverse. But it's part of the same thing, isn't it – what we were talking about earlier. I want to be here; John expects me to come home. What's my obligation, really?'

Mary shot me a look but spoke mildly enough. 'Didn't you promise something, all those years ago at the altar? Before God and the congregation?'

I groaned softly. 'Yeah. I did. But I've kept them, you know, those promises: in sickness and health, rich or poor, forsaking all others – I've done all that. It's the "till death us do part" bit that's giving me grief at the moment.'

'Ah, Fen.' Mary shook her head. 'I can't advise you; you're not a teenager any more. This is something you're going to have to work out for yourself. I sense your frustration, but where people are in the mix there's no escaping muddle. All I'd say is, if in doubt, be generous-hearted, as I know you really are. Annoying as they can be, none of us can do without other people, and we should be thankful that there are those who care for us.'

I heaved myself out of the chair. 'You're right, of course, Mary. Now I'm going to leave you in peace, unless there's something I can do to help. You're looking very tired.'

She yawned. 'Yes. I'll see if Peter wants anything, then I'll turn in.'

I pulled my coat down from the hook behind the door and put it on. I could hear the steady patter of rain outside. 'Thanks for dinner, Mary. And the chat. You know where I am if you need me.'

I LEFT IT a day, and then with an inward sigh I rode down to Chibley. The weather at least had improved, if only a little. At least the almost constant rain had decided to give it a rest, and there was even the odd weak ray of sunshine breaking through the cloud. It probably wouldn't last, given the latitude and the time of year, but I told myself February was almost in sight: the year had turned, spring was coming.

I'd called Liam briefly the previous evening and we'd agreed to meet up with Martha at nine-thirty. 'Olive won't be conscious that early,' he said. 'We'll have a couple of hours at least. She'll need to have her bath and get her face on. I think she has some arrangement with the taxi firm in town. And a specially-favoured driver – poor bloke.'

As I parked my bike against the house wall, I heard a door slam and looked up to see Liam clattering down the wooden stairs that led to his flat above the barn. He put his arm round my shoulders and gave me a squeeze. 'Fen, good to see you. You were missed.'

'Not by Olive, I imagine,' I said as we opened the door.

Inside, the fire was already lit and giving out warmth. 'Your handiwork?' I said to Liam, looking up at him.

'Yeah. Martha feels the cold these days, being so slow on her feet. I thought I'd try to get it a bit warmer before she came down. I was awake in the dark – did a bit of work in my flat, though it's not easy, drawing while wrapped in a blanket!'

'Pretty much the same with me,' I said. 'Though I've been working at Mary's table too.' I shed my coat and looked around. 'What's this?' A large sketchbook lay on the big kitchen table. 'Olive's?'

Liam was about to answer when we heard Martha's stick tapping on the flags of the hallway. The door creaked open, and she came in, dressed as always in her voluminous black. I noticed straightaway how much more bent she seemed; I hadn't seen her for a while and she already looked older, the lines of pain deeper in her face. But her eyes were bright as she looked over at us and said in her growly voice, 'Haven't you youngsters got the coffee on yet?' Liam shook his head and went to the sink. 'Good to see you, Fen. You've finished the painting.'

'Yes. Have you seen it?'

Martha shook her head. 'Not yet. Maybe later today. But I've heard about it.'

I pulled out her chair, and she eased herself down.

'Liam! Thank you for the fire,' she called. 'You're a good boy.'

'You're welcome, Mother dear.'

'You're also cheeky. Where's that coffee? I need to wake up.'

'Coming.' A moment later he brought three mugs on a tray, with milk and a plate of biscuits. 'I haven't had breakfast,' he said. 'My bread was mouldy.'

I leaned over and put a hand on Martha's arm. 'Are you really better?'

'Well,' she said, blowing on her coffee before taking a sip. 'That pesky cold has gone, but I feel washed out. Every year of my age making itself felt. And that's not the whole story – but we'll come to that in a moment. Pass me that sketchbook, will you.'

Liam stretched over and slid the book across the table to Martha. 'Just look at these,' she said. 'I think she's improving.'

Liam leaned over me as I sat, and we looked at Olive's sketches and watercolours, chiefly scenes from around the house, in snow and thaw, and some of the town, seen from her hotel room. 'The pen and ink ones are quite effective,' I said.

Liam looked across at Martha. 'But will they make a permanent exhibition?'

'They'll have to,' Martha said sombrely. 'These, and some others she's brought with her, plus the ones she left here about two years ago. If she gets decent frames they may look just about all right.'

I frowned. 'Are you two going to enlighten me?'

'It's like this, Fen. You know things have been pretty tough here lately. If we can't get an injection of funds, Chibley Art will fold – that's the stark fact. Olive is our only likely lifeline at the moment. She and I've been talking, while she's been working here the last little while. She wants to turn the small barn – the one behind where Liam's currently dossing – into a room for a permanent exhibition of her work. There'd be good light there, if the windows were right. She'd put up the money to get the building repaired and shipshape, which I certainly can't afford. It's basically not in bad shape, but there are bits of roof that need fixing, and other work – heck, it's an old farm building and it hasn't been used in a long while, so that's all we can expect – so it won't come cheap. But she's willing to pay for it, on condition we show her work in there. For ever, more or less. In an ideal world I'd be dubious, because I don't really think her stuff merits that exposure. But then I say to myself, without Olive we're up the creek anyway.' She paused, looking at us, and when we said nothing she grunted and continued. 'Also, just so you know, I may be out of the picture too for some time. I saw a specialist yesterday, up at the hospital.' She jerked her head in a northward direction. 'I need another operation, and soon, or I'll be in a wheelchair.'

'I have a feeling this plan involves us,' Liam said.

Martha nodded. 'Someone has to supervise all this work. Look, Olive will start the process of sorting out architects and planning permission and builders and so on, with my help while I'm available. But when I'm not, someone needs to be on hand, and she isn't capable. Full of ideas, but she's not up to it. I'll be around for a while yet, and even after the op, whenever and if ever I have it, I'll be back recuperating and able to jerk the reins occasionally. Between you I reckon you two could see to things, keep an eye on progress, liaise with workmen, when I'm *hors de combat*.'

'Wait a minute, Martha,' I interrupted. 'I don't know how long I'll be here, and this looks like a long-term project. Anyway, Olive won't approve of me being involved with something of hers. She really doesn't like me.'

'I thought of that,' Martha said, a glint in her black eyes. 'As far as she's concerned, Liam will be in charge. You can back him up without her knowing. Just keep on with your own work and be available if Liam needs help. This is the only way, I reckon. If we do this for her she's got reason to keep on coming back, and if she feels committed to Chibley there'll be more money. Plus, she'll be recommending us to visitors, just to come and see her great works.'

I was silent for a moment, digesting everything she'd said. 'It's positively Machiavellian.'

Martha shrugged. 'Needs must.' She grinned. 'As to why she's got it in for you, Fen, you know it's because she has her eye on this handsome fellow.' She glanced at Liam. 'And she thinks you're a rival.'

'Well, I'm not,' I said firmly.

Liam groaned. 'It makes me want to crawl into a hole and hide.'

Martha hauled herself onto her feet, using the arms of the chair. 'This gal needs a bathroom break. And when I get back, more coffee.' She looked at Liam, grinning wickedly. 'You know what would be an ideal solution? You marry Olive. She'll buy a sweet little love nest nearby and you can set up house.'

Liam scowled. 'Martha, I love you, but not that much. *You* marry her if you think she's the answer to all our prayers.'

'I don't think I've got what she wants, dear boy. But you definitely have.' Even when she'd left the room, closing the door behind her, we could hear her laughing.

I turned to Liam, frowning. 'Why don't you just up sticks and go? Anywhere. This is intolerable.'

He shook his head. 'She likes to tease, but really she's desperate. She promised her old grandpa – or was it her dad? I forget – and she'll move heaven and earth to save this place. She'll feel she's failed if she has to sell up. And I owe her, Fen. You don't know the half of it.'

※

Foolishly perhaps, I felt something had soured my life at Chibley. Had I been naïve, unrealistic? No doubt I had, all of that, and maybe self-absorbed into the bargain, but Olive's arrival and all that flowed from it had changed things, and from my point of view not for the better. Lying in bed that night, sleepless despite weariness, I pondered. The prospect of Chibley being turned into a building site, ringing with the voices and loud radios of the workers, the track and the land around turned into an impassable sea of mud, was deeply unwelcome. I'd told Mary that this was reality for me, where I wanted to be – but now I wondered. Could I really work like this? Sighing, I turned over in bed, clutching my hot water bottle to my chest, and prayed for clarity.

The next morning I felt poorly rested and bleary, but as I boiled the kettle and looked out of my window onto the grey morning, some better thoughts began to form. This, after all, as far as my work was concerned, was my one chance. I had to go on in the assumption that this one year was all I had, and I must make the most of it. No place this side of the great divide was perfect – not Yorkshire, not Brant, nowhere on earth. Surely the studio was big enough for us all. While the weather stayed inclement, I imagined Olive would keep out of my way, whether at the hotel or in Martha's kitchen, and I would put all my energy, even my doubting thoughts, my very uncertainty, into the second panel. What was stopping me? Nothing. I would start today, and I would also contact Steve the vicar and make concrete arrangements for the hanging of the first panel. It was time to stop brooding and push on.

※

True to my resolve I rang Steve that morning, and he invited me to the vicarage the following day. The front door was ajar, and I found him in his study, its door wide open, loud music emanating from it – some kind of Irish folk band, it sounded to my untutored ears.

'Come in, Fen, if you can stand it!' he called.

Another voice hailed from the kitchen. 'Ignore him – it's a lot warmer in here.'

I put my head round the door and saw Jane sitting at the table in their vast kitchen, her long dark hair up in an untidy knot, her elbows on the table where an open book lay. 'Hello, Fen,' she said. 'I was thinking of making some scones, but I got carried away reading instead. Steve, turn that racket off and come in here! We'll have some coffee, shall we? I promise it's a better brew than that rather terrible stuff they dish up in church. Pull up a chair, Fen.' Leaning on the kitchen counter, waiting for the kettle to boil, she turned to me. 'I don't suppose you play the piano, do you?'

'Afraid not,' I said.

'Pity. I have to go to a funeral, and there's no one to rehearse the choir. Can't be helped.'

Steve shambled in, cleaning his glasses on a large handkerchief. He looked strange without them.

When we were settled, coffee gently steaming at our elbows, he said, 'I've been thinking. I thought it would be rather nice to have your painting in church before Lent. The subject matter might well lend itself to a sermon or two on the end times. What do you think?'

I raised an eyebrow. 'It's not the most popular subject.'

'He likes a challenge,' Jane interjected. 'And, to be fair, quite a few of our regular congregation might welcome it.'

Steve leaned forward. 'If your painting has been on view for a few days, maybe a week, they'll have a few questions, I imagine. Can you get it to us by the end of the month?'

I thought. 'It has to be sealed, and I need to arrange framing. It'll be tight, but I'll certainly try.'

'I know a good framer locally,' Jane put in. 'If it's us asking, he'll give it priority.'

I nodded. 'Sounds promising.'

'Can we agree a date for this question-and-answer thing I mentioned to you?' Steve said.

I smiled. 'My calendar is not exactly bursting at the seams. You arrange it to suit you.'

'Thing is, we can't actually hang it just yet,' Steve said. 'We'll have to jump through a few official hoops first. Get the right permissions, all that. This is the church we're talking about here. You can't just do as you please.'

'I know.'

'But I have a plan,' Steve said. 'While we're waiting for all that to grind away, we can put the painting up on a sort of temporary framework, like a giant easel, only safer. We have a carpenter friend I can ask. I'll see what he says.'

'That sounds good to me.'

'I wonder,' he murmured, staring at the ceiling, his coffee cup tilting alarmingly in his hand, 'maybe, if people are interested, we could do a study on Revelation at home group.'

'Steady on, love,' Jane said. 'Aren't you getting a bit ahead of yourself?'

'I'll try anything once,' Steve said. 'Would you be prepared to come along, Fen, if I set it up? You must have done a fair bit of research.'

'Well, yes-ish,' I said doubtfully. 'I've read it, and a commentary, a few times, but I wouldn't call myself any kind of authority.'

Steve laughed. 'More than most, I'd say. I might learn something myself.'

As I rode away from them down towards Chibley that morning, I was in better spirits than I'd been for a while. Whatever machinations Martha and Olive might cook up between them, I had a focus: to prepare the first panel for its public outing, and to make a start on the second.

I arrived and parked my bike against the studio wall, not waiting to greet anyone. Smoke was curling out of the farmhouse chimney, and the lights were on. As I opened the door a black taxi ground up the lane and came to a halt in the yard. I watched Olive climb out, swathed as ever in her furs, with a matching hat pulled well down over her ears. She marched up to the farmhouse door and let herself in as the cab turned and trundled back the way it had come. There was no sign of Liam.

Over the next few weeks, as January came to an unlamented end, I worked more intensely and for long hours. I felt such absorption that when Liam came up behind me soft-footed and discreetly cleared his throat I jerked and spilled a small pot of gold paint onto the floor.

'Sorry!' he pleaded. 'Yes, I know, that's expensive paint. I'll get something to clean up.' In the event he made more mess than he cleared, and my concentration was broken. 'You can make some tea as a penance,' I said.

He looked up at me wide-eyed from where he squatted on the floor, rag in hand. 'You were absolutely not in this world.'

'No, I was in the courts of heaven,' I said sarcastically. 'Contemplating the sapphire throne. Until some oik came along and broke the spell.'

He straightened up and inspected the section of my painting I'd been working on: the gold doors of the Temple's inner court, with tiny detailed figures of fantastic creatures, palm trees and exotic flowers. 'There's a bit of artistic licence going on there,' I said. 'Anyway, to what do I owe this visitation?'

'Let's get the kettle on, and I'll tell you.'

In the back room with two fan heaters on full I began to thaw out. Up to that moment I hadn't felt cold, but now I found my fingers were cramped. I wrapped them round the hot mug of tea. 'Where's Olive?' I whispered.

'Closeted with Martha and a solicitor. At least, that's who I think he is. Smart suit, slicked down comb-over. Later, as far as I can gather, they're talking to an architect. I came to let you know I'm going away for a while. Olive is on my case, Fen – the whole time. When she's not in some meeting she's after me for help and advice, supposedly about her work, but it's all a blind. She's all tarted up and simpering. I can't stand it much longer. I can't settle to any of my own work.'

'Where are you going?'

'If I don't tell you, you won't have to tell any lies to Olive. The thing is, for Martha's sake, I can't tell her, Olive that is, to back off. Which I would very much like to do. These negotiations are at a delicate stage, apparently.'

'Good grief. You make it sound like some international peace treaty! They're both abusing you, Liam, I hope you realise. Clear off while you have the chance.'

'I will. I've packed my rucksack. But I'll be back in time to help you seal the first panel. Is the frame going to be ready?'

'Yes, Jane's arranging it, plus the wooden framework it will be mounted on in the church. Then we have to think of a way to transport it down to St James's. Who's got a big enough boot?'

'We'll sort something out.' He finished his tea. 'Right – I'm aiming to catch the next train south.' He stood up, squeezed my shoulder, and loped towards the door.

An hour later I was back to work. This time there was no discreet entrance, no attempt to minimise disturbance, but a clatter of heels, a banging door and a strident demand without preamble: 'Where's Liam?'

I put my brush in a pot of water and turned slowly. Olive stood in the open doorway, clutching her fur coat round her. The door swung in the wind, banging against its frame.

'Were you speaking to me?' I said.

'Who else is here?' she growled. Clearly she was enraged, about what I had no idea. Her face was unusually flushed, her eyes narrow.

'Perhaps you could close the door,' I said. 'It's chilly in here.'

With an impatient mutter she pulled the door to.

'What was it you wanted?' I asked, hoping she could hear the frost in my tone.

'Liam – where is he?'

'How should I know? I don't keep track of his movements.'

Suddenly she strode across the room until she was barely two feet from where I stood. 'You two are as thick as thieves,' she hissed.

I tried to remain calm. 'No, we're not. I've hardly seen him. If we're friends, what's it to you?'

Her eyes bulged at this, and I thought she might actually explode. 'You know perfectly well,' she said. 'If it wasn't for you…'

'If it wasn't for me what?' I demanded.

She took a step back, her shoulders heaving. Her fists were clenched.

'If you'll excuse me,' I said with exaggerated politeness, 'I have work to do.' I turned back to my painting and ignored her. A moment later I heard the door banging again where she had left it open. I crossed the room and closed it firmly, trying hard not to curse her.

After this unheralded piece of animosity, I saw no more of Olive for almost a fortnight; in fact, she didn't reappear until Liam returned. Left in peace, I forged ahead with the second panel. The gold doors were done, and I'd sketched in the throne and the rainbow, the elders and their thrones, and the positions of the four living creatures.

As I cycled to and fro, from Whitepost to Chibley and back, I began to see tiny signs of approaching spring. It was now mid-February, and in Brant there would be snowdrops clustering round the trunks of trees that lined the streets, and daffodils would be in flower. Here I had no expectation of such early blooming, but in town, in pockets of gardens sheltered by stout stone walls, where the sun gave occasional warmth, to my surprise there showed one or two brave yellow trumpets, dancing wildly when the wind blew. In the open churchyard they were still in tight bud, huddled against the elements. Still, I was encouraged, hoping that winter was on the run. I should have known better. By the third week of February, we were beginning to hear warnings of a great storm brewing; yellow alerts, then amber, were issued. It was called Doris – such a comfortable name, something that might have been suitable for a beloved aunt given to knitting – and it was approaching from the west. Ireland and Scotland were already experiencing some buffeting; we would be next and we were very exposed.

As if blown in, Liam reappeared as the afternoon darkened, and he came into the studio with coat tails flapping and hair flying.

'Hello, stranger,' I said. I was packing up to leave.

'Wow, it's wild out there!' he said. 'And by all accounts it hasn't actually arrived yet. Please don't tell me you're planning to ride your bike in this wind!'

'I don't have much option, do I? I'll be fine. Anyway, I need to get to Whitepost. There are some things Mary needs in town.'

'What about tomorrow? Are you planning to come back?'

'Yes. Someone promised to help me seal my painting.'

He grinned. 'So they did. Please, Fen, be careful. And when you come back, it might be an idea to bring some things with you, like spare clothes and a toothbrush, in case you have to stay over. If it's as bad as they predict there could be fences down, power lines as well, and trees blocking the roads. It wouldn't be the first time.'

'I'll be careful,' I promised. 'Did you have a good time away?'

He smiled. 'I did. I feel like a new man.' He looked around and lowered his voice. 'Have you seen Olive?'

'Not since you left. Then she came over here in a fit of temper, demanding to know your whereabouts and practically accusing me of deliberately cramping her style.'

Liam shook his head. 'Honestly, Fen, sometimes I think she's just a bit deranged.'

'Maddened by uncontrollable passion, maybe?'

He groaned loudly. 'Don't you start!'

THE BUILDING STORM found all of us – Martha herself, Liam, Olive, and me – gathered in the kitchen at Chibley. I'd made it back that lunchtime at breakneck speed, the wind following and hurling me onward, an elemental monster carrying everything before it. Already on my way I'd seen branches down. On my bike I could skirt round them, but it would need a tractor to shift them sufficiently for a car to pass, and the worst of the storm was yet to come. We huddled round Martha's small TV, keeping track of the news and weather.

'Make the most of it,' Martha said. 'There's every chance we'll lose electricity. You'll have to stay here tonight, Olivia, Fen.'

'What? No, I can't!' Olive wailed. 'I've got a really important hospital appointment tomorrow – I've booked the taxi.'

'Well, I'm sorry, but Doris says you'll have to reschedule. According to the weather people the worst of it'll hit us in the small hours. Not to worry – we've got plenty of logs, so we'll keep warm, I'm well supplied with torches and candles, and we can cook with gas. The bedrooms may need some airing, but there's space for you all, and if someone fancies volunteering you might investigate the freezer so we can have a decent meal.'

Olive scowled. 'I tell you, I can't stay here. I must get to see my consultant. I'm going to ring Barry Cockerill. He always comes out for me. He won't be deterred by a bit of wind.' She got up, grabbed her bag and went through the door into the hallway. In a few moments we heard her speaking, her voice rising in shrill remonstration.

'He won't come out,' Martha said. 'Not even if she offered him triple the normal fare. He's a local man born and bred, and he respects the weather. Even if he weakened, Brenda Cockerill wouldn't let him leave the house. He puts up with a lot from Olive, but this time she's out of luck.'

Olive returned, the picture of furious misery. 'Now I'll have to ring the hospital,' she muttered as she sat down again at the table.

'They won't be expecting you,' Martha said. 'I think you'll find your consultant will stay put as well, if they've got any sense. There's dangerous weather coming, Olivia. People get killed, you know – trees falling on cars, cars washed into rivers.'

Olive glowered and said nothing.

'There's nothing for it, I'm afraid,' Martha said. 'Why don't you go and check out the bedrooms? There's plenty of linen and blankets in the cupboard at the top of the stairs.' She turned to me. 'Looks like you might be our cook for tonight, Fen. I don't think these two look very likely.'

Olive got up, scraping her chair against the flagged floor. 'Well, don't look at me!' she said. 'I can't cook for all of you.' She left the kitchen, banging the door behind her, and we heard her clumping up the stairs.

'Useless woman,' Martha muttered.

'I'm no expert, but I can be your sous-chef if you like,' Liam said. 'Put me on peeling duty.'

'Let's go and see what there is,' I said. 'There might be something we can use in the fridge.' A thought struck me. 'Before we start, shouldn't we check the studio is secure? Did we shut the window in the kitchen? We probably need to lock the main door as well – it's inclined to fly open.'

'I'll go,' Liam said. He put down his empty cup and went out, grabbing his coat as he went, and the wind nearly pulled the door out of his hand. Five minutes later he was back. 'All battened down,' he said. 'It's a howling gale out there, and it's started to rain as well. Martha, while I've got my coat on, do you need any more logs?'

'No, I think we're OK. You got me plenty yesterday.'

A querulous voice came from upstairs. There were no audible words, just a plea.

Liam sighed. 'I'll go and see what the problem is.'

'She's probably never made a bed in her life,' Martha said caustically.

In the fridge I found the remains of a lamb joint that needed using up and decided to make curry out of it. Martha had most of the ingredients in her pantry, and in a rack I found a box of random vegetables to supplement the meat. In a short time, the pot was simmering on the range, which luckily was powered by a gas bottle.

'Liam's been a while,' Martha commented, a wicked twinkle in her eyes. 'I hope she hasn't got him pinned down somewhere.'

'Poor bloke.'

A moment later Liam appeared, shaking his head. 'Olive now has a bed.' He closed his eyes, inhaling. 'That smells wonderful. Can I help?'

'No need,' I said. 'I'll just do a pan of rice later.'

'Close the curtains, someone,' Martha said. 'It's practically dark out there. Are you going to sleep in your eyrie, Liam? It's none too sturdy, that roof.'

'I aim to be all alone tonight,' Liam said, narrowing his eyes. 'As far away as possible from you-know-who.'

Neither Martha nor I were able to suppress a childish giggle.

Half an hour later Olive reappeared. She had brushed her hair, changed her top and put on makeup. At least she had made the effort; I, on the other hand, was unkempt, flushed from cooking, hair all over the place, and as I glanced in the mirror on the mantel I saw a sooty smudge on my forehead, no doubt from when I mended the fire.

Olive wrinkled her nose. 'What's that smell?'

'Lamb curry – that OK with you?'

'Good heavens, I can't possibly eat that, not with my delicate digestion,' Olive said, making a face. 'Can't someone do me some eggs?'

'Feel free to do your own,' Martha said with some asperity. 'You know where they are. Gin, anyone?'

As I dished up our meal, I tried not to notice Olive's loud, exasperated fumblings as she concocted a pan of scrambled eggs and a piece of toast. Watching her mangle a loaf of bread as she tried to cut a slice had been torture enough. Martha found a bottle of cider in the pantry, and we soon became quite merry, with a sort of survival mentality, as if sheltering from invasion.

'Let's put the TV on again,' Martha said. 'See how dear old Doris is shaping up.' We'd barely tuned in when there was a loud bang outside, the TV went blank, and all the lights went out.

There followed a dead silence, punctuated only by a moan from Olive. 'Seems like our lines are down,' Martha said. 'Ah well, I expect they'll fix it in the morning. We'll all just have to get an early night.'

'What?' Olive said. 'Can't you ring somebody?'

There was a tiny pause, and we held our breath.

'Perhaps it hasn't occurred to you, Olivia,' Martha said silkily, 'living in the city as you do, that the chaps are already out there in the storm, risking life and limb to reconnect people, not to mention the emergency services dealing with real disasters. I hardly think we're a high priority. Let's light some candles, shall we?'

By candlelight and with the aid of torches, we cleared the table. 'Leave the dishes,' Martha said. 'Tomorrow'll do.'

'I'll say goodnight, ladies,' Liam said, and he made a hasty exit.

'Shall I shine a torch so you two can get upstairs?' I offered.

'I've got my own,' Martha said. She heaved herself up out of her chair and took the torch in one hand and her stick in the other. I glanced enquiringly at Olive. She was standing quite still, her arms wrapped round her skinny torso, and she looked utterly terrified.

DORIS RATTLED AROUND us all that night. Used as I was to the noises of the natural world through the walls and windows of my little cottage at Whitepost, the racket didn't stop me sleeping, huddled in a lumpy single bed in one of Martha's smaller bedrooms at the back of the farmhouse facing the lane. But as the storm reached its height and moved direction, some time after two in the morning, there was a loud bang and a piercing scream. I sat up, blinking away the fog of sleep, and tried to guess where the sound had come from. I put my feet on the ratty rag rug beside the bed and shuddered at the cold. Then I heaved myself up and switched on the torch I had taken up with me; it cast eerie shadows across the darkened room. I'd flung my coat on a chair near the door; now I put it on and went out into the hallway, listening for any sounds that might penetrate the howling wind.

I heard what sounded like a banging door or shutter and padded along the landing. Unsurprisingly there was no sound from Martha's room – I knew she took strong pills for pain that knocked her out – but from the room over the kitchen, now occupied by Olive, came the sound of sobbing.

The door was slightly ajar, and I pushed it gingerly. 'Olivia? What's up? Can I come in?'

I heard a gulp and a moan, which could have borne any interpretation. I pushed the door wider. By the searching beam of my torch I saw Olive, sitting up in bed, her hair straggling across her heaving shoulders, a wadded handkerchief in her fist, her red-rimmed eyes wide with fright.

'What is it?' I whispered. 'What's the matter?'

She didn't answer – perhaps she couldn't – but even in the dim light I could see she was shivering.

I crept up to the bedside. 'You look frozen,' I said, my voice low. 'Your blankets are on the floor.' I picked up one of the covers and draped it round her shoulders.

Now she found her voice, and it was weak and slurring, as though she was drunk or drugged. 'I heard a noise. It was so loud. I woke up and I didn't know where I was. I was scared.'

I heard a bang and saw Olive flinch. I shone the torch round the room and saw that her window had blown open and with every gust it beat on the frame. The curtains were sucking in and out, and I could see they were wet. I went to the window and pulled it shut, showering myself with freezing rain in the process: outside a torrent was lashing down, and as I closed the curtain a brief flash of lightning brightened the sky and then, after a pause, came a soft thundery rumble.

I turned back to Olive. 'It was just your window,' I said, trying to sound comforting. 'The storm's moving away – it should be quieter now.'

To my dismay she began to weep, pressing the handkerchief into her eyes. I came back and sat on the edge of the bed.

'Have you always been afraid of storms, Olivia?' I asked gently, and she nodded. 'I think the worst is over now. Do you think you can get back to sleep? Is there anything I can get you?' She didn't answer, and I tried again. 'Do you have a hot water bottle?'

That slurred voice came again, and I realised it was because of all the crying. 'Yes.' Her arm came out from under the covers, holding the water bottle in its blue floral cover. 'It's cold.'

I took it from her. 'I'll fill it up for you. Would a drink help? What about some hot milk with a spoonful of honey in it?' I saw her nod and pull the blanket tighter round her shoulders. 'Back in a minute.'

By torchlight I made my way down the stairs and into the kitchen. I put a pan of water on the gas ring for the hot water bottle. While it heated, I put milk into a smaller pan and started to warm it. I thought of making her some toast but realised that without electricity and with the fire nothing but embers it might be difficult. I found a tin with biscuits in it and put two in my pocket – not very hygienic, but I only had two hands. I tucked the hot water bottle under my arm and carried the milk in one hand and the torch in the other. Its light wavered all over the stairs, and I remembered the stair carpet was a trip hazard.

I found Olive as I had left her, but visibly calmer. The wildness outside had abated a little, but perhaps also it was the comfort of another person; knowing she wasn't alone in the dark.

'Here you are,' I said. She tucked the hot water bottle under her arm as I put the milk on the bedside table. 'I brought you a couple of biscuits as well,' I said. 'I won't be offended if you don't want them, as they've been in my pocket! But you didn't have much to eat this evening.' She took them from me with no sign of revulsion and ate them between slurps of the milk. When she had finished, she put the empty cup in my hand like a child.

'Thank you,' she said in a small voice.

'That's OK. Do you feel a bit better now?'

She nodded and slithered down in the bed, clutching the hot water bottle to her chest. I rearranged her covers, heaping the blankets over her.

I was going to leave her, but then she said, 'I don't know why you've been so nice to me. I haven't been very nice to you.'

I suppressed a laugh. 'Well, that's true. Want to tell me why?'

She was silent for a moment, clearly struggling with her thoughts. 'I know I wasn't fair. But, I don't know, I was surprised, I didn't expect anyone else to be here. And somehow you seemed to have, to be… all the things I'm not. Strong – all that cycling! – healthy, happy, successful.'

'Hold on a minute – you couldn't possibly know all that.'

She blinked. 'No, of course I couldn't. But that's how it seemed. And then there's Liam. I'm not stupid, you know. I could see how he avoided me, and when he couldn't, oh, yes, of course, he was always helpful, always polite, but that was all, where with you he seemed free and at ease…' A sob choked her to silence.

I risked putting a hand on her arm as it lay beneath the blankets. 'Look, Olivia,' I said softly, 'there's absolutely nothing going on between me and Liam. We talk about art. And as I'm sure you're well aware, I'm married. In almost twenty-five years I've never once cheated on my husband, and I have no intention of starting now. I'm not your rival.'

She took this in for a moment. 'Well, I did wonder, and I know it's none of my business, but here you are for months on end and he's far away and never comes…'

In this line of questioning, I wasn't about to indulge her. I felt sorry for her, much to my surprise, but there was something about Olive I didn't quite trust. 'Well, let's say he's a very generous man.' I smiled with as much warmth as I could muster. My bare feet were getting very cold, and I was ready to go back to bed. 'Do you think you might get some sleep now, Olivia?'

She didn't speak for a moment, and when she did it wasn't an answer to my question. She looked up at me. 'I was married once, you know.'

This I hadn't expected – not just the information itself, but the desire to confide. 'Oh, were you? But you aren't now?' I felt the need to tread warily, to choose my words with care, but she seemed unfazed, clearly ready to tell her story. 'No, he died. It was a long time ago,' she added as I made some sympathetic sound, 'fifteen years, and he was very old. Ninety-one.'

'Oh.' I hardly knew how to respond. 'How old were you?'

'When he died? Twenty-four. We'd been together four years.'

'That's quite an age gap.'

She nodded. 'Huge. But it wasn't a normal sort of marriage. I'd gone to America. That's where I met him.'

I was beginning to feel dazed. 'America?' I repeated.

She smiled at my confusion. 'I'd better go back a bit. I was a student, eighteen years old, studying history of art. It was a good course, and I was enjoying my life. I hadn't had a very happy childhood, but I won't bore you with all that; lots of people have unhappy childhoods, don't they? Anyway, I was delighted to be away from home. I liked the work, and I'd made a few friends. During my second term I got ill – just a nasty throat infection, or so I thought, and I didn't get it checked out soon enough. It's not just storms I'm scared of – I really hated doctors and hospitals as well, which was a lot to do with what my mother made me go through… it got worse, and I developed rheumatic fever. I had several bouts of it, and it damaged my heart valves, so it was ironic really because after that, of course, I had lots of medical interventions. It messed up my university life; I missed so much that I had to give it up, and even though I hated the idea I had to go home to recuperate because there was nowhere else. Well, I did get better, after a fashion, and as soon as I could I went to America. I had the idea that there would be lots of opportunities there – I was terribly naïve. So, to cut a long, dreary story short, there I was, twenty years old, with no qualifications and in fragile health, doing all sorts of awful jobs just to stay alive, and that's when I met Vinnie.'

'So he was, what? Eighty-seven? And you married him?'

She nodded. 'At first it was just a sort of convenient arrangement. He was unbelievably rich, you see. Property all over the world. But he was lonely. Sometimes rich people don't know who to trust – do you know what I mean? There are so many spongers.' She sighed. 'I suppose in a way you could say I was the same, but I did try to look after him, to be a kind friend and ally, as far as I could, and in the end we did become very fond of each other. I did my best, and it gave me a home and comfort. After a while, odd as it may seem to you, I did come to love him, in my own way.' She frowned suddenly. 'The trouble was, Vinnie had a family. A son and a daughter. But they'd fallen out with him over some business deal, and the only person Vinnie got on with was his grandson. We'd been together for a couple of years when Vinnie started seeing a lot of lawyers. And the upshot was he made a new will and in it he left me a huge amount of money and property. He left some to his children too, and a lot to George, his grandson. After he died it all got very nasty, and the son and daughter tried to contest the will. They said it couldn't possibly have been a proper marriage, but they couldn't prove anything, could they? Anyway, the will was all watertight, and George stood up for me, saying I had been a real companion to Vinnie, which I had. I took some good advice, made some canny investments – Vinnie would have been proud! And suddenly I was a very rich woman – and lonely too. I missed him dreadfully.'

She heaved a sigh, and I saw her eyelids were drooping. 'When you're very rich,' she said, 'you can do lots of things – get the best medical care, indulge all your whims. But it doesn't get you the important things – friends, people who really care about you. I was in the same position as Vinnie – taken for a ride a few times and trusting no one. Perhaps that's a story for another day. I'm feeling sleepy now.' Suddenly her eyes flew open. 'Please, say you won't tell anyone what I've told you. Not even Liam, or Martha.'

'If that's what you want, of course I won't,' I said. 'But how can you know I'm trustworthy, after all the disappointments I suspect you've had?'

Her hand came out from under the covers, and she gripped my wrist with surprising force. 'You're a Christian, aren't you? Yes, well, I've met some very dodgy individuals who've claimed to be Christians, but somehow I don't think you're like them.'

'I hope I'm not,' I said softly. 'I'm not perfect, Olivia, but I try to keep my promises. And what you've told me will stay just between us. Look, it's almost three o'clock. I'll leave you to get some sleep, if you can.'

She yawned widely. 'Thank you, Fen. Goodnight.'

Settling back in my own bed, now cold, pulling the covers up over my shoulders, I pondered. I wondered why Olive had told me her tale; perhaps waking scared in the night had led her to lower her guard. What was it that she didn't want others to know? Was she afraid of ridicule? It would have been nice to think that these confidences might mark a turn for the better in our relations, but somehow I felt sure this was merely a chapter, not the end of the story. There were, I thought, many levels to Olive.

In the gloomy light of morning, the only one awake, a mug of tea in my hand, I looked out of the kitchen window at the wreckage wild Doris had wrought. To my relief the studio appeared unharmed, but there were bits of tree and fence, a wheelbarrow, even a whole gate, strewn across the yard, and some of the tiles over Liam's flat were missing. The worst of the wind had passed, but its remaining flurries and eddies caused flowerpots and buckets to roll around noisily on the flagged courtyard.

I saw Liam emerge, warmly dressed, at the top of the wooden steps that led up to his quarters. He waved when he saw me and started to descend. The handrail, never secure, wobbled alarmingly, and when he reached the bottom step the whole staircase swayed. He let himself into the kitchen, rubbing his hands. 'Someone – probably me – is going to have to fix those steps. I'm in danger of breaking my neck. Did you make a pot?'

'Just. It should still be hot. Did you manage to sleep?'

'For a few hours. I woke up to a lot of rattling – window frames, probably. So I sat up and did a few drawings. You?'

'Yes. Storms don't bother me. I quite like elemental fury, as long as I'm not out in it.' I drained my cup. 'I think I'll just go up and get some warm clothes on. Then do you think we should go and see if the studio's OK? It looks all right from here, but there are precious things in there.'

He smiled. 'Including a painting needing sealing.'

'Today?'

'Why not? Once we've done the first coat, we can do a bit of tidying up around the house while it dries. It's still too windy for cycling, so you're stuck here for the time being. Is the electricity still out?'

'I'm afraid so.'

Ten minutes later we were in the studio, surveying the scene. The wind was still moaning around the building, which I supposed was particularly vulnerable because of its height. The first panel still rested against the wall, held in place by the lengths of timber I'd placed against its bottom edge. Luckily, I'd also lowered the second panel from its rather rickety support of two easels and placed it, too, against the wall. Liam went up close and looked at what I'd done. The edges of the gold doors were well-enough executed, but I hadn't yet decided how to approach the throne. 'I might need some advice,' I murmured.

'About what?'

'Painting the sea of glass. How do I make it look like glass rather than water? Water's difficult enough.'

'Mm.' Liam bit his lip. 'Maybe we need to check out some books. Let's go into the back room and see if we can find an expert.'

On the table, where I'd left them, were several fat art books open at pages showing some of the works of Caravaggio: the two renditions of the *Supper at Emmaus*, the famous one with St Peter's outflung arm reaching into the audience, and the basket with the lifelike fruit beginning to rot; the full-faced Christ, half in shadow, his eyes downcast; and the second, painted some years later, and quite different: much darker, with barely a chink of relieving light, and even less idealised than the first. Then there was the remarkable and strange painting of the *Conversion of St Paul*, with its baffling composition – so much horse, so little saint! – and the man holding the horse's rein almost invisible in the artist's trademark shadow.

I turned to Liam with a sigh. 'I would give my right arm to paint like Caravaggio.'

Liam laughed, his eyes bright. 'If you gave your right arm, you probably wouldn't be painting anything.'

'And if I used my left arm, all my work would look like a five-year-old's.'

That's how Olive, entering soft-footed in slippers, must have seen us: standing with our backs to the door, shoulders touching, chuckling foolishly.

The next thing we knew was a loud, harsh, accusing voice: 'You absolutely despicable snake in the grass, Fen Bailey!'

We both turned, drop-jawed. Olive stood in the doorway, her face as ever ghostly but with a scarlet spot on each cheekbone. 'I should have known you couldn't keep your mouth shut! As for you, Liam, I shouldn't be surprised – listening to tattle for a cheap laugh! You both disgust me.'

Liam found his voice first. 'What on earth are you talking about?'

'Don't tell me you didn't find it funny,' Olive said scornfully. 'Poor old Olive, what a story! Don't make out she hasn't told you everything I told her last night.'

Now I understood. 'Olivia, I haven't said a word. You haven't even been mentioned. We were talking about Caravaggio.'

Her voice rose to a shriek. 'I hate liars and traitors!' She turned and stormed into the main studio area and, sensing she was out of control, we both ran after her, but we were too late: like Nemesis herself she strode across the room, and to our horror we saw her kick away the pieces of wood at the base of my panels. Then with a jerk of her arm she sent them crashing face down to the floor, accelerated by their own weight.

'No!' Liam yelled and raced towards her. As he passed, Olive gave him a hard shove, making him stagger. 'Weak-minded little toady!' she hissed. 'Making up to your latest squeeze! You are shameless.' Before he could right himself, she swept past him, draped clothing trailing, and disappeared out of the door. She left it swinging in the wind while the two of us stood transfixed, gaping with astonishment and dismay.

Without thinking I made to follow her, but Liam recovered his wits. 'Leave her!' he barked. 'We need to rescue your panels, find out what the mad bitch has done. Help me lift them.'

We took an end each, and I found I was trembling, nausea roiling in my gut. Gently we lifted the first panel and leaned it back against the wall. To my astonishment it was relatively unscathed apart from a missing flake or two round the edges.

'It's a good job we left it to cure this long,' Liam said, his tone uncharacteristically grim. 'The other one may be more damaged.'

He was right: some of my newly applied paint on the Temple doors had come away. 'I can redo that, I guess,' I said shakily.

Liam turned to me and put a consoling hand on my shoulder. 'I can help,' he said. 'But for now, the best thing we can do is seal the finished one. The sooner that's had two coats and dried, the sooner we can organise getting it down to the church, where it should be safe. Didn't you say something about the framer coming to the church and measuring it up in situ?'

'Yes, that's what Jane suggested. Seemed a better idea than him coming out here.'

'OK. First of all, I'm going to get the kettle on. You're in shock, and I'm about to explode with rage, so we both need more tea. She won't show her face in here, but if she did I can't answer for my self-control. Look, why don't you get the polycrylic and the brushes and get started? If I help you, it will take half the time.'

I looked at him, my eyes filled with unbidden tears. 'Haven't you got your own stuff to do?'

'Don't be daft,' he said roughly and disappeared into the back room.

We were about halfway done when we heard the rumble of a car engine approaching. Liam, brush in hand, went to look out of the door. 'It's that hero, Barry Cockerill. I thought Olive might disappear as soon as she could. I suppose they must have cleared any debris off the lane.' He scowled. 'Good riddance. I hope we never see her nasty washed-out face again.' He closed the door with an audible click, and at that moment the lights came on.

'Thank heaven for brave men up poles,' I said. I paused for a moment as Liam came back. 'You know, I don't understand what's going on in Olive's mind. I didn't tell you, because she asked me not to divulge what she said, but I was up at half past two this morning with a very frightened Olive, making her warm milk and filling her hot water bottle, and she told me something of her life. She's a very strange lady, and a sad one, despite her wealth.'

Liam stared. 'I don't know how you can be so charitable, Fern.'

I shrugged. 'Maybe it's because I've got you to do the angry bit. It could be worse – the paintings are retrievable with a bit of work. And I really appreciate your loyalty, and your help.' He looked embarrassed at this and mumbled something unintelligible. I heaved a sigh and smiled. 'Not to mention she's gone! The atmosphere's lighter already. Do you think she'll be back?'

Liam shook his head. 'I doubt it. Once she calms down, she'll be cringing. She may come back one day, but my guess is she'll wait till you're not here. On the other hand, she may have gone for good, in which case I imagine her deal with Martha will be off the table.'

I stared at him. 'Isn't there a contract?'

‘They were still negotiating. Nothing signed.’

‘Oh. That’s not good for Martha, or for Chibley. If it wasn’t for me, she might have had her solution.’

‘It’s hardly your fault!’ Liam said. ‘Yes, Martha’s back to square one, but part of her will be relieved. She never thought Olive’s work was really worth a one-woman permanent exhibition. Come on, let’s get this coat finished, then we can lock up and leave it to dry. I didn’t have any breakfast, and my inner man is protesting. Maybe we can find out from Martha what went on before Olive left.’

AN HOUR LATER we were done. It was good to have Liam helping; I was able to copy his brushstrokes, which were so much more confident than mine. I was getting the hang of it by the end and thought I could probably be left to apply the second coat by myself. We left the brushes soaking, locked up, and walked down to the farmhouse. There we found Martha, in her favourite chair at the table, speaking haughtily into her phone. I found some bread and ham and started to make sandwiches while Liam brewed coffee. Martha finished her call, breathing heavily. ‘Stupid cocksure little man. Full of his own importance.’

I put a plate and a cup next to her. ‘Who’s got your goat?’

‘The architect we were having talks with. Chap called Ambrose, not local. Annoyed I’m dispensing with his services. It was all preliminary talks, nothing settled. And without Olive, I can’t afford him. Luckily the solicitor was more understanding.’

‘So Olive’s pulled out?’ Liam said. ‘I thought she would.’ He took a sandwich and began to munch.

‘I’m sorry, Martha,’ I said. ‘I know this is because of me, though it isn’t my fault.’

‘You’re just the excuse, Fen,’ Martha said. ‘There’s something wrong with Olive. I’m sure she has some syndrome or other. The one where people think everything revolves around them. I’m glad to see the back of her. She was in a heck of a state when she came back here. What was going on?’

We told her the bare facts, and Martha was appalled. 'You say you can repair the damage?'

'The first panel's had its first coat,' I said. 'We'll get it down to St James's as soon as it's done and dry. Not sure what I'm going to do about the recent work, though.'

Martha looked at me levelly. 'Liam and I will both help and advise, won't we, Liam? You shouldn't have to defend your work against lunatics like Olive. I feel responsible.'

I laughed, a little shakily. 'Thanks. With you two on hand, all will be well.'

'I'LL GO AND see what repairs I can do,' Liam said after lunch.

'I'll give you a hand,' I said, getting up from the table.

'No, you won't,' Liam said sternly. 'Your job is to get that second coat on, preferably while there's some daylight left. You never know if the lights are going to go off again.'

'I,' Martha said, 'shall put my feet up and shut my eyes. With all that racket going on last night I'm short of sleep and likely to be grouchy.' She smiled beatifically. 'Isn't it nice and peaceful!'

We chuckled and separated to our various tasks. I deliberately switched my phone off so I could concentrate, and the second coat went on smoothly.

It was beginning to get dark as I left the studio and went back to the farmhouse. The yard was clear of debris, and as I looked up I could see that Liam had replaced the slipped tiles on the roof of his barn. In the kitchen Martha lay sprawled in her easy chair, gently snoring. The fire had burned down, showing just a dull orange glow; I put a couple of logs on and opened a vent. I thought I would make a meal for us and then think about returning to Whitepost; I was starting to feel uneasy about Mary and Peter, wondering if there had been damage to their buildings.

Liam appeared, windswept and flushed. 'It's getting cold out there. Shall I make some tea?' He sniffed. 'Something smells good.'

'I've thrown a meal of sorts together for us this evening,' I said, 'but then I really should get back to my cottage. What have you been doing?'

'Fixing things that got loose,' Liam said. 'There was part of a fence down along the lane.' He paused, thinking. 'If you find there's damage at Whitepost, give me a ring. I might be able to help.'

'Thanks, that's kind. Should we wake Martha up?'

'I'll put the news on. See how the rest of the world is faring. Have you had any communication from home?'

I felt a pang of guilt. 'No idea. I turned my phone off.'

THE SIX O'CLOCK news told a dramatic tale of the destruction caused by Doris, which they were calling a 'weather bomb'. The coasts had had it worst, as well as the high ground to the north. Eighty-mile-an-hour winds had been recorded in Leeds, and there was the usual chaos of roofs ripped off, whole trees or huge branches fallen and power lines down. Some places were still in the dark, and inevitably there'd been injuries and fatalities. Teams of engineers were out, working round the clock to restore electricity supplies. Schools were closed. Rivers were dangerously high. The news majored on the local area, but the effects were widespread, and I remembered finally to turn my phone on, intending to contact John and Alice and see if they were all right. However as soon as I was connected my phone went crazy with pinging, and I saw I had many messages.

I sent a text to John, Dan, Alice, and Grace, thinking that would be enough to assure them of my safety before the next time we spoke; but a few minutes later my phone rang.

'Kind of you to let us know you're still alive.' John's annoyed sarcasm was absolutely destined to produce the wrong response. Had he said, 'Fen, thank heavens you're all right' – which is what I knew he actually meant – I would have been suitably remorseful. As it was, he made it sound like yet another failed obligation, and created nothing but bristling indignation. However, I swallowed the words that came to my lips. 'Sorry if you were worried,' I said, unable to control a level of frostiness. It irked me that I had spent so many years choosing words to avoid quarrels, whereas he sprayed them around like a scattergun heedless of the consequences. For an intelligent man he could be pretty stupid; but maybe that was something that applied to most of us, me included, in one way or another. As it was, I sighed inwardly. Here was yet another tedious example of our continued failure to communicate.

'Of course I was worried,' he said. 'It's been all over the news – where you are was one of the worst-hit areas. Please tell me you weren't out riding your bike in it.'

'No,' I said. 'I stayed over at Chibley last night. How are things in Brant?'

'Noisy and messy,' he said. 'A fair bit of damage, but all cleared away now.'

'I've texted Alice but not heard back. Has she contacted you?'

'Yes. Said she's OK.'

'That's good. So, storms aside, are you all right? You sound tired – aren't things calming down a bit at work? You expected them to.'

He grunted. 'I've had a few days off. Been a bit under the weather.'

'No surprise,' I said. 'All that jetting about.'

'It's not that. I've had a bit of tummy trouble. Probably just a bug.'

'Are you eating properly?'

'I haven't got much appetite at the moment. But don't worry – I'm sure it'll pass in no time.'

'Literally.'

'Ha, ha. So, what have you been up to?'

'Mostly painting. The first panel is sealed, and we're about to get it framed and take it to the church.'

'Progress indeed.' There was a very small pause. 'Remind me when you're coming home?'

I gritted my teeth. Nothing changed, it seemed; his interest in my affairs was so obviously minimal. 'I told you – the Tuesday after Easter.'

Now he sounded woeful. 'That's more than six weeks away. What's so important you have to stay away for six more weeks?'

'If you are really interested, I'll tell you. I want to see the first panel on display in the church. If at all possible, I want to finish the second one and leave it to cure while I'm away. And I want to ask Will Wharton if I can help get his ewes down from the high pasture, with help from Sadie, and be on hand for lambing.'

'*Lambing?* What are you now – a farmer?'

If only. 'Just making the most of my time here, that's all.'

'I miss you,' he said mournfully. 'I don't think you miss me, us, at all.'

'Of course I do,' I said briskly. 'I'm just very busy, that's all. Look, John, it's getting late, and I need to get back to Whitepost. Let me know how you are over the weekend.'

I expected him to wind up the call and ring off, but after a pause he said, 'What would you do if one of us – Alice, Dan, me – was really ill?'

'I would come and look after you,' I said. 'Of course. Though it might be a bit difficult if Daniel was still in America. If it was him, I suppose I'd have to fly out there. Daft question, John – it's obvious.'

He said nothing, but I heard his unspoken doubt.

I AND EVERYONE I came in contact with was longing for spring, especially after the savagery of the storm and the sometimes protracted clearing up operations that followed; but we still had some time to wait. Snowdrops were appearing under trees, and the early daffodils began to proliferate in sheltered spots, but March was unsettled, with days on end of steady rain and depressing low cloud. Occasionally we were teased by an hour or two when the sun broke through, but then came strong winds and even the odd snow flurry up on the high hills. Farmers, including the Whartons, looked out frowning, wondering and worrying about their pregnant ewes, trying to decide when to bring them down; but it was early yet for lambing this far north, and the weather was not in their favour. We had to wait for April for a more settled period, and then there was a flurry of activity in which I was, to my delight, included.

Meanwhile, the last of winter had to be seen out. I had no quarrel with the weather, apart from one occasion when, on my way from

Whitepost to Chibley, my bike got a puncture and I had to fix it in a layby while being drenched in a sudden squall. When I got to Chibley I was so wet I had to borrow clothes from Liam – some ancient patched jeans and a very old brown sweater, which he said were all he had and not either in the wash or being worn by him. They were good enough for painting in and who was looking at me anyway?

Those weeks through March and April were among the happiest I could remember. Of course, through the years I had had moments of joy – the birth of healthy children probably foremost. But I couldn't remember such a long period of being both contented and driven, a deep upwelling of a peculiar kind of peace in the midst of intense activity.

In the wake of Olive's destructive attempts, Liam and I worked to repair and salvage the work I'd already done, and I continued with the second panel with renewed energy. I managed to create an effect with the sea of glass that, while far from perfect, or even especially accomplished, came close to the effect I wanted: the idea of God's unapproachable holiness. As March came to an end I'd started on the lower part of the panel, which could have been tedious with its rank upon rank of angels similarly attired (though with the odd eccentric detail: one angel sported a tartan scarf, another was playing a trombone), but I went to it with a persistent commitment I didn't know I possessed.

The first panel was framed – at considerable expense because of its size, but expertly done – and securely mounted. To be visible, yet safely out of the way, Steve had decided to put it in one of the side aisles where there was space for people to stand back and gaze. For some weeks it was there for anyone to view, whether members of the congregation, the idly curious among the town dwellers, or even a scattering of hill walkers passing through. There was a hum of fascination, some of it baffled. Steve chose a date for me to answer questions, and it was advertised around the town and beyond. I thought I'd better take another look at the relevant chapters of Revelation and the notes I'd taken from the commentary. I didn't want to look ignorant, though I suspected there'd be some questions I couldn't answer from folk more Bible-literate than

I. This event happened one murky Sunday afternoon between services when both Steve and Jane could be there, and when for some it might make a change from dozing in front of the fire or the TV after a hefty lunch.

To a surprisingly large audience – perhaps fifty people – I gave a little prepared talk. This was not something I'd ever done, and I was nervous, but I was on familiar ground, and most artists of any stripe were in my experience happy to talk about their work. I wanted to tie in what I had done with the reason for it – to explain the message in terms that could be understood by people of my own time. The modern touches: car parks and playgrounds and shops, were generally appreciated. I told them how St John sought to twitch back the curtain between this world and the next, giving his readers a notion of the world we live in as the scene of a great ongoing battle between good and evil. Nodding heads told me that this was an easy concept for anyone who watched the news or read a newspaper. I mentioned St John's emphasis on the need for repentance, which was greeted by one or two blank faces, and told them that despite the later visions of violence and destruction Revelation was essentially optimistic, not because of human character or activity but because of God's purpose and work in history. Finally, I pointed out the dominant figure of the risen Christ, left and centre, gloriously shining in triumph. 'Most writers of works like Revelation,' I said, 'look forward to the Messiah. But of course for John he had already come: the man John knew as a beloved friend, the man he had followed to the cross.'

I left it there, and for a moment there was silence, and I wondered if anyone would ask me a question; but I needn't have worried. The questions and comments were as varied as the people asking them: some were puzzled, others wanted to show off their knowledge, some were sceptical, some whimsical. Some wanted to know my motivation; and one lady, almost invisible beneath a high coat collar and an enveloping hat, wanted to know who was my favourite artist, and why was that?

At a point in the proceedings, I noticed that Liam and Martha had quietly come in at the back of the church, and now I caught Liam's eye and saw him grin.

'I like and admire many artists,' I told the lady. 'Some worked centuries ago, and some are much more recent. One I admire and envy is Caravaggio, and he died way back in 1610. I wish I could manage some of the effects he achieved, even though he had to work with materials far less convenient than the ones we use now. And although he was of his own day, he had a vision that transcends his time. He didn't idealise his subjects – he showed them as recognisably human, even when he was painting Jesus, which scandalised some of his contemporaries. One of his most famous paintings is his *Supper at Emmaus*, and it's a dramatic, lively work with extraordinary use of light and shade, showing both Jesus and the apostles as real people.'

When the formal part of the afternoon came to an end, and (as is usual) tea and cake were being served, a number of people from the audience shyly approached and asked me more questions. I tried to answer them, but in the end I was thankful that the evening service brought it all to a natural end. I found I was both energised and exhausted.

An uncomfortable thought struck me. As I put on my coat to leave, I said to Steve, 'I hope I didn't commit any heresies. I wouldn't want to lead anyone astray, and I'm no theologian.'

He laughed. 'I don't think I'm much of one either! Don't worry. If anyone thinks you strayed from orthodoxy, I'll set them straight. Remind me again: what's in the second panel?'

'Heaven, essentially. But I'm beginning to realise from my reading that I might have to deal with something rather more alarming in the third, if I ever get to it.'

Steve raised his eyebrows. 'Oh?'

'Hell. Judgement. It's not popular, I know, to think about God in terms of punishment. But St John makes no bones about it – we may think we've got away with our wickedness, probably because our personal sins seem so flimsy compared to the horrific things perpetrated by tyrants and warmongers, but even so the consequences will have to be faced, if not in this world, then in the next. You may not be quite so keen on that painting.'

Steve nodded. 'Well, we'll see. These things must be faced, of course, as you say. But I'm in favour of tempering the wind to the shorn lamb.'

I smiled wryly. 'An apt saying for the farmers. I'll let you get on, Steve. Thank you for this opportunity.'

'Not at all, Fen. I rather think you've put St James's on the map!'

COMMUNICATION WITH THE family was a bit sketchy as spring approached. Alice and Dan sent brief messages from time to time, and both seemed to be getting on with their lives, happy in their work and relationships, so I was pleased. John rang me, or I him, with some regularity, but briefly; it seemed we had little to say to each other. I sensed he was peculiarly distant but put it down to work pressures. The person who caused me greatest puzzlement was Grace. She'd been a fairly regular emailer when I was first away but now seemed increasingly reticent. I knew she was actively contemplating emigrating and that, I supposed, must be taking up all her thoughts. I was so involved in making maximum progress on the second panel that I put concerns about life in Brant to one side. I would have to think about them, but not yet. And, apart from painting, to my great joy I had my wish: going up onto the green hills with Sadie, and Will Wharton with his dogs, and young Thom once he was free of school, on foot or by quad, bringing the pregnant ewes down to the farm. Then, on several nights and days, weary but elated, I got to watch and learn as the experts attended to labouring ewes. Finally, they let me deliver a lamb – closely supervised – pulling the wriggling slippery little creature free of its mother, rubbing it with a handful of straw, hearing it breathe and bleat. It was an experience I had coveted and would not forget.

EASTER SUNDAY STARTED off with a short shower, as if to remind us humans not to get too complacent. But by the time Mary and I piled into Will Wharton's venerable Rover, brought out of its barn for special occasions, and sank into its slippery leather seats, the sun came out, sparkling on the grass of the fields as we rumbled down to the town and gleaming on the puddles that washed the road.

'Even the daffodils look yellower today,' I said.

Mary simply raised her eyebrows.

Will dropped us off and went to his favourite hostelry to wait. Mary and I walked up the long approach to the church, seeing daffodils in yellow drifts all along the path's edge and clustered round the gravestones. Flowers were a big theme inside the church as well – pots of them on every available shelf and window ledge. The pews were full of people, including many we'd never before seen within these walls, and the small choir of little girls, accompanied on the keyboard by Jane, were singing something unfamiliar to me but very rhythmic and sung *fortissimo*. Steve emerged from the vestry, resplendent in a scarf worked in gold, which lost none of its magnificence for being draped unevenly over his bony frame.

The service was as ever slightly disorganised – it was for me part of the charm of this place. But whatever it had been like couldn't have dimmed my joy. Easter Sunday had long been my favourite day of the year: today, whatever the circumstances, hope triumphed over hopelessness. Today I couldn't avoid thinking about things eternal.

I said as much, in an undertone, to Mary as we sipped a cup of coffee afterwards.

She heaved a small sigh. 'I'm sure you're right, Fen. But it's sad when you think of the people who can't be part of it.'

'You're thinking of Peter.'

'Not just him. There are folk at the nursing home, for instance. Mrs Mellor, who's blind. She can't see the daffodils, can she?'

I nodded. 'I get that, of course. But there was something I found in that commentary on Revelation that's stuck in my mind – something along the lines of ultimate reality not being subject to, or limited by, what was it exactly? Circumstances. No, appearances. Sorry, I made a mess of that.'

'I think I know what you mean,' Mary said softly. 'And if we can't think about ultimate reality today, when can we?' She glanced over at the side aisle. 'People are still looking at your painting, Fen.'

One or two of those people had obviously been at my talk; they came up and asked me questions. How was I getting on with the second panel? Would that be in church too? Was I still hoping to do a third? I answered as best I could, grateful for their interest. It was still a surprise – I'd come here less than a year ago with a vague idea for a series of pictures; now, rather embarrassingly, I seemed to be a bit of a local celebrity.

I spent the rest of the day with Mary and Peter, quietly festive. As dusk approached I went back to my cottage, full of food and wine, content to think about very little. I kicked off my shoes and lit a fire. With a cup of tea on the small table beside the armchair I opened my laptop to check my emails, and I was happy to see there was one from Grace.

In moments my pleasure evaporated, and to my shame all those lofty thoughts about ultimate reality were rendered void by what she had to tell me.

> Dear Fen,
>
> I've thought very hard about this email, but there's nothing for it, and nothing can sugar the pill. A few days ago I was shopping in town, and went into that little coffee shop in Friary Row to take the weight off. I was very surprised to see your Alice in there. I thought she would still have been at her university, especially as her boyfriend is there, but I supposed she'd come home to see her father. I went to sit at her table, and when I did I could see she was very upset. I didn't want to stick my nose in, but as soon as I sat down she burst into tears.
>
> Fen, I have to warn you. She said you would be coming home after Easter, and you had no idea what was going on. She'd only discovered it by accident, she said. Fen dear, John is ill. I mean, very ill. At the time I spoke to Alice he hadn't told you, and he'd forbidden Alice to say anything, which he

really shouldn't have. Apparently, he told her he would tell you himself, before you came home, but time is running out.

I can't say any more, Fen. I hope I haven't done the wrong thing by interfering, but I couldn't in all conscience have you coming home to a shock. Perhaps he's told you by now, but if not, please, Fen, ring home.

When you get back to Brant, if you need me, you know where I am.

With love from Grace.

In those few moments, as I tried to digest Grace's news, I couldn't have said how I felt. The ceiling hadn't fallen in, I hadn't fainted; but I realised I'd forgotten to breathe, and when I did it was with a gasp, a rasping in my throat. I got up and poured a glass of water, gulping it down till I spluttered and choked. Then I took several deep breaths and picked up my phone. I barely noticed that the fire had gone out.

When he answered, I said, trying not to sound reproachful, 'John. When were you going to tell me?'

'What? Oh! Has Alice been talking to you? I asked her not to. She promised.'

'No, not Alice. She's always loyal, you know that. But you shouldn't have given her that burden, John.'

'No, I shouldn't. It was wrong of me. So if not Alice, who?'

'I just got an email from Grace. Apparently, she bumped into Alice in town and saw she was very upset.'

I heard him sigh. 'It wasn't supposed to be like this. It's all got away from me. Everything's gone wrong.'

'Hadn't you better fill me in?' I said quietly.

'Alice came home last weekend.' I heard the abject misery in his voice. 'I wasn't expecting her. Rory was in Scotland at some relative's funeral. They were already on their Easter vac, and she was at a loose end, so I suppose she decided she'd come and check on her old man.' I heard a bitter little laugh, and then there was a silence. 'I'd left a letter from the hospital half open on the kitchen work surface. Alice just turned up without warning and let herself in. Perhaps she wanted to surprise me. I was in the garden; I didn't know she was there. She saw the heading from the oncology department. She shouldn't have read the letter, but she did.'

'Oncology?' My voice was barely above a whisper.

'Yes. Fen, I have cancer.'

For a long moment I found I could say nothing. My very brain seemed to have frozen over.

'Fen?'

'Sorry. I'm just… trying to take it in.' I took a deep breath. 'Where is it, John?'

Again, that laugh that contained neither humour nor joy. 'God alone knows where it is now. It started in the head of my pancreas.'

'Oh, no. No. That's not good, is it?'

'As cancers go, it's a bad one, yes. I'm learning more about it every day – from reading, and from first-hand experience.'

'Oh, John.' I bit my lip. 'I'm so sorry. I don't know what to say. Or do.'

'Just come home,' he said. 'You can't cure me, you can't make it go away, I don't think anyone can. But I'll feel better if you're here.'

'Should I come tomorrow?'

I heard him sigh. 'I don't think there's any need for that. You'll have ends to tie up, people to tell. I doubt I'll peg out in the next twenty-four hours. No, stick to the plan.'

'How is it making you feel?'

'Sick. But we can talk about my horrible symptoms and what's going to happen next and the frankly rather gloomy prognosis when you're here. It'll be easier then.'

'OK.' I thought for a moment. 'How long have you known?'

'For sure? A couple of weeks. I felt unwell for a while, but I went to the GP when I turned a bit yellow. After that I had a battery of tests, some quite unpleasant, and they confirmed the diagnosis.'

'So you didn't know, way back in February – do you remember? It was after storm Doris, and you asked me whether I'd come home if one of the family was ill.'

Again, that quiet, bitter laugh. 'Oh no, that was purely hypothetical. I don't think I'm quite so devious.'

'But you've known something was wrong for quite a while, by the sound of it, and you didn't think to tell me?'

'Oh, I thought about it,' he said. 'But I didn't want to spoil things for you, not until it was unavoidable. I knew you were doing stuff that was important to you. And I thought now would be soon enough. I was wrong about that too. I didn't know it would progress this rapidly.'

'Does Daniel know, John?'

'I haven't told him. I don't imagine Alice has either, or he'd have been in touch.'

'Let's call him when we're together,' I said, 'as soon as possible after I get home. But I must ring Alice straightaway. Poor child! This must have been so hard for her.'

'Yes. I'm sorry I made her promise not to tell you. I wasn't thinking straight at that moment.'

'I'll call her as soon as we hang up.'

'Let's leave it there, Fen. You'll be here soon.'

'All right.' I took a steadying breath. 'Look, love, whatever happens, whatever we have to face, I'll be with you, for as long as it takes. You know that. Nothing else matters, not now. I don't know what else I can do.' The initial shock was wearing off, and the sheer horror of it all was beginning to dawn on me. My eyes blurred with tears.

'There isn't anything you can do.' He spoke so gently that I felt a huge thing like a fist clench in my chest. 'But believe it or not, just you being here with me will help.'

After we'd rung off, I gathered my chaotic thoughts before calling Alice. I relit the fire, feeding it until I was sure it was established, and I made a cup of tea. Then again I picked up the phone.

'Alice? It's Mum. I've been talking to Dad.'

As soon as she heard my voice, Alice burst into a torrent of tears. I heard a soothing voice in the background and assumed it was Rory. I was glad she had some support.

'Sorry,' she gulped. 'It's been a tough few weeks. I wanted to tell you.'

'Of course you did,' I said. 'But you promised. You've been very loyal, sweetheart, and brave. I'm proud of you.'

She sniffed. 'Yeah, well, I've had Rory to help me. He's been great.'

'I'm very glad to hear it. I shall look forward to meeting him. It's just a shame it has to be in such awful circumstances.'

'I know, Mum. I'll bring him down to see you soon. Whenever you tell me it's a good time. I don't want to give him a swelled head, but I think he's a keeper.'

I heard a louder voice, with a Scottish accent, protesting in the background.

'In that case, I shall be all the more keen to meet him.'

'Dan doesn't know, Mum,' Alice said, sounding anxious.

'Don't worry,' I said firmly. 'I'll ring him as soon as I get back to Brant. You've done your bit.'

'OK, that's good. But Mum, you should know, seeing Dad may give you a bit of a shock. He's lost a load of weight, except he's got a weird pot belly. And he's yellow. He said they might have to unblock something to deal with that. He looks pretty bad, Mum.'

'Thanks for warning me. See you soon – and Rory.'

EASTER MONDAY WAS very far from how I'd imagined. I'd thought it would be a day of packing a bag with little hurry, buying a train ticket, making sure my second panel was stored safely, and saying a casual goodbye to Mary, Liam, and Martha – after all, I planned to be back in a couple of weeks. Now, with everything so open-ended, the goodbyes were heavy with uncertainty: would I even be back at all?

Before going down to the farmhouse to speak to Mary, I cleaned the cottage as best I could. I put bedlinen in the wash and left everything spotless. Then, taking a deep breath, I walked down the path and into the house.

When I told Mary about John, she was silent for several long seconds as she dried her hands. She turned to me, and her face was grey and lined. 'This is terrible news,' she said. 'I'm afraid your family is in for a very hard time. I'm so sorry, Fen.'

'Yes, it's not great, is it? I've tidied up as best I can, Mary. I've put my sheets on the washing line as it's breezy. I'll take all my belongings with me – I don't know when I'll be back, or even if I will.' I felt my eyelids prickle with tears and blinked them away.

'You'll be back, Fen,' Mary said quietly. 'Of course you will, whatever happens. There's work for you to do here.'

I nodded. 'I hope so.'

I DECIDED TO call in on Martha on my way to the station; it was a way of avoiding a long, painful goodbye. I rode my bike down to Chibley, intending to take it with me: I'd probably need it in Brant. I found Martha and Liam in the farmhouse kitchen; Martha was in her favourite chair reading out loud from a magazine while Liam stirred something on the hob. Both were chuckling. They reminded me of a mother and son, at ease in the other's company with no need for pretence, and seeing them so, and knowing I wouldn't be part of this for a long time, made the tight feeling in my chest all the more painful. But then I told myself not to be so self-pitying. This whole state of affairs was about my suffering husband, not me.

'Hey, Fen! Lovely day. Are you ready for the trip south?' Liam was smiling, but what I then told them sent the smile into oblivion. He dropped the wooden spoon into the pot, crossed the room and wrapped his arms round me. 'Oh, Fen!' He pulled away, looking down at me with eyes full of sympathy, and I remembered he was no stranger to pain. 'What terrible news.'

Martha was heaving herself up from her chair with difficulty. I went over to her. 'Don't get up, Martha.'

She grabbed my hand. 'I'm so sorry, Fen. How grim.' She frowned. 'What of the future?'

I heaved a sigh. 'That's just what I don't know. I'll have to see what the situation is when I get there and do whatever I can to help John. I don't even know yet any details about what tests he's had or what treatments are on offer.' I swallowed. 'And I guess if I do come back, it won't be for a very long time. But as for that, no one knows.'

'As far as is humanly possible,' Martha said heavily, 'do your best to return, Fen. You're part of Chibley now. And you've got so much more in you to do.'

'Yeah, I know, Martha,' I said, my voice low. 'But John has to be my priority now. In sickness and in health, and all that.'

'Well, I've never had occasion to speak those words,' Martha said. 'Never wanted to be married.'

'Married or not, we're all supposed to keep promises, I think.'

'Look,' Liam said, 'I'm going to be around for a while. If it helps, I'll cover your unfinished work and store it safely. Then if and when you do come back you can take it up where you left off.'

'Thanks, Liam.'

'And,' he stumbled on, 'leave us your contact details. You may be a few hundred miles away but, as Martha says, you're part of us now, whether you like it or not. We're going to want to know how you are.'

'Of course. I'll text you. Can someone tell Steve the vicar? I haven't got time now. My train's at midday.'

'I'll see him in church,' Martha said.

We all fell silent.

I gathered my scattered wits. 'Ah well, I guess I'd better be on my way.' I went to the door. Looking back, I saw them together, Liam standing by Martha's chair, looking back at me, their faces full of sadness. 'I'm going to miss you.' I gestured, a wide sweep of my arm. 'And all of this.'

So THERE I was once again on the train, gathering speed across the valleys and the viaducts, seeing now, as spring advanced, hills just beginning to be covered with green. In time they would be ablaze with the yellow of the lesser celandines. In some of the fields the yows were accompanied by tiny offspring, playing with their friends in the sunshine like any other carefree young things. Travelling away from them, and towards horrors and sorrows unknown but all too easily imagined, was the last thing I wanted. I thought with some embarrassment of the pontifications about ultimate reality that I'd regaled Mary with so recently. Yes, I still believed in it, and in what I'd rather smugly said, and maybe one day I'd be able to square such notions with the raw realities of my earthly life, but for now it all seemed astronomically distant, and as meaningless.

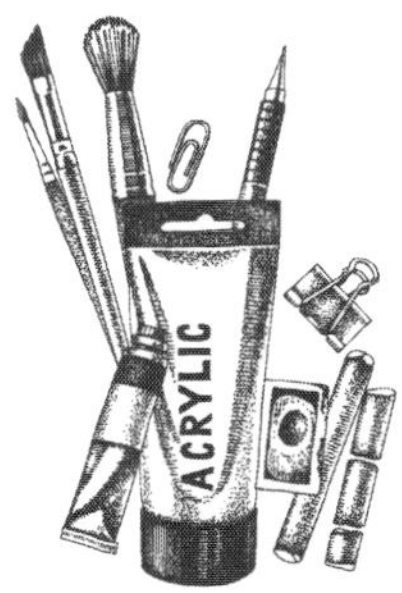

PART FOUR

I didn't really know what to expect when I let myself into our house in Brant, but when John appeared out of the kitchen, a tea towel over his shoulder, I didn't think he looked too bad. I hugged him rather gingerly, and he gave that half-smile I knew well; it usually meant he was holding something in – as well he might. When I looked more closely, I saw the yellow tinge in his skin and the whites of his eyes, and he was alarmingly thin.

'I'm not too fragile,' he said, 'not yet. I probably won't snap in two.'

'How are you feeling?'

'Not much different really. I'll make you a cup of tea, shall I? Journey OK?'

'Yes, fine,' I said faintly. To be exchanging small talk when my husband was almost certainly dying seemed bizarre.

We sat at the kitchen table, steaming mugs before us. My bulging backpack was still in the hall, and I hadn't even stowed my bike. I took a sip; the tea was scalding.

'Something smells good,' I said. 'Have you been cooking?'

'Just for you. I've been trying to extend my culinary skills, although it's a funny time to start, as I have very little appetite these days.'

'I noticed.' There was a pause, and it felt full of unspoken things. I took a deep breath. 'John, hadn't you better tell me what's been happening? From the beginning?'

He was silent for a long moment, staring down at the table. 'I put it down to all the stress,' he said finally. 'All those flights and meetings and reports, late nights, early mornings, snatched meals. I knew I didn't feel great, but I thought it would sort itself out once the merger was up and running, or once I could leave it to others to flesh out the details. But then one morning I was shaving, and I looked in the mirror. I didn't like what I saw. My eyes were going yellow, and my skin was flaky. So I made an appointment with the GP, and she didn't like the look of it either. Long story short, I had a whole raft of blood tests. I was thankful I was under that private health scheme at work – otherwise chances are I'd still be waiting now. What they saw in the blood speeded things up even more. I had an MRI. Didn't much like it – as you know I'm a bit claustrophobic – but I shut my eyes and gritted my teeth and tried not to panic. They're ninety-nine percent sure of the diagnosis, but I have to have another investigation. It's called an ERCP, which is short for some long string of medical-speak – I won't bore you with it. Anyway, I have an appointment for Friday. I probably won't be knocked out completely, but I'll be sedated, so I'll need you to drive.'

I frowned. 'So, what's it for?'

'They stick a tube down into your gastric area, with a light on it, to take a closer look. To make sure what they suspect is right. Probably to take a biopsy. Then they put a dye down there, and I'll get an x-ray. But at the same time, they'll put a stent in to clear the bile duct. With any luck I might lose this golden glow.' He looked up and saw my expression, and he reached across the table and took my hand. 'Fen, I'm sorry. I've had a little while to take this all in, and it's still hard to come to terms with. You've been thrown in at the deep end.'

I tried to smile. 'I'm not the one who's ill, though, am I? Oh, John. This is a nightmare. I want to wake up.'

He nodded. 'I know,' he said softly.

I breathed deeply for a few moments, trying to marshal my chaotic thoughts. I swallowed down the tears that threatened – how could they help? 'So you have this test. Then what?'

'As I said, they're pretty sure of the outcome, so they probably won't wait to confirm it. I've got some chemo booked.'

I noticed his voice shake, and also the effort it took to control it. I squeezed his hand. 'Look, love, if you feel like screaming and kicking the walls, you're entitled. Don't mind me.'

He pressed his lips together. 'Not yet,' he said at last. 'That'll probably happen at some point. But for now I'm trying to hold it all together.'

Seeing him gather up the shreds of his courage in the face of disaster almost broke me. I whispered, 'Then I'll try to do the same.'

We sat there for a minute or two in silence, just breathing deeply, still clutching each other's hand.

'Have they told you about the chemo? When you'll have it, what's involved, what drugs?'

He nodded. 'I had an idea anyway. In my line of work you do, or you can find out pretty easily. In a week or two I'll have to go into the hospital once a week for three weeks. They'll pump something strong and nasty called Gemcitabine into my arm. Then I'll come home and take some pills every day – Capecitabine. After three weeks I get a break for a week. Then it starts all over again – I'm not sure for how long. They'll be monitoring me to see how it's going.'

I felt a wash of heat rise up in my body, and my hearing seemed to grow faint. I wondered if I was going into some kind of shock. 'John,' I stuttered, 'do you think I could have another cup?'

He looked at me keenly and released my hand. 'Coming up. Do you want to talk about this later? It's a lot of bad news all at once.'

I swallowed hard and shook my head. 'No, I want to know.'

'OK.' He busied himself with the kettle, and I took the opportunity to collect myself. When my second cup was in front of me and John had sat down again, I said, 'What are they hoping the chemo will do – apart from probably make you very tired and cause your hair to fall out?'

John smiled faintly. 'They're hoping it'll kill at least some of the cancer cells,' he said. 'Wherever the nasty little creatures have got to, wherever they're lurking. But I know and they know there's no actual cure, Fen. It's gone too far – all the while I was passing off my symptoms as something and nothing, the tumour was sending out streams of diseased cells. The chemo may help with the worst of the symptoms.

They'll try and make life a bit more comfortable. They may even succeed in prolonging it for a while. But we have to face reality here, I'm afraid. I'll be lucky to make our birthdays, our anniversary.'

My eyes felt too big, and I could hardly get words out. 'So soon?'

He nodded. 'And before you ask, I cancelled the cruise. They were very good about it; they said in the circumstances they'd return the deposit.'

This finished me. The cruise I hadn't wanted, but which with such enthusiasm he had chosen with a view to my interests, and which he'd looked forward to with such boyish delight; even this was denied him. I held my head in my hands and howled.

After a few minutes of hiccupping sobs, I took the wad of tissues he was holding out to me. 'I'm sorry,' I said. 'This isn't helping.'

'Feel free, my love,' he said sombrely. 'I've done a fair bit of crying myself.'

'We have to talk to the children.'

'Not tonight,' he said firmly. 'That can wait one day. Tonight we'll have a meal and a bottle of wine, and later we'll go to bed and console each other. While I've got a bit of strength left.'

I laughed shakily. 'You're incorrigible. I'm glad you are. So, tell me, what about work? Are you signed off?'

He nodded, 'Yes, for however long I need. But at my request they'll probably send me the odd bit of paperwork, just so my brain doesn't totally turn to porridge.'

A cold thought struck me. 'John, do you think this might have its origins way back? With that awful place you worked at when we first met?'

'Hawkes?' His face was grim. 'It's altogether possible, at least as a contributory factor. But you know, Fen, there's a lot about cancer and its causes that's still a huge mystery.'

I nodded, feeling now hollowed out and utterly bleak.

'I'm going to check the meal is OK,' John said. 'Then there's some stuff I need to tell you, things you absolutely must be prepared for.'

'I'll put my bike in the shed,' I said. 'And I'll take my bag upstairs and unpack.'

'I've done some housework,' he said with a small smile. 'It should look reasonably tidy.'

'There was no need. As things are, a bit of dust doesn't seem very important.'

I had a wash and put on some clean clothes, and when I came down John was laying the table. 'Shouldn't be long.' He uncorked a bottle of red and poured me a generous glass; his own glass, I saw, contained very little. 'Tonight I just want to enjoy you being home,' he said. 'Even before I knew all this was going on, I was looking forward to it. There'll be plenty of opportunity for horrors – let this evening be a bit of an oasis. But before that I have to tell you how it's all going to affect you. That's if you're planning to stay.'

'What?' I was horrified. 'You think I would abandon you – *now*?' He said nothing, and I sighed. 'OK, I suppose I kind of deserve that. No, John, don't be an idiot. "In sickness and in health" – remember?'

He nodded. 'Of course. And I didn't really think you'd march out of the door saying "You're on your own, sunshine." But here's the deal, Fen. Chemo is toxic. It kills cancer cells, and healthy ones along the way. For two or three days it'll be seeping out of me in every possible bodily fluid. You have to take great care not to come into contact with it. We'll have to use separate bathrooms – I suggest I'll take the en suite. We'll need to sleep separately too. Scrupulous hygiene will be the order of the day – keeping my laundry separate, cleaning bathrooms within an inch of their lives, wearing double gloves, every precaution. I hope I can clean up after myself for as long as possible, but inevitably some of that will fall to you. I don't want you contaminated.'

'I get it.'

'They'll help you at the hospital. Give you a leaflet or something. Spell it out.'

I took a large gulp of my wine. 'You're right, John. We can't make this go away, can we? I can't make you better; I wish to God I could. We can pray, and I will do that, every day, of course. As I hope they're also doing at St Swithin's. But meanwhile we have to do the best we can and make the most of the time we've got.'

'Exactly.' He raised his eyebrows and winked in the most ludicrously lecherous way, and despite myself, I laughed.

LOOKING AT THE time difference between London and New York, I decided to ring Dan just before we went to bed the following evening, when he would be back from work and perhaps cooking a meal or preparing to go out. We agreed it might be best for me to tell Dan the bad news and leave it to him to speak to his father when he'd had time to digest it. As it turned out, though, John was so tired that he was showered and asleep soon after the ending of the evening news. I decided to ring Daniel anyway; I felt something of such import really couldn't be delayed. But when he answered I felt immediately that it was a bad idea.

'Hey, Mum! To what do I owe this lovely surprise?' He was full of bubble, loud, almost febrile, most unlike my son.

'Hello, Dan. How are you?'

'I am very well, Mother, yes, extremely well!' He burst out laughing as if he had cracked the funniest joke ever heard.

'That's good. Dan, listen – I have some news, and it's not great.'

He didn't seem to be listening, or at least he was distracted. In the background I heard voices and strident music.

'Daniel, is this a bad time?'

'A bad time? Of course not, darling Ma! We've got a few friends round, a few bottles opened, that's all!'

There was something wrong with this gaiety, and I admitted to myself I preferred my son in a more prosaic mood. A suspicion began to form.

'Dan, are you *on* something?'

'What? My goodness, whatever can you mean?' He chuckled, then sobered. 'As it's you, Mother, I suppose I can confess to just a little, a very little, weed. And alcohol, of course. Don't be cross. We're having a small celebration, you see.'

Suddenly I felt a weight of weariness descend on me. 'Look, sweetheart, it obviously is a bad time. No, of course I'm not cross. You're old enough to make your own decisions, supposedly. You enjoy your evening, and I'll ring you about this time tomorrow, if that suits you.'

'But it's so lovely to chat!' I heard someone speak to him. 'Well, apparently I have to go. Yes, please do ring me tomorrow. It won't be so hectic. Bye, Mum.'

I sat on the sofa, my phone in my hand, and asked myself why I suddenly felt so intensely miserable. Was it because my son indulged in drugs? Of course he did, didn't most of them? I hoped it wasn't too much of a habit, that's all. No, it was because he wasn't as he usually was, and I realised how much I depended on the idea of Daniel as sensible, thoughtful, kind. Of course, at that distance he couldn't *do* anything, but without consciously realising it I'd counted on him to share our situation, take on its implications and offer words of support. I felt a tear leak out of my eye and run down my cheek. I dashed it away impatiently. It was no time for self-pity, I told myself sternly. We shouldn't rely on our children anyway.

I trudged upstairs to the bathroom, feeling heavy, dispirited and profoundly alone. As I slipped into bed, trying not to disturb John, who was already turning restlessly from side to side, I told myself I would ring Alice at lunchtime, when she might be back from lectures or the library. She'd left us in peace today, but now she'd need to be updated.

However, around noon, before I had a chance to ring her, the phone rang.

'Mum? Did you ring me last night?' Daniel, sounding worried.

'Yes, briefly, but you were busy.'

'Busy? God, Mum, I was full of… er, substances! I'm so sorry you got no sense out of me.'

'You weren't expecting me to call.'

'Look, I have to go to work in half an hour. Did you say you had news for me?'

I sighed. 'What are you doing at this moment?'

'Sitting at the kitchen table, with a cup of coffee and a headache. Clyde's in the shower. When he's ready we'll go together.'

I took a deep breath. 'Son, I'm sorry to land this on you, but you have to know. Your Dad is seriously ill.'

'What? Dad? What's wrong with him?'

I told him, and I heard him suck in his breath, but he said nothing. I let the silence gather.

His voice, when it came, was barely audible. 'I can't believe it. How long have you known?'

'Just a few days,' I said. 'He's known for a few weeks, but he'd suspected for longer.'

'And he didn't say anything?'

'No.'

'God, Mum, that must have been a bloody awful shock.'

'Yes, it was.'

'Are you with him now?'

'Yes, I came back on Tuesday.'

'Are you staying this time?' he blurted.

'Good grief, Daniel! How can you even ask? Of course I am. For as long as it takes. He's got to go to the hospital tomorrow for what sounds like a quite unpleasant procedure. They'll know more then. In the next week or two he'll start chemo. But Dan, they can't cure this. Don't get your hopes up, will you? I hope they can make him more comfortable, that's all. And I'll be here to back him up.'

When he next spoke, Dan's voice was rough, and I realised he was crying. 'Sorry, I shouldn't even have asked you if you'd be staying. That was unkind, and stupid. But it just hit me: my dad's going to die.' He gave a long, low groan, then inhaled deeply. 'Sorry, Mum. Are *you* all right?'

I sighed. 'As far as I can be, I suppose. At least I have a job to do, looking after him. Don't cry, Dan. You'll set me off, and I have to stay on my feet.'

I heard him say something, not to me.

'Sorry, that was Clyde. Does Ally know?'

'Yes. He didn't want to tell her, but she found out by accident. I'm going to ring her in a minute.'

'Look, Mum, should I come home?'

'I don't think that's necessary, sweetheart, at least not yet. I'll let you know if things get suddenly worse, of course. But I'm sure he'd love to hear from you.'

I heard him speak again, but not to me. 'I have to go, Mum, or we'll be late. Please give Dad a huge hug from me. Tell him I'll call him as soon as I get in from work.'

'OK. Are you going to be all right?'

'I don't know.' He sounded bleak. 'But I've got Clyde. He won't let me fall apart. Sending you love, Mum.'

Minutes after I'd hung up my phone rang again.

'Mum, it's Alice. I've been trying to get hold of you.'

'Sorry, love. I was talking to Dan. I just told him about your dad.'

'How did he take it?'

'Just how you'd imagine. Horrified. In tears.'

'Yeah, well, I know all about that.' She sounded hollow. 'You're home now, though – that's good. How is he? – Dad, I mean.'

'He's not too bad – or at least that's what he's telling me. He doesn't sleep well, though, tossing and turning, and last night he was crying out in his sleep – dreaming, I suppose. I hope it wasn't because of pain. He says not, but I don't know if I believe him.'

'And what about you, Mum? Are you OK?'

'Not really. But I have to be, if that's not a contradiction.'

'I get it. Mum, can we come round this evening? Me and Rory? Will Dad be up for visitors?'

'I'm sure he'd love to see you, sweetheart. Come in time for dinner.'

'I know it's not the best time for you to meet Rory, but it's an opportunity, and I want you both to meet him, because he's going to be around for a while. Maybe a long while.'

'Of course he must come. It's a good time. Your Dad has to go into hospital for a procedure tomorrow. We hope it will make him feel a bit better, but he's bound to be groggy for a few days.'

'OK, Mum, we'll leave here about five. No need to come to the station – Rory brought his brother's car down from Scotland when he came back from his uncle's funeral. He thought we might need our own transport. I'd better go. Best love to Dad, and see you later.'

❈

It was a strangely understated evening. If John had been well, his usual self, he would no doubt have subjected Rory to polite, but in-depth, scrutiny, verging on interrogation. As it was, Rory had an easy time of it, and so did I, released from my usual status of go-between. John's conversation was at best languid, and there were moments when he didn't seem to be fully present. As a result there was an atmosphere of gentle ease, underpinned by a deep, unspoken sadness.

Alice's description of Rory didn't really prepare me for the reality. Alice herself is moderately tall and willowy, and Rory dwarfed her: tall, broad, solidly fleshed, the whole impression intensified by his enormous black ex-military greatcoat. Even when he'd removed it he was a big presence, with baggy corduroys, even baggier sweater and huge boots. His chestnut hair curled round his shoulders and his face was clear-skinned and ruddy, his jaw fuzzed with a scrubby beard. In contrast to his appearance, his voice was deep but soft, mitigating his strong Scottish accent.

I liked him from the outset. He was respectful to me and very gentle with John, without any trace of condescension. Even in his weakened state John would have resented being treated as an invalid, but Rory's questions were well-phrased and entirely appropriate. Alice, I saw, looked on him with quiet pride. She spoke little but sat huddled up to her father on the sofa, her arm through his. I saw this, and my heart hurt. Alice and John had always been close; losing him would be a world-shattering blow.

I'd tried to make a good meal for us all, hungry students and sick man alike, but John ate very little, and when Alice and Rory had gone I heard him throwing up in the downstairs toilet. He emerged so pale he was practically transparent, his eyes shadowed, his mouth pinched.

I took his arm. 'Come and sit down.' I led him to the sofa, and he collapsed with a shuddering sigh. 'You're in pain.' It was no longer a question.

'Yeah. Right here.' He pressed his hand to the right side of his stomach.

'Was it too much for you, this evening?'

'Maybe a bit. But I wanted to meet this fellow of Alice's.'

'What did you think?'

'He seemed a decent young man. Intelligent.'

'She'll be glad to have your approval,' I said wryly.

He opened one eye. 'You think?'

'John, this pain – will what you're having tomorrow help, do you suppose?'

'I hope so. Maybe when they're poking around in there they'll make some adjustments.'

'Don't forget to tell them where it hurts.'

'You know you'll have to drive me. What will you do while you're waiting? It could take a while.'

'I'll think of something. Don't worry about me.'

I DELIVERED JOHN to the hospital on time, though it was a struggle. He seemed to be up and down half the night, and then he sank into sleep that was more like stupor and was difficult to rouse. As he was led away to be prepared for the procedure, I took my laptop out of my bag and connected with the hospital's internet. I was determined to find out as much as I could about John's illness, and there was a great deal of information, too much for my non-medical brain. I discovered that most pancreatic cancers start in the cells that produce digestive juices and are called exocrine tumours. Picking apart the technical stuff, I deduced that nobody really knows why a cell turns cancerous, but there are suggestions, and the fact that one of them was exposure to toxic chemicals gave me a cold frisson as I remembered John's time at Hawkes. I wondered if that dreadful place was still there next to the river; I knew it had been closed, but had the buildings been demolished? Perhaps I would find out, though I was sure that looking at the remains of that poisonous installation would fill me with fury. I dragged my mind away from these fruitless speculations and went back to my research. What I found fulfilled my worst expectations. John's symptoms – his nausea and pain, his loss of weight and appetite, the jaundice, the swollen stomach, all pointed to advanced cancer and widespread metastasis.

Taking a deep breath, I plunged into descriptions of what we might expect, including survival rates, but it was all too detailed and confusing and I gave up and sat back, eyes closed. What came inexorably through the fog of charts and stages and measurements was the stark knowledge that John didn't have long on this earth. He'd tried to tell me, but I had to find out for myself, and here it was, a profoundly unpalatable reality. At that moment I was engulfed by pity for him: not even fifty years old, with so much more he wanted to do, and leaving behind so much that he loved. Breathing deeply, I prayed for him and for us all.

I wondered if, alongside medical interventions, there might be something I might be able to do to help him, and as well as dietary recommendations I found there was medication he could take to aid digestion. I decided I would ask about this if I had the opportunity.

It was a long, tedious morning. I could have gone out into the city, but I wanted to be there waiting when they released him. I bought a cup of coffee from a machine in the foyer, but it did little to stop me drifting into a shallow doze. The night had been disrupted for me as well.

'Mrs Bailey?'

I snapped awake and almost spilled the dregs of my coffee. A tall, middle-aged man in a white coat stood in front of me, smiling kindly. He stooped a little to speak to me, and the light from the tall windows glanced off the rim of his glasses.

'Sorry,' I mumbled. 'I must have dropped off.'

'I thought I'd speak to you,' he said, 'as your husband may be a bit confused. I decided to anaesthetise him rather than merely sedate, as I suspected there might be things we needed to do that would take a bit longer. So he's awake, but a bit out of it, and may not take things in.'

'OK.'

He indicated the chair next to me. There was no one in the waiting room. 'May I?'

'Of course.'

'If we are disturbed we can go to my office, but it's a few corridors away. The plan this morning was to have a look inside Mr Bailey's abdomen generally, to confirm what we thought following the tests he's had, and to see what we could do to alleviate symptoms. I hoped to put a stent into the bile duct to release fluid and reduce the jaundice, and we've done that. But I also discovered the tumour is impacting the duodenum, and all this will be causing the pain and nausea, so, not to load you up with incomprehensible details, I've done a bit of tweaking around that and I hope, once he's recovered from today, he'll feel considerably more comfortable.'

'I hope so. He doesn't say much, but it's clear he's suffering.'

The doctor – was he a surgeon? I didn't know – nodded. 'He's due to have chemotherapy, I think – in about ten days' time?' He lowered his voice. 'You do realise, don't you, that it won't actually cure him?' I nodded, letting out a long breath. 'The treatment we can offer at this stage is, I'm afraid, only palliative. But it should help him feel better, at least for a time. Of course, every patient, every cancer, is different, and I can't predict how Mr Bailey will react. But we will monitor him, and I hope what we can do for him will help.'

'I hope that too,' I said quietly. 'What can I do to support him, apart from emotionally? Is there any food I can make, for instance? His appetite is poor.'

Again, he nodded. 'I'd say give him whatever he feels like eating, in small quantities. There are things that can help digestion. I'll write him a prescription and you can take it to the pharmacy today.'

'Thank you.'

'Is there anything you need to ask me?'

I shook my head. 'I can't think of anything at this moment.'

He got to his feet. 'Don't hesitate to contact us if there's anything you need to know, or some concern, an unusual symptom, for example. He'll leave here with a few sheets of information, and the phone number to ring will be there.' He hesitated for a moment, and he spoke more quietly still. 'These situations are very testing for patients' families, of course, especially for spouses and carers. You need support too. There are people here at the hospital who can help. Do feel you can call on them.'

I swallowed, momentarily unable to speak. When I did, it was a croak. 'Thank you.'

He nodded and smiled, and then he was gone, his white coat flapping.

THAT SUNDAY I went to St Swithin's alone. John had been asleep most of the weekend, and when the time for the morning service arrived he had just woken up. I suspected he didn't want to see anyone given the state he was in; their very compassion would have unmanned him.

I was greeted effusively by my old-lady friends, twittering sympathetically, asking me many questions, expressing their worry and sadness, offering solace as best they could; and I was grateful. Gilbert took me aside at coffee time and assured me of his continuing prayers. Of course, John, along with other sick people of the parish, had been communally prayed for, and hearing the genuine concern brought a tear to my eye. I was very tired.

I knew John would be asking who was doing his treasurer's duties, and I asked Gilbert, who told me he was attending to them himself, with the help of one of the vergers, who was probably at least ninety but had been a teacher in another life.

'Of course, it's not the same,' Gilbert said solemnly. 'But we're coping, tell him, in our own bumbling way.' That, I thought, would be small comfort to John.

Monday morning brought a distinct improvement. The effects of Friday's anaesthetic were wearing off; John had had a relatively peaceful night and made it to breakfast before ten o'clock.

'The pain's gone,' he said thoughtfully as I handed him a mug of tea and a plate of toast. 'Or almost.' He felt his stomach gingerly. 'Just a tiny twinge now.'

'And you're decidedly less yellow.'

'Whatever Mr Dawson did seems to have worked. For now, anyway.'

I looked at him with a critical eye. 'Maybe, when you're feeling stronger, we could go for a short walk. The fresh air will do you good.'

John groaned. 'You sound like my granny.'

'Obviously a wise woman. And it's spring, John! There are daffodils, crocuses, even a bit of early blossom! Good for the soul.'

As I rounded the table, in search of marmalade, he caught me round my waist and buried his face in my shirt. 'I love you, Fen,' he said indistinctly. 'Thank you for taking care of me.'

'As if I wouldn't,' I said. I spoke gently, and I understood, but I felt a pang of alarm at this new, sentimental version of my husband, and I realised I'd have much preferred the usual cranky sarcasm.

We did manage a walk, mid-morning a few days later when nobody was about. As we turned into our road on the way back, we caught sight of a neighbour mowing his front lawn. John was appalled. 'Ours needs doing,' he said, 'and I can't do it. I'd forgotten about it.'

'You're going to have to forget about quite a few things, I'm afraid,' I said. 'Anyway, I am perfectly capable of mowing the lawn.'

'I know you are,' he said, and I winced at the sheer dejection in his voice. 'But it was always my job.'

He was very quiet all that day, and I think he was processing all the things he would no longer be able to do. Somehow, he managed to gather up his courage and face it philosophically, and as a result those few days, a little over a week, before the chemo started, were a strange oasis of calm. I was happy to see him more at peace, but meanwhile I was working: shopping, cooking, filling the freezer with nourishing small meals, cleaning the house and blitzing the garden, which with the arrival of the warmer weather was taking off with rampant growth.

In his slightly other-worldly state he had little idea of what I was doing while he dozed on the sofa or in the conservatory. 'You know,' he said one afternoon when I'd stopped to put the kettle on, 'if it weren't for me being ill, this would be rather nice. I don't feel too bad at the moment, and we seem to be getting on better than we used to.' He turned to face me. 'Don't you think so?'

'Hm, maybe.'

'Do you think this is what it would have been like if I'd made it to retirement?'

I had to laugh. 'Absolutely not! If you were well, my love, you'd have been rushing around with all sorts of projects. I'd never see you. But I agree, as it is, it is nice. And most unexpected.' *We had to wait for you to be dying to arrive at a more harmonious relationship: me less restless and discontented, you kinder, less dismissive.* I didn't say any of that to him.

The children phoned regularly, and I saw a change in his talks with Daniel. Of course, Dan had spoken to his father as soon as he could after I'd told him the news, and I think that had been a difficult conversation, but now I often heard John chuckling, and when Dan spoke to me he was amazed. 'Mum, he's so different. It's just a terrible shame that it took a terminal illness for us to get along and be an affectionate father and son without me feeling judged and found wanting.'

'I know, sweetheart. He's being nice to me as well.'

'Wonders will never cease,' Dan said shakily.

That week John also insisted on going through paperwork with me – the will, the house, the cars, the insurances, the investments – in minute detail. When I protested, he became quite anxious. 'I need you to be on top of these things, Fen. You've never needed to be bothered with them before.' *But I am not incapable. And I can read.* Of course I said nothing.

Gradually during those days, I found myself being inexorably reabsorbed into my life in the city that had been home for almost a quarter of a century. I went to see Grace a few times, and she asked after me, and John, and the children, but mostly she was preoccupied with the prospect of moving to Australia. 'There's so much to deal with,' she said. 'You just wouldn't believe.' She showed me photos of a small bungalow which, with her daughter's help, she was in the process of buying, just around the corner from Andrea and her family. 'Of course,' she said thoughtfully, 'if things really take off and I go soon, it'll be coming up for winter there. But Andrea says the house has good heating. Did I tell you? – this house is on the market now, and I've had two viewings already.'

I realised with new clarity the difference between my life in Brant, past and present, and the one I had been making for myself in Yorkshire: here, no one seemed interested in me beyond the superficial civilities. But here was current reality, and the reality as it loomed nearer was indisputably grim: John would undergo harsh treatment which, even if it worked to a degree, would cause unwelcome side effects; and I, as ever, would be squarely in the path of the fallout. I had heard not a word from Yorkshire, and unless I was feeling especially sorry for myself I recognised they were probably giving me space. As time went on Yorkshire, and all it meant to me – the friends, the painting, the dogs and the sheep, the weather and the landscape – began to fade, as if it existed as something on a distant planet, a nocturnal figment that vanished with the morning.

THE WEATHER STAYED fine into May, but by the time John started his first dose of chemo heavy clouds loomed over our heads and there were rumbles of thunder and sudden squalls that tossed trees about and soaked the unwary. I went with him to his appointments, because I suspected he wasn't safe to drive, and for once he didn't protest. We had been directed to a different part of the hospital and didn't see the sympathetic Mr Dawson. Instead, there were specialist nurses, some kindly in their manner, others briskly efficient, and I wondered if this was a way of insulating their humanity against the scenes of daily pain, weakness and fear that constituted so much of their working life. At the first appointment, as they took John away, one of the staff handed me a leaflet giving details of the treatment, how it would be administered and what side effects he might encounter. As I read through the list I was appalled. Chemotherapy would cause a reduction in the number of white cells in the blood, so the risk of infection was increased. The patient might suffer breathlessness, bruising, bleeding, anaemia, nausea and loss of appetite. He might develop an itchy rash. After one or two doses his hair might begin to thin and fall out. He might have a sore mouth or throat; his digestive system could be impacted. He might suffer from muscle or joint pain, and headaches.

I waylaid one of the nurses as she crossed the waiting area. 'This list,' I said, indicating the leaflet. 'I could almost wonder if the side effects of the drugs aren't worse than the illness.'

She smiled faintly. 'People say that. But we hope no one gets *all* those things. That would be very unlucky. We have to include everything, so you aren't unduly alarmed.'

I thought for a moment, while I had her attention. 'What would happen if chemo wasn't given? If the patient refused it, for example?'

Unfortunately for me this wasn't one of the kindlier nurses. 'The cancer would accelerate.'

'Oh.'

There was little more to be said. She nodded and went on her way.

FOR A TIME, John seemed to be bearing up both physically and emotionally, though he was distant, almost dreamy. I guessed it was his way of coping with the intractable horror of his situation. But there were moments of greater sharpness of mind. One wet morning I was looking out of the kitchen window, contemplating the rain and wondering if I could defer doing a load of laundry, and I heard him calling from the lounge where he was half-lying on the sofa. His laptop was beside him, open, threatening to slide onto the floor. I picked it up and put it on the coffee table. 'Did you want something, love?'

'I was thinking,' he said. 'It's almost your birthday.'

'So it is.' I'd forgotten; it didn't seem important.

'I'd like you to get something you really want. I can't get out by myself, and I wouldn't get you the right things anyway.'

'Do I want anything?'

'Yes,' he said firmly. 'You need some art materials. I know you're up to your eyes running around after me, but there must be some times when you can do something for yourself. It would make me happy if I thought you had some decent paints and brushes or whatever you need. Maybe you can get away from all this illness for a while. When the nurse comes would be a good moment, wouldn't it? Then you don't have to worry about leaving me.'

'All right, I'll go into town tomorrow, as soon as she arrives.'

'Good.' He smiled. 'And don't worry about the cost.'

'You might regret saying that.'

'I won't.'

The following day I let the nurse in and said I was going out at John's insistence. I had my phone if he needed me and would come straight back.

'Good idea,' she said. 'You need a break once in a while. He'll be OK for an hour or two.'

It felt strange to be in the car on my own; I had thought I would be glad to be free, but I felt anxious and distracted. I hadn't realised quite how bound up I had become in the minute details of John's care; it was as if we had both become prisoners of his illness.

The wind was blowing hard as I parked the car, and whisks of rain spattered my face. No one would have thought it was almost June. I walked down two streets, passing people with umbrellas and coat collars turned up against the unseasonable weather, till I came to a pedestrianised area where the shop I wanted was located. It was a relief to close the door behind me. At once I felt my mood lift. The very smell of the place reminded me of the back room at Chibley, and I felt a fleeting pang of longing.

The proprietor was someone I knew from many past visits. He'd been sitting behind his desk reading a catalogue; now he leapt up, pushing his glasses onto his forehead. 'Mrs Bailey! I haven't seen you in quite a while.'

'Yes. I've been away, in Yorkshire.'

'Is there something particular you're looking for?'

'I don't really know. Mind if I browse?'

He made an expansive gesture. 'Be my guest.'

I made my way to the stairs, at the bottom of which was a huge room containing shelves and cupboards full of canvases of all sizes, paints, brushes, pencils, sketchbooks, thinners, varnishes – everything to gladden an artist's heart. I took a deep breath and smiled.

I wandered about aimlessly for a while, looking, admiring, wondering. Finally, I took an oversized basket and filled it with several small canvases already stretched, a dazzling spectrum of acrylic colours in fat tubes, six different brushes, some very expensive pencils and a pad of paper so deliciously tactile it seemed a shame to draw on it. At that moment I had little idea what I would do with such treasure, but John was right: just having it was satisfying. Given his apparent indifference through the years his intuition was astonishing, but I wasn't complaining.

As I headed towards the stairs to go up and pay, I heard the shop's owner talking to someone, and the other voice was familiar: deep, with a local accent, sparking with humour. I arrived at the top and rounded the corner. There he was, unmistakably unkempt, laughing through his beard: Ronnie Milburn.

'Ronnie!'

He turned, and recognition dawned. 'Fen Bailey, as I live and breathe! You're still alive!' He bounded towards me and enveloped me in a rib-crushing bear hug.

'Whyever would I be dead?' I said, laughing, as I pulled free.

'Have you been in Yorkshire all this time?' he demanded. 'Have you been working on some masterpiece? And what about Martha? I need to know everything.'

'It's a bit of a long story, Ronnie.'

He frowned. 'Then we shall go to my favourite café,' he said. 'I will buy you a good cup of coffee, and you can bring me up to date. I only dropped in here to see if something I'd ordered was in, and it isn't. Shall we?'

'Let me pay for my extravagant purchases,' I said. 'And I haven't got long.'

'Neither have I. You'll have to give me a summary.'

The café was only in the next street and down a narrow alley whose flagstones were uneven and wet from the rain. As we waited for our order I told him, as briefly as I could, what I'd been doing in Yorkshire, how things were at Chibley, and why I was back in Brant.

The coffee arrived, and he blew on it before taking a long, hot gulp. He wiped his moustache with the back of his hand. 'Well, Fen,' he said soberly. 'That's some story. Your old man on his last legs. I'm very sorry for him, and for you. I can't imagine where I'd be without Tanya.' He shook his head. 'Anything I can help with?'

'Thank you, but I don't think so.'

'Will you go back to Chibley, you know, after…?' His attempt at delicacy was almost funny.

'I honestly don't know, Ronnie. Right now, all I can think of is the here and now, today and tomorrow, how John is, what I can do for him. The future is pretty blank. I barely know I exist.' I indicated my large bag full of things from the shop. 'What I'll do with this lot I have no idea. Even if I had time. My creative well is empty.'

He shook his head. 'No,' he growled. He stretched over the table and patted my hand. 'The springs that feed it are still flowing, you'll see. Maybe not now.'

'Look, I must go,' I said. 'I've left John long enough. I don't imagine the nurse will have stayed. It's been good to see you, Ronnie. You've reminded me I used to have aspirations.'

'Used to have?' he bellowed. Other clients looked up startled from their teapots. '*Used to have?* We'll see about that.' He pushed his chair back and loomed over me. 'Seems to me you've barely begun. That second panel needs finishing, and nobody else can do it.'

As I drove home, I wondered: could he be right? It didn't feel like it, certainly; but there was at least a little comfort in knowing that someone believed in me, even if he was only trying to be kind.

I BEGAN TO notice the effects of John's treatment after the second session of chemo. He was no longer yellow – more grey. His hair started to come out – first wispily, then in handfuls. As well as doing his laundry (separately) I had to take over cleaning his bathroom (wearing double gloves, as instructed), and I found hair everywhere. There was no doubt in my mind that his condition was deteriorating.

He knew it too, and for days he was silent, brooding, angry. Finally he said, 'Fen, I've decided. I'm going to stop this treatment. I feel worse. And I hate what you are having to do – cleaning up after me, all those precautions. It's disgusting, and I'm putting you in danger. I'm going to take charge of my own life, what's left of it. I've already spoken to our GP, while you were shopping yesterday. If I have to die, I want to have a shred of dignity left. It's time to call the children. I was only waiting for Alice and Rory to finish their finals. But Dan will need time too, to square things with his work.'

'Are you certain?'

He nodded. 'Do this for me, Fen.'

I RANG DANIEL; I tried to be calm but choked on the words. When I gained a bit of control, I told him, 'Your dad wants to go into The Lawns. That's the private hospice off Marley Way. His work's insurance will fund it.'

'Oh, Mum. Sounds like things have got really bad.'

'He said he wanted to take back a bit of control. That's the old John coming out – it's his way of fighting. He never was going to lie back and let it all happen, was he? I have to do what he wants, Dan. At least he'll be more comfortable there.'

There was a long silence. 'I'd better come home.'

'Yes, I think so, sweetheart. Seems like it's time. I'll talk to Alice – at least she's finished her exams.'

NOW THAT JOHN had made his decision, he seemed to relax. As far as he was concerned, his life was his to live and to relinquish, in his own way. Through the turmoil of my own feelings and the need to make many arrangements, I admired him for it, and I recognised the last expression of the decisive, sometimes rather overbearing, man I had married.

The children came home for a few days. More than that he probably couldn't have managed. Rory said he would stay away, but John would have none of it. 'One day you may be a member of this family,' he said. 'And whatever happens, Alice will need your support.'

We held it together for John's sake, and even managed to laugh at times. When he went to bed, exhausted, I said to them, 'This needn't be the last time you see him – you can come any time, and you can visit when he's in the hospice. But we don't know what's coming, so it's an opportunity to say goodbye.' Both Dan and Alice were sobbing, and even Rory was red-eyed. I was too worn out to feel much at all.

AFTER THE SWELTERING heat of June, July was all over the place: torrential downpours, thunder, even flash flooding in places. John suffered a downturn and was admitted to hospital for a few days. When I went to collect him Mr Dawson the surgeon shook his head and said, 'I'm afraid to say I think the cancer is winning.' I needed no medical training to agree with him.

Before his time in hospital John had asked me to organise his admission to the hospice. At the end of the first week in July, at a rare moment when the rain had stopped, a discreet private ambulance took him away. It was thought best if I didn't accompany him. 'Come tomorrow,' they said, 'when we've got him assessed and settled.'

That evening, I felt a scratchiness in my throat and a dull headache and put it down to weariness and stress. But in the morning it was clearly a full-on cold, with eyes streaming and a sore throat. I was and am hardly ever ill, but it was obvious I was infectious. I rang the hospice and asked them to let John know I'd be in to see him as soon as I was better. It took almost a week of hot lemon, painkillers and sleep to see it off, and as a result I missed his fiftieth birthday. I rang him and croakily wished him as happy a day as could be managed. He seemed unfazed, almost upbeat. I guessed they were managing the pain, and maybe he felt safe there, able to lie back and let others do the running around and worrying.

I was well in time to celebrate – if that was an appropriate word in the circumstances – our twenty-fifth wedding anniversary. The hospice had made considerable efforts to mark the day with balloons, champagne and a cake, and John gamely ate a tiny slice. His bed was surrounded with cards on every surface.

'We made it, then,' he said when they tactfully left us alone.

'Did you think we wouldn't?' I asked.

He was thoughtful. 'I don't know. For my part I was in it for the long haul, but you hear of so many people giving up or finding someone else. The golf club's a prime example.'

'Hm. Hotbed of infidelity, the golf club.'

His eyebrows – what was left of them – shot up. 'Do you think so? Worse than other sports? How come I wasn't aware?'

'Do you mean to tell me you had no offers from predatory women?'

'Can't say I noticed.'

By this time, we were chuckling at our own silliness.

'So you were never tempted to stray?'

I saw a fleeting gleam in his eye. 'I didn't say that,' he said with a small smile. 'But no, honestly, there was never anyone else. Only you.' He lifted my hand and brushed it with dry lips. 'Even when you were being difficult and distant.'

I sighed. 'Yes, I guess I was, and I'm not proud of it. But you were pretty unapproachable at times too.'

'Guilty as charged,' he said with a grimace. 'I suppose nobody gets it right all of the time, do they? And I guess it's not easy to recreate the early days. Not when there's work and children and all that to think about.'

I laughed. 'Just as well – we'd be exhausted!'

Now his grin was broad, and momentarily he closed his eyes. 'I remember.'

'Actually,' I said slowly, sober now, 'there was something I wanted to say to you.'

'What, before it's too late?' he said, so gently my eyes welled up.

I heaved a huge sigh. 'Yes. Something I've been thinking about. I wanted to thank you.'

He frowned. 'Whatever for? I should be thanking you. All the things you've done through the years, and especially in the last few months.'

'No, not that,' I said. 'Of course I'm grateful for all those things – your hard work, your not carrying on with other women, your care for the children, but I played my part too and that's what you do, you do it for your family. No, the best thing you ever did for me was introduce me to God.'

'That was a privilege,' he said quietly.

'Of course, at the beginning, when we first knew each other, I thought you practically *were* God.'

'What?'

'Slight exaggeration, but you seemed so wise, knowledgeable and grown up.'

'For which read boring and full of my own importance?' he said, trying not to laugh.

'Not at all. Anyway, I soon realised otherwise.'

He blew out a breath. 'Thank heavens for that. I definitely have feet of clay, and maybe more than feet.'

We were quiet for a moment, then he squeezed my hand that still rested in his and said, 'I've been doing some thinking the past few days too. Not much else to do, really, and I think I've done you an injustice.'

'Oh?'

'Well, probably many, but this is what has been pricking my conscience. I haven't taken enough interest in the things that are important to you, especially your art. I'm probably a bit thick, a bit slow on the uptake, but it came to me that if you wanted something badly enough to take off and spend months at it, perhaps I should know more about it. You've mentioned it a few times, and I wondered if there was any way I could see this triptych of yours.'

This was new, and it took me a few moments to swallow my astonishment. 'Well,' I said cautiously, 'it isn't actually a triptych yet. There's one finished panel, framed and displayed in the church. I did tell you about that. That's the one of St John on Patmos and the cities that got letters, with Christ shining in the centre. And the second one's still unfinished, propped up at Chibley; that's the one that gives us a glimpse of heaven. I'm still thinking about number three.'

'I should have come and visited when I had the chance,' he said sadly. 'I could have seen them then.'

I thought. 'There might be a way,' I said. 'I've got a few photos on my phone, but they aren't very good. Maybe I can organise some better ones.'

'That would be good.'

He seemed to be tiring. 'Look, love, I'm going to leave you to get some rest,' I said. 'God willing, I'll see you tomorrow. I should have told you, you were prayed for at St Swithin's on Sunday. Quite a few people said they were praying for you privately as well. As am I, of course.'

He smiled. 'What for, precisely?'

'Peace, mainly.'

'Well, in that case, your prayers are answered. I've been doing a lot of praying too since I've been in here. It was something I never really got the hang of before I was ill, and I confess I neglected it. Now I realise how much I have been forgiven, and how much I still need it.'

'As we all do.'

He gave my hand a last squeeze. 'See you tomorrow.'

THAT EVENING, AS I was washing the last of the dishes I'd left to accumulate all day, the phone rang. I was delighted to hear Mary's voice.

'Well now, stranger, how are you? And how is John?'

'I'm OK, thanks, Mary. And John is still with us – just. He's in the hospice now. How are you? And Peter? Oh, and how's Sadie?'

'I'm fine, and Peter is much as ever. Sadie is well, working a lot for the Whartons these days.'

'Mary, I'm afraid I've neglected you. I'm sorry. It's been pretty fraught here at times. But it's so good to hear your voice.'

'I thought I should wish you a happy anniversary.'

'You remembered? I didn't know you even knew the date.'

'You must have mentioned it,' she said. 'But talking of neglect, I think your friends at Chibley are missing you.'

'Oh. Yes, I've neglected them too, shamefully.'

'I expect they understand. They were both at church last Sunday.'

'Liam too?'

'I think he must have brought Martha in her car. Maybe she's finding driving difficult these days.'

'I'd almost forgotten, bad friend that I am,' I said. 'Martha was due to have one of her hips done. That's probably why she got Liam to drive her.' I sighed, thinking. 'It's odd. Of course, it's not as if I didn't even have one minute to ring, or write an email. I could have, of course I could, but somehow I've felt so sucked into everything that's been going on here it's almost as if Yorkshire ceased to exist.'

I could hear her smile. 'I assure you it does, and we're all well and truly alive and breathing.'

'Thank heavens! But you were saying you saw Martha and Liam?'

'That's right. After the service they were looking at your painting. I did notice Martha was walking with two sticks, so perhaps she has had her operation. Anyway, I went and spoke to them, and they asked me if I'd had any news of you.'

'Oh dear. I feel very guilty. I didn't honestly think they'd be giving me much thought at all.'

'Well now, that's silly. You're friends, aren't you? I'm sure they realise you've been up to your eyes with a sick man to look after, but it's my belief they'd be very glad to hear from you.'

'I shall rectify my poor behaviour right away,' I said. 'There's a favour I need, so I'll drop Liam an email and let him know some of my news at the same time.'

'That's good,' Mary said. 'Well, dear Fen, I do hope we'll see you back here at some point.'

'I don't know, Mary. I just don't know. And I can't think about the future yet.'

After we'd rung off, I opened up my laptop and wrote an email to Liam, apologising for not having contacted him before, asking after him and Martha, giving a very brief summary of my own situation, and then asking him if he could take photos of my paintings and email them to me. Less than an hour later I had a reply: 'Leave it to me.'

Halfway through the next morning, as I was getting ready to go to the hospice, he sent me an attachment with photos of both paintings from a number of angles. He must have dropped everything to do it, because he would have had to get Steve to open the church. I replied at once. 'Thank you. It's for John.' A few minutes later he sent me a thumbs-up. I wondered if the terseness of his communications meant he was aggrieved at me. I hoped not; but for now I put it out of my mind.

John seemed a bit brighter that day. He spent quite some minutes examining the photos Liam had sent. 'I truly didn't realise,' he muttered. 'I know less than nothing about art, but even I can see how astonishing these are.' He looked up at me wonderingly.

'No surprise, really, that you didn't know – these are the first big things I've ever attempted.'

'You absolutely must finish them. You do plan to, don't you?'

I shook my head. 'I don't know. I have no plans.'

Over the next weeks I saw John decline – at first gradually, then with greater rapidity. There was nothing to do at home, and I took to sleeping at the hospice, going out only to take a walk for fresh air and a change of scenery, while the staff did things to make John more comfortable. He wasn't eating, and barely drinking; his skin was like tissue paper, and I could almost see his bones. The thought of the cancer eating him away from inside was deeply distressing. One night in mid-August I felt he was slipping away; the staff were in and out a lot more, keeping an eye on him, but his drips and tubes had been taken away.

'I'll stay here tonight,' I said to the nurse on duty, a rotund young woman with fine fair hair and rosy cheeks called Tabitha.

'Whatever you want, my love,' she said.

I sat by his bedside. He was propped on several pillows to aid his breathing, which seemed unnaturally loud and rough in the silence of the room. I held his hand that was more like a claw, with prominent blue veins and yellowed nails, and watched him breathe, thinking of the vigorous man he had been, and I prayed for his release with tears in my eyes. I must have dozed despite myself, because as the first light of morning came through the uncurtained window I came to groggily and knew at once that something was different. My head had dropped onto the edge of the bed; now I raised it and saw that John's hand was slack in mine. I looked at his face and saw that even when someone was as sick as he had been there was all the difference in the world between a living person and a dead one. John was gone.

THE WEEKS THAT followed, between John's death and his funeral, were among the oddest I have ever lived through. I was like half a human being, with all feeling leached from heart and soul, capable of little but automatic responses. I was rational; I made small decisions, I replied civilly to enquiries. What was going on in the depths was invisible to everyone, myself included. I caught the children exchanging anxious glances, but I had no spirit either to let them behind my defences or to console them. They had both been in touch with their father during his time in the hospice, Dan by phone, and Alice in person, sometimes with Rory, sometimes by herself; these visits had given me respite, and I knew John took comfort from them, although they wore him out.

At the time of John's death Dan was, of course, still in the States. Alice and Rory were in Scotland, visiting his family. Dan flew home,

Alice and Rory cut short their trip, and they were all there, living with me in the house, for several days before the funeral. They were helpful and solicitous, but I felt suffocated and longed to be alone. I could think of few other times when I had wished my children away; but so it was.

John's funeral amazed even me. St Swithin's was so full there were people standing in the aisles and crammed into the choir stalls: people from his work, from the golf club, and what looked like the entire congregation of the church. I wished he could have seen it. Dan and Alice had composed a tribute, with a little help from me, and it was full of affectionate anecdotes so that there were ripples of laughter as well as tears. I did not weep, though I was aware of something monstrous within me biding its time. I prayed that today I would be calm.

Once the inevitable gathering had dispersed, the five of us – Grace was helping too – cleared up the house. Grace hugged me, assured me she was there for me, and went home – with, I thought wryly, a sigh of relief. The young people were clearly unsure what they should do next, waiting for a lead from me. I sat them down in the lounge.

'My dears, you have all been wonderful, and I am thankful. There's no more for you to do, and I would very much like you to go on with your own lives as soon as possible. No, Daniel, let me finish. I need some space to process everything that's happened – I hope you understand. I came here in mid-April; now I find it's September, less than five months have passed, and yet there's been a sort of volcanic eruption in my life – in all our lives. I need time to think, and I need to be on my own to do it. I've been so, I don't know, *submerged* in your father's care that I haven't given any thought to what I want the future to look like. You don't need to worry about me – I'll be perfectly all right. We'll be in touch frequently, of course. I promise not to do anything rash or forget to eat and waste away. The fact is, I am exhausted. Dan, you've been away from your work long enough. Book your flight as soon as you can. Alice and Rory, finish your Scottish trip. Your family is grieving too, Rory, after your uncle's death. In the next day or two, no longer, I want to know you are getting on with life. I'll still be here, and I won't do anything major without talking to you about it.' They were all in tears, and I was sorry to be so little help to them, but at that moment my reserves seemed utterly depleted; besides, each of them had someone to support them, as I did not. Without too much protest they did as I asked, and barely forty-eight hours later I was blessedly alone.

I spent the next two days walking round the city – the city I'd so desperately wanted to leave behind. I didn't like it any more than I had, but there were places that, over the course of more than twenty years, had become comfortingly familiar: a coffee shop I'd often frequented with Grace; a playground I'd taken the children to when they were small; shops, streets, parks. At some level I realised why I was doing this – these places connected me with John and our life together, and I was reluctant to let it go. I told myself I was foolish, because after all Brant would still be there wherever I went, and would change as places do, but perhaps subconsciously I was saying goodbye to my life here, because whether I stayed or departed it was over beyond recall, just as John himself was. The very self that had inhabited these places no longer existed.

In the house I did nothing beyond the necessary, cooking meals and washing up, showering and sleeping. My sleep was fractured, full of violent dreams, some of an intensely sexual nature – why? I had no idea. During the day I did nothing of consequence; the art materials John had wanted me to buy for my birthday were still in their bag, untouched. Then, a few days after the children had gone, I had a visitor.

I was in the garden, half-heartedly pulling up weeds from a flower border, when I heard the doorbell. I frowned in puzzlement: I wasn't expecting anyone, I'd ordered nothing from the internet. I wiped my dirty hands down my trousers, kicked off my muddy boots and tramped through the house in my socks. I opened the front door. Standing on the doorstep, looking out down the front garden, his back to me, was Liam.

I must have uttered some strangled exclamation, because he whirled round. 'Fen!'

I gulped. 'Come in.' I shut the door behind him, and we stood in the hall, staring dumbly at each other. Seeing him, as himself, alive, breathing, healthy, flushed from walking, but also as an envoy from another life, was stirring something terrifying within me. I sensed the monster moving, its yellow eyes flashing, and I felt myself coming apart. I wanted to say something banal like 'How lovely to see you! I'll get the kettle on,' but nothing came out of my mouth.

His voice was rough with some undefined emotion. 'Hello, Fen. I had to come.'

I could not have predicted my response to hearing him speak, seeing him standing in my house, wearing his usual worn shirt and baggy trousers, the representative of something I thought lost. My chest heaved, and I was weeping so hard I could barely breathe. I tried to swallow, but it was no good.

'Oh, Fen.' He closed the gap between us and wrapped me in his arms, rocking me gently as if I was a heartbroken child. For minutes I cried, soaking his shirt. Then he put me away from him and looked at me, his bright blue eyes full of compassion. 'You got anywhere nice to sit in this establishment?'

I laughed shakily at this and led him into the lounge. 'Sorry, Liam. It was just such a shock seeing you on the doorstep, like two planets colliding. I'm very happy to see you, despite that rather watery welcome.'

His eyes narrowed. 'Would I be completely wrong if I assumed you'd been keeping everything under tight control till now?'

'No, you'd be eerily right.'

'In that case, I'm glad I freaked you out. Ah, Fen, we were so sad to hear what happened, Martha and me. We've been worried.'

'I'm sorry. I really did abandon you, didn't I? But I'm glad you haven't abandoned me.'

'Of course not. Now, were you ever going to offer me a cup of tea after my epic journey?'

'Yes, of course. Come into the kitchen so we don't have to shout.' He followed me and planted himself on a stool at the table while I put the kettle on. 'Have you come down from Yorkshire today?'

'No, I was exaggerating – a foible of mine, so I'm told. My epic journey started at Thripp's Ford. I've been staying with Ronnie and Tanya the last few days.'

'Oh! I didn't know you knew them.'

'I didn't. Ronnie called Martha and talked about you. And I invited myself. So now we're great chums. I love that ramshackle barn he keeps his paintings in. It reminds me of Chibley. And his latest series is something amazing.'

I made two mugs of tea and passed one across the table to him. 'It's very kind of you to come and see me, Liam.'

'No, it's not kind, it's absolutely selfish. We need you to come home.'

I stirred my tea and looked at him bleakly. 'Where's that?'

He frowned. 'If you don't know by now, I despair of you. Just tell me, where are your friends? Mary, Peter, Steve, Jane, the Whartons, Martha, me? In Yorkshire. What's keeping you here, anyway?'

I stared at him. 'On the face of it,' I said, my voice low, 'absolutely nothing. My children are getting on with their lives, as they should. Oh, of course they are grieving for their father, they are concerned about me, but I have no need to keep a base for them, not any more. And my friend Grace is preparing to emigrate to Australia. So no, not much. But it's weird, I've found myself reluctant to go, Liam, even though I know what you say is true – my friends are in Yorkshire.'

He nodded. 'Not only that. Potentially there's a whole new life there, if only you'd reach out and take it up. Not what you planned in the beginning – not some sort of fantasy, not an escape, not a holiday, not something that would come to an end and you'd come back here where your real life was. Not that. I mean something you could commit to wholeheartedly, without reservation. Because now you can. Now you can build on what you started.' I made to speak, and he held up his hand. 'Look. You're thinking, since when is he an expert? He's never settled to anything, a serial drifter. And you'd be right.' He leaned across the table, fixing me with an unnervingly intense stare. 'But Fen, I'm saying these things to myself just as much as I'm saying them to you. It's time I grew up. Stopped sitting on some kind of fence, forever hedging my bets. Martha has a plan, and it involves us both. You have to come back and hear what she has to say. Please.'

'A plan?' I said. 'I don't doubt she has, but why me?'

He smiled. 'I've been instructed to call it that. What Martha calls it is a last roll of the dice. And as for you, don't underestimate your considerable abilities, Fen, because Martha doesn't, and neither do I.'

I pondered for several minutes, and Liam was silent. I took a breath. 'Liam, did you buy a return ticket?' He shook his head. 'OK, how about this for a plan? Just in case I want one day to sell this house, it needs to be sorted out. We accumulated, just like most people do. You help me clear out the loft, or the garage, or both, depending on time and energy, and in return I'll give you a lift back to Yorkshire. And meals while you're here.'

He beamed. 'Done. Shall we start now?'

FOR THREE DAYS Liam and I worked. We brought down many boxes from the loft. Some contained precious things, like photographs, children's drawings, christening gifts. These I set aside. Others were full of the sort of thing that made me exclaim, 'Why on earth did we keep *this*?'

Liam grinned. 'Unlike you,' he said, 'I don't keep much. You don't when you have no fixed abode.'

We made numerous trips to charity shops, mostly with John's clothes, and I tried not to mind as I packed cases full of his familiar things. There were also many journeys to the local dump, and I found someone at the golf club happy to buy John's clubs. In the end the only things still in the loft were the boxes for keeping or distributing to Dan and Alice. As I swept up the dust I marvelled at our progress. Then I turned my attention to the garage, and that was trickier. Here were cupboards and shelves with boxes large and small, wooden, cardboard and metal, containing tools whose use was a mystery to me. Liam identified some of them and claimed a few for himself; much of the rest he managed to sell online.

Each evening I fed us a good meal and then drove him back to Thripp's Ford. Considering how helpful he was being it was the least I could do, since he had arrived at my door in the first place by two buses.

He made a very mild protest: 'It would save you all this driving if I just stayed over. I promise I'd behave myself.'

'Absolutely not a chance. However well-behaved we were, Ronnie and Tanya would come to one conclusion only. If my reputation is to be shredded, I would rather it was for something I'd actually done. And perhaps you're forgetting I buried my husband barely a week ago. Some more puritanical folk might think me unbelievably hard-hearted to be entertaining a strange man so soon.'

He sighed. 'OK. You win.' Then he grinned. 'If anyone asks, you can say I am your handyman.'

Eventually the garage looked as bare and dust-free as the loft. Liam stood and surveyed our handiwork, hands on hips, nodding. We were both filthy. 'I don't suppose you'll need two cars.'

'No. I'll keep the big one and let Alice and Rory have the smaller one. They can't borrow his brother's car forever, I guess. So – are we ready to go north?'

'You tell me.'

'Tomorrow. I'll collect you in the morning. Perhaps you can let Martha know we'll be on our way. I'll alert my children.'

I FILLED THE boot of the car with clothes and supplies and shut up the house. By nine o'clock I was banging on the Milburns' door. Ronnie opened it, his feet bare, a coffee mug in his hand. 'Come in for a minute, Fen. Liam's just getting his stuff together.' Tanya was sitting at a huge table in the middle of the kitchen, munching on toast. Now she got to her feet. 'Fen, how are you?' She gave me a hug. 'We were so sorry to hear your sad news.'

'Thanks. Yes, it's been a bit tough.'

'Come and sit for a moment. So, how long do you plan to be in Yorkshire this time?'

'Long enough to hear what Martha has in mind and how I fit into her fiendish plan.'

Ronnie helped himself to his wife's toast and narrowly escaped having his hand whacked with her knife. 'Fiendish it may well be, knowing Martha.'

'Whatever happens, I have to come back here. Even if in the end I decide to stay in Yorkshire I'll have to come back and sell the house. There's a lot to think about.'

'I'd absolutely love to live up there,' Ronnie said. 'But moving all my gear doesn't bear thinking about.'

'And my work's here,' Tanya said with some asperity. 'Without my salary we couldn't cope. Besides which, I actually enjoy my job.'

There was a clattering on the stairs and Liam appeared, carrying a battered leather holdall. 'Morning, Fen.'

Ronnie grinned, and there was a salacious glint under his bushy brows. 'It's a good job you insisted on bringing this reprobate back each evening,' he said, 'considering his reputation.'

'I wish,' Liam retorted. 'Anyway, how would you know?'

Ronnie merely beamed and tapped the side of his nose.

'Ron, give over trying to make trouble,' Tanya said. 'You're a terrible old scandalmonger. And this poor soul's a new widow. She doesn't need your off-colour insinuations.'

Ronnie held up his hands. 'Sorry, Fen.'

'You ready, Liam?'

'As I ever will be.' He turned to Ronnie and Tanya and hugged them both. 'Thanks for putting me up.'

'Any time, Liam,' Tanya said. 'And maybe we'll come and see you in Yorkshire one of these days.'

'Great idea,' Ronnie said. 'I'd love to see old Martha again.'

'If you call her old your life won't be worth fourpence,' Liam said. He turned to me. 'Are we on our way?'

'We will be.' I took out my phone. 'I'm going to put you on the car insurance. Then I won't have to do all the driving. It's a long way.'

Ronnie pretended to be shocked. 'You trust him?'

'If I had boots on, Ron,' Tanya growled, 'I'd kick you under the table.'

❋

THE JOURNEY NORTH didn't seem as long as it often did, now that I had company. We stopped at a service station for a leisurely lunch and to refuel the car, and while Liam drove I slept. He told me I'd dropped off mid-sentence.

'Hope I didn't snore,' I said.

'Like a clattering locomotive. Absolutely deafening.'

We drew into the yard at Chibley in the early afternoon. 'I'm just going to drop you off for now,' I told him. 'I'll come back later. Martha may be having her post-lunch nap anyway, and I want to see Mary.'

As I drove through the town the clouds began to gather. All the way the weather had stayed fine; now a mist descended from the hilltops. But nothing, it seemed, could dampen my rising spirits. The very air smelled different, and I realised I'd forgotten just how much I loved this place.

❋

I PARKED OUTSIDE the Whitepost farmhouse. Mary must have heard the crunch of my tyres; she looked out of the window and waved. As I got out of the car, still stiff from the long drive, she opened the door.

'Fen dear, how lovely to see you.' She gave me a hug, then stepped back and looked at me keenly. 'I think you've lost weight.'

'So have you!' I said and laughed. I took her arm, and we went inside. 'How are things? Peter?'

'It's hard to say if he's worse or not,' she said with a small sigh. 'I see him every day. What do you think?'

I went over to where Peter sat in his favourite chair, apparently fast asleep. I took his hand, warm and heavy.

'About the same, I think,' I said quietly, so as not to wake him.

Over tea and scones we caught up with news. I told her about the children, John's last days, the funeral, and she gave my arm a sympathetic squeeze. I described Rory to her, and she smiled.

Again that small sigh. 'I have news too,' she said. 'I didn't want to go into it on the phone. Mrs Wills, Ruby, she passed away in August. She was very deaf and was losing it a bit, poor soul. I've known her since I came here. Anyway, Peter's next on the list and now there's room for him at the nursing home. We'll be out of here by the end of the month. The Whartons have been very good, said take as long as you like, but we've waited a long time and now I want to get him properly settled. He needs more care than I can give him.'

'What about you?'

'I'll move in with my friend in town. She's got a spare room, and she's always said I can live with her if I like. It's just round the corner from the home so it'll be handy for visiting.'

'It's such a shame, Mary.'

She nodded. 'I know. But it can't be helped.' She lifted the teapot and looked at me enquiringly.

'I won't, thanks. Even I don't have your capacity for tea.'

'If you live here long enough, you will.'

'So, what happens to the farm?'

'Well, you know it belongs to the Whartons – land, buildings, the lot. If they can't farm it themselves, they'll sell some of it off.'

'What about the eighteen old ladies?'

'They've taken them on already.'

I looked around the room. 'And Sadie? I don't see her.'

Mary blinked rapidly. 'I had to sell her, Fen.'

'Sell Sadie?' I was horrified. 'But Mary, she's your dog! You had her from a pup, you trained her!'

'Yes, but I can't work her. She's still young. It wouldn't be kind to keep her. The Whartons have her, and young Thom is training her for trials as well as using her every day with the sheep.' She shook her head. 'Anyway, I needed the money. Nursing homes don't come cheap.'

'I guess not,' I said. 'And sheepdogs like Sadie are worth a king's ransom.'

Mary smiled sadly. 'Pretty much. But you know,' she said, brightening, 'the great thing is I still see Sadie. And I know she'll be well looked after.'

'Everything looked shipshape when I drove in, Mary,' I said. 'Have you managed to get out, or was that the Whartons too?'

'Neither,' Mary said. 'I forgot to tell you. Your friend Liam came round out of the blue, asked me if I needed anything done, and he fixed a fence that was down and a splintered gate. I offered, of course, but he wouldn't take anything for his trouble.'

'That was neighbourly,' I said. 'But I shouldn't be surprised. He has a good heart.' I frowned. 'He never mentioned it.'

I hadn't meant to stay so long, but by the time I left Whitepost it was getting dark. I phoned Liam. 'Do you have some culinary delight lined up for this evening, or shall I get a takeaway?'

'No, I don't, and yes please! Martha says get a move on.'

Martha was pleased to see me, it seemed, to the point of impatience. Sitting round her big table, we demolished the takeaway in short order.

'Good,' she said, lifting her glass of red wine. 'Now that the inner woman is dealt with, we can proceed to business. Except,' she added, looking at me, 'where are you planning to sleep?'

'Mary said I could have my old cottage back until they have to move.'

Martha grunted. 'If you're still here then, you'd better move in here till you can sort out something more permanent.'

'Thank you,' I said. 'But that's a very big if. So, Martha, Liam tells me you have a plan.'

Martha leaned forward, picked up the half-empty bottle and refilled my glass. She caught my look. 'Don't worry. I doubt the local law will be around this evening between here and Whitepost. I happen to know there's a major football match on TV.' She settled back in her chair. 'The thing is, Fen, as you well know, Chibley has been limping along the past few years, and sometimes I think it's a bit of a miracle it's still going at all. I was hoping, or to be more honest relying, on an injection of funds from Olive Wastwell, who definitely has more money than talent, but please don't say I said so. Anyway, as we all know, that's fallen by the wayside. In one way I'm relieved, but it leaves us right back where we were.'

'Unfortunately, that was because of me.'

'It was because of Olive's envy and insecurity,' Martha said. 'For which you are clearly not responsible. Whatever, Olive is out of the picture as a benefactor.'

She leaned forward. 'I want to have one last try, Fen. To get Chibley up and running again. Maybe I won't manage it, but I want to try. And for that I need money, a lot of money. So I'm going to America. I've been meaning to for years, to see my cousins and their families before I'm too crippled to travel. I'm getting over my op now, and doing the exercises when I remember, but my other hip's still dodgy. They see me as their eccentric English relative, and are quite well-disposed towards me, so in the course of my long-overdue family visit I'm going to major on that – my lifetime's work, my promise to my forebears, this unique place in a glorious part of the old country, poor handicapped elderly lady with a bee in her bonnet – you get the picture – and see, not if any of them are wealthy, which I know they are, but if someone can be found who's willing to back my project. In hard dollars.'

'I hope it works, Martha.' I said. 'But what if it doesn't?'

'Then I'll have to sell up,' Martha said. 'I don't know who'd be interested in this place; perhaps some developer.' She shuddered. 'I hate the idea of it, but I don't have much choice.'

'And how do I fit into this scheme?'

'Nowhere, unless I come back with the goods,' Martha said. 'And then you will be instrumental. You and Liam.'

I shook my head. 'I don't see that I have any skills here.'

She tapped the table impatiently. 'Nobody's asking you to become a builder overnight, Fen. Or at all. This time we have to have a proper business plan, a scheme of works, and a team of experts, and it all has to be costed to the last cent. This is my last chance, and I have to prove it's viable. You and Liam are my overseers, my deputies, representing Chibley to outsiders who don't understand what it's about, keeping an eye on things. You're both capable people, and I know I can rely on you. That's worth at least as much as the money. Dollars pave the way, but trusty people are beyond price.'

'Thank you for your confidence, Martha,' I said faintly. 'But it's a big ask. My husband has just died, there's everything to do, and I haven't decided yet what to do with what remains of my life. If I agree to your suggestion, it means I am committing myself to moving here for the foreseeable future. I'm not sure I can do that just yet. If at all.'

Martha nodded. 'I understand. But please don't hesitate too long. In my eyes you're a big part of this crazy undertaking, and if you aren't willing to come on board I'll have to think again.'

'I'll do my share of thinking as well, Martha. I'll stick around for a day or two and see what comes to me. I'll probably stay with Mary tomorrow, see what she thinks. I'll be in touch, of course.'

Liam walked me to my car. 'I know how you feel,' he said. 'Well, I think I do. About not being much use in this project. I think Martha feels she needs backup, dealing with all the bits of the project. It's a lot for one person, keeping an eye on something so complicated. She's not getting any younger, and she's not in the best of health. I just hope her relatives in the US aren't a massive disappointment.'

I leaned on the roof of the car and felt a drop of rain hit my cheek. 'Honestly, Liam, I don't know what to do. It's a very big step, and I admit to being scared.'

He patted my arm. 'I get it. I feel scared myself most of the time.'

THE NEXT MORNING when I got up I saw the nurse's car parked in the yard at Whitepost and decided not to bother Mary till later. I'd slept well, tired from the journey, but also I suspected because before I went to bed I'd spent some considerable time battering God's ears with my indecision. No clear answer had yet come to me, but I believed it would, and that instilled a sense of something approaching peace in my troubled spirit. Thinking along the same lines, I picked up my phone and rang Steve at the vicarage.

'Fen, how nice to hear from you! Where are you?'

'About three miles away,' I said. 'I was hoping to come and have a chat, if you're not too busy, or about to go out somewhere in your vast parish.'

'No, I'm right here at home in my study, thinking about preparing a sermon,' he said. 'Come and welcome.'

I sat with Steve at his kitchen table, drinking coffee and eating Jane's homemade biscuits. 'I think she's popped into town for some shopping,' Steve said vaguely. 'Fen, we heard about your husband, and we're very sorry. It must have been a tough time for the family.'

'It all happened unbelievably quickly, Steve. He seemed more or less OK at Christmas, though looking back he wasn't really himself, but I put that down to the stress of work and all the travelling he had to do. Perhaps he was ill even then, but nobody knew, including John himself. Then when I got home in April it was obvious he was quite poorly. After that, even with treatment, it just galloped away.'

Steve nodded. 'I've had parishioners with the same illness, and it's very cruel. Jane and I have been praying for you.'

'Thank you.'

'What are you going to do, do you know? I hope you're going to finish your painting project. The panel in church has caused quite a stir! Oh, and I didn't tell you, we got the permission and it's hanging up now. You should see it. Finish your coffee and we can go to the church right away if you like.'

'That would be great, Steve.'

Together we walked down the rain-slicked path round the back of the church and to the door, which Steve opened. 'We put it in the side chapel,' Steve said, 'where there's a nice blank wall. But if you complete the series we might have to think again. They'd need to be together, side by side.'

I was amazed. 'You mean you'd want them all in church?'

He turned to me, smiling. 'Of course we would, Fen.'

'But you don't even know what will be in them.'

'You said something about the second one being a glimpse of heaven,' Steve said. 'How could I object to that?'

'I suppose. But… well, I haven't planned the third one in any detail yet. Actually, I didn't really think about painting at all until I came back here. There just didn't seem any room in my head… sorry, I'm rambling. What little I do know is that in the third panel I will probably have to deal with judgement, and that's not an easy subject for people.'

'No,' he said soberly. 'We have to face it, of course. But that's not all Revelation's about, is it? Among all the judgement images, is there something you could include that speaks of hope, forgiveness, redemption?'

'I'm sure there is. And I'll think about it, of course. But Steve, please don't think you are obliged to take any of them. You've been very generous, but I don't take it for granted. I wouldn't want any work of mine to frighten the congregation.'

He laughed. 'Don't worry. And you know, Fen, there's a lot in it for me.'

'There is?'

'Yes, apart from the people your painting brings into the church who normally aren't seen within a mile, it's given me quite a few preaching opportunities.'

I COLLECTED MY car and reparked it near the centre of town. I rang Martha and offered to bring some supplies so that we could have lunch together, and she gladly agreed. Then for several moments I sat in the car park behind the town's one big grocery store and pondered. What was I going to put in that third panel, if I ever began it? Talking to Steve had ignited something in me, and although I still felt like an imposter, I had to admit that the Revelation triptych might actually one day hang in the church for all to see. It was an overwhelming prospect; when I'd come to Yorkshire more than a year ago I could never have foreseen it.

Plunged in thought, I got out of the car and made my way into the shop. I was examining the contents of the cheese counter when I heard a familiar local accent. I looked round, and there was Will Wharton, looking out of place with his shopping basket. 'Will, how are you?' I smiled inwardly, thinking he must have come straight off the hill and Bess would not approve. He was in his customary rig of battered boots, patched jacket, flat cap and trousers held up with baling twine, and the ruddiness of his cheeks spoke of his outdoor life.

'Well now, I'm all right, but how about you?' he said. 'We heard your sad news, and we were sorry to hear it.'

'Thank you, Will.'

'Are you here for long?'

'Not this time. Just a flying visit for now. Lots to do at home, as I'm sure you can imagine. But maybe I'll be back. How's Bess? And young Thom?'

'Ah, they're grand,' Will said, beaming. 'Lad's in sixth form now. Seems he were a baby only yesterday.'

'Mary says you have Sadie now.'

'We do, and she's doing well. Thom's after training her for trials. Out there every weekend when I can spare her, never mind the weather. She'll do well, I don't doubt.'

'She's an exceptional dog.'

'She is that.' He must have seen my expression, because he added, 'We take her down to Whitepost most weeks to see Mary. Well, young Fen, I'd best be off, or Bess'll be wondering. Good to see you.'

I paid for my shopping in a daze. Seeing Will, the quintessential farmer and shepherd, had caused something to come together in my muddled mind. As I drove to Chibley I knew what must go in my third panel, and my hands itched with impatience. I couldn't wait to get hold of pad and pencil and start to sketch it out. It occurred to me with a small shock of realisation that this was all I'd needed to make my decision to stay. Whatever happened at Chibley, whether Martha's plan worked or not, whatever became of me in the long run, this was the place where I would bring my scrappy original vision to fulfilment. After that, I had no idea.

I flew into Chibley farmhouse like someone propelled by a gale. Martha was standing at the table, putting out plates and cutlery. 'At last!' she said. 'I am faint with hunger.'

I put my bag on the table. 'Well, here's your remedy: bread, cheese, pâté, tomatoes and a big bottle of Amos's cider. Will that do?'

'Very well indeed. But what kept you?'

I sat opposite her. 'Martha,' I said breathlessly, 'I have had an epiphany.'

'Good heavens, what brought that on?'

I cut a thick slice of bread. 'Will Wharton.' I looked round the room. 'No Liam?'

She stared at me, cheese knife in hand. 'No, he's out sketching somewhere. Did you say Will—? Are you kidding me?'

'Perhaps not Will as himself, but as he represents something. I went to see Steve too. We talked about the third panel. We agreed that too much emphasis on judgement might be gloomy and off-putting. Something kinder needs to be included as well. I'd already decided to stop with the seven seals, or to be exact, six. It's faithful, but not in sequence. I'm taking some artistic licence.'

'Just as you have in the second panel,' Martha said, clearly amused. 'I like the little effects. The angel with the trombone, for instance. Nothing wrong with a touch of humour, and who knows what instruments the angels play? You should put a few more in like that.'

'Maybe I will,' I said, 'because I've got a lot more angels to do. But let me tell you about the third one while the wind's in my sails, Martha. I had plenty of trouble with the sea of glass, and I still don't know if I pulled it off. But now I've got to learn how to paint horses.'

'Plenty of subjects round here,' Martha said. 'Anyway, I've seen some of your juvenile work, and you already can draw horses.'

'Maybe, but painting them is different. Think of it – four horses! – a white one with its rider carrying a bow and wearing the victorious warrior's wreath. The red, with his huge sword, bringing civil war. The black with his scales, signifying famine. And the pale one, yellow-green, such an unnatural colour for a normal horse, meaning death.'

'I see why you need some less frightening images.'

'Not got there yet. I also want to include the seven angels with their trumpets, and the one angel with his incense burner, the prayers of the faithful rising to the throne, but I want to have them *waiting.* It's not their time yet. There are still the martyrs under the altar, pleading with God, and the terrifying images of the black sun and the red moon and the stars falling like figs from a tree.'

Martha took a swig of cider to wash down the buttery doorstep on which she had laid several slices of Stilton. 'So where does Will Wharton come into all this?'

I took a deep breath. 'I had the idea of including the Good Shepherd. Perhaps the ultimate image of protection and consolation, and this section of Revelation is supposed to be about the worship of the Redeemer. But I didn't want a Victorian sanitised Jesus, all shiny hair and white robes and soulful eyes raised to heaven. And when I saw Will, in his stained flat cap and his terrible trousers, I thought, here's a real shepherd, and someone people round these parts will instantly recognise. Something, someone, for the here and now, like the car parks and shops in the first panel. I'll paint him in the left foreground, I think, stick in hand, nice and traditional with the orphan lamb under his arm, and of course a dog at his side, modelled on Sadie. I won't make him *look* like Will, of course. Otherwise he won't be symbolic. But, so nobody is in any doubt as to who he represents, I'll have both his hands pierced.'

Martha was silent for several long moments, thoughtfully chewing. 'If I didn't know you better, I'd swear you were on some illegal substance.'

I laughed. 'Nope, just high on Revelation.'

Martha gave me one of her narrow-eyed, considering looks. 'So, does this mean you're staying?'

'I suppose it must.'

'Does it mean you'll be with me on the Chibley revival project?'

'It probably does. But the triptych's the priority for now.'

Martha grunted. 'Well, you'll have plenty of time for it while I'm in the States. And it'll give you a deadline, maybe.'

'But first,' I said, sobering, 'I have to go back to Brant and put my affairs in order. There's still a huge amount to do. If I'm back by Christmas it'll be an achievement.'

'I'd like to think we would all be here for Christmas,' Martha said. 'But like you, I have a lot to do in the US, and not all the outcome depends on me.'

'When are you hoping to go?'

Martha sat back in her chair. 'I'm just waiting to hear from my cousin Walter,' she said. 'Then I'll buy a ticket. Sooner the better.'

I nodded. 'That's how I feel, too. I'll go back south tomorrow. But this afternoon I shall go out and find a horse to draw.'

THE FOLLOWING MORNING found me driving down the motorway into sunshine. I'd said goodbye to Mary and Peter and asked Martha to say the same to Liam, who hadn't reappeared. I broke my journey at some services and sat outside to drink a cup of coffee and phone Alice.

'Hi, Mum, where are you?'

'Somewhere on a southbound motorway. I just made a very brief visit to Yorkshire.'

'Ah. Don't tell me – it's inspired you to move back there.'

'How did you guess?'

'Not difficult, Mum.'

'You don't mind?'

'Why should I?'

'I thought you might find the removal of your home base unsettling.'

'Maybe once I would've. Not now.'

'Well, that's good, love. Where are you?'

'On a train. We just left Edinburgh. Rory's brother needed his car back. Maybe we'll all get back together.'

'Good, because there's a lot we need to talk about.'

ALICE, RORY AND I sat in the lounge with cups of coffee after our evening meal.

Alice yawned. 'I'm knackered. Too much running about. And this fellow—' she nudged Rory, who was sprawling beside her on the sofa, '—says we have to start looking for jobs.'

'We don't have any money,' Rory said mildly. 'It's kind of an incentive.'

I put my empty cup down. 'Don't be in too much of a hurry,' I said. 'Because I have a plan. I've been thinking about it all the way down from Yorkshire.'

Alice sat up. 'Go on, then.'

'Well, it seems to me I have no reason any more to be in Brant. I've never liked it much, as you know. Dan's in America for the foreseeable, you two will be going wherever life takes you, and here am I, on my own and rattling around in a house that's way too big. Why do I need four bedrooms, two bathrooms, a conservatory, a garage and a sizeable garden? I don't. So, unless someone gives me a good reason for staying, I'm thinking I'll sell up.'

'OK.'

'But I really want to go back north as soon as possible. I told you about Martha's plan, which may or may not work, but in the immediate future I have some paintings to finish. So, what I thought was, we clear the house of all the junk. We put the furniture I don't need into storage. Once I've gone, which won't be just yet, you two stay here and supervise the sale, and I'll make it worth your while. Then when the house is sold and we have the money, I want to give you and your brother a goodly sum from the proceeds. Obviously, what you do with it is up to you, but on the basis that money is easy to spend but hard to come by, I hope you'll be grown-up and sensible. Invest it, put a deposit down on a flat, start a business, whatever.'

Alice looked at Rory with her eyebrows raised, then back at me. 'How about travelling the world?'

'Sounds good to me,' I said. 'Bearing in mind you may end up with nothing but memories.'

'Because,' Alice said, 'that's what we've been thinking about. Only we don't have any money, so we thought we'd better find work, save up, and go when we can. Meanwhile having to pay rent and bills, so it would probably take years. If we could stay here rent-free, and act as your agents till the sale went through, and then had some serious cash, we could do it very soon.' She clapped her hands. 'Shall we start tomorrow? Clearing the house, I mean. I bet the loft is floor to ceiling in stuff.'

'Nope. It's got nothing in it but a few boxes of photographs.'

'You've started already?' Alice said, wide-eyed.

I nodded. 'Last week my friend Liam came down and we slaved for two or three days. Made inroads in the garage as well. Sold a few things online. Now that you're here you can decide if there's anything you want to keep.'

Alice was silent for a moment. 'I wonder what Dad would think?' she said in a small voice.

'Your dad was a practical man,' I said. 'He did his share of hoarding, for sure, but I reckon he'd be cheering us on.'

Alice looked round the room and sighed. 'There's so much of him here.'

'Yeah, I know,' I said. 'Maybe it all seems a bit soon to you. But what remains of your dad isn't confined to this house. It's in our memories, and those go with us everywhere.'

Alice smiled sadly. 'You're right, Mum. OK, let's not dither. You go to the estate agent tomorrow, and Rory and I will start on the house.'

IN THE END I didn't make it back to Yorkshire till the end of October. It soon became apparent that while I had no need for a four-bedroom, two-bathroom house with a garage and a biggish garden in a leafy suburb, plenty of others did, and as soon as the house found its way to the internet we had several viewings from interested parties. I realised that with all the decisions that had to be made it would have been unrealistic and unfair to leave it in the hands of two inexperienced young people. They were, however, very helpful in the disposal of the contents, whether to the charity shops, the tip, or storage, and seemed to take on their house-clearance role with relish. Of course, I'd been in touch with Daniel, who approved our activities and looked forward to his slice of the profits.

'What will you do with it, do you know?' I asked.

'I shall chew it over with Clyde,' he said. 'We've been talking about one day getting some little place by the sea for holidays – when we're about eighty at current progress! Now maybe we can do it sooner. But what about you, Mum?'

'I think I'll see if I can find a small place near to Chibley,' I said. 'I can stay in the farmhouse for the time being, but in the long run I want to be independent.'

I'D BEEN BACK in Brant only a couple of days when Liam phoned. 'I'm sad I didn't see you before you departed,' he said. 'I came back and you'd gone.'

'Yes, I'm sorry. I really thought I'd be back in no time, and you'd hardly notice my absence.'

'There's no way,' he said, 'that I wouldn't notice your absence.'

'Why, because I am too loud?'

'For once, darling, I am perfectly serious.'

'Oh.' I changed the subject; it all felt a little uncomfortable. 'Have you heard from Martha?'

'Not yet. She's only just flown out.'

'I hope I'll be back soon, Liam. Soon as this place is sold and no one needs me here.'

'That's what I hope too. I miss you.'

THE HOUSE TOOK less than three weeks to sell, to my astonishment. 'These houses are in demand, Mrs Bailey,' the estate agent said. 'It's in good order, and I think we've priced it realistically.' I nodded, inwardly smiling. He was a very young man who took himself and his occupation extremely seriously, to the point of pomposity. I began to be hopeful that I could move on. Meanwhile, with the prospect of homelessness even for a short time, Alice and Rory found themselves a tiny basement flat in town and dull temporary jobs – Rory in a laboratory at the hospital as some kind of pseudo-scientific dogsbody, and Alice in a busy restaurant. I felt it would do them no harm. They told me they would probably spend Christmas with Rory's family in Scotland, visiting me on their way north, and would begin their epic journey in the New Year. Every spare moment was taken up with excited planning.

'Mum, you'll never guess where we want to end up!' Alice crowed.

'Surprise me.'

'Well, we'll already have been round quite a lot of southeast Asia, then Australia, so what's to stop us hopping over to New Zealand and giving the grandparents a shock? We could be there for the apple harvest. Anyway, it's time someone from the family visited them. I haven't seen them since I was very little.'

'Yes,' I said. 'Great plan.' Inwardly, though, I felt quite strange at the prospect of my daughter hooking up with the parents I hadn't seen for so long. I wondered what they would make of my going back to our old haunts and our old ways among the hills and farms of Yorkshire.

The night before I left, I had a meal with Alice and Rory in their tiny flat. My house was empty, and I was staying the night with Grace. Her bungalow was also looking very spare, but at least she had beds. I'd given our smaller car to the children, and the estate car was parked outside Grace's loaded to the roof with things I thought I might need.

'How are you feeling about it now?' Grace said. 'Moving, leaving it all behind?'

'I could ask the same of you.'

She shook her head. 'I'm ready to roll, Fen. I associate this place with an unhappy marriage and a messy divorce. Australia seems all sunshine by comparison. Isn't it different for you?'

'Hm, maybe in the details. Here's where the children grew up, but it's also where I looked after a dying man. There are always some regrets, I suppose, when you've been in a place for years. But in my case, not many. I feel a bit apprehensive, of course. Is it all going to be OK? But then, whoever knows that? Anyway, I trust in God's providence, and maybe it's time I stepped out on my own account.'

She didn't reply, just grunted – a little sceptically, I thought.

THERE WAS ONE last task I had to do before leaving Brant behind. Grace had gone shopping, and I took the opportunity to ring Gilbert at the rectory. He seemed pleased to hear from me and said I might call in that morning. I walked down to his house with my small portfolio under my arm.

'Come in, Fen,' he said and ushered me inside. 'I'll make us some coffee. No biscuits, I'm afraid – I haven't had time to go to the shops.'

We sat in his lounge, he on an upright chair, me on a lumpy sofa covered in some velvet-like maroon material. The room had a dusty, unlived-in look.

'No Norma?' I asked.

Gilbert sighed. 'She's in hospital,' he said. Seeing my look of alarm, he waved a hand. 'No, nothing too dreadful. She'd been having more of those turns I mentioned, and they took her in for a few days' observation. I'm hoping she'll be discharged soon. Apparently, they've adjusted her medication.'

'I'm sorry, Gilbert. That must be a great worry.'

'It is, yes.' He smiled. 'But we soldier on, don't we? Now, what about you? How are you coping?'

'I'm all right, Gilbert. Tired, of course – I think worry and dread wear you out as much as anything. But I've come to see you to tell you that I'm leaving Brant. You probably know the house is sold.'

He nodded. 'Yes, I'd heard. And I can't say I'm surprised.'

I took a deep breath. 'I don't know how things will pan out. But such life as I have seems to be centred in Yorkshire, at least as far ahead as I can see. I have friends there, and work to do.'

'Those things are blessings in themselves.'

'Yes, they are. And although I have friends in Brant, I don't have anything that feels like meaningful work. Also, as I dare say you know,

I'm no lover of cities. But I wanted to come and see you, to say goodbye, and thank you for all your kindness to me and to John, and to wish you all the best in your retirement.'

'Thank you.' He beamed. 'Not long now! As long as Norma is stable, I think we'll enjoy our flat by the sea.'

'I hope you do, Gilbert. You've laboured long in the vineyard, and I'm sure you'll be an influence for good wherever you are.'

'That's kind of you to say so, Fen,' he said modestly. 'I wish you well too, of course. Perhaps we can pray for each other.'

'Gladly.' I finished my coffee. 'I have a small present for you to remember me by.' I took up my portfolio and slid out two pen-and-ink drawings. 'There's one for you, and one for the church. I'm hoping you'll say goodbye to folk at St Swithin's for me.'

Gilbert held my drawing almost reverently on his outspread hands. He took in the simple scene of a church in the snow, with hills rising behind, and sheep looking through the slats of a fence, and exclaimed in pleasure. 'This is lovely, Fen. I will treasure it.' He took up the second one, a flower-filled hillside and slate-roofed cottages in a row. 'And this will hang in the vestry.'

ABOUT A MILE and a half down the eastbound road out of town, a right turning led to a small, undistinguished cluster of houses that hardly merited being called a village. It had a disused chapel and a tiny shop that was open less than half the week. But it was here I found my new home, and it was ideal even in its imperfections. At the end of a short terraced row of similar houses, it was built from the grey stone that seemed to rise out of the landscape, with a darker grey slate roof that shone with rain or sun. Mine was distinguished by a gravelled space alongside where I could park the car, leading to a ramshackle garage that hadn't been used in years judging by the amount of vegetation that had found its way inside through the many cracks and the warped door. Indoors, however, it was sound, having been used as a holiday let for about a decade. The floors were wood, there was a functional log burner as well as central heating, a smart kitchen and bathroom, even a small conservatory, and upstairs two bedrooms, one looking to the front, over the quiet road and the small patch of grass in front of the shop, the other to the back overlooking the garden. Attached to the side of the main house was a one-storey annexe, which I thought would be handy if ever I had visitors. Here there was a bedroom, a kitchen corner, a shower room, and room for a table for two against a wall and a two-seater sofa. I thought with some amusement of Rory trying to fit into the shower; he definitely wouldn't be able to turn round. At the back of this building was an area of decking where a couple of garden chairs might fit. The garden sloped down towards a small stream, but I thought the house was far enough away, and high enough, to be safe from floods. I had seen enough of roaring waterfalls and flooded fields to be extremely aware of such hazards.

The purchase didn't take long; it was eminently affordable, leaving me with enough to live on for a considerable time, and I was able to carry on staying at Chibley while all the arrangements were made.

November was a busy month. Not only was I moving house, but also working all the hours I could on the second panel. I wanted to have it finished so it could have its month of curing and be sealed and framed ready for hanging by Christmas. I knew this to be ambitious, but I was fired up and full of energy. When I was at the Chibley studio Liam was often around, working on a series of landscapes that I could see departed from earlier work and were seriously good. He seemed to be flowering as an artist, even to my untutored eyes, and I was interested to hear what Martha thought when she saw his work. When the weather was kind enough, he was out on the hills sketching and came back frozen and famished. I made vast pots of soup that I put in the Chibley freezer in batches, and this with a loaf of bread and some cheese kept us going most days.

We'd had emails from Martha, and the news seemed promising. She'd met up with relatives, some of whom were distant both geographically and in their knowledge of her, but whose interest had been piqued. She told us about her plan to gather as many as possible at the huge place belonging to her closest cousin, Walter Emery, where she was based, and unfold her predicament and her plan. 'I'm having to attend quite a few gatherings already and ooze charm,' she wrote. 'Walter is using me as a sort of exhibit: eccentric old Brit with more wacky ideas than money.' The idea of Martha oozing charm sent Liam and me into peals of laughter.

Alice and Rory phoned from time to time, reporting that the new people had moved into the Brant house. 'Mrs Prout is a bit of a worrier,' Alice said. 'She's been ringing me up with all sorts of questions I can't answer. I've given her your number, so don't be surprised if you get a call.' A few days later I was just washing brushes when my phone buzzed, and there indeed was Mrs Prout wanting to know how old the central heating boiler was.

When I could, when nothing was to be done at the new house, or when I had to wait for paint to dry, I invited myself up to Tubside and offered my services on the farm. The weather was often horrible, but I had good all-weather clothes, boots, torches, scarves, even a hat with a battery-operated light sewn into it at the front. When I'd arrived in October it was a particularly busy time for farmers, with the ewes ready for tupping. Humans, dogs, quad bikes were all roped in to bring them down to the farm fields, and even I was useful as another pair of legs and hands. It was often blowing a gale so that the dogs couldn't hear commands, or foggy so we couldn't see the dogs. At the same time lambs were being prepared for sale, weighed and tagged. With the ewes close by for a week or two, and with no pasture to speak of, they were now being fed on hay and silage, and I helped with that job too. Some of the lambs had already been sold at auction, to lowland farmers for fattening up or to use as breeding stock. I was sorry to have missed the tup sales, but I consoled myself that now I would be on hand all year round and would, with any luck and the indulgence of the Whartons, be part of it all. I was especially looking forward to lambing, now that I'd had a very tiny bit of experience.

It was young Thom, a sheep farmer in the making and happy to share his knowledge, who supplied me with information when we sat in the kitchen at Tubside, taking a break from work and warming ourselves by the fire, which was kept going night and day at this time of year. He reminded me of some of the terminology that I'd known as a teenager: male lambs were called tups, females were gimmers, and a sheep path, used time out of mind, was a trod. He told me about the clipping of the eighteen-month-old hoggs in July, and how it was fiercely competitive. He also blew away the notion of sheep being docile to the point of stupidity. 'You've got to be joking,' he said. 'Some of them are escape artists, some are crazy, some can jump over walls, some are good mothers and others just aren't. Isn't that right, Grandpa?' And Will would sip his coffee and smile. 'But you know,' Thom said solemnly, 'you couldn't do this job without the dogs.' At this Will nodded. 'Did you realise,' Thom said, leaning forward, 'them dogs know up to a hundred commands? But I reckon Sadie knows what you want even when you don't tell her.'

Bess came to the table with a plateful of biscuits, still warm. 'Thom reckons Sadie is a wonder-dog.'

'That's because she is,' Thom said. 'You wait till you see her at trials. Not only that, but I'm sure she knows them eighteen old ewes that were her own flock down at Whitepost. Grandpa doesn't believe me, but I've seen her keep a special eye on them.'

Will grunted. 'She works all the sheep the same, Thom.'

'I know,' Thom said. 'But she looks on them old girls as her responsibility.'

'Aye, well, Sadie's a fine sheepdog, fair enough. But a wonder-dog? A bit of a fancy of yours, I reckon, lad.'

I hardly saw Sadie except when we were working the sheep with the other Tubside dogs. Bess wasn't having four muddy dogs in her kitchen, and Sadie, with the others, was housed in a small barn attached to the farmhouse. It was a stout stone building, equipped with straw and wooden crates lined with blankets for beds, but the dogs, valuable as they were, were seen as part of the farm's work, and Sadie was no longer the beloved friend who slept by the fireside. As we went out again into the weather I muttered, 'I'm with you, Thom. I think Sadie's some kind of canine genius too.' I was rewarded with a broad grin.

When I could I dropped in on Mary, now living with her old friend Anne Welland. They were comfortable, and Mary could visit Peter in the nursing home, which was a short walk away. She was stoic as ever, accepting whatever was thrown at her, but I thought of the old Mary, shouldering the tough work of a hill sheep farm alongside her husband, and the contrast was stark. As my own life was expanding, so hers had shrunk, and I was saddened.

UNEXPECTED NEWS ARRIVED from America. 'Walter seems to know everybody,' Martha wrote, 'and has numerous useful contacts. As a result of which I had my second hip replaced, at his expense, and am writing this from my hospital bed. I still hope to be back for Christmas, but I have to recuperate, so it won't be just yet. In the meantime, perhaps you two idle loafers could make a start on finding the necessary experts. But please don't use that chap we had before. He's all wind.'

'Is that what we are, Liam – "idle loafers"?'

He snorted. 'She's got a cheek. Good job she's the other side of a big ocean.'

'Does she say anything else?'

Liam consulted his phone. 'Not a lot. I guess she doesn't want to count her chickens. But from what she does say, I reckon she's got what she went for. Can't say I'm too surprised; Martha is very determined.'

'Maybe she does have charm and knows where to deploy it.'

Liam laughed. 'Just not on us.'

THROUGHOUT DECEMBER THE weather continued unsettled, even for Yorkshire: we had rain, high winds, fog and a scattering of snow. Temperatures dropped, and Liam was driven indoors. We both spent most of our time in the studio until the cold drove us to the farmhouse where we kept a fire going. I worked wearing fingerless gloves, hat, coat and scarf and still froze, but I was keen to get my myriad angels done. It was a test of my resolve, and I went at it with gritted – and sometimes chattering – teeth. I decided after all not to overdo the quirks of humour in the angelic ranks. While unbroken solemnity wasn't a goal, I felt that to have an angel knitting was probably a step too far into frivolity. However, a small group of cherubs with sheet music, conducted by a forbidding seraph, I thought would be acceptable, considering the number of times singing is mentioned in Revelation. I had just the final highlights to do when Martha rang and told us she'd be back some time in the fortnight before Christmas.

Meanwhile, I became increasingly worried about Liam's state of mind. The weeks we had spent together at Chibley since my return to Yorkshire had been almost carefree, both of us working on our projects, trying to keep warm, sharing meals and either talking excitedly or side by side in a friendly silence, happily occupied. Now, with Martha's return imminent, he seemed to descend into an altogether gloomier place, by turns morose and irritable. If I asked him if he was OK, he'd mutter something incomprehensible, his normally open face darkened and scowling. If I – however mildly – observed he seemed not quite his usual self he'd snap and tell me to back off. I was baffled, but left him to it. I'd never seen him in this mood before and felt I didn't know him well enough to understand what might be the problem. I hoped that when Martha returned, she – who knew him better than anyone – could get to the bottom of it. Apart from anything else, I was also having a few moments of my own of acute uncertainty. My first night at my new house was sleepless, although I was tired. The bed had come from Brant, and was comfortable and familiar enough, but the very room seemed strange, and I felt alien in it. I knew how foolish nocturnal alarms often were, and I still asked myself, 'What am I doing here? I don't belong here! I hardly know anyone. Have I made a terrible mistake?' In the end, around three in the morning, I got up, put on numerous layers with a fluffy bathrobe on top, thick socks and slippers on my feet, and made a cup of tea. I opened the curtains and looked down the garden, but of course all I could see was darkness. It was a cloudy night with no moon, and all my neighbours' lights were, unsurprisingly, off. At that moment I felt very small, vulnerable and alone. Much as I had wanted to leave Brant, much as my life there seemed suffocating, it was familiar and safe. John himself was safe. From the time we met, when I was an ignorant adolescent, he had been my bulwark against life's uncertainties. I was no longer that girl; I had matured and learned many things, and would normally have considered myself to be competent, self-reliant and positive. But that night nothing seemed sure. In the stillness of a windless night, I heard the rushing of the stream at the bottom of my garden and felt the earth itself tremble – which of course was nonsense. Was it because I had left behind everything I knew well? Was it just because John was no longer there, a steady reference point, even if one I'd wanted to shrug off? I was no stranger to survivor guilt, though rationally I knew I couldn't have changed the outcome for him; but now in the silent dark I plagued myself with useless questions that had no answer: had I really done my best for him? Not so much in the last few months before his death, but before, when I was remote: had he known just how much I was chafing at my humdrum, even meaningless, existence? Would he have seen it as a rejection of himself? I didn't want to think this, not now, in the light of all that had happened. Inwardly, uselessly, I told him I was sorry. He could be thoughtless, sometimes overbearing, occasionally insensitive, but he was very far from being a bad man, or a bad husband, and for a long time I had thought him the sum of all I had wanted. Now I felt I no longer knew what I wanted, or where to find it – if indeed it was to be found.

❖

THE NEXT DAY, gritty-eyed from broken sleep, with a headache threatening, I cycled to Chibley. I'd decided to plough on, in the teeth of my insecurities, with sketching in the third panel. After an hour or so the door banged and there was Liam, narrow-eyed and frowning. He grunted a greeting, made no attempt to start work, but stood behind me with his arms folded, watching me make tentative pencil strokes.

Eventually he cleared his throat. 'It'll be down to you to collect Martha from the airport,' he said abruptly. 'Seeing as you're the one with a car.'

I turned to him and spoke as mildly as I knew how. 'Yes, of course I'll collect her. But you'll come too, won't you?'

He shook his head. 'I'm going south, to my friends at Theasby. I'll probably stay there for Christmas too.'

I was baffled. 'Why, Liam? Don't you want to see Martha? Especially now, when she's got all these plans for Chibley?'

He shrugged, half turned away. 'That's just it,' he muttered. 'There'll be nothing for me here now all this is going on. It's good for Martha – she's got what she wanted. Not so good for me.'

'I don't understand.'

He gave a bitter little laugh. 'Don't you?'

I tried again. 'Surely Martha will need you, won't she?'

'Will she? As what? I can't see her needing an odd-job man, a hanger-on, in her new dispensation. And when the building work starts, my old barn will be one of the first to go. So I'll be jobless, homeless and broke – as usual. No, I can't stay. I have to look after my own interests. There's someone down in Leeds who's taking an interest in my work. I've got to go and talk to him, see if anything will come of it. I wish Martha well, but I don't belong here any more, if I ever did.' He looked up then, and I was grieved to see him look so wretched; but as I didn't know what Martha's plans were, there was little I could say to encourage him. 'I'll need to come back one more time,' he said. 'I'll have to leave some of my paintings here for now – there's only so many I can take with me. So I guess I'll see you again, Fen. Hope you get the triptych finished.' He smiled sadly. 'Oh yeah, Happy Christmas and all that.'

I shook my head, puzzled and aghast. 'Can't you just stay till Martha gets back?'

He shook his head. 'I don't want to be any kind of embarrassment. Best I go now.'

The loss of Liam's companionship, especially now that I too was feeling lost and adrift, was a huge blow – but what could I say? I had no claim on him. 'I'll miss you,' I managed.

Again that small, bitter smile. 'Will you? Well, I expect you won't for long. Bye, Fen.'

A FEW DAYS later I picked up Martha from Leeds Bradford Airport. I watched her as she left the customs hall, and she looked different: still using her stick, but more upright, her gait more fluent. She had even abandoned her usual black and looked quite smart in a blue and white jumper, a long navy-blue skirt and ankle boots, with a huge coat in some hairy fabric over the whole ensemble.

'Fen! There you are.'

I gave her a hug as I relieved her of her enormous suitcase. 'I see you've been shopping.'

She grinned. 'Just a bit.' Then she frowned. 'No Liam?'

'Ah. I'll bring you up to speed in the car.'

As we found our way out of the airport area, I told her what Liam had said. 'I tried to dissuade him, but I'm afraid I failed.'

Martha nodded and sighed. 'Don't worry. I'll do my best to sort him out. But I have a packed schedule. I've organised meetings so I can get the formal stuff under way before Christmas – my solicitor, for instance, and the surveyor and the building firm. We're bound to be held up by weather so the sooner we can get work started the better.'

'What exactly did you agree with your cousin?'

'Well, we had a lot of talk. In the end we decided on something quite simple. Walter is going to make me a substantial loan, as a private benefactor. That way we can avoid tax. There are other family members involved, but he's the chief contributor. Then when Chibley Art starts to make money I repay the loan, and that's where I need to make detailed arrangements, a contract if you like. There were some distant cousins who got quite fired up about the whole thing – said they wanted to come and visit. Good, I thought, spread the word! But I did put them off coming to Yorkshire in the winter. They need to wait till things are properly up and running.'

'And what about you? You seem to be walking so much better.'

'You can't imagine! The stick's just for a bit of extra support, as the op was so recent. I hope I'll be ditching it before too long.'

I signalled and carefully joined a thundering stream of traffic. 'From your messages I gather you were quite the honoured guest.'

'My dear, I was positively fêted! They were all immensely kind. I did feel a bit like an exhibit at times, but I'm not complaining. I couldn't have hoped for a better outcome.'

'I'm glad, Martha.'

She turned towards me in her seat. 'And what about you?' she asked. 'Are you holding up? You've had a fraught few months.'

'It's hard to say. Up and down. One minute enjoying freedom, the next terrified. I feel huge sadness for John, though – cut off so early, when there was so much he still wanted to do.'

'And the children?'

'They are grieving too, of course. But I'm looking forward to a visit very soon – Alice and Rory are coming to see me on their way to Rory's people for Christmas. I hope you'll meet them.'

Martha nodded. 'So you're staying?'

I took a breath. 'I guess I am. I've bought a house.'

Martha clapped her hands. 'Have you indeed! Where?'

'It's the smallest of places, Knapp's Bridge. Do you know it?'

'I know where it is. Did you know you can get from there to Chibley across country?'

'I didn't. And I don't know why it's called Knapp's Bridge when there's no bridge in sight.'

'Ah, now there I can help you. Way back there used to be a very inconvenient stream that made access to the village difficult, especially when it rained. So a local farmer, one Mr Knapp, built a bridge. This was at the beginning of the nineteenth century, I believe. The bridge wasn't a great success – it got washed away. Since then the stream has been diverted, but the name stuck. What's your place like?'

I told her. 'The annexe is currently full of furniture from my old house. Piled up against the walls, tables on top of cupboards – you get the picture. I got rid of some of it in Brant, but I'm not too sure what to do with the rest. I'm thinking of dropping a note in to all my neighbours inviting them to come and help themselves. I thought it would be a good way of getting to know them. I might do the same at church, if Steve agrees.'

'There's a charity in Richmond if there's stuff you can't shift. Takes furniture in good condition. I can give you the address.'

'Thanks. I really can barely move.'

For a long moment Martha was silent as I negotiated the narrow roads above the valley, the steep climbs and descents and sharp bends typical of the journey to Chibley. Once we were again on an A-road we both breathed more freely. I came to a grateful halt outside the farmhouse as the evening drew in. 'I lit a fire in your kitchen, Martha, but it may have gone out.'

She climbed out of the car and looked round. 'It feels as if I've been away a long time.' She turned to me with a thoughtful expression. 'Has Liam been working in my absence? On his art, I mean.'

'Yes, he really has. He took some stuff with him, but there's more in the studio. Why don't you come and look before it gets too dark?'

She followed me up the track, and I unlocked the door and switched on the light. She went straight up to where my third panel rested on its rickety support. There was little on it but sketchy pencil marks. 'Where's the second one?' she demanded.

I showed her where it rested against the wall, and she scrutinised it minutely. 'You've learned a lot,' she said. 'Maybe you can tell me what you have in mind for the final one.'

'I will – when we're indoors in the warm. Liam's stuff is over there, and there's some more in the back room.' I was intrigued to know what she thought. I believed Liam's work to be excellent, but I was not much of a judge, whereas Martha was.

I saw her nod as she looked. 'He's really upped his game,' she said quietly. 'This is some of the best work he's done. And he's probably taken what he thinks is the best away with him.' She looked up at me. 'Is this what he's been working on while I was away? There's so much of it.'

'Yes, he was out sketching when the weather wasn't too bad, and back here when it got too fierce. He certainly worked incredibly hard.'

'What was his mood then?'

'Oh, he was happy. Full of ideas, full of energy, on a high. Which made it even weirder to hear him so… I don't know, bitter, defeated, the other day. I'm worried about him, Martha. Will he be OK?'

She nodded. 'I'll make sure of it. Right, time to warm up my old bones. Let's get the kettle on.'

FOR THE NEXT few days, before things started to close down for Christmas, Martha was extremely busy with meetings. She was hardly ever at home, and now she was able to drive herself. Once I had finished in the studio I'd light a fire for her and put a meal together. On this evening I'd made a start on a wash for panel three, my brushes were soaking and I was preparing to leave when my phone rang – Martha's gravelly voice. 'Fen, I'm on my way back. Don't rush off – there are things I want to run past you.' I had barely ended the call when my phone buzzed again. 'Mum, it's me. Rory and I will be with you some time on the twenty-third.'

'It will be lovely to see you, sweetheart.' Then I had a moment of panic. I had hardly any time to buy presents, and I hadn't thought about it at all. I didn't even know what I, or anyone else, was planning for Christmas.

The next few days were frantic. I'd been invited to Christmas with Mary and Anne, but I didn't want Martha to be alone, and at that time I'd thought Liam would be with us as well. One day I piled my boot up with supplies and stocked Martha's freezer. The next I decided to drive up to Richmond for a better selection of shops where I might find something approaching suitable Christmas presents. At the same time, I thought, I would visit the charity that Martha had recommended. I'd already searched their website and went armed with a list of items I wanted to dispose of and some photos. The sooner my little house in Knapp's Bridge was free of clutter, the sooner it might feel like home – or so I told myself. I didn't expect any movement till well into January, but it wouldn't hurt to get the process under way.

It was cold, that day I drove north, a hard, grey cold with no wind. I was unfamiliar with the town, and it took me a while to find a parking space. With Christmas so close the pavements were thronged and the car parks full. I spent half an hour with the charity, who decided on what they wanted and when they would come to collect it. Much thought went into the size of the van that would take my things away. I looked at a few shops, but ideas were in short supply. Eventually I found some local crafts, gift-boxed wines and cheeses, and books on travel for Alice and Rory, including a quirky one full of pitfalls to avoid and humorous anecdotes. My bags were heavy as I trudged back to the car. I debated whether to stop here for lunch but decided to go home instead. My last port of call was a shop selling all things seasonal, where I picked up wrapping paper, decorations, and a few cards.

As I left the shop, I saw something that made my skin prickle. On the opposite side of the road stood a large, traditional country hotel, once probably a coaching inn, and undoubtedly the foremost place to stay in this modest Northern town. In the small parking area in front of its main door a sleek black car had drawn up, and out of it, one skinny leg at a time, unmistakable in her calf-length fur coat and matching hat, stepped Olive Wastwell.

I was bare yards away, and I called out, 'Olivia!' She looked in the direction of my voice, and I was certain she'd seen and recognised me, but she merely turned away, adjusted her handbag and disappeared through the door with her nose in the air. Did I imagine it, or did I really see her expression before she blanked me – a look of guilty discomfort, almost of fear?

I called in at Chibley on my way home and found Martha sitting at the kitchen table surrounded by papers. 'I just saw Olive in Richmond,' I told her. 'Marching into that big hotel in the market square. A bit of a change, I imagine, from those grand places in New York I've seen pictures of, with their gilded entrances and obsequious doormen.'

'Ah, she's back, then.'

'Where did she go?'

'Word is she disappeared off to Europe somewhere, just after all that business after Storm Doris and her trying to smash your panel, stupid woman,' Martha said. 'Did she see you?'

'I'm sure she did, though she pretended she didn't. And she looked horrified.'

'Small wonder.' She got up from the table. 'But let's not think about her, Fen. She's history, or so I hope. There's someone I'd like you to meet.' She picked up her phone and tapped in a brief message. 'Chibley's new artistic director.'

'Oh! You worked quickly, Martha.'

She grinned smugly. 'No, not really.'

The door opened, and Liam appeared in the doorway. 'May I come in?'

'Don't stand on ceremony, foolish man,' Martha said irritably. 'What do you think, Fen?'

My mouth fell open and I blinked. 'Liam – you're back!'

He was smiling broadly. 'So I am.'

'And you – you're the artistic director?'

'Well, I will be, once there's somewhere to be a director of,' Liam said. 'But I'm already about to collect a salary, so I'm told.'

'Martha, you are extremely devious,' I said. 'But probably a genius. I can't think of anyone better.'

'Told you I'd fix things,' Martha said. 'But there's another reason why he's grinning like the Cheshire cat.'

Liam crossed the room and hugged me. 'Remember that bloke I was seeing in Leeds?' I nodded. 'He liked the stuff I showed him, and in the spring I'm going to be part of an exhibition he's staging.'

'Wow,' I said. 'That's brilliant news! I'm so pleased for you. You've worked unbelievably hard recently, and you deserve recognition.'

I saw a flush stain his cheekbones, and he looked down, shoulders hunched. 'I'm sorry I was such a whinging fool, that day before I left,' he mumbled. 'I hate to think what you must have thought of me.'

I patted his arm. 'I felt sorry for you, that's all. You were like me – a bit lost and lonely and vulnerable. I empathised.'

He looked startled. 'You? But you always seem so together.' Then he checked himself and looked embarrassed. 'I'm forgetting, aren't I? How could I do that? You just had your old man die on you. I'm sorry, Fen. I'm a self-obsessed insensitive moron.'

I laughed. 'You're no such thing. Now if you'd claimed to be an exaggerating drama queen, I'd be more inclined to agree.'

'Hear, hear,' Martha interrupted. 'It's a good job his work is so damn good, because I couldn't put up with all this poor-me posing. Now, children, enough of all this frivolity. What do you reckon – is the sun over the yardarm? I'm parched.'

As DUSK FELL I heard the familiar sound of my small car that I had given to Alice and Rory, its engine labouring as it came up the steep incline of the Chibley track from the road. I looked out of the door of the studio, where I'd been working all day on the third Revelation panel, and saw lights bouncing around as whoever was driving – I suspected Rory, as Alice was a hesitant driver – took every muddy corner at speed, spraying gravel right and left. I watched bemused, expecting at any minute to see the wheels skid uncontrollably. Clearly the driver had no notion of the perils of farm tracks in winter. The car came to a lurching halt outside the farmhouse. A door opened, and Rory clambered out. He stretched his arms up, and I thought how confining my car must have been to a man of his bulk over a journey of many hours. The passenger door opened, and Alice folded herself out rather more gracefully. I noticed that the back seat was piled high, obscuring any view out of the rear window. Seeing Alice look round I waved until I caught her eye, and she bounded up the track to where I stood in the lighted doorway and into my waiting arms.

'Agh, Mum, we should have been here so much earlier!' she wailed. 'We got horribly lost. Rory swore he knew where he was going, but he really didn't. And these little lanes are a nightmare!'

'Well, you're here now,' I said.

Rory lumbered up to us and gave me a more decorous hug.

'I think my little car must be a bit uncomfortable for you,' I said.

He noticed my smile and returned it wryly. 'I probably need to ease off on the beers.'

'Come inside while I clean up,' I said. 'Then we can go down and meet Martha and Liam.'

I left them wandering around the studio while I cleaned brushes and tidied up. I heard Alice exclaim, 'Mum, is this yours?' I emerged from the back room, brushes in hand, and saw her standing in front of the second panel that was still curing, awaiting sealing and framing; I hadn't managed to get it finished in time for Christmas.

'Yes, panel two. The first one's in the church, of course. And I've just begun blocking in some of the third one.'

Alice's eyes were round behind her glasses. 'It's amazing. I don't understand it, but it's fascinating.' She indicated smaller canvases that were stacked to dry. 'What about these? They're really different.'

'They're Liam's. Newly appointed artistic director, and twice the artist I will ever be.'

❋

It was a merry evening with the five of us in good spirits. Martha was a different woman since her operation, almost free of pain. I'd prepared a meal earlier, and Liam was finishing it off, making sure potatoes were roasted to a turn and nothing burnt. Martha opened a couple of bottles of wine and the party became quite loud, ice well and truly broken, with everyone talking at once.

'Steady!' I protested as glasses were refilled. 'Two of us have to drive tonight.'

'Hah!' Martha said. 'Nobody will bother you between here and Knapp's Bridge.'

After we'd eaten, the men volunteered to wash up. Alice leaned back in her chair, puffing out her cheeks. 'I'm totally bloated,' she said. 'I haven't eaten and drunk this much in weeks. Mum, can we take a walk outside? I'm feeling in need of fresh air.'

'Gladly, but I think you'll find it a bit more than fresh.'

Outside, well wrapped up, Alice tucked her gloved hand in the crook of my elbow and we walked slowly up beyond the studio to the grassy area beyond. I had my torch; I knew just how dark it would be.

Alice shivered. 'You weren't kidding, Mum. It's freezing! But it was really hot indoors with that fire blazing.' She looked at me sideways. 'Are you OK?'

'Yes, I'm fine.'

'I mean, not sad or lonely?'

'Sometimes, I guess. I've made a big change. And of course I am sad when I think about your poor dad and all he suffered.'

'Yeah, me too.' She was silent for a while as we walked along the side of the fence that separated the studio from the fields behind. 'Do you think you would have come back to Brant? I mean, if Dad hadn't got sick, if everything had gone as he hoped, like the cruise?'

'I suppose so. That was the plan.'

'What about your life here?'

Now it was my turn to take a moment to think. 'I don't know, love. I guess I'd have wanted to come back here a fair bit. It's hard to know how things would have been.'

She pondered this, then she took me by surprise. 'Do you ever think you might remarry?'

I laughed. 'Not really, no! It's a bit soon to be thinking such thoughts, if I ever do. Why, do you have a candidate in mind?'

She grinned. 'Liam's nice.'

'Alice! Are you matchmaking? I'd have thought you'd be the last person to be happy seeing me with someone else.'

She sighed. 'I guess it would be a bit weird. But I've changed in the last year. The time with that total rat Ormerod taught me a lot. And you're human, aren't you? And not so very old. Well, quite old, but not completely finished.'

I pretended to box her ears, and she ducked out of the way, grinning.

'I thought you'd hate it,' I said, sobering. 'You were always such a daddy's girl.'

'Yeah, I was,' she said sadly. 'And in some ways I always will be. But I'm Rory's girl now, and the fact is Dad's not here, and you are, and I care what happens to you.'

'Thank you, sweetheart. The feeling's mutual. Aren't you cold? Don't you want to go back?'

'They should have finished the washing up by now,' Alice said, a sparkle in her baby-blue eyes. We turned back down the track. 'Going back to Liam, he's really quite attractive for an older guy.'

'*Older?* Alice, he's not even forty!'

'You know what I mean. And it's pretty obvious how he feels about you. He watches you all the time.'

'Nonsense.'

'No, it's not. He's probably holding back to spare your feelings, seeing as you are a grieving widow.'

I laughed. 'Honestly, child, you are ridiculous!'

Alice shook her head. 'We'll see.'

WE ALL TRIED to sober up with coffee, and then Alice and Rory followed me in their car as I led them back to Knapp's Bridge, where the annexe was now more or less empty.

'I haven't had much time to clean up properly in here,' I said. 'The van only came yesterday to take the furniture away, so it's a bit dusty.'

Alice yawned. 'We're used to it, aren't we, Rory?' She gave him a meaningful look. 'Rory's a slob. He leaves his dishes mouldering in the sink all day.'

'And you,' Rory retorted, 'leave your underwear dripping in the bathroom for days on end.'

'Right, you two. Here are some towels. You go and take up residence and do your bickering out of earshot. There's tea and coffee, and milk in the fridge, plenty of hot water if you want a shower, and I'll see you in the morning.'

AFTER A GREAT deal of unnecessary flapping about they finally got on the road by late morning. 'It's a fair way up to Scotland,' I said. 'And you don't want to arrive in the dark if you can help it.'

'No,' Alice said, frowning in Rory's direction. 'We might get lost again.' She gave me a hug. 'It's going to be a weird kind of Christmas, isn't it?' There were tears in her eyes. 'Not like last Christmas, when we still had Dad. Do you think he was ill even then?'

I heaved a sigh. 'I think maybe he was, love. He was so tired, and he didn't have much of an appetite. I thought he'd just been overdoing it at work with the merger, and all that batting back and forth to America. Nobody knew, then, that there was more to it than that. And then I was back here, and Dan in New York, and you and Rory at uni, and whenever I spoke to him on the phone he said he was OK. Honestly, I don't think he knew himself – not until much later.'

Alice nodded. 'Yeah, and then it was too late.' She was silent, staring at her feet, scuffing the ground with the toe of her shoe. 'Things won't ever be the same, will they?'

'No, they won't,' I said as gently as I could. 'But there'll be happy times for us all even so. And your dad won't be forgotten, whatever happens. He'll always be a part of us.'

'Yeah, he will. Oh well, better get going, I suppose. We'll see you before we start our travels.' She hugged me again. 'Happy Christmas, Mum.'

BY THE TIME I saw them again Christmas and New Year were over. They called in for a few hours on their way south, with their plans laid and tickets bought. 'First stop Bangkok!' Alice said gleefully.

'You will keep in touch, I hope,' I said.

'Of course we will. We'll send photos as well. But now I guess you won't see us for a few months.' She looked around at the bleak environs of Chibley, a grey sky under a scattering of melting snow, and shivered. 'I'll be very glad to be somewhere warm.'

THE BEGINNING OF the year was, on the whole, mild, wet and changeable, but by mid-January, at least for a time, we enjoyed more settled weather. This coincided with the first sheepdog trial Thom had entered with Sadie. He explained that while Sadie was already a fine sheepdog she had yet to enter any trials, and she had to win a maiden trial before she could compete in something more advanced. Winter was traditionally the time when inexperienced dogs and handlers were encouraged to improve their skills, and in mid-January Will piled Thom and Sadie into his truck and drove them to Penrith, which was the nearest trial they could find. I'd asked Thom to let me know how they got on, and in the middle of the afternoon I had an excited phone call from him to say that Sadie had swept the board. I was not at all surprised. 'She did so well,' Thom said. 'Even when I messed up a command, she kind of interpreted.'

'So, where to from here, Thom?' I asked.

'I'll probably put her in for a couple more over the next few months,' Thom said. 'So we can keep our hand in. Because I'm learning, just like she is. Then in the summer we can probably take on an open.' In the background I heard Will – not his words, but his note of caution. Will took nothing for granted.

At Chibley, as soon as the holiday period was over, and fuelled by Martha's impatience, building work began with excavations prior to turning the farm track, which at times the weather rendered impassable, into a proper road. If in the future clients came to Chibley they would need reliable access and somewhere to park, and meanwhile a good road would be vital for supplies and workers coming and going. The architect, surveyor and the man in overall charge of the proposed works were often on site, and I watched them tramp through mud and grass and puddles, heads together in deliberation, sometimes with Martha in rubber boots and waterproof, waving her arms around as she tried to convey her vision.

I was keenly aware of all this going on, because I had finally started on the third panel, and heard voices outside almost every day. The second panel, now cured, I had sealed with a little help from Liam, and it was due to be transported to town for framing.

Liam was often in the studio working on his own projects. 'There's not a lot of call for an artistic director yet,' he said with some irony. 'Since there's no school to be director of. So I might as well get this series finished for the exhibition.' He often paused, sometimes to make coffee, sometimes simply to stand and watch me work.

'You've come a long way,' he said.

I smiled. 'That's thanks to you to a considerable degree.'

'No, you're a quick learner. Want to talk me through the composition?'

'OK.' The stretched canvas was supported on its easels, and I took a moment to adjust it. 'That should be all right, I think.'

'Just as long as we don't have a vengeful Olive creating mayhem,' Liam said.

'I wonder what she's doing back here,' I murmured. 'She could go anywhere.'

'I know,' Liam said. 'It's like this place has some kind of magnetic quality for Olive. Before she was ill this last time, she used to come regularly, almost every summer.'

'Yep, she's a funny one, for sure,' I said. 'Anyway, here we have a blank canvas – just a nice brownish wash all over and a few pencil marks. It's going to be the usual mishmash of images, but there are two overarching themes.'

'Two?'

'Yes. We're looking at the end times here, so there has to be the theme of judgement, God calling us all to account. But also there's the theme of redemption. Up the top here, on a throne, the Lamb. And here—' I gestured, '—the great angel holding the scroll with the seven seals that no one but the Redeemer can open. As each seal breaks, a horseman appears: white, red, black and yellow-green, the colour of death.'

'So that's why I've seen lots of sketches of horses.'

'Yes, but I still don't think I've got them quite right.'

'I've got a book that might help,' Liam said. 'I'll look it out for you. So, horses, angels, and Martha said martyrs under the altar – is that right?'

'Yes, and the cosmic drama too – falling stars and so on. But then the more homespun Good Shepherd. Somewhere down here, on the left.' Liam was silent, staring at the canvas, probably trying to imagine what I had described. 'Well, you've set yourself another mammoth task, Fen.'

'I know. Can I pull it off?'

'I have faith.' He smiled kindly. Then he said, 'Any news from your young travellers?'

I pulled out my phone and found the latest photos they'd sent: a carefree Alice leaping into a tropical pool, palm trees in the background. Liam peered over my shoulder as I clicked through.

'You're very lucky, Fen. To have a family like yours.' There was sadness and longing in his voice.

'All grown up and scattered across the globe,' I said lightly.

'Even so.'

❋

We were warned. Anyone who'd listened to the national or local news would have known that unusually ferocious weather was expected. Farmers started to lay in extra feed for their animals well before the bad weather struck, especially because there was little hay to be had: the summer of 2017 had been a particularly poor year for it. Trailer-loads of sheep cake and fodder beets arrived at Tubside, where the problem was where to store it. There were empty barns at Whitepost, but if the anticipated snow was deep it would be difficult to get across the fields. Will Wharton was concerned to time the moving of his flocks at just the right moment: too late and they could be stranded in inaccessible snow drifts; too early and he would be giving them expensive bought-in feed for longer. While the worst of the weather held off, they were best left on the high moors where there was still some pasture, supplemented daily by dwindling hay-stocks carried on two quad bikes with trailers.

The deep cold started to set in on February the twenty-second, with steeply falling temperatures and sharp overnight frosts. A couple of days later Will began to bring in his flocks in batches, down to the low pastures surrounding the farm where he could keep an eye on them, rescue them if necessary, and ensure they were fed.

The snow arrived just when it had been predicted, on the twenty-seventh. All day we waited. The sky felt heavy, as if it were sitting on top of our heads, a dark, uniform grey. It had been windy the previous few days, but now an ominous calm descended. The last batch of sheep were gathered off the moors as the first flurries of snow whirled down, and by the time they came in sight a howling wind was blowing stinging sheets of snow in all directions. I was at Tubside that day, and I heard one of the men say to Will, 'I think there are still a few more up there. But we couldn't risk hanging around.' Will shook his head resignedly. 'Well, if we lose some, it can't be helped. I'm not sending you out again, neither man nor dog. Let's get them penned, and you get home while you can.'

I stayed at Tubside that night at Bess's insistence, sleeping under the eaves under a gaily patterned patchwork quilt made by someone's grandmother, and before I turned in I looked out into the storm. Already drifts were piling up against walls and gates, some of which had almost completely disappeared, and the noise of the wind was like an army of angry ghosts.

I thought it would never end – but the next morning there was a lull, and by the afternoon the snowfall and the wind had abated.

'It'll be back,' Bess said. 'It might give us a rest for a few hours, now that the wind's changed direction. But it'll be back. It's not spent yet. You're welcome to stay, Fen, but if there's something you need to be doing or somewhere you need to be now's the time.'

'I've been invited to a meal at Mary and Anne's this evening,' I said. 'I reckon I can walk down there. They might even have gritted the main road by now. As long as they don't expect me to arrive in my party dress! This bad-weather gear is all I've got.'

Bess nodded. 'You should be all right. It's not above a mile down to the road. Will's cleared the worst of it off the track. But get going before dark. And if it comes down hard again, stay at Anne's. We don't want to lose you in a drift.'

I put on my many layers topped with a waterproof jacket, scarf, gloves, grippy boots and my hat with its built-in light. I had to wrap my scarf over the lower half of my face, because the air was so cold. I pulled my hat down well over my forehead so all you could see were my eyes, and they were watering freely.

The road had been gritted, but only through the town, and now where heedless cars had passed there was slush which would turn to solid ice if the temperature fell any further. Anne's cottage stood just back from the road, but it was a battle just crossing her small front garden to her door. Someone had cleared the area immediately in front of the door, but there was snow piled halfway up her windows.

'Oh, Fen, there you are! Come in, come in. We thought you might not come.'

I peeled off my outer layers and left my boots in her porch. 'I'd have phoned, Anne. Anyway, I wouldn't willingly miss a meal cooked by you!'

I greeted Mary, who was putting logs on the fire. The little sitting room was warm.

'What's the road like?' Mary asked.

'Not too bad. The gritters have been out. But I haven't come from Knapp's Bridge, just from Tubside. I stayed with them last night.'

'I hope Will got his sheep in all right,' Mary said.

'Most of them, I think.'

She hesitated. 'Did you see Sadie?'

'No,' I told her. 'She's shut up safe with the others, and they've got plenty of straw and old rugs. Will looks after his dogs.'

'I know,' Mary said.

ONCE WE'D DEVOURED Anne's excellent pie and washed it down with Amos's cider, our talk turned inevitably to the weather.

'Bess says there'll be more,' I said.

Mary and Anne both nodded. 'She's right there,' Anne said. 'Once the wind changes direction again it'll be back – probably worse. Still, we're all right, aren't we, Mary? Plenty of logs and a full larder and freezer. We can sit it out. I'm keeping my eye out for some of the older neighbours, though, the ones who aren't so sprightly. If the snow doesn't stop me I'll pop round and see if they're OK. I just hope the pipes don't freeze.'

'Me, I hope we can still use the phone,' Mary said. 'If the winds get high we could have lines down.'

'Do you remember that terrible winter, Mary? 1947?'

'Not really,' Mary said with a smile. 'I were just a toddler. But I've heard it spoken of many a time.'

'Ah, well, I'm a bit older than you,' Anne said. 'I can remember being quite happy when I didn't have to go to school! We were cut off for a week. They had to come and dig us out in the end, us and our neighbours. My mother told me they found old Jim Pickett dead in his bed when they finally got to his place. Mind you, he was pushing ninety, poor old chap.'

'But you lived up on top of the moor when you were a kid,' Mary said. 'They always get it worst up there.'

'I dare say the families who live that way now kept their children home,' Anne said. 'Otherwise they'd not get them back.'

'I've heard talk about that winter too,' I said. 'Do you think this time will be as bad?'

'According to some of the old folk where Peter is,' Mary said, 'the ones in their eighties now, they reckon nothing could be as bad as that. They remember it well – they'd have been teenagers then. But the older you get, the more you think things were better – or worse! – than now. I hope they're right. I don't fancy being snowed in.'

'What will be, will be,' Anne said stoically. 'Anyway, if we lose the electric I've got a little camping gas, so we can make tea. There's a deck of cards and board games in the cupboard. We'll just have to manage. There's plenty worse off.' I saw Mary roll her eyes – discreetly. Anne got up from her squashy old armchair whose defects were hidden under layers of patchwork blankets. 'Let's see what it's doing.' She went to the window and twitched back the curtains. 'Look at that – not a flake of snow in sight! And there's a moon. Lovely and bright it is – like a picture.' She turned back to us. 'I wouldn't want to be out in it though. What do you reckon – is it time to put kettle on? While we can?'

She was in her kitchen, singing quietly to herself, when I heard the phone ring in the hall. 'Anne – that's your phone.'

'Oh, is it? I didn't hear it – must be getting deaf.' She left the room, and Mary said, 'I don't know about "getting". She doesn't hear half the things I say to her.'

We heard Anne's voice from the hall, and then she came back in. 'It's Will Wharton. Wants to speak to you, Mary.'

Mary got up, frowning. 'Now what does he want?' she murmured.

'He didn't say.'

Mary went out, and the next thing we heard was a distinct 'What? What do you mean, Will?' Then there was nothing but a low voice that sounded distinctly alarmed, but no clear words. Anne and I looked at one another, puzzled and anxious.

Mary came in and closed the door carefully. She turned to us, leaning on the back of a chair. 'I really don't know why he told me,' she whispered. 'What am I supposed to do? Except go off my head with worry?'

I jumped up and helped her back to her chair. She was shaking. 'Whatever is it, Mary?'

'It's Sadie. She's gone missing.'

'What?' I said stupidly. 'But she was shut up in the barn with the others.'

'That's what Will said. But she found her way out somehow. Maybe somewhere there was a hole, or a loose bit of timber, behind something where nobody'd noticed, and we know Sadie isn't a big dog.' I saw her clench her fists. 'Will was asking me if she were here, with us.'

'But why, Mary?' Anne said. She took a large handkerchief from her apron pocket and wiped her eyes. 'Why would she venture out – in this?'

Mary and I looked at one another, and I knew we were thinking the same thing.

'When they got the sheep down yesterday,' I said, 'I heard one of the men tell Will that some of them were still up on the moor. The snow was coming down in blinding sheets, and Will said no one was to go back to look for them.'

'That's where she's gone, isn't it?' Mary whispered. 'Were her eighteen old ladies among the missing sheep, Fen?'

'They didn't say, Mary.' We were all quiet for a moment, even Anne. Then I said, looking at my old friend, 'But I reckon I know where she'll be. If, God forbid, she's not buried in some snowdrift, if she managed to track down those sheep somehow, we know where she'll be heading for.'

Mary looked up at me, and a tiny gleam of hope sparked in her eyes. 'Do you think there's a chance, Fen?'

'I'm no shepherd,' I said. 'But I believe in that dog. And I'm going to see if I can find her.'

There was a gasp. 'No, Fen!' Anne wailed. 'You can't go out up on the moor in this! It could change in a moment. We could lose you as well.'

I said nothing, simply went into the chilly hallway and started putting on my outside gear. Holding my boots in my hand, I came back into the warm room. 'Look,' I said quietly to the two old ladies. 'There's nothing you can say to stop me. But the moon is up, so I'll see where I'm going. I'm well wrapped, and I have two torches and my phone. That won't be much use for communication, but it has a powerful light. I will be careful, because I don't want to end up buried in a drift either. And I promise to go no further than the barn. If she's not there, then I'll accept defeat. But I have to try.' Mary reached out and wordlessly grabbed my hand. 'Anne dear, if you want to help, how about you put up a sandwich and a flask of tea? If the weather turns and I have to spend a night in a freezing barn, I'll need some sustenance.'

Anne, now visibly weeping, nodded and took herself into the kitchen.

'Fen,' Mary said, 'I beg you, take care. No sheep, no dog on earth, not even Sadie, is worth your life.'

'I know.'

'But if you truly are determined, don't go over the fields from here. Don't head to Tubside. Go down to Whitepost. It's a bit further, but you know the way from there. In this snow it'd be all too easy to get disoriented. Landmarks – gates, walls, anything you might recognise – could be covered up. And you'll need a stick. Anne will have one you can borrow.' She sighed. 'If I had the words that would dissuade you, I'd speak them now. But I know you. You always were a headstrong lass.'

Twenty minutes later, amid more advice from them and more promises from me, I stepped out. The pavement was iced up and slippery, so I walked in the road. The moon, almost full, sailed in a sky so dark it seemed as if you could stretch out and touch it, and it would feel like black satin. A sprinkling of stars was visible too. I looked at my phone: it was half past eight. As I walked, not one car passed me, and I saw no one. It was a beautiful night in a hard, lonely way, but the air was frigid, and I wrapped my scarf twice round my face.

At the turning to Whitepost I took a deep breath. Now the going was much more difficult. Someone in a tractor had been here, and I tried to follow the tracks, but they soon turned off. I slipped and slithered and waded through drifts. It was hard going, and I soon felt weary, with aching calves and raw chest. I made it up to the bridge where, on the left, the land sloped down. Here the sign to Whitepost was up to half its height in snow, and I could see the roofs of the cottages below me, and beyond them the farmhouse, white in a white landscape. They looked as they were – uninhabited; no cheerful light shone from those windows.

I paused for a moment, trying to get my bearings. Everything was different under the snow: where was the gate to the hill? I looked both ways but could see nothing. Using Anne's stick to keep me on my feet, I plunged right and up, hoping my memory wouldn't cheat me.

In the end the stick found the wall before I crashed into it and injured myself. Now I crept along the wall, feeling my way with the stick, and eventually I found the gate, further along than I'd thought and half buried in snow. There was no possibility of opening it, so very awkwardly, stick in hand and backpack bouncing, I managed to clamber over. My foot slipped at the top and I fell gracelessly into a drift. For once I was grateful for the cushion.

To my surprise, through the dead silence of the night, I heard the sound of running water off to my left – the beck that flowed crosswise down the hill. Not all of it was frozen, so it seemed. Now I knew where I was, and my spirits lifted. I struck across the hill, always upwards but slanting left. But my mood was soon to be shattered. A ripple of wind brushed across my face, strengthening to a gust. In a moment heavy cloud descended, blotting out moon and stars and obscuring my vision. With fumbling fingers, numb despite my gloves, I switched on the light in my hat, and the view it gave made my stomach drop. Fat flakes of snow were whirling down, propelled by a driving wind that seemed to change direction every few seconds, so that I was rapidly becoming disoriented. The going was less heavy, because the wind was blowing the lying snow as well, and from time to time I could even see brief glimpses of green under my feet. But the noise of the wind was deafening and terrifying, howling and wailing like a host of souls in hellish torment.

My stick found a large rock – suddenly, so that my arm was jarred. I crouched down beside it, on the side I thought must be away from the wind, but it offered little shelter. I tried to think. Where had I come to? I guessed I was about halfway up, and I told myself all I needed was to reach the crest, and then the barn would be close. I staggered upright, almost blown over by the force of the wind, and ploughed on. The snow was blinding – I could see nothing, and I risked veering completely off course. I turned and began to trudge backwards, keeping my eyes on the ground, inching back with painful slowness. The wind was freezing as well as wild, gusty and loud, and I felt my face turn to ice. My feet were already without any feeling. In the end I had to turn round and go forward, and to my surprise and relief the hill came to an end before me, and there was nothing but snow-whipped blackness. I felt my feet lurch forward as the ground dipped, and I knew I had reached the crest. I peered into the darkness, hunting with ice-crusted eyes for the solid shape of the barn, but there was no sign of it. Had I gone completely astray? All my confidence drained away. I had thought I knew the way, but now I was lost on a bleak hill in a blizzard, frozen and frightened. I fell to my knees, oblivious of the freezing snow, and prayed – incoherently. I said to myself that this was what I should have done before I began, but in my ridiculous pride I'd stepped out: not heedless, but trusting too far in my own powers – which, in the face of this tempest, were as nothing.

I got to my feet, slow and stiff, and looked round in a circle. For a few moments, miraculously it seemed, the wind dropped with unnerving suddenness, and the snow slowed to a steady fall. High above me, somewhere where there was no storm, no biting wind, no featureless landscape, a solitary star twinkled before it too was extinguished. In that tiny moment I heard a familiar sound: a sheep bleating. Somewhere near was another living being, and I plunged on towards it. Moments later a great wall reared up before me, darker even than the surrounding darkness: the barn. My eyes filled with tears of relief, and I muttered heartfelt thanks as I laid my hands on its solid bulk.

I felt my way round it, because I seemed to have come from the side, and there was the door, leaning outwards on its broken hinge. I edged along the wall and slipped inside, into the relative peace of a stout building made to resist the wildest of elements.

I squatted on the cold earth floor, away from the door where snow had blown in and piled up, and wrapped my arms around my body, shuddering and wheezing. For that moment I was only thinking about myself, somehow alive, uninjured, safe – despite my folly. But then bit by bit my brain unfroze, and I remembered what I had come for. I stood, reluctantly went out and back the way I'd come. This, I thought, was where the bleating had come from. As I rounded the corner of the building several pairs of eyes met me, gleaming in the light from my head torch. From the red marking on their rumps I recognised them as Tubside ewes, and there were about ten of them. I spoke to them in a low, comforting voice. 'I'll see about some hay in a moment, ladies.' I edged further round the building where the walled enclosure was and found my way along its edge to the opening. There was movement within it, and under a blanket of snow, huddled together, were the Whitepost ewes, looking at me hopefully. But where was Sadie? Could it be, small as she was, that she had driven her charges to safety and then, overcome with exhaustion, lost her own life in a deep, suffocating drift?

In the end I nearly fell over her. She was lying across the entrance to the enclosure, almost entirely swallowed up in the snow, just an ear and her nose showing.

'Oh, Sadie!' I breathed, almost choking. I bent down and gathered her up in my arms. She was light, stiff, and deadly cold. 'Please, please don't be dead.' But I was terribly afraid that my mad attempt had met with the worst of failures.

I carried her into the barn and laid her down. I pulled handfuls of precious hay from the bales stacked there and rubbed her body from head to tail till she seemed drier. On the shelf were some rough grey blankets, and I swaddled her, paws and all, and held her hard against me, trying to share such warmth as I had. 'Please, Lord, let her not be dead.' Her eyes remained closed, and I couldn't detect any breathing, but with the wind now increasing in ferocity outside I probably wouldn't have heard a choir of angels singing. I smoothed the fur from her forehead. 'Come on, Sadie. For Mary, for Thom, for me. You wonderful, brave girl. We need you to live.'

In all my life, before and after, there can have been no better moment than when that heroic creature opened liquid brown eyes, gave a little cough, struggled a bit in her wrapping of blanket, then looked up at me and licked my hand. 'Oh, Sadie! Thank God. You did it.' I hugged her close and wept.

Not for long. I recovered myself; I needed to act. I pulled off my backpack and, leaving Sadie swaddled, I pulled huge armfuls of hay from the stacked bales. Holding it close so it didn't blow uselessly away, I slipped out of the door and round to the side as quickly as I could. I scattered the hay at the feet of the Tubside ewes first, and they fell to eagerly. I went back inside, grabbed more hay, and found my way to the enclosure where the Whitepost ewes were waiting, bleating anxiously. 'That's your lot for now,' I told them. 'Now I have to see to your saviour.'

Gratefully I went inside the barn, where I found Sadie trying to throw off the blanket. 'Hold on a minute,' I said to her. 'Stay where you are. The sheep are OK.' I remembered seeing an old metal bowl when we'd been here in better weather. I took it down and once more ventured outside. The wind was fiercer now, and savagely cold. With hands that had no feeling, I scooped up snow into the bowl. Inside again, I squatted beside my backpack and took out the flask of tea. I poured some into the bowl, melting the mound of snow. Shivering, I took off one glove and dipped my finger into the liquid, checking the temperature. It was freezing. I added more tea until it seemed drinkable. 'Right,' I murmured to the dog, 'Now I'll unwrap you. But we have to keep you warm.' When she was on her feet, I offered her the bowl of tea-warmed snow, and slowly she drank. 'Good girl. Now for something more substantial. How do you feel about ham and cheese sandwiches?'

I pulled a sandwich apart and offered her a chunk. She must have been ravenous, but she took it politely. I ate the other half, washed down with tea, and it tasted better than the most sumptuous feast. We shared a second sandwich and the remains of the tea. 'That's it, I'm afraid, my love,' I told the dog. 'Until some angel brings us supplies, or we manage to stagger out of here in the morning. Now the challenge is to see the night out without freezing to death. I'd bring the sheep in, but I don't think they'd come. So we'll have to huddle together as best we can.' I looked at my watch before I put my gloves back on, even though they were so cold and wet they probably weren't much use. It was almost eleven o'clock. Under the hay bales, as far from the door as I could get, I made a nest of the old grey blankets and called Sadie to me. Her legs were a bit wobbly. I covered us both up as best I could, and prepared to wait out the long, cold hours of darkness. Between my body and Sadie's, a little warmth slowly grew. I was cold, wet, aching and alone – but nothing could take away my thankfulness.

Frozen as I was, I was also exhausted, and gradually I slipped into a fractured doze. Blearily, I became aware of my phone making odd noises, and remembered I hadn't tried to contact anyone. I expected no success, but I had to try. My sodden gloves fumbled Mary's number, but there was absolutely no signal. I hugged Sadie closer, feeling her warm breath on my cheek, and slipped into oblivion.

I wouldn't have called it sleep, and when it ended it wasn't like waking. Something brought me back to half-consciousness – most likely the deep cold that seemed to be stiffening my very bones. The only tiny patch of warmth was where Sadie and I connected. I struggled to a sitting position. The blankets had fallen away, and I wrapped one round my shoulders and round Sadie. But she broke free, and as I blinked away the shreds of darkness I saw her eyes were open and her ears pricked. A low rumble came from her throat – not quite a growl, more a quiet warning. I listened intently, and what I heard was nothing. Silence. The wind had dropped, the howling was gone.

Stiff and frozen, I got to my feet, numb inside my sodden boots. I staggered to the door, and Sadie stretched and came with me. She too was unsteady on her legs. I peered out of the door into the darkness, and saw only snow, falling in fat flakes softly, vertically down to the earth. The air was full of snow, and if I had not been so cold I might have found it beautiful. The stark thought came to me that if I had fallen, somewhere out in all that whiteness, if I hadn't found Sadie when I did, we would probably both be dead. I shuddered, and acknowledged again my own prideful folly, but in the same moment I knew I would have done it anyway.

Sadie crept up beside me and put her nose out into the falling snow. Again I heard the rumble in her throat, louder now, and frowned, puzzled. Then I heard it – with no wind, a voice, distant and hollow, eerie, without words. I felt a spasm of shuddering fright – irrational, perhaps, but alone on a frozen hill, in an old stone barn with a door that wouldn't close, in a whiteout of blinding snow, it felt as if anything could happen – anything could be out there – some ravening creature out of myth, a tale to scare the children. I listened, every sense alert. For a few minutes there was silence, then it came again. And this time there were words – a word – my own name. 'Fen!'

When I thought about it afterwards, I wondered at my reaction and decided I was half-demented from the strain of the last few hours. Far from feeling a sense of relief that perhaps someone was out there looking for me, I was terrified. My breath caught in my throat, and a ripple of fright swept over me from the rim of my hat to the edge of my wet socks. Gradually I came to my senses and told myself sternly not to be an idiot. But at that moment, believing in malign otherworldly beings was all too easy.

The voice came again, nearer now, hoarse and frantic. 'Fen! Where are you?' I didn't recognise it, but I heard the fear in it. Someone out in that wasteland was as lost, maybe, as I had been.

Regaining a sense of reality, I went back into the barn and retrieved my torch. The light in my hat was weak now; obviously the battery was fading. I stood in the doorway, which Sadie was still guarding, and switched on the torch. Its light seemed very feeble against the wall of dropping snow. But after a moment the voice came again, harsh and hoarse: 'Fen! Please, answer!' I swung the torch in a slow circle. I still saw nothing, but the voice came back immediately, fractured and hard to understand. I thought, I hoped, it said, 'I see your light!' Again, I moved the torch beam slowly through the whiteness. The voice came again, louder now: 'Hold it there!' In both trembling hands I held the light steady, and a dark shape emerged from below me, down the hill – not the hill I had climbed, but the one that descended from the barn on the other side. I heard panting and grunting, and I tried to call out, but my throat was raw and no sound emerged.

Then suddenly the shape resolved into a human form and was almost on top of me, hands outstretched. I flinched and jumped back, and I heard Sadie growl.

'Fen! Thank God! Are you OK?'

In my fright and bewilderment, I still didn't recognise the voice. I stumbled back into the barn, Sadie round my feet, the torch beam wavering wildly, and the figure followed, sidling through the doorway.

'Fen! Don't you know me?' A gloved hand came up and tugged the scarf away from where it covered most of the face. A pair of blue eyes, blinking away the ice that crusted their lashes, a face red from the cold, a stubbled chin, a curl of dark hair escaping from the hat.

My voice was no more than a croak. 'Oh! Liam, is it you?'

He strode over to me and wrapped his arms round me. 'Who did you think I was? Who else would it be?'

I couldn't speak; my eyes were full of tears.

After a moment I came to what was left of my senses and stopped crying. It was too cold for a wet face. I laughed shakily. 'Stupid, I know. When I heard you yell, I didn't recognise your voice. I was terrified. I think I've gone a bit mad.'

He smiled. 'I thought you might be lonely out here, so I've come to offer my company.'

'You're as mad as me.'

He looked down at Sadie. 'This dog doesn't like me. She has a most baleful look on her face.'

'That's because she doesn't know if you are friend or foe.' I squatted down. 'Sadie, this is Liam. Liam, Sadie. Be friends.' And Sadie stopped growling and went to the pile of blankets and lay down.

'So, this is the famous sheepdog that you thought worth risking your life for,' Liam said sternly.

'I know I was foolhardy,' I said, my voice low. 'But she's special. To have lost her would have broken Mary's heart, and Mary has already got quite enough sadness in her life.' I lifted my chin. 'I didn't enjoy it. But I'd do it again.'

'If I have anything to do with it, you won't ever have the chance,' Liam said. His voice cracked. 'Oh, Fen, it was grim. I thought we'd lost you.'

'Well, here I am,' I said. 'Alive. In one piece. With a blessedly living dog. And you won't have noticed, but on two sides of this barn there are sheep. Ewes that Sadie brought down off the high moor where they would probably have perished. They'll be hungry. I want to know how you found out where I'd be. But first let's take them some hay before the weather worsens.'

Together we pulled down armfuls of hay and fed the famished sheep, and with the snow still falling I couldn't count them, but I saw they were all on their feet and had some shelter, either from the stout barn wall or the enclosure.

'That'll have to do till morning,' I said. 'Let's go inside. It's not cosy with that door half open, I'm afraid.'

'Let's see if we can close it, even if only a bit,' Liam said. 'With both of us heaving we might manage it.' He kicked away the snow that had collected at the foot of the door and braced his hands along its edge towards the base while I took the top. We struggled and strained; the door moved a few inches and then stuck in the snow.

'That'll have to do,' Liam panted. 'I'm frozen to the bone and worn out from climbing that hill.'

We slid back inside, and I noticed he had a pack strapped to his back. 'Do you have anything edible in there?'

'Of course!' he said triumphantly. 'A flask of coffee, a slab of Bess Wharton's fruit cake, a bottle of water, and some kibble for the dog.'

We sat down on the floor, the second blanket under us to defend us from the frozen earth. 'I didn't know you knew the Whartons.'

Liam extracted the flask, unscrewed the cap and poured a cup of steaming coffee, which he handed to me. 'I didn't, but I do now.'

I took a long gulp of coffee, and the heat seared my gullet. 'That is a wonderful feeling,' I said, wiping my mouth with the back of my gloved hand. 'I feel almost human. Now you have some.'

Before pouring a second cup, Liam took out from the pack a bottle of water and a bag of dry dog food. I put this into the bowl we'd used earlier and gave it to Sadie, who wolfed it down with amazing speed. With the bowl empty, I refilled it with water and she drank till the bowl was dry. I replenished it, and she drank again. Then with a sigh she lay down, her head on my leg.

Liam poured himself a cup of coffee and handed me a foil-wrapped package. As I peeled back the layers a rich, fruity smell arose. I inhaled gratefully. 'Nectar,' I said. 'Bess's fruit cake is legendary.'

'Didn't you bring anything with you?' Liam asked between sips.

'Yes. Sadie and I shared a sandwich, and I melted snow with some tea for her to drink. But that seems a long time ago. Now, are you going to tell me how you got here?'

Liam wiped his fingers down his trousers. 'I will. But shuffle over a bit closer. I'm cold.' I did as he asked, and he put his arm round my shoulders. It was a most comforting feeling, and I was in danger of being weepy again. I bit my lip and tried to squash my feebleness.

'When the weather turned,' Liam said, 'I was anxious about you. I remembered you were supposed to be with Mary and Anne for dinner yesterday evening. But I didn't know whether you'd gone or decided to stay at home. I just wanted to make sure you were OK. So I rang your number – many times. And I got no answer. So I started to be really worried. In the end, about nine-thirty I suppose, I rang Anne Wendall, and that's when I heard you'd gone out in search of Sadie. At that point it was calm, the snow was lying deep but the moon was up, so I wasn't utterly without hope. But I was scared.' His arm tightened round me.

'I wasn't at home at all,' I told him. I explained that I'd been at Tubside, helping to bring the ewes down. 'We knew then that some of them were still up there. And so, of course, did Sadie.'

'I'm beginning to understand why you think this dog is special,' he said. 'Not that I think any dog is worth your life. Anyway, I couldn't rest, thinking of you out in the snow on your own. I got well layered up, put on my stoutest boots, and walked from Chibley up to Tubside.'

'Liam! That's got to be, what, six miles?'

'Probably. No great distance in normal circumstances, but slow going in snow. A part of it was on the road, though, and the weather held – for a while. But by the time I got to Tubside there was a howling gale and lashing snow, and I hate to think what the temperature was, but my teeth felt like frozen tombstones in a churchyard.'

'You must have regretted even starting out.'

He looked at me and frowned. 'No way. But I was very afraid you were buried somewhere, and that kept me going. I have to admit, though, I was relieved to get to the Whartons'.'

'I guess they were a bit surprised.'

Liam laughed. 'Just a bit! It was a miracle I found their farm at all. There wasn't a light anywhere, and I found out when I finally roused them that their power was out – a line was down somewhere. Mary and Anne had power, but I guess people further up the moor didn't. I hammered and hammered, almost turning to ice in the blizzard, and eventually I saw a light over the door, and back went a load of noisy bolts, and there was this old guy in his pyjamas and dressing gown holding a lantern, and behind him a formidable-looking lady with grey hair down her back in a plait. But humanity overcame suspicion, and they ushered me in. When my teeth stopped chattering, I introduced myself and told them I was concerned about you. Bess made me a mug of tea on their old gas range, and bit by bit I started to thaw out. Of course, they had no idea what you'd done, and they were appalled. They didn't put it into words, but I realised they thought you were a goner. There was a lot of muttering and head-shaking. But when I told them I intended to go after you they thought I was stark staring mad. 'You'll be lucky to survive in this,' was what old Will said. Anyway, they could see I wasn't going to be put off. I told them where Mary said you were heading for, and they told me the best way to get there from Tubside. Bess got busy with the food and flask, and Will went upstairs – I hadn't thought the old boy could move so fast – and he came down wearing proper clothes over his nightwear and took me out into the yard. He and his stockman had done some clearance, but obviously the snow was piling up again. Anyway, bless him, he offered me their quad. He held the lantern up and pointed away up the hill, and told me to ride to the gate. I couldn't see any gate, but I had to hope for the best. After that, he said, there was a steep climb up a field full of boulders, so it wasn't safe to take the quad – I'd have to leave it at the gate and go on foot. Bess handed me the pack, and her expression said it all. They were clearly convinced that when the snow thawed they'd find two humans, a dog, and a few dozen sheep scattered across the moor, dead of exposure.'

I heaved a sigh. 'It's a catalogue of craziness, Liam. First a dog who had to do her job to the utmost and round up a bunch of sheep. Then a mad woman who couldn't bear to lose the dog. Then a madder man who couldn't let the woman die in the storm.' I looked up at him; his face was in shadow. 'We're lucky, you know that. But maybe it wasn't luck. I reckon my faithful friend Mary would have been praying for us all.'

Liam grunted. 'That's what she said. I don't know what I think about that, but I'll take the outcome.'

He fell silent, but I had the sense he was struggling with something enormous, and I didn't know how to help, what to say.

At last he said abruptly, 'You know I wouldn't have come out in a snowstorm for anyone.'

'I get that,' I said gently.

'Oh, God, Fen, what am I going to do?' he cried out. 'I'm more confounded than I've ever been in all my disorderly life. I just know for me a world without you in it would be unbearable.' He took a deep breath and rushed on. 'I didn't say anything. I was pretty sure you thought I was some kind of lightweight, unreliable, callow even.' I made to protest, but he waved me away. 'Like a fool I opened my mouth and said what I didn't mean, propositioning you that evening at your cottage. Even then I was dimly aware that a night of meaningless romping wasn't at all what I wanted, though I couldn't have said what I did want. And then your husband got sick, and you vanished from our lives. And then he died, and you were free, but now you were a grieving widow, so I kept on saying nothing, and pretending we were just arty friends, and I tell you, it was sheer bloody torture.' He ground to a halt.

'That's what Alice said,' I murmured wonderingly. 'That you were holding back because I was mourning. Of course I didn't believe her.'

'She's wiser than you. Or me.'

I shifted round to face him. 'Liam, listen. I don't think you are a lightweight, or callow, or whatever else you said. I think you are a stalwart friend, and you've made everything better for me here. You turning up in Brant was a wonderful thing to do. I didn't want to think what it really meant, not then, because I simply didn't have any room for anything in my head at that point. But even now, I hope you understand, quite apart from me grieving for John, and concerned about the children, I don't even know who I am. Am I Fennel Mayne, that ignorant, precocious, lonely child bride? Am I Fen Bailey, supposedly respectable Christian widow and mother, wanting she knows not what out of life, not even now? Or will I find some mixture of those two, or someone that's new? I don't know. I need time to process it all and make sense of my life.'

He reached out and very tenderly brushed my damp hair away from my forehead. 'As far as I'm concerned you can have all the time you need. I can be patient when I have to be. As long as you don't just tell me to take a running jump into the nearest beck.'

I laughed. 'If you were the last person in the world I'd want to be with – if you were hideous and graceless and charmless and a thoroughly bad egg – I wouldn't be saying any such thing to a man who'd just risked his neck for me.'

'I guess not,' he said, smiling faintly. 'You're much too polite.'

'Oh, Liam.' I reached out and pulled him to me and kissed his cold mouth. 'Stupid man. Politeness really doesn't come into it.'

He gave a frustrated moan and drew me closer. 'Please can we repeat that?' He kissed me with a mixture of gentleness and fervour that was practically irresistible. 'I think,' I said, catching my breath, 'it's probably a very good thing we are both wearing innumerable layers in an icy barn in the middle of nowhere.' He said nothing, just smiled and held me close.

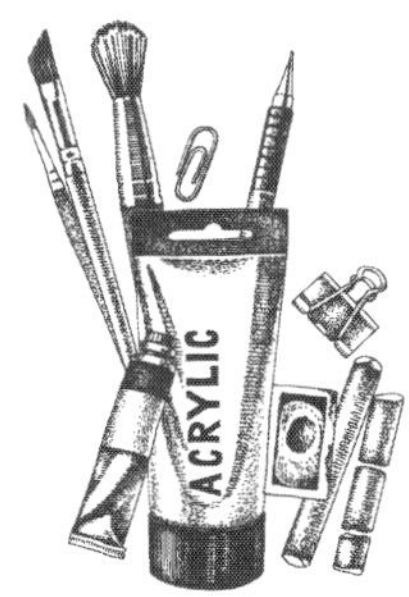

PART FIVE

THE BEAST FROM the East, as it was popularly called, didn't sheathe its claws for another ten days. The snow continued to fall, the wind blew it into towering drifts, and the cold was bone-biting. For weeks it lay, unmoving, sometimes many metres deep, in valleys where the sun couldn't reach. When the thaw finally came, people began to count the cost, which was high: drystone walls flattened, gates washed away in floods, dead sheep.

There were brief lulls when the sun came tentatively back, and we said hopefully, surely now that March is here spring must be on its way. Farmers worried about their pregnant ewes, because lambing time was near. The extreme weather had caused a lot of damage, expense and worry, and we were clearing up for weeks after it was over.

Liam, Sadie and I were rescued the following day, along with twenty-nine sheep. Will Wharton and a gang of helpers, including his three other dogs, battled up the hill on foot and quad bikes, and rounded us up. Subsequently the local press got wind of our escapade and ran a story, but we tried hard to restrict it to the heroism of Sadie, minimising my part in it and, to his relief, barely mentioning Liam at all. There were many stories emerging over the following weeks of tragic losses and miraculous escapes, and we were absorbed into them; but in our own circle of friends there was much head-shaking and sheer disbelief.

The vet examined Sadie and pronounced her unharmed but said she had spent herself to her limits and must have a week of rest and good food to build up her strength. She spent the time at Anne's being watched over by Mary. When I led Sadie into their cottage the look on Mary's face made every moment of my efforts a hundred times worthwhile. Before the week was over Sadie was keen to be back to work, and Mary reluctantly walked with her through the snow to Tubside, where she was reunited with the other dogs in a flurry of noisy exuberance.

March continued wet and dreary, with that sad flattened look that fields get when snow is finally gone, but soon enough new grass began to appear, and farmers heaved a sigh of relief to know that their ewes would have some pasture before they gave birth.

Meanwhile at Chibley the receding snow and subsequent thaw were bringing unwelcome developments. Some progress had been made in January and early February, and a half-decent road now led from the lane up into the farmhouse yard – sufficient at least for the trucks bringing materials to get in and out. But there were also more troubling things left behind, chiefly a landslip in the sloping area behind the farmhouse leading down to the lane. The surveyor returned, and his report was a huge blow to Martha. The weight of snow that had piled up in great rippling drifts had caused the land to slide down, and revealed more water than could be accounted for by a mere thaw. An unsuspected underground stream, swollen by meltwater, was making the stretch of land unusable, and it was adjacent to this that Martha had planned to renovate two barns and turn them into small residential units where people could stay when they came to Chibley to learn and paint. Now this was impossible, and new plans would have to be made, but Martha knew that even with Walter's loan funds would be tight. 'I can't ask Walter for more,' she said. 'He's been unbelievably generous already. And the costing has all been worked out for the original plan.'

We were sitting round the farmhouse table, Martha, Liam and I. We'd told her only the barest outline of our time on the frozen hill, and she didn't ask, because she was so bound up with the fate of her renovation. We were pleased to have it that way, and set ourselves to brainstorm solutions in the hope of salvaging something of her plans.

'Martha, what about this?' I said. 'I don't know if it's possible, but could you pull down the barns and use the stone to build the units further up? Say, in the field to the north of the studio? There's a good bit of room there. Those barns are probably going to have to be demolished anyway – they're too close to the landslip. You could have gravelled pathways from the new cottages to the studio and make it pleasant with plantings.'

Martha frowned, saying nothing for a while as she sipped her coffee. 'Well, maybe. It's certainly firmer ground up there. Obviously, I had it surveyed when the studio was built and there's solid rock. But that's demolition and rebuilding, which would cost a whole lot more money. I'll talk to the surveyor, but I'm not hopeful. It's a good plan, Fen, I'm not saying it isn't – it would give us the chance to start afresh and get things as we wanted, and with a look that was in keeping, using the original stone – but I don't think we can afford it.'

Meetings with the surveyor, the architect and the building firm followed, and endless discussions, but it was as Martha feared – it could be done, but more funds would be needed. When she told us the estimated cost, we were dismayed. 'I can't see where I'm ever going to get that sort of money from,' Martha said heavily. 'I'll just have to return Walter's loan unused, and Chibley will have to be sold.' She sighed. 'Ah well, it was a good dream while it lasted.'

Liam and I also chewed over the problem when were alone; we were sad for Martha, for Chibley, for ourselves.

'Such a good plan,' I mused. 'And down the pan because of mere money.'

Liam grunted. 'You wouldn't say "mere" if you'd ever been short of it.'

That night I lay awake in my cottage at Knapp's Bridge, thinking. I had a lot to think about, but the problem of the works at Chibley dominated; and when I woke to a morning of tentative sunshine, and looked down my garden to the river, noticing with a frisson of pleasure a clump of daffodils just beginning to open, I had an idea.

I made a phone call, and on the basis of the answer I took my car and drove to Richmond. I said nothing to Martha or Liam except that I wouldn't be around that day. I didn't want to raise anyone's hopes – it could all be a complete failure; but I had to try.

At half past ten on a grey morning I parked outside the hotel where, a few months before, I had seen Olive Wastwell flounce inside. I hoped my interpretation was right: that Olive had cold-shouldered me because she felt embarrassed and ashamed; and I also had a notion as to why she was still in the vicinity. I enquired at the desk, and they rang her room – or, to be more accurate, rooms. Olive, it seemed, was out. I bought coffee from the bar and sat in reception where I had a clear view of the front entrance. Half an hour later Olive arrived, carrying several large bags. She couldn't avoid seeing me, and her expression was one of sheer horror. I tried to smile encouragingly. Before she made for the lift I got up and barred her way.

'Hello, Olivia. I wonder if I could take a little of your time. There's something I'd like to run past you. I promise it's nothing to worry about.'

People were looking up, and Olive clearly didn't want any kind of scene. 'Well… I suppose so. I have a meeting later, so it'll need to be quick. You'd better follow me.'

The few minutes in the lift passed in strained silence, but I kept up the fatuous smile. Once in her rooms she flung the bags down, pulled off her coat and perched on the edge of her enormous bed. She didn't invite me to sit. 'So, what's all this about?'

'Olivia,' I said quietly, 'a year ago, during storm Doris, you took me into your confidence. You asked me not to tell anyone what you'd said, and I agreed. I wasn't sure why it needed to be a secret, but I promised, and I must tell you now I haven't told anyone, and without your permission I never will. Please accept that as truth.' I waited, but she said nothing, her face stony. 'OK. The next day, apparently in a fit of rage, you tried to damage my unfinished painting. Let me tell you that I managed to fix it, and it's all finished now. I was horrified at the time, of course, but I've thought about it since, trying to understand why, especially after what we talked about the night before, and I thought that rage was fuelled by jealousy. I understood you were miserable. It was a stupid, unkind and unnecessary thing to do, but if forgiveness is required you have it. We can put it behind us.' I waited for her to respond, but she simply sat with her head bowed. 'I wanted to get that out of the way, because I have a proposition for you.'

Now she looked up, and her eyes were red. 'A proposition?'

I nodded. 'Before I tell you what it is, can I ask you a question? It's relevant. I don't know if you've been here all the time, or whether you've been away and come back. But it seems to me you always do come back. Why, Olivia? You feel the cold – you could be somewhere warm. Is it perhaps because, over the years, you've come to see Chibley as a sort of second home? Somewhere where people are kind to you? I know you regard Martha as a friend, or at least you used to. But you know, if anyone should be annoyed with you, it's not Martha. She was disappointed, of course, that you withdrew your offer of funds, but your money is yours and you can spend it as you wish, obviously.' I looked down at Olive and saw tears running down her cheeks. She pulled a tissue from her pocket and blew her nose.

'For heaven's sake, sit down,' she muttered. 'You look too tall.'

I found a chair. 'Let me tell you what's happened, Olivia.' I explained about Martha's trip to America, how she'd come back triumphant, seeing her beloved Chibley rescued from the brink. How things had been progressing, if not quickly, then fairly surely, until the weather revealed the fatal weakness in her plans. How now she was on the point of giving up all she had worked for. 'Tell me if I'm wrong, Olivia. I think that place means a lot to you. But now you feel you can never go back.'

She sighed. 'Is it money you want? It usually is.'

'Yes, it is. Martha could change her plans, and they would work. But it would all cost more. Please see this is not for me, but for her.'

Now Olive frowned. 'OK, let me get this straight. Are you saying you want funds, and if I decline you'll tell everyone what I told you – about me and Vinnie?'

I slapped my hands down on the arms of the chair, and she visibly flinched. 'For goodness' sake, Olivia! What are you accusing me of – blackmail? I said I wouldn't tell, and I never will. Don't you know anyone who can be trusted? If that's the case, I'm sorry for you. And as for your "secret", it's really not much of one, is it? It seems to me you're just afraid of being laughed at. How silly is that?' I made a huge effort and lowered my voice. 'Look. I'm sorry I yelled. I forget you are lonely and vulnerable and trying to cover it up. I'd just be glad to see Martha's dream realised. You have money, but you don't have friends. Or at least you think you don't. But you could have. You could have them without the money, but I don't think you believe that. I'm asking you to help, and there are no strings. Martha doesn't know I'm here – nobody does.'

'Most propositions have advantages for both parties,' Olive muttered. 'Where's mine?'

'Are you honestly telling me you don't know? You could come back to Chibley as a welcome guest. One who had the privilege of being involved in its revival. Martha would be grateful. You could come and go as you used to. She may even agree to your private exhibition space, but that'd be up to her. This could be your opportunity to spend your money in the cause of your own happiness.'

'They always told me it couldn't be bought,' Olive said. 'I've found that to be true.'

'It usually is, but spending in a good cause can be rewarding. Like giving to charity.'

She said nothing, twisting her handkerchief in her hands, sniffing. Then she looked up, and she seemed to have come to some resolution. 'I'll have to think about it. I promise I will. Meanwhile, I want to say I'm sorry I did that to your painting. I don't think I'm normally a vindictive person, and I felt very bad about it. That's why I ran.'

I nodded. 'I understand. Thank you for the apology, but as I said, it's done. We can begin again: eventually, I hope, as friends.' I stood up. 'I'll leave you in peace now, Olivia. There's just one more thing. I feel the need to be completely honest. I don't want you to think I've kept anything back from you that you should know. Forgive me if I'm clumsy – it's a bit delicate, I know.'

She interrupted me. 'You're talking about Liam, aren't you?'

I nodded. 'When I said to you, that morning after the storm, that there was nothing between me and Liam, I told you the truth – at least from my point of view. Not long after that, I had to go home, because my husband was very ill, and some months later he died.' I heard her gasp, and her handkerchief covered her mouth. 'I'm not looking for sympathy. But obviously things have changed. Nothing is certain, but… you get the picture, I hope. I wouldn't want you to come back to Chibley, if that's what you decide, thinking that Liam wants to pursue anything but a friendly relationship with you. But that shouldn't stop you, and I truly hope it doesn't.'

She nodded, and I saw she was resigned. 'I get it. Thank you for your honesty. And I'm sorry about your husband.' She got up. 'So,' she added shyly, 'are you and Liam an item now?'

I smiled. 'Not yet. Maybe. Too soon to say.'

'And—' She hesitated. 'Are you sure we can be friends? You, and me, and Liam, and Martha?'

'It's a very distinct possibility,' I said. 'And that doesn't depend on the money. Though I can't pretend it wouldn't be a great relief.'

AFTER THE GRIMNESS of the Beast from the East, April and May and the subsequent months were warm and dry. By the end of March most folk had cleared up the mess and counted the cost, though repairs were still ongoing. I was looking forward to lambing, especially as I'd seen so little of it the previous year because of the need to hurry back to Brant.

When to bring the pregnant ewes off the high moors and down to the fields surrounding the farm was always a judgment call: too soon and they'd eat up all the new grass before the lambs arrived. Inevitably some got left behind. One Sunday in April, just before the school term began, Thom Wharton and I were given the pleasant task of looking for the strays. Sadie, now fully recovered, came with us, and she seemed happy to be out and involved in her favourite activity.

Whatever his elders may have thought about my foolhardy behaviour in February, to Thom I was now a hero.

'It's a good job I didn't know anything about it,' he said feelingly. 'I'd have done just what you did.'

'I'm glad you didn't know,' I said. 'I'm sure your grandparents would have been appalled to have me perish in a snowdrift, but to lose their only grandson would have been a far different order of disaster.'

'I suppose. Was it very scary?'

'When I couldn't see for snow and I didn't know where I was, yes.'

'It's hard to remember what it was like, now that the sun's out and the hills are all green.'

'Except for all the damage. Everyone's out these days fixing broken walls. So, Thom, what are we looking for this afternoon?'

'We just need to get the strays down to the farm. Sadie will round them up, and I've got nice tasty sheep cake in my bag. That'll tempt them.'

'Do you think any of them will have lambs already?'

'They might have.'

We arrived at the crest and looked down over the panorama that spread out before and below us as far as the eye could see. I breathed the cool air and marvelled at the magnificence of the landscape; it was a sight I would never tire of. In the middle distance the fields were dotted with sheep.

'How do you know they're Tubside sheep?' I asked Thom.

'Because all this area is their *heaf*, their home territory. The sheep know, and they teach it to their lambs.' Sadie was looking at us enquiringly. Thom put his shepherd's whistle to his lips and blew a shrill signal. Sadie bounded off, at first a fast ground-covering gait, then as she got nearer to the sheep she flattened herself against the grass and made a wide circle behind them, slow and patient.

'She's trying not to spook them,' Thom said. 'They can be quite skittish when they've got newborn lambs.'

'Are there any lambs? I can't see them.'

'They're probably lying down.' He handed me a pair of binoculars. I adjusted them and peered down the hill.

'Yes,' I said. 'I can see one or two, not many.'

We watched as Sadie brought the sheep together and set them off in our direction. But one ewe refused to be rounded up. Try as she might, Sadie seemed unable to persuade her to join the others.

'I don't know why people think sheep are silly,' Thom said. 'Ours definitely have ideas of their own.'

I adjusted the focus of the binoculars and looked again. 'Thom, it looks to me as if that ewe has lambed. There's blood on her – at least, I think so. Maybe she's refusing to follow because she's lost her lamb.'

Thom took the binoculars from me. 'I don't know,' he said. 'I think we'd better go down there and see.'

Sadie came back to us with all the rest of the sheep, plus four lambs, in a tidy bunch. She kept looking down the hill, clearly anxious. Thom spread the sheep cake out in front of them, reserving one chunk, and they were soon feasting. He told Sadie to stay and watch them, and then we trudged down the hill to where we had last seen the ewe – because by now she had disappeared.

There were, we knew, gullies that criss-crossed the moor, but rendered invisible by the vegetation growing up in them. As we approached, we heard loud bleating, and rounding a scrubby patch of bushes we saw the ewe.

'You know, I think you're right,' Thom said. 'Somewhere around there's a lamb in trouble. But how are we going to find it?'

'Let's follow the mother.'

The trouble was, this sheep was going nowhere. She stood, looking at the bushes, and bleated. If we got too close, she skittered away, but always came back to her one spot.

'Maybe the lamb's stuck in these bushes,' Thom said. He stowed the binoculars in his pack and extracted some sheep cake. While the ewe was munching, he began to pull the brushy branches aside.

'Thom, let me. You'll tear your hands to shreds. I've got my gloves.' But Thom wouldn't stop, and together we hunted through the vegetation.

'I thought so,' Thom said. 'There's a ditch in here. What Grandpa calls a grip. What do you bet me the little thing's down here? I hope it isn't dead, Fen.'

In the bushes, down into the ditch, it was dark. I couldn't see anything, but I thought I sensed movement. Behind us the ewe was still bleating plaintively, and suddenly, from somewhere below us, we heard an answering bleat, weak and pitiful.

'It's down here all right, Thom.'

'I'll do it.'

In a moment Thom was down in the ditch, and I heard his boots squelching in the mud. 'I can see it!' Thom cried out. 'But I'm not sure I can get hold of it.' I heard him grunt with the effort, and then there was a sucking sound and a splash. Moments later Thom emerged, soaking wet and covered in mud, and in his arms a lamb that should have been white but was now completely black. Its thin bleats were answered by strong bleats from its mother.

'Take it, can you?' Thom said. I grabbed the lamb, plastered with mud, and Thom heaved himself out of the ditch. 'A nice sturdy tup,' Thom said. 'You never know, this one could turn out to be a champion one day. Grandpa will be pleased.'

I carried the lamb, and Thom saw to the rest of the flock, ably helped by Sadie. Lamb and humans were all covered in sticky filth. The ewe dogged my heels, her eyes on her baby, and gave the occasional bleat, as if to say, 'I'm still here.'

'How's the training coming along, Thom?' I asked.

The lad flushed with pleasure, his fair-skinned face glowing. 'Really well! I think we'll make a good team.' He sobered. 'I wanted to do a trial in June. I'm sure Sadie's well ready. But Grandpa said we had to wait till July, when all my exams are over. Which means we'll have to go south, somewhere near Huddersfield.'

'That's not so far, is it?'

'No, but it means not many of my mates at school will come.'

'But your parents and your grandparents will, won't they? And I'd like to come too, Thom, if you let me know when and where.'

'Would you?' Thom's grin was broad. 'That would be grand, Fen. Do you think Mrs Hipkin would come?'

'I'm sure she would. Why don't you ask her? I could take her in my car.'

The mention of Mary must have sparked something in my memory, because I suddenly realised I had no idea what had become of Peter's dog, Old Joe.

'Thom, maybe you know – what happened to Mr Hipkin's dog? I don't suppose they allow dogs in the nursing home. But they were always together. How can I have forgotten?'

'I expect you had a lot on your mind,' Thom said kindly. 'But yeah, when Mr Hipkin went into the home Old Joe went to stay with Mrs Hipkin and Mrs Welland. But he pined, they said. And they came down one morning and found he'd died in the night. But he was old, you know – twelve I think – and almost blind. Sheepdogs don't live as long as normal dogs that are just pets, especially the ones that work the hill sheep – did you know that? But I reckon they have the best life.'

'Maybe you're right,' I said to Thom, and almost to myself, 'I wonder if Peter knows.'

'Mrs Hipkin said he asked after Joe, when he first went into the home. He hasn't asked since, but Mrs Hipkin said if he does she'll tell him the truth. Course it's sad, but no dog goes on for ever.' He looked behind him, watching Sadie keeping the sheep together. 'I'm glad Sadie isn't old yet. I don't like to think of her dying.'

The next few weeks were full on, with lambing taking all our time day and night. I got to go home for a shower and a good night's sleep more often than Will and his helpers. Will, I knew, was seventy-six, a hill farmer all his life, hale and ruddy and tough as baling twine. Even so, when I arrived back for another shift, I saw how weary he looked.

'Will,' I said, 'you look worn out. Was it a busy night?'

'One or two difficult births,' he said with a smile. 'Some twins and triplets. But we didn't lose any.'

'Will, I know I'm a greenhorn, but would you trust me to spell you? Your stockman will be here, won't he? Jeff? You look as if you need a good few hours' rest.'

He looked at me, considering. 'All right, lass,' he said. 'But only if you promise to wake me if there's any problems.'

THAT EVENING, I rode my bike back to Knapp's Bridge on a high. I was covered in sheep birth fluids and blood, and I was exhausted, but with help I'd seen a score or more lambs born alive and healthy, and we hadn't needed to disturb Will. Bess came into the barn with a tray of tea at five o'clock and told us Will had been heard snoring loudly. Of course, they all thought I was a rank amateur playing at farming, but I didn't care. I had a long shower, wrapped myself in a cotton bathrobe, and rang Liam.

'Hey, you sound happy,' he said.

'You could say that.' I told him about my day's work. 'Twenty-six! I'm sure it was twenty-six. Some out in the field, and some twins in the barn. Healthy lambs, and I delivered them myself. Well, with Jeff. And the ewes did most of the work.'

Liam laughed. 'Who else would be so chuffed after a day of sheep midwifery?'

'What have you been doing?' I asked.

'I've been at Chibley all day,' he said. 'In between watching the builders work, and keeping Martha from interfering, I've made good progress with that series of landscapes for the exhibition.'

'Do you want to come over? I could cook.'

'You say the nicest things. I'll come across country – it's a beautiful evening. And I've got things to tell you.'

'Give me an hour.'

BY THE TIME Liam arrived, flushed from his walk, I was dressed and combed, a fire was warming the room, and the casserole I'd thrown together was filling the cottage with rich scents. I went into the garden as the light began to fade, a large glass of red wine in my hand. From there I could see Liam striding along the footpath between the fields, his loping gait instantly recognisable.

'It's been a beautiful day for sure,' he said, unwinding his long scarf as he came indoors. 'But it's still chilly. That breeze is brisk.'

For any other friend, perhaps we might have hugged one another, or even planted an amiable kiss, but there was a tension between Liam and me that seemed to preclude such innocent civilities: the tension of knowledge that was still foggy, and at least one unanswered question. Privately, I veered between the extremes of believing, at some level, that we could do well together, and of clinging to my liberty, that heady illusion. So instead of a better greeting, I handed him a brimming glass.

'Take the weight off,' I said. 'Not that there's a lot of it in your case.'

He smiled. 'Judging by that amazing smell of cooking, there might be a bit more of it after this evening.'

'You said you had news,' I said, settling myself on the sofa opposite him.

He leaned forward. 'Yes – a surprise visitor.'

'Let me guess – Olive?'

'The very same! We've been kind of expecting her, but she hasn't shown up in person till now. She was disappointed not to see you.'

'Really?'

'Yes, she really was. You never told us in detail what you and she talked about that time you snuck off to Richmond, what you said that brought her round, but she certainly regards you as a chum now. We know she contacted Martha on the phone, and Martha went to see her, talking business, and of course there wasn't really any bad blood between Martha and Olive anyway. Then Martha reported that sudden hike in her funds at the bank, and the rest is history. And I, for one, am grateful, because now I have a job. But I wonder why she's left it so long to come and inspect her investment.'

I shrugged. 'Maybe the weather put her off. We know she doesn't like squelching around in mud, and I imagine Chibley is a building site. Unless you've provided a nice little path up to the farmhouse door.'

Liam laughed. 'It can't be that. She was wearing waterproof boots, not the usual elegant flimsy sort but great clunky rubber ones.'

'Good heavens! Well, if it's not the mud, maybe it was the problem she has with you.'

He shook his head thoughtfully. 'I wondered that. But it was strange. For Olive, she was almost natural. Greeted me like an old friend, no batting of eyelashes or trilling giggles. I almost felt comfortable. It makes me question just what you said to her.'

'I just told her what I thought was the unvarnished truth.'

He raised his eyebrows. 'Which is?'

'She asked me if you and I were an item. And I said no, at least not yet. That it was too soon after losing John. That was how it was, I thought, at the time.'

He frowned, and fell silent. Did he want to ask, 'What about now?'

I got up. 'I think this meal is ready. Shall we?'

For the rest of that evening I sensed an unusual reserve in Liam, something that he was holding away from me, and I wondered. But I was already ahead of him as the level of wine in the bottle dropped, and he declined a refill. Perhaps my brain was a little fuddled. I told myself I was celebrating the arrival of healthy lambs to Will's flock; but what Liam had to say as we sat, replete, with cups of coffee, came as a shock.

He spent a few moments staring at the floor, and then he looked up at me, as if gathering himself. 'Martha and I are a bit worried about you, Fen.'

'Worried?' I echoed stupidly. 'Whatever for? I'm fine. I'm having the best time.'

He took a breath. 'It's just… we've hardly seen you. You haven't been at Chibley for weeks. The third panel is lying around unfinished. Yes, I know, you've been busy up at Tubside, being a shepherdess. But Fen, you're *not*. OK, I know that's been your way of getting to know people, blending in with the community, helping out. And, according to you, having fun. I get that. But you already were part of the community, even before you had to go back to Brant. You might not have been here in person, but everyone who went into the church saw your work, and you know that people outside the church, outside the area even, know about you. You didn't have to prove anything.'

I gaped. 'I wasn't—'

He waved a hand to stop me. 'It's not just that. I realise I'm straying into territory where I'm quite ignorant. But Martha also said you haven't been inside St James's for weeks either. Fen, I'm no expert, but that doesn't seem right. People, Steve and Jane, the congregation that have begun to get to know you, they're wondering. Knowing those charitable folk, they may be thinking you're staying away because you're grieving and want to be alone – and that would make them sad anyway, thinking you felt unable to ask for some kind of comfort – but I'm sure that's not why. It's not, is it?'

I shook my head, speechless.

'You know what worries me, Fen?' he pursued. 'I'm afraid that because you're here, in this place which you love, which you associate with your childhood, because you feel free, free to choose what you do, how you live, you're slipping back into your old pagan ways. I know that sounds overly dramatic. Please tell me I'm wrong.'

For a moment I could say nothing. Then I heaved a great sigh. 'What puzzles me right now,' I said slowly, 'is why you of all people would care if I was backsliding.'

'What do you mean, "of all people"? Because I am undecided, I don't count?' His voice was sharp, but in a moment it softened. 'Can't I care what's going on with you, even in a sphere where I am a stranger? If you had a physical illness, I wouldn't need to be a doctor to care about your symptoms. Besides—'

I frowned. 'Besides what? There's more to this?' I felt anger rise up within me, and at some level I knew I was unreasonable, but I gave the anger its head.

'Please, don't jump in and judge,' he said softly. 'That's all part of your new self – if it is new. The part that wants to brush off everyone's thoughts, that's hard and self-sufficient, the part that wants its own satisfaction, no matter what.' He swallowed. 'I just thought maybe – this is hard to explain – I wondered if you could be to me what John was to you, all those years ago.'

'What? I'm not with you.'

'Someone who could explain things,' he stumbled. 'A guide, a mentor. You said you were grateful to John, didn't you? For the insights, for introducing you to God. Now it looks like you're shedding all of that, and it makes me worried for you, and a bit bereft for me.'

'Stop, please stop,' I said. 'I can't handle this, not now. This isn't how I wanted this evening to go. I even thought – no. That won't be, not now. I think you'd better go. I'll think about what you said, but right now, and maybe the wine is heating up my brain, I just feel annoyed and persecuted.'

He stood up. 'I had to say what was on my mind, and not just on mine. But I'm sorry if I have offended, overstepped, whatever. I need you to know that it's because I love you. But you knew that. I'll go now, Fen. It's OK, I have my torch – I won't fall in the river. Thanks for dinner.'

The door closed quietly, and I heard his footsteps fade into the darkness. Like an automaton I got up and closed all the curtains. I put a log on the embers of the fire and refilled my coffee cup. Then I went to the kitchen and began to run hot water into the sink. My head was throbbing.

Later, with the dishes draining, I lay in bed. It had crossed my mind, much earlier, that Liam might have stayed. But something was batting at me, an insistent voice, small and almost inaudible, and it was asking: Was he right? I felt a shudder, a cold prickling of my skin, although the bed was warm. Was I walking away from something that had been – no, still was, surely – so important to me? Something I would have said was the very bedrock of my life?

My anger dissipated as I began to see it for what it was – a malign intrusion. I found myself silently saying over and over, 'I'm sorry.' I believed I would be forgiven, but I mourned what I now wondered might be something broken between me and Liam, and I found that I was weeping.

THE NEXT MORNING the fair weather broke, the sky was a dark uniform grey, and as I thought about getting my bike out the rain started to fall, steady, unrelenting, wetting. I gave in and took the car to Chibley.

As I drove up what had been the track and was now a road, my eyes widened. Already the two barns, plus the nearer one that had been Liam's hideaway, had been razed. It was, apparently, too early for workmen, but there were diggers and other businesslike machines all round the studio perimeter, trenches had been dug, there were lines of string stretched out between wooden posts, and great heaps of stones lay up against the fence.

I found Martha sitting in her kitchen, a pot of coffee on the table, paperwork spread out.

'Hello, stranger,' she greeted me with a smile. 'How's our shepherdess?'

I winced. 'Not much of one, I'm afraid. Not much of anything, probably. Is there any coffee in that pot?'

'Help yourself.'

'No Liam?' I asked as I poured.

'No, he went out early, house-hunting.'

'What?'

Martha pushed her papers aside. 'I expect you noticed he no longer has his shabby little dosshouse. He's been staying in the farmhouse with me, but that's not a good permanent situation. So he's gone to find somewhere to live, much as you did, except I imagine he'll be renting for now.'

'Oh.' I felt oddly dismayed.

'I expect he'll be back some time this afternoon. So, no lambs being born today?'

'I'm sure there will be,' I said. 'But Will and Jeff will be fine without my bumbling help. I left a message to say I wouldn't be at Tubside today.' Martha said nothing, faintly raising her eyebrows. 'I thought it was high time I checked out what was happening here,' I said. 'And I need to get that third panel finished.'

'Indeed you do,' Martha said firmly. 'Well, you know where it is, and you know where I am if you need help.' I finished my coffee and got to my feet. 'Oh, and Fen, we had Olive here yesterday.'

'So I heard.'

Again, she made no comment. 'I want to thank you again for what you did, from the bottom of my crusty old heart.'

'You did the lion's share of schmoozing in America, Martha.'

'Perhaps I did, but it would all have been for nothing if not for you.'

'Well, I'm glad. And you're welcome.'

IT WAS STRANGE, working again on my painting, almost as if I was starting afresh; and I'd forgotten how cold the studio was when no one was there. I put on some overalls that were lying in a crumpled heap, spattered with paint, more to warm up than to protect my clothes. I took the sheet off my third panel and eyed it critically. The area at the bottom left, which I had earmarked for the Yorkshire version of the Good Shepherd, was still only pencilled in. It was time to give Will Wharton and his like a touch of celebrity, if such it was.

I assembled my materials, mixed my paints, and got to work, and somehow, despite my neglect, my ideas seemed to come together. I left the shepherd's face till last and concentrated on his clothes: the patched jacket with half its collar turned up, the ratty scarf knotted at his throat, the heavy trousers folded into muddy boots. I left a space between his body and his right arm, curving round a small space where a black-faced lamb would be held, its head and chest and dangling front feet all that could be seen. I paused as I sketched in his other arm, doubting that I could render it convincingly with its weathered hand grasping a stick. That might have to wait. I was so absorbed in what I was doing that I forgot the cold, and I failed to hear the door open.

'Fen!'

My heart lurched, and I almost dropped my brush. Liam was standing in the doorway.

'Ah, Liam, close that door! It's freezing in here. My breath's coming out in clouds.'

He smiled and obliged. 'You're right – it's like the inside of a fridge. Why didn't you put the heaters on?'

'Forgot.'

'Time for tea? We can put the heaters in the kitchen and close the door. You're practically blue.'

'Done.' Now that I had stopped work, I was aware I was shivering.

He came and stood beside me, gazing at my painting. 'What have you been doing?'

'Giving Will Wharton an airing. But I need some help with his left hand.'

Liam turned to me suddenly and put his arms round me, ignoring my filthy overalls, loaded palette and dripping brush. 'Oh, Fen. I'm beyond glad to see you. I was afraid you'd never want to speak to me again.'

I pulled away and looked up at him. 'What nonsense! You're exaggerating. Anyway, it's me who should be apologising. For being so cross when you were trying to help.' I looked away from his bright blue gaze. 'Anyway, I asked myself some hard questions and concluded you were probably right. So here I am.' I allowed myself a small smile. 'And I will be back to St James's on Sunday. I need to talk to Steve about this panel – as well as seek some spiritual nourishment. I'm not going to give up on being a part-time farmer, though.'

'I wouldn't want you to when it makes you so happy.'

'Anyway,' I said as I unbuttoned the overalls and stepped out of them, 'there are sheep in the Bible. Sacrificed at every festival. Not to mention the Good Shepherd himself.'

Liam grinned. 'I know. And with all your close-up experience you should be a dab hand at painting them.'

'I wish. Let's get that kettle on before I turn to ice.'

We huddled in the kitchen, the two fan heaters blasting out round our feet, mugs of tea in our hands, and slowly I thawed.

'I didn't get to say everything I wanted to, last night,' Liam said. 'I thought I'd better beat a diplomatic retreat.'

'Before you arrived,' I said, feeling a wash of heat rise up from my throat, 'I was even contemplating asking you if you wanted to stay over.'

He sighed. 'Really? And I would have declined, madman that I am.'

'Would you?' Now I was astonished. 'Why? Am I suddenly so unappealing? Or is it only the version of me that's half-dead in a frozen barn that fires you up? That seems a bit perverse.'

He closed his eyes and groaned. 'Don't tease, Fen. Nothing has changed. Not very long ago I'd have shouted 'Hurrah!', thrown you over my shoulder and carted you off to the bedroom. And I wouldn't have let you out for at least a week.'

'I'd like to see that,' I murmured. 'You'd probably do yourself an injury. So, what's changed?'

'I'm not sure I can explain it very well,' he said, his voice faltering. 'It's to do with you as well as me. Thing is, I have a job now – I'm an *artistic director*.' He bowed in mocking self-parody. 'Which means I get paid. And as of today, I have a place to live that's not on someone's charity or someone's sofa.'

'I heard you were looking.'

'Well, I now have a tiny one-bedroom place in a side street just off the market square. I don't have any furniture, but that's OK. I don't need much. What all this means, well, what it means to me, is that I am trying to be a proper grown up. Not really tried it before. And that's your fault in some measure. I don't want to be aimless any more, Fen. I want to have some purpose.'

'That all sounds great. If it's what you want, I'm very pleased for you. But I'm not seeing the connection.'

'I've been thinking about you as well,' he battled on. 'I think about you most of the time, and a lot of that is not to be rehearsed in public. But also I've been thinking about your painting, especially your

Revelation triptych, and where it might lead you. Because I think you have some kind of calling.'

'What? What as?'

'I know it maybe sounds crazy to you, but all this research you've done… once you finish the triptych, and it's hanging up there in church in all its glory, you could do some other stuff, perhaps not as big, but on equally prophetic themes.'

I gaped. 'Have you been reading, Liam?'

'A bit, yes. Revelation is about lots of things, isn't it? Judgement, the end times… and it's full of fire and flood and blood, warfare, angels and demons… eagles and lions, and a lamb with a sealed scroll. I didn't need to read, just to look at your panels. And then, and this is the thing, Fen, why I think you should do more of this prophetic stuff and bring it up to date and make it accessible to people today.'

'Enlighten me. I'm listening.'

'Well, just think about some of the things that have been happening in the last year or so, terrible things, so much human suffering, and not just humans – animals, the planet itself. Even just recently, that Russian guy poisoned in Salisbury with his daughter, and the absolute firestorm of horror that's erupted from that. And at least two school shootings in the US. That horrific fire in London last year when so many people were killed, and everything it said about cynical slipshod building practices and the negligence of government. Persecuted minorities, whole peoples wandering stateless and homeless. Nuclear tests in unstable countries. Famines and conflict in Africa, the Middle East and Asia. Social media scandals. And on top of that, the sinister and steady warming of the planet, and everything that's flowed from it – devastating hurricanes, loss of life and livelihood and property, everything people have worked for. Wildfires in California, mile upon mile of forests destroyed. Did you know last year was the warmest year on record? And it's only going to get worse.' He ground to a halt, his voice hoarse.

'So you're saying this is the sort of thing you want me to paint?' I said uncertainly.

'Yes,' he said simply. 'I know you could do it. You have the eye for such things, and the knowledge – I've seen it. And there's endless, *endless* material – surely you see that.'

'Why not you?' I asked. 'You are a far better artist than me by any standards.'

He shook his head. 'Maybe technically. But I'm a landscape artist principally – and that's kind of connected, if you look at it that way. I paint the things I want us all to preserve: the hills, the rivers, trees. You do the warning, the fire and the blood.'

'Wow,' I said shakily. 'You really have been thinking. I had no idea.' Then I frowned. 'But why would all that stop you yielding to my seductive wiles?'

He shook his head. 'It's just the other side of the same coin. Being true to your calling. Because your calling is also as a Christian, Fen. And like it or not, you're well known down at St James's, and there are young impressionable people there who probably think of you as some kind of role model. Anyway, if you're painting the consequences of sin, you can't be leading a less than honest life and not be accused of the rankest hypocrisy.'

For a moment I gaped, completely stumped. 'Am I talking to the real, the original Liam Audley?' I demanded. 'Or has some alien abducted him and sent a very unexpected lookalike in his place?'

'No, it's the same battered old model,' he said. 'Maybe with a reconditioned engine and a new tyre or two. I've still got a long way to go. I hoped you could help me. Reconnect with the spiritual, and all that.'

I shook my head. 'I very much doubt I'm qualified. We'll have to muddle along together for now.' Once again I stopped short. 'That is, if this self-imposed celibacy isn't permanent. I'm not sure I could cope with that.'

He laughed, his whole face lighting up. 'No, no, no and no again. Of course not. I'm not made of stone, and neither, I'd bet every penny I haven't got, are you.'

'So, what's the answer?'

He sighed. 'If you can bear the idea, we have to make it legal. But please know this – I have no wish whatsoever to clip your wings, restrict your autonomy or turn you into something dull and domestic.'

Now I was frowning again. 'Is this a proposal?'

'I suppose it is.'

'Good heavens. Aren't I a bit old?'

'Silly. Will you?'

'I suppose I will, otherwise I might implode with sheer frustration.'

'I thought a year would do it. What do you think?'

'A year? What, from now?' I was frankly horrified.

'No, a year from your widowhood. August.'

'Hm. Maybe I can manage that, if you can. It won't be easy.'

'You're absolutely not kidding. Darling one, put that tea down. It must be cold anyway.' He pulled me off my chair, gathered me up in his arms and held me very tight. 'You know what, ever since I first saw you on your bike, I was blown away.'

'On my bike?'

'Yes, it was the sight of those toned and shapely calves.'

'Calves?'

'What's this, some kind of echo?'

'I'm just amazed, that's all. To think that it was my calves that struck you so forcibly.'

'And your hair. The way it bounces and catches the light. It must be the artist in me.'

'I think it's more like the idiot in you.' I bit my lip, suddenly afraid. 'Liam, do you think this… all this, is wise?'

'Nope,' he said. 'It isn't, and maybe it never is. All I know is I adore you. And I don't think you're completely indifferent to me. For now we restrict ourselves to chaste kisses. And in August we set the bed on fire.'

I'D ARRANGED TO pick up Mary after breakfast. At the last minute, Anne also decided to come with us, though she grumbled about the early start.

'It's a good two hour run down to Huddersfield,' I told her. 'And I plan to take the cross-country route. The weather's set fair, and down across Wharfedale the fields will be smothered in wildflowers. It'll be a sight to see. Once we get to Skipton we'll have to use the A-roads, but let's make the most of summer while we have the chance.'

I pulled up outside Anne's house and the two friends appeared, wearing flowery summer dresses and big hats, but with a cardigan handy, just in case. Each carried a capacious bag and a folding chair. Mary took the front passenger seat, and Anne, who was a big, heavy woman, folded herself into the back seat with a great deal of puffing and muttering as she fumbled for her seat belt.

Finally, we were on our way. Mary glanced over at me. 'You're very brown, Fen.'

I smiled. 'I've been up at Tubside, helping with the hay making. They let me drive a tractor.'

Anne leaned forward. 'I thought today we might see you in a dress,' she said, looking askance at my cotton cut-offs and sleeveless top.

'Not sure I own one, Anne.' I flashed a grin at Mary, who shook her head.

'But surely you'll wear one for your wedding, won't you?'

'Hm, maybe I will. I haven't got one yet, though.'

'But it's only a few weeks away, Fen! Aren't you leaving it a bit late?'

'Don't you worry. I'll find something, probably in a charity shop. I'll try and look the part.'

'A charity shop?' Anne almost choked. 'Whatever next?'

Mary looked back at her friend. 'She's just teasing you, Anne. Take no notice.'

'Well, I know young folk have different ideas these days.'

I laughed aloud. 'Thanks for the "young", Anne. But I'm actually forty-three, and should probably have arrived at an age of discretion by now. I'm a lost cause.'

All we got from the back seat was a flapping of voluminous skirts and a disbelieving harrumph. For a while she was quiet, then she said,

'Mary's been telling me what young Thom has to do, all that fetching and driving and penning and whatnot. I hope Sadie does as she's told.'

'No question about that,' I said. 'Although she has been known to make her own mind up. As we know.' As we climbed up out of the town and onto the narrow road that struck out south across the moor, I said, 'How do you think they'll do, Mary?'

'Well, Thom's been practising a great deal, according to Bess. And we know Sadie's one in a million. But they'll be up against some very stiff competition, and as far as trials go they're novices.'

'I have faith.'

Anne had obviously lost interest in the finer points of sheepdog handling. 'So, where's your young man today, Fen? Didn't he want to come?'

'Liam's in Leeds all day. He's talking to someone about another exhibition in the autumn. The spring one was well received, and the gallery owner wants to build on that.'

'Hm.'

I wasn't at all sure Anne approved of art, except as a hobby. Presently we became aware that she'd stopped asking questions, and we heard a gentle snore.

'Anne makes me want to laugh,' I said. 'She likes to make her views known.'

'She does,' Mary said. 'And she's nothing if not traditional. But she has a good heart.'

'She probably thinks I'm a bit shocking.'

Mary smiled. 'She hasn't figured you out, that's for sure.'

The road rose, levelled, rose again, then at the top of the rise veered sharply left then right before it straightened out. We were now high above the valley and the beck that ran through it, and everywhere we looked the fields were alive with colour.

'You just can't believe, can you,' Mary murmured, 'that less than six months ago you were risking your life in one of the worst storms in years. Look at us now – cloudless skies, and it's really warm. Even Anne won't need her cardigan today.' She breathed deeply.

'These days don't happen very often,' I said. 'But this place is beautiful in all seasons. I wouldn't want to be anywhere else.'

'So tell me, Fen,' Mary said after a moment, 'if I'm not being too nosy, how are you feeling about being married again?'

I slowed to take a steep downward slope. 'Most of the time,' I said, 'I'm cautiously optimistic. The rest of the time I'm terrified.'

'What of?'

'Oh, you know, the usual things: will we be ok, is this the worst decision of my life, etcetera. Didn't you feel scared when you got married?'

'I did. Nearly called it off. But my future mother-in-law, who was a most formidable woman, told me not to be a feeble fool. She was right, of course.'

I laughed. 'I can just see it. That's something I won't have – in-laws. Liam has no one. It's a very different feeling to the first time, though. I'm not an over-confident seventeen-year-old any more. There's some truth in ignorance being bliss!'

'Are Dan and Alice going to be there? They don't mind?'

'They don't seem to. And yes, they will, and not only them, but Rory and Clyde as well! I'm honoured.'

'Do you really not have a dress?'

'I really don't. Sorry, Anne.'

After only one missed turning we found the farm and the field in plenty of time. Thom and his entourage had been there since mid-morning. I parked the car, and Mary and I helped Anne negotiate the rough field and the tussocky grass. We took an arm each, with Mary holding the bags and me in charge of the chairs, and after a lot of groaning, panting and stumbling we made it to the barrier and found Will and Bess, and Thom's parents, already in position. Space was made for us, I unfolded the chairs, and we slid Anne into one of them, where she subsided, fanning her red face with a large white handkerchief. Mary was ready with a flask of tea, and before long Anne had recovered her spirits and was engaged in lively chat with Bess Wharton. Thom's mother, Bess and Will's daughter-in-law Vicky, came to stand alongside me at the barrier.

'Is there some kind of running order?' I asked her.

'Oh, yes, here.' She handed me a flimsy piece of paper. 'There are six dogs this afternoon. Thom's somewhere in the middle. I'm really nervous for him. He's worked so hard, and I know it means a lot.'

'It does to all of us. But Thom has done so well. He's very dedicated.'

She smiled shyly. 'He thinks the world of you, you know.'

'Does he?' I said, surprised.

'Yes. Because of how you went out into the snow to find Sadie. So brave.'

'So bonkers, more like.'

She nodded. 'Well, yes. It was really crazy. It could have been tragic, you know.'

'I know.' I smiled. 'I won't be doing it again, I promise.'

In an abrupt change of subject, she said, 'I saw your work in church the other week. All three panels, all together at last, side by side. They look wonderful. I don't really understand what they're all about, but there's so much to see in them, and they're so vivid and colourful. Is it really true you used my father-in-law as your inspiration for the shepherd?'

'Yes. I met him in the shop in just that get-up, and I thought he'd make the perfect model. I changed the face, though.'

'Will you be doing more paintings? Like, from the Bible?'

'I hope to be doing more, but what they'll be about I haven't decided yet.'

'You're getting married soon, aren't you?' I was having trouble keeping up with her.

'Yes. In three weeks. What do you think – another reason to suspect my sanity?'

She gave a little gasp and giggled, casting a sidelong glance at her husband, who was leaning on the barrier, smoking and looking faintly bored. 'I think you may be right,' she whispered.

The trials began, and we were asked to be quiet. There was an atmosphere of friendly tension, with supporters leaning over the barrier, craning to get a better view, and people taking photos. Nearly everyone knew what was required of both handler and dog, and between each trial there was a great deal of knowledgeable muttering and wagging of heads.

Then we all took a collective breath as Thom and Sadie were announced. Sadie's coat gleamed in the sun, and Vicky whispered to me, 'He was brushing her for ages yesterday evening. Poor dog!'

The crowd fell silent. Away in the distance a man in a broad-brimmed hat and two dogs had seven sheep under control. Now there was a sharp whistle from Thom, and Sadie streaked away, a black and white blur across the grass, fast and completely focused. I had to remind myself to breathe. I watched as she gathered the sheep and brought them back to where Thom stood, crook in hand. She kept them trotting without hurry, only moving to one side if a sheep started to break free from the group. Now it was time for the drive, when Sadie had to take the sheep on a prearranged route, through a set of gates and round a huge boulder. The sheep seemed to want to break loose and go round the boulder on each side, but Sadie corralled them, then fell back and crouched low as they skittered round in a bunch. I heard a collective sigh from the crowd. Now Sadie turned them back towards Thom in answer to another whistle. Thom moved slowly and deliberately to a fenced pen, pulled the gate wide and stood aside. As Sadie came towards him down the straight, with the sheep in front, I saw one of them balk and try to make off. There was a bundling in the ranks, a sense of agitation, and Sadie circled left and dropped to her belly, watching the sheep intently. One sheep in particular seemed to want to challenge Sadie, and the sheep was a lot bigger than the dog. But Sadie didn't flinch.

'This is the difficult bit,' Will whispered to me. 'Sadie is resourceful, but she's small and doesn't have that mean eye some of them have.'

Thom now approached the sheep and divided the little flock with his crook, three and four. The sheep clearly didn't like this at all, especially the big bolshy one, and the three tried to break away and rejoin their fellows, but Thom kept them divided, Sadie drove the four towards the pen, and with the only quick movement I'd seen him make, Thom swung the gate closed.

There was a moment of silence, then loud applause, cheers and catcalls. Will turned to me, his expression speaking of both pride and surprise. 'I can't believe that wasn't a perfect round,' he said. I watched as Thom stood there, his hand on the gate, the dog by his side, her tongue lolling in the heat but clearly not at all out of breath.

We all heaved a relieved sigh as Thom and Sadie disappeared from the field. We watched the other trials now with keen interest, and noted the small mistakes, the flustered handler, the over-powerful dog, but also the immense skill, and remembered that all these dogs would have been working sheep all week as they did every day. The trial was just a showcase of normal working ability.

Thom's scores came up. He had been docked just two points, for the little blip at the boulder and the minute loss of control at the sort. Every one of us was jubilant, talking all at once. Anne had dropped off to sleep, but the racket woke her. Then something happened none of us expected. The trials were over, Thom had been presented with a small silver cup to warm congratulations from the judges, and we were free to go home. We saw Thom across the field, his award clutched in his hand, a huge smile on his face, and as he walked towards us he bent down and said something to the dog. Sadie left him and loped towards the barrier to where we stood. She made straight for Mary as she sat in her folding chair and put her muzzle in Mary's hand as it rested on her lap. For a long moment they simply looked at one another; then Mary murmured something inaudible to the dog she had trained. We all looked on, awestruck. After a moment Sadie looked up and moved along the barrier, and to my immense astonishment she raised her forepaw and put it on my knee as I stood. 'Sadie,' I whispered, 'you're an absolute wonder.' Tail up and furiously wagging, she bounded back to Thom.

I SAT IN the vicarage kitchen, light pouring in at the big windows. For once Jane wasn't baking but kept company with me and Steve at the table, cups of coffee in front of us.

'Jane, you look weary.'

She yawned and smiled. 'I always find the school holidays a challenge. Thinking of something for the kids to do. Plus all the other things I do anyway.'

A thought struck me. 'I could do an art day with them, if you like. Give you a break.'

'That would be brilliant!' Jane said. 'But haven't you got enough to think about, with the wedding and stuff?'

I shrugged. 'We're not going overboard. I have a dress, Liam – so he tells me – has a suit. Steve's doing the service, members of the congregation are organising the party. All we have to do is turn up.'

'You're very relaxed about it all.'

'About the day, yes. Why not? I hope everyone will have fun. Not so relaxed about afterwards, though.'

Steve frowned. 'You're not getting cold feet, are you?'

I sighed. 'Not as such, but I'm not a starry-eyed adolescent like I was the first time round, and I'm very aware there'll be challenges ahead. It's a complicated business, marriage.' I saw Jane grin and raise her eyebrows. 'As is any relationship, of course. It's Liam who's the starry-eyed one. But then he has no experience!'

'Maybe you're over-thinking,' Steve said gently. 'I'd just let it all happen without worrying.'

'You're probably right.'

'So, Fen, how's it all going over at Chibley?' Jane asked.

'Apace! Now that the weather's improved they're making headway. Three of the four units are already up, at least the shells. And Martha has taken up my suggestion of turning her little parlour, which she almost never used, into an office for herself as director. It's not that big a job, but it'll make a difference to have all the paperwork in one place as well as being a good centre for the business side of things. She's also seeing about getting the marketing stuff done – posters, business cards and so on. The next job is to construct a website. She's hopeful they'll be up and running and taking bookings next year.' I looked at Steve. 'What I really wanted to talk about this morning though, and I hope you can help me here, is the problem of evil.'

Steve almost choked on his coffee. When he recovered, he said, 'I should know you'll always throw me a curveball, Fen. Want to unpack that?'

'Sorry, that was a bit abrupt.' I took a breath. 'Well, of course Revelation is full of it. You might even call it the culmination. And I could go on mining Revelation till I'm a hundred. But I want to do something that flags it up in our own day, in ways people will recognise. Actually, I've already begun; I've got a few things stacked up waiting at Chibley. You've been so supportive, especially hanging my monster panels in the church, but where am I going to put all the new stuff, if anyone's ever to see it? I need a bit of guidance with the content and the approach. I want my work to mean something to people – to make them think, even change their minds. It's what you do every Sunday, of course – in a different way.'

'Hm,' Steve mused. 'It's true, I did wonder about that inscription on the third panel: "The terrible day of their anger is here, and who can stand against it?" But then I thought about it, and I saw it was right and necessary. We have to raise these unpopular and uncomfortable things; it's part of our responsibility. Sin is real, and every one of us will have to face the consequences of it. And in some ways it's harder to do here – making people aware of the threat – in this peaceful backwater, where most folk in general don't do anything too terrible day by day.'

Jane got up out of her chair and collected our empty cups. 'It doesn't feel so much like a backwater with all the tourists about,' she muttered. 'And wicked things can happen anywhere – thievery, rape, murder, abuse. We know that, don't we, Steve? You never know what's going on behind other people's front doors.'

'That's just it, though,' I said. 'Those things are what people think of as evil, and rightly. But Steve has a point – we live here in peace with our neighbours. There are no doubt threats to our security, but we're often oblivious. Evil is more obvious in a war zone, say, where innocents are slaughtered and people lose everything to greed and violence. But those aren't the only ways wickedness takes shape.'

'And it's easy to forgive ourselves for what we see as little things, peccadilloes,' Steve said.

'Doesn't it say somewhere in the Bible that more is expected of those of us who have so much?' I asked. 'So how do I do this, in a way that will strike a chord with people?'

Steve shook his head slowly. 'I can't really tell you how to do it, Fen. I'm no artist. But as to where you could show the paintings, there's always the church hall. As long as they're not as big as the triptych! And people use the hall all the time.'

'Once again, you're most kind to this amateur,' I said.' And it's hugely appreciated. But clearly it'd all be subject to your approval.'

'Sure. Tell me something about what you're thinking, what you've done already.'

I frowned, collecting my thoughts. 'It's to do with the idea of the city as the hive and hub of evil,' I said. 'Not that bad things don't happen in the country. Of course they do. And many good things happen in cities, for sure. That's not the issue. It's symbolic, to a degree. But I see the great city as the place where wrong can flourish in a spectacular way, partly because of anonymity, but also just because it's often the place where human creativity is most active and concentrated. I'm not thinking so much of art and poetry and music, but of dreaming up schemes. Sometimes they aren't bad in themselves, sometimes they are meant for good. But there are somehow more opportunities for deceiving greed, for self-congratulation, for engulfing pride in human achievement, the celebration of life without God.'

'Wow. Yes, I see,' Steve said. 'How do you portray that in a painting?'

'That's my question. I have some ideas, and I don't want to make it seem that just because a place is beautiful, like here, it's necessarily innocent! Privately, of course, I think of ugliness as an abomination in itself.' I fell silent for a moment, thinking. 'There's as much potential for pride, for instance, or greed, or selfish ambition, or putting other people down, in a meeting of the local council as there is in Parliament, except on a smaller scale. And I shouldn't forget the pride of the artist who gives herself too much freedom. I have to remind myself I am also capable of doing harm, even when I intend good.'

Jane came back to the table, drying her hands, and she was grinning broadly.

'Fen dear, with all this going round and round in your head, I can quite understand why well-meaning queries about your wedding dress are a bit of an irrelevance.'

I WOKE WITH the sun in my eyes and pulled the pillow over my head. For a moment I was fuddled; the sheets smelled different, this was not my bed. Then, of course, memories started trickling back. Pulling the pillow off I sat up too suddenly and registered a twinge in my temples and the need for fluids. I fleetingly thought I must have over-indulged.

There was no sign of Liam, but a moment later I heard the front door bang and loud singing came from downstairs, something that sounded suspiciously like a well-known operatic aria, but dangerously off-key. I got up and staggered to the bathroom, where I drank a copious draught of water from a toothmug. Feeling in need of at least a week's sleep, I made my sluggish way back to bed. I registered my pretty, but terminally crumpled, apricot-coloured dress in a heap in one corner. Liam's dashing, but decidedly non-traditional, sky-blue linen suit had been tidily stowed on a hanger on the curtain rail. He had neither curtains nor a wardrobe.

I sat up, wrapping the sheet under my armpits, and remembered. It had been, after all, a happy and unthreatening day: the sun had obliged, the guests were merry, Steve made several jokes during the service, the music was deafening, the refreshments were first class and the drinks flowed liberally. I seemed to recall I had drunk sparingly at the party; my headache was no doubt due to the fizzy that awaited us when we got back to Liam's little house in town. Above all Liam was in buoyant spirits, and if I had any needling doubts I had no intention of raining on his parade.

Part of my own pleasure was in seeing my children and their partners, and meeting Clyde, and introducing Liam to the ones who hadn't met him. Alice, of course, was full of triumph and crowing I-told-you-sos. I'd made over my cottage at Knapp's Bridge to the younger generation, with some caveats. 'If you plan to roister, do it in the annexe away from the neighbours. Remember I have to live here after you've gone, so no weed on the decking.' They promised most solemnly to behave, but I was not convinced.

A clumping on the stairs brought me back to the present. Liam appeared, fully dressed and carrying a tray. He put it on the floor, flung himself on the bed beside me and pulled me into his arms. 'Awake at last, Mrs Sleepy.' He scooped my tumbled hair off my forehead, nuzzled my neck and kissed me all over my face. I didn't resist.

'Where have you been so early?'

'Not early at all. It's nearly ten. I went to the baker's – I thought croissants would be good.' He leaned down and produced the tray where not only croissants but jam and coffee leaned at a precarious angle.

'That looks wonderful. Might it be an idea to take your boots off?'

Several silent minutes were spent eating, drinking, getting jam on our fingers and trying not to get flakes of croissant in the bed.

'You don't normally sleep this long, do you?' Liam said. 'Was it the champagne that knocked you out?'

I frowned theatrically. 'No. Champagne just makes me giggly and uninhibited. I think I must have been *very, very tired.'*

Liam broke into peals of laughter. 'Uninhibited is an excellent word.' But then his face fell.

'What?'

'I'm disappointed,' he said.

'Are you? Why?'

'We didn't have to call the fire engine. After all my boasting.'

I pretended to examine the sheets. 'No sign of charring, I'm afraid.'

'Well, good! I bought the best ones I could find, and they cost a small fortune.'

I'd noticed, before we started on the champagne, that he'd made a huge effort with his house. Everything was sparkling, the towels were new, there was food in the fridge. He'd even put fruit in a bowl and flowers in a milk-bottle, and I was touched.

'You're very careless with your clothes,' he said, looking at my dress screwed up on the floor.

'I think that might be part of uninhibited.' I looked at him sideways. 'Speaking of clothes, I'm wondering why you still have yours on.'

'Brazen hussy.' But he was already loosening his belt and kicking off his socks.

'I thought we might have another go at combustion. Anyway, it's supposed to be good for you.'

His shirt came off with the buttons still done up. 'What is? Arson?'

'No. Sex.'

'Sex as therapy – now there's a thought.' He started to kiss me slowly and languidly, and I felt my skin grow warm. 'Well, if you ever feel a bit under the weather, I'm your man.'

'Darling, as of yesterday, you most definitely are.'

IT WAS WELL into the afternoon when I came back to consciousness and realised my phone was buzzing. I'd left it on the floor, and when I finally located it whoever it was had given up. The number was vaguely familiar. But it would have to wait – I needed the bathroom. I heaved Liam's arm off me, and he barely stirred. While I was there I decided to shower – I was sure I was less than fragrant. Liam had already showered; I could tell from the damp towel as well as his shaven chin. Feeling a lot fresher, I scrabbled in my bag and found some clean underwear, jeans and T shirt. Then I decided I needed tea, and this time I'd play waiter. Realising we'd had no lunch, I made a couple of sandwiches and took it all upstairs.

'Wake up, Mr Slug. It's almost five.'

Liam groaned and sat up, running his hand through his disordered hair. 'Whose crazy idea was it to spend all day in bed?'

'Mine. But you were more than willing. Tea is served.'

'Oh, good. My mouth feels unsavoury.'

I remembered my mysterious phone call and decided to ring the number back. 'Hello. You called me.'

'Oh, yes! Mrs Bailey.' (But I'm not, am I? Not any more.) 'It's Annabelle Prout here.'

I looked at Liam and rolled my eyes. 'Hello, Mrs Prout. What can I do for you?'

Liam grinned and mouthed, 'The boiler?'

'I'm sorry to bother you. But I just needed to check. This past fortnight there's been a large ginger cat visiting my garden.' I felt my mouth drop open and a prickle race all the way down my arms. But Mrs Prout was still talking. 'It looked very thin, so I've been feeding it, but it's extremely shy and if I go anywhere near it bolts. Yesterday I mentioned it to Mr Drake next door, and he told me you used to have a ginger cat, but it vanished. Some years ago, he said. I know it's probably a long shot, but could it be yours?'

I found I could barely answer, and when I looked up at Liam he was frowning in puzzlement.

'Well, er… as you say, it seems terribly unlikely, but… what would you like me to do?'

'I know it's a long way for you, but would you come down and see? The thing is, we're going on holiday soon. I'm not a huge cat lover, but I wouldn't want the poor creature to starve.'

'No, of course not. Look, Mrs Prout, thank you for letting me know, but you've caught me rather on the hop. Can I ring you back, say in half an hour?'

As I ended the call Liam said, 'Fen, what is it? You look as if someone just died. I gather it's not the boiler.'

'No.' My voice seemed to have disappeared; it came out as a hoarse croak. 'There's been a ginger cat frequenting my old garden, so Mrs Prout said.'

His eyes widened. 'What?'

I felt my eyes well up. 'Do you think – it could be, couldn't it? Could it be Wesley come home? I never thought I'd see him again, Liam. It's been more than three years. I thought he was dead for sure.' I choked and fell silent; tears were running unchecked down my cheeks.

'Oh, sweetheart. Don't cry. We'll have to go and find out.' He put his arms round me and stroked my hair.

'It's not what we planned. Do you mind?'

'Did we plan anything?'

'No,' I said huskily. 'But I don't think we were contemplating a long drive down a motorway. To inspect what may be just some stray.'

'If there's any chance it could be your old chum we have to go,' he said firmly. 'But not now. If we went now, by the time we got to Brant it would be dark, and you wouldn't see anything, and then we'd have to find somewhere to stay. Besides which we're supposed to be meeting your offspring and partners at the Indian in a couple of hours.'

'So we are. They'll be astonished. And probably disbelieving.'

'Well, it really is quite hard to believe,' Liam said reasonably. 'Where has he been all this time?'

I pulled away and looked at him. 'I've asked myself that question countless times.'

'Darling, ring Mrs P back and tell her we'll come down tomorrow morning. First thing.'

I put my arms round his bare chest and rested my head in the hollow of his shoulder, taking in his very particular scent. 'Thank you.'

He laughed softly. 'Can I drink my tea now? And is that a sandwich I see? I'm absolutely ravenous. I feel as if I've just run a marathon.'

'I guess you kind of have.'

THE TOPIC OF maybe-Wesley dominated our conversation with the children that evening for the first half hour. But they also wanted to tell us all their doings. Alice and Rory had kept me updated during their long absence, sending regular photos, including some of them with my parents in a sunny pear orchard. 'They're very well,' Alice reported. 'Send their love. Even said they might come over some time, but they were a bit vague about it. They're lovely, and just a tiny bit batty.'

'That sounds about right.'

Dan and Clyde filled us in on their lives, and Clyde with his wacky humour kept us laughing immoderately. For them the subject of my long-lost cat was soon forgotten, but my mind kept circling back to what I might find when we got to Brant – or, indeed, what I might not find. Perhaps the cat had moved on; perhaps I wouldn't see it; perhaps it wasn't Wesley. Perhaps, I told myself stupidly, I didn't deserve this extra bit of joy when I had so much already. I caught Liam looking at me with an expression that combined concern and encouragement, and I loved him for understanding.

With an early start and a long drive ahead of us, we paid the bill and made our excuses. We wouldn't see the children again this trip; all of them had work to get back to.

'We'll leave the key under the flowerpot, Mum,' Alice said as she hugged me goodbye. 'We'll see you soon. Let us know how you get on tomorrow.' There were hugs all round, and we parted company.

We walked the short distance from the restaurant to Liam's, and he kept his arm tightly round my shoulders.

'I hope you're not going to lie awake fretting,' he said. 'Perhaps I need to think of something to distract you.'

'What, a tap dance?'

'That's not what I had in mind.'

'I thought you said you were exhausted.'

He shrugged and put his key in the door. 'I seem to have got my second wind.' He adopted a terrible gangster accent. 'You game, doll?'

'Always.'

WE SET OFF after breakfast.

'We have to go to Knapp's Bridge first,' I said. 'Somewhere in all my junk is a cat basket. Just in case.'

'You kept it?'

'Yeah. I thought even if Wesley never came back, you never know, I might have another cat one day.'

He shook his head and said nothing, and for a longish time we were quiet, busy with our own thoughts. We stopped for coffee at a motorway services and pushed on.

We were approaching the slip road to Brant when Liam said suddenly, 'How confident are you, if you even get a sight of this cat, that you'll know if it's Wesley? Or isn't?'

'I'll know him,' I said. 'I don't have any doubt of that. He has unusual markings – a Z on one flank, and tufts on his ears.' I bit my lip. 'What's not so certain is whether he'll know me.'

We drew to a halt outside my old house. At once I saw changes: they'd had the drive paved, and the tubs of flowers had gone. It was at once familiar and strange, like something from a different country I'd not visited for many years; and yet it was a bare year since I'd left. I took a deep breath and rang the doorbell.

After a moment we heard a clacking of heels inside, and Annabelle Prout opened the door. 'Ah, Mrs Bailey. Do come in.'

We stepped inside. 'Mrs Prout, this is Liam. My husband, as of Saturday. I'm no longer Mrs Bailey. If I'm anything at all, I'm Mrs Audley.'

'Oh.' She seemed flustered. 'Well, ah, congratulations.'

She led us into the lounge. It looked very different, as you would expect. But I wasn't interested in the décor.

'Have you seen the cat today?' I asked.

'No,' she said. 'I put a bowl of food out for it last night, and this morning it had gone, but whether the cat had it or the hedgehogs I can't say.'

'May I go outside?'

'Of course. Would you like coffee?'

'Thank you, that would be nice.'

I slid back the patio doors. On the terrace there was a smart set of outdoor furniture and leaning up against one of the chairs a new-looking bag of golf clubs. It seemed there was a Mr Prout, though I'd never met him. Or maybe the clubs were hers.

I circled the garden, making little noise. Mrs Prout had disappeared, but Liam stood in the doorway and watched me, as if unsure what to do, what his role was. I saw a small bowl, empty now, by the old timber shed. I tried the door; it was locked. I peered in at the dusty window, but there was little to be seen: just the shape of a lawn mower and some flowerpots. There seemed no way a cat could get in. Quietly, I skirted the shed. Behind it was a space, perhaps a foot wide, where dead leaves collected from the tree at the end of the garden, where it was difficult to get to if you felt the need to clear the leaves away. Clearly nobody had.

And that's where I found him, my Wesley, fast asleep, curled into a ball with his nose under his tail. As soon as I saw him, even without checking his markings, I knew it was him. I stood absolutely still. After a moment he must have caught a scent, or a sense, of me. He raised his handsome head and gazed at me with his deep green eyes.

'Wesley.' I spoke softly. 'I've come for you. Do you remember?'

He lay still for a minute or more, unmoving. He yawned widely, got to his feet and stretched, arching his back. I saw how thin he was. Then he gave a little shake and padded towards me, without hurrying, and apparently without fear. I held my breath. He arrived in front of me, looking up, and to my surprise and delight, because he'd always been a bit stand-offish, he rubbed his face against my leg.

I squatted down. 'Oh, Wesley,' I said brokenly. 'Ever since I heard you might be back I've been ridiculously weepy. Now I'm starting all over. Sorry.'

For a while we just hung out, and I spoke to him, and he seemed relaxed. Then I started to feel stiff in my unnatural position, and I straightened up. 'Would you let me carry you, Wesley?' I bent down, my arms outstretched, and he didn't flinch. I gathered him up, and by this time I was actually sobbing. I was becoming shamefully tearful, but I thought perhaps I could be forgiven. It had been an emotional few days.

Of course, Mrs Prout and Liam were astonished to see me coming up the garden with a rangy ginger cat in my arms. 'So, this is the famous Wesley,' Liam murmured. 'Are you quite sure it's him?'

'Absolutely,' I said, sniffing. 'The only thing that might make me doubt is that he's unusually placid and affectionate.' I turned to Mrs Prout, who was hovering with a tray of coffee cups. 'I'm so grateful to you for feeding him and letting me know he was here,' I said to her. 'Thank you.'

Wesley, most uncharacteristically, reclined on the sofa beside me while I drank Annabelle Prout's watery coffee. Then Liam fetched the basket from the car. Wesley balked a bit as we put him inside, and howled pitifully for a few moments, but I spoke to him softly, murmuring comfort and encouragement, and at last he settled. We put him on the back seat, strapped him in and started for home. When Liam was driving, I turned round in my seat from time to time and watched Wesley, and he looked back at me with his unwavering green stare until he gave up and slept.

We left the motorway as the light was fading and took the A-road home.

'We need to stop somewhere and get cat food,' I said. 'And something for our supper. I don't want to go out and leave him tonight.'

'OK,' he said. He paused. 'You know, I was surprised today.'

'What by?'

'That you called yourself Mrs Audley. I quite like it, but I didn't think you would.'

I yawned. 'I've stopped worrying about such things. Anyway, I'm no longer Bailey, and I need to be something. If you think about it, most of us inherit our father's or mother's name; we don't have one that's distinctly ours. But when it comes to work, I'm going to go by Fennel Mayne. Two artists called Audley in one town would cause confusion.'

We were a few miles away when a thought came to me that made me feel ashamed and embarrassed.

'Liam,' I said. 'I have just realised I haven't even asked you if you like cats. I'm very selfish.'

'Hm, no, I wouldn't say that. Maybe a bit preoccupied.' He thought for a moment. 'Actually, I've never had a pet.'

'Never?'

'No. I worked on the farm, as you know, and in general I like animals, and I certainly don't have a hidden loathing for cats. I think I would have said.' He turned to me, and his expression was solemn, but there was a wicked gleam in his eye. 'But you know, simply because I am so devoted to you and committed to your happiness, if you had a pet cockroach that you adored, and took out for walks on a little lead, I'd do my best to live with it. I just wouldn't want it in the bed with us.'

'A *cockroach?*' I spluttered.

Which was why, as we drove up the town road towards home, I was laughing till I could barely breathe.

Printed in Great Britain
by Amazon

48562999R00198